A SARO COMMUNITY IN THE NIGER DELTA

ROCHESTER STUDIES in
AFRICAN HISTORY and the DIASPORA

(ISSN: 1092-5228)

Power Relations in Nigeria: Ilorin Slaves and Their Successors
Ann O'Hear

Dilemmas of Democracy in Nigeria
Edited by Paul Beckett and Crawford Young

Science and Power in Colonial Mauritius
William Kelleher Storey

*Namibia's Post-Apartheid Regional Institutions:
The Founding Year*
Joshua Bernard Forrest

*A Saro Community in the Niger Delta, 1912–1984:
The Potts-Johnsons of Port Harcourt and Their Heirs*
Mac Dixon-Fyle

Forthcoming:
*Thwarted Power in Angola: The Ovimbundu
and the State, 1840s to 1997*
Linda Heywood

A SARO COMMUNITY IN THE NIGER DELTA, 1912–1984

The Potts-Johnsons of Port Harcourt and Their Heirs

Mac Dixon-Fyle

 UNIVERSITY OF ROCHESTER PRESS

First published 1999

University of Rochester Press
668 Mt. Hope Avenue
Rochester, NY 14620   USA

and at P.O. Box 9
Woodbridge, Suffolk IP12 3DF
United Kingdom

ISBN 1–58046–038–0
ISSN 1092–5228

Library of Congress Cataloging-in-Publication Data
Dixon-Fyle, Mac, 1948–
     Saro community in the Niger-Delta, 1912–1984 : the Potts-Johnsons of Port Harcourt and their heirs / Mac Dixon-Fyle.
        p.   cm. — (Rochester studies in African history and the diaspora, ISSN 1092–5228 ; v. 5)
     Includes bibliographical references and index.
     ISBN 1–58046–038–0 (alk. paper)
     1. Creoles (Sierra Leone)—Nigeria—Port Harcourt—History—20th century.   2. Port Harcourt (Nigeria)—History—20th century. 3. Potts-Johnson, L. R. (Lionel Randal), 1886–1949.   4. Potts family—History.   5. Johnson family—History.   I. Title. II. Series.
     DT515.9.P67D59   1999
     966.9'42—dc21   98–54324
                                                                                  CIP

British Library Cataloguing-in-Publication Data
A catalogue record for this book is
available from the British Library

Designed and typeset by Cornerstone Composition Services
Printed in the United States of America
This publication is printed on acid-free paper

For Joyce, Wandini, and Monze

The late Rev. L.R. Potts-Johnson.

The author and his wife (seated 4th and 6th from left) with their children, Wandini and Monze, photographed with the officers and members of the Sierra Leone Descendants Union, outside Wesley Church, Port Harcourt, in April, 1988. Principal informant, W. Byron, is seated 4th from right.

CONTENTS

TABLES

MAPS

ACKNOWLEDGMENTS

Work on this study began in 1985 while I held a position in the History department of the University of Port Harcourt. I am deeply grateful to my students and colleagues at that institution for providing the stimulation and the support that sustained my interest in this project for many years, even as our collective material condition suffered significant decline. The 1980's will be recalled as the season of Nigeria's progressive exposure to the initial travails of structural economic adjustment. It is indeed remarkable that Port Harcourt's Uniport kept up a spirited regime of seminars, debates, and inaugural lectures throughout this period to sustain a culture of intellectual disputation from which many of us derived great nourishment.

In a study that has been this long in gestation, the author inevitably incurs many debts. In several years of research and travel in Port Harcourt, Enugu, Ibadan, and London, I have relied heavily on the support of many colleagues, compatriots, friends, and other associates who unfailingly relieved the tedium of scholarly toil, while often pointing the way to new paths of exploration, and much-needed avenues of social reproduction. In Port Harcourt, I will always be grateful to the following individuals and their families: "E.J." and Mercy Alagoa, J.U.J. and Rose Asiegbu, Hannah Benstowe, David Blaney, George Caffentzis, Ade and Marie Corkson, Philippe Dah, Nick Faraclas, Silvia Federici, Willfried and Mary Feuser, Sahr and Hawa Gbamanja, Feh and Florence George, Sherry Gray, Robin Horton, Patrick and Joan Kakwenzire, Cecil and Clementina Manly-Rollings, Sahrfillie and New-Year Matturi, Alamin Mazrui, Hector and Marion Morgan, Kay Moseley, Charles Nnolim, Nwobodike and Judy Nwanodi, Bio and Muna Nyananyo, Bob and Lettie Ogali, Sam and Diane Okiwelu, Ola and Hazel Rotimi, Ademola and Ore Salau, Bobo and Abba Tekenah, Kay Williamson, and Okogbule Wonodi.

Work in Enugu would have been impossible but for the invaluable support of Igwe Njoku, Ogbonna Onwosi, and Gabriel Njoku. My thanks also go to the officials at the National Archives in Enugu, for their promptitude and patience over many months, as my file requests multiplied, and my goal seemed ever more elusive.

This study drew heavily on the passion and the resilience of the Saro residents of Port Harcourt. Their story and their fortitude were beacons of inspiration at every turn as research progressed. For the joy and trust with which they shared their heritage with me, and the warmth they showered on my family throughout our sojourn in Port Harcourt, I will be forever grateful.

I wish also to register my gratitude to the officials at the National Archives at Ibadan for their unfailing support. LaRay Denzer, Chris Ikporukpo, and Tonye Ibisiki were my principal hosts in Ibadan, and I will be in their debt for many years.

The authorities of the Public Records Office, London, were extremely supportive of my many requests, as were those of the library of the School of Oriental and African Studies. I wish to record my appreciation of these invaluable services. I also thank Andrew Roberts for his advice and support with accomodation and research arrangements in London in the spring of 1996. I owe a special debt of gratitude to President Robert Bottoms of DePauw University (whose vision of diversity resuscitated the position I now hold on this faculty) for his encouragement of this project, and for the financial support which made it possible for final archival review to be undertaken in London in 1996. Funds from DePauw's faculty development committee also supported this sabbatical stint in London, and I thank my colleagues for their trust and confidence.

My interminable interlibrary loan requests at DePauw were always handled with despatch by Bizz Steele, and I thank her for many helpful suggestions. I am also grateful to Pete Akey, Fred Soster, and Scott Wilkerson for their help in the production of the maps. To Peg Lemley who patiently deciphered my handwriting to type the entire manuscript, I will be forever indebted. My gratitude also goes to John Dittmer for the inspiration of his example, and for the many words of encouragement this project received from him.

I derived great benefit from the trenchant critique of an earlier draft of this material by Christopher Fyfe and Paul Hair. I am extremely grateful to these pioneers for the many hours they devoted to my typescript. But for their guidance, I would have erred in many more areas, and overlooked many a promising field of exploration.

In the production process, I have received generous assistance from Toyin Falola and from Sean Culhane, Louise Goldberg, and Jane Toettcher of the University of Rochester Press, for which I am very thankful. My gratitude also goes to that anonymous reader of the manuscript for the very detailed and incisive comments which ultimately shaped the final product, and proved invaluable in the revision process.

I wish to acknowledge, with thanks, the support of the following for the use of two of the maps in this book: E.J. Alagoa, T.N. Tamuno, and Heinemann Educational Books (Nigeria Ltd.), for the use of map 3; and C.V. Izeogu, A.T. Salau, and Butterworth and Co. (England), for the use of map 4. I have made every effort to locate all copyright holders of these maps; if anyone has inadvertently been overlooked, necessary arrangements will be made at the first opportunity.

Finally, let me record my gratitude to my wife, Joyce, and my children, Wandini and Monze, for their devotion and spirited support throughout this project. Their patient resignation to my prolonged absences on archival duty was, in itself, emotional comfort, and this study would have come infinitely more painfully to final fruition without their robust and unstinted encouragement.

Mac Dixon-Fyle
DePauw University
Greencastle, Indiana
June, 1998

ABBREVIATIONS

ACL	African Community League
APA	Abandoned Property Authority
APU	African Progress Union
CBE	Commander of the British Empire
CMS	Church Missionary Society
CO	British Colonial Office records
HTU	House Tenants Union
MBE	Member of the British Empire
MBHS	Methodist Boys High School
NAE	National Archives of Nigeria, Enugu
NCNC	National Council of Nigeria and the Cameroons
NYM	Nigerian Youth Movement
OBE	Order of the British Empire
PEHA	Proceedings of the Eastern House of Assembly
PRO	Public Records Office, London
RDPL	Rivers Division Peoples League
SLDU	Sierra Leone Descendants Union
SLDUPH	Sierra Leone Descendants Union, Port Harcourt
SLGS	Sierra Leone Grammar School
SLU	Sierra Leone Union
TAB	Township Advisory Board
WMMS	Wesleyan Methodist Missionary Society
WTWF	The Win-the-War Fund

A NOTE ON SOURCES

This study draws heavily on an extremely valuable and a much underutilized source in Niger delta studies—the Nigerian Observer newspaper. This is not fortuitous. The bibliography supplies a listing of the various sources consulted at Ibadan, in Enugu, and in London, and the text refers to the paucity of SLU documentation due to the ravages of the Nigerian civil war. In the absence of detailed reporting on the minority Saro population in the official colonial records (emphasis naturally went to the local Ijaw groups, and the Igbo), and with no collection of Saro private papers in Port Harcourt, heavy, but not uncritical reliance on the Nigerian Observer, was inevitable. Moreover, no source covered the Saro in such punctilious detail as did this paper. The local indigenous-owned press relayed Saro activities occasionally, but this was not, for them, compelling terrain. The Nigerian Observer thus became the daily journal of Saro life, and it reflected its diverse vicissitudes of fortune—its angst, joys, frustrations, and sundry emotional experiences. Scholars of the Niger delta's colonial history have a mine of socio-economic and political data in the pages of Potts-Johnson's paper, and critical reading of its numerous offerings should illuminate many an elusive element in the colonial records.

The Church Missionary Society (CMS) collection in Birmingham (England) was reviewed only cursorily for this project. This was due to constraints of time and funding. The collection seemed, in many areas, to corroborate social commentary as found in the Methodist archives located in the library of the School of Oriental and African Studies (London University). For future work on the Saro, however, I do intend to explore the CMS papers more extensively.

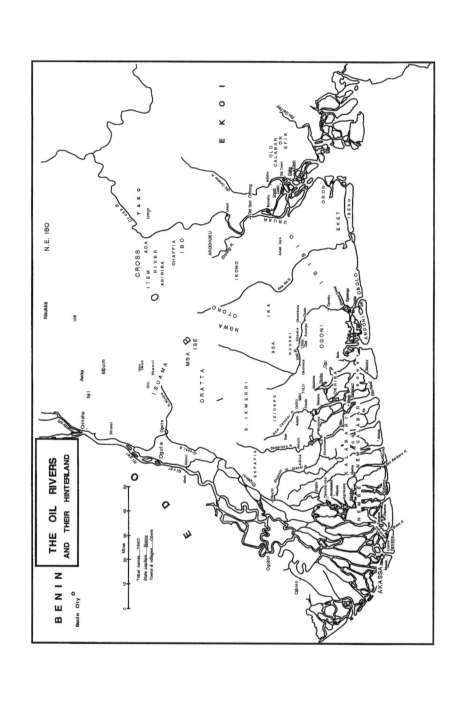

THE OIL RIVERS
AND THEIR HINTERLAND

Tribal names......YAKO
State capitals.......Bonny
Towns & villages.......Okrie

Miles
0 10 20 30 40 50

BENIN

Benin City °

N.E. IBO

Nsukka

Nri   Awka

Udi

Mbom

OFFO

Onitsha

Nnewi

Oguta

Ndoni

Aboh

Ogobiri

Ogbion

AKASSA

I S U A M A
Oru   Ngwerri
Ugwu
Oturu

ORATTA

MBA
ISE

S. I K W E R R I

EKPAFIA

ORON

EKET

IBENO

URUAN

ARQCHUKU

OHAFFIA
IBO

CROSS
RIVER

ITEM   ADA
ABIRIBA

Umor

YAKO

EKOI

OLD
CALABAR
OR
EFIK

IKONO

OTORO

NGWA

IKA

ABA

NDOKKI

OGONI

ANDONI

OBOLO

IBIBIO

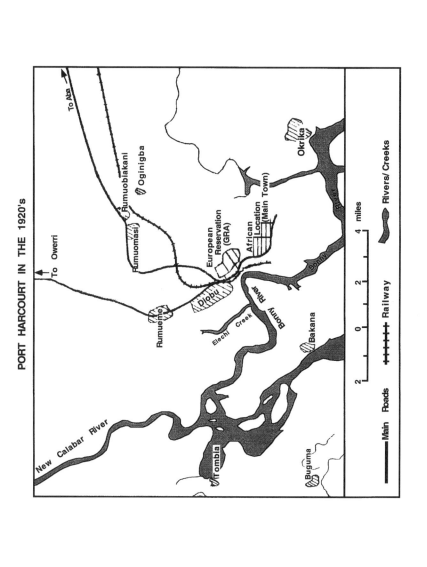

PORT HARCOURT IN THE 1920's

To Aba

Rumuobiakani

Oginigba

Rumuomasi

To Owerri

European
Reservation
(GRA)

African
Location
(Main Town)

Rumueme

Diobu

Elechi Creek

Bonny River

Bonny River

Okrika

Bakana

Trombia

New Calabar River

Buguma

—— Main Roads   ++++ Railway   Rivers/ Creeks

2   0   2   4 miles

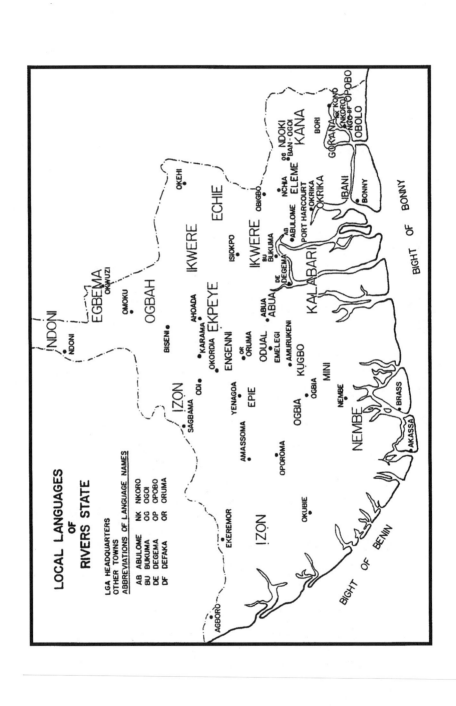

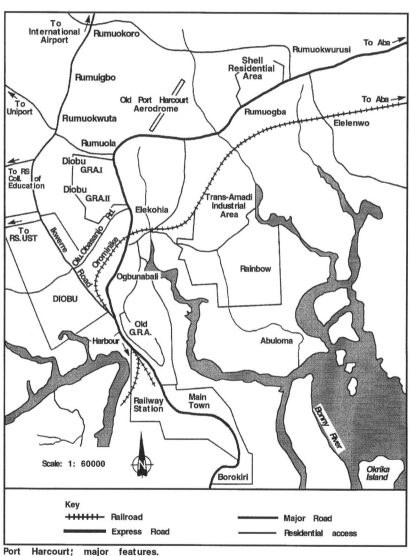

Port Harcourt; major features.

INTRODUCTION

The diligent observer of the diaspora history of the Krio of Sierra Leone is undoubtedly to be struck by the dearth of published material on the activities of Sierra Leonean immigrants in the environs of the Niger river. Unlike the adjacent Yoruba enclaves, which have attracted much patient scholarship over the years to emerge as the premier centre of Krio exertions outside Freetown, the Niger Delta communities to which Sierra Leoneans also ventured, have received scant review. This study is a corrective in that direction as it seeks to examine Sierra Leonean immigrant contributions in diverse fields of endeavour in this region of southern Nigeria during the first eight decades of the 20th century.

The Krio society of Sierra Leone, to be reviewed in more detail presently, was an amalgam of ex-slaves from England and the New World, liberated slave captives who never left African continental waters, and acculturated local indigenes who had been absorbed into the group over the years. Although much emphasis has been placed on Krio embrace of European values and ideas, and their willingness to be seen as "black Englishmen", a matter that has drawn much criticism,[1] Krio society was highly differentiated. Within it were self-confessed and deeply conservative anglophiles, much enamored of the educational opportunity provided by the British, cultural nationalists in various stages of a nostalgic return to lost roots, and the not sufficiently remarked community of the poor and the generally disadvantaged. Though most Krio took to Christianity, a segment of the group held tenaciously to Islam, with both sides, often with consanguineal ties, participating actively in a regime of rites of passage

encompassing birth, marriage, and death ceremonial that featured prominent elements of principally Yoruba culture.[2] The ties with Nigeria were
strong as will shortly be evident, for many of these ex-slaves considered that
territory the home from which they had been captured. While most Krio
would content themselves with cultural identification with Nigeria, others
would pursue emigration to Lagos, Abeokuta, Ibadan, and other Yoruba
towns for that much-sought reunion with kin group members. It is this
latter group that became the Saro, a distinctive element of that emigre
band of Krio that fanned out of Freetown over the years, not only to Nigeria and other locations on the coast of West Africa, but even into the Congo
and Southern Africa.[3]

Commenting on the evolution of the Krio society in Sierra Leone,
Akintola Wyse once noted the following characteristics of the group: "Its
high cultural attainments, its modern outlook, the sometimes ambiguous
relationship with the white men, its political consciousness, the continual
struggle with authority, its religiosity, its litigiousness, its individuality, and
that unfortunate capacity to fragment".[4] A study of the Saro of Port Harcourt,
a secondary, perhaps even a tertiary diaspora of the Krio, provides an opportunity to evaluate these attributes away from the traditional geographic
milieu of the community. A host of questions inevitably emerge, and ought
to be confronted. What were the circumstances of the departure from
Freetown, and how crucial a variable was this for the cultivation and maintenance of the home ties? What was the nature of the reception in a Niger
Delta of such pronounced ethnic fragmentation? To what extent did a pro-
longed sojourn in the delta modify the Krio values and beliefs in the Saro?
How did the Saro respond to acts of European racism in colonial Port
Harcourt? How were the anti-colonial activities of the Saro received by a
British presence that had come to regard these immigrants as vectors of
European values and sub-imperial subalterns of the realm?

The decision by the British to establish Port Harcourt in 1912 as a
port for the export of coal from the neighboring Udi fields, and the handling of European manufactured goods, marks the beginnings of emigration into the fledgling township. Although unskilled labor was drawn predominantly from within Nigeria, and particularly from the surrounding
mainland and riverine Ijaw communities, the need for skilled labor in construction work and early administration provided many opportunities for
Saro already resident in different areas of the territory. We do not know
precisely when the first Saro arrived in Port Harcourt. Kuczynski and Amaury
Talbot are not particularly helpful here,[5] and the unreliability of early cen-
sus activities in the southern Province of Nigeria further exacerbate our

difficulty. Up to 1911 (a year before Port Harcourt's debut), enumerators of the "non-native" elements of the southern Nigerian population concentrated only on the European residents. The black, non-native count featured Brazilians and West Indians more prominently than it did West African emigres, whose numbers in the years up to 1938 appear to have been too low to warrant much interest.[6]

It would appear that the earliest Saro to reach Port Harcourt, c. 1912, came from Bonny where they had served as clerks, teachers, pastors and traders. This initial nucleus would later attract other Saro from Calabar, Lagos, some towns in Igbo country, and, lastly, it would seem, from Freetown itself. We are equally reduced to speculation in the matter of population growth, but judging from what we know of the better documented 1930's, the Saro count in pre-World War I Port Harcourt could not have exceeded 20 households.

Their insignificant numbers apart, the Saro immigrants, by virtue of their education, were entering Port Harcourt with a distinct advantage not open to most indigenes. As in Lagos, they would easily dominate the clerical field in both the government and private sectors, and rise to positions of influence in the schools and churches that were introduced in the early years. This pioneer population of Saro was all Krio (members of other ethnic groups in Sierra Leone were not represented in the early years),[7] with the available jobs going predominantly to the male heads of households. Saro women were mostly housewives, and though significant hearth-hold heads, central to the social reproduction of the family,[8] their lives revolved around the home, with husbands dominating public space. Saro society was, from its inception in Port Harcourt, a patriarchal assemblage, modelled on Lagos and Freetown, with women and children operating within relations of great material dependence on the men folk, a matter of great relevance to our review.

Towering over the colonial developments of the period in a British-ruled Port Harcourt, is the personality of the Rev. Lionel Randal Potts-Johnson, a Saro pioneer of an immense innovative range. A review of early Port Harcourt invariably becomes one of the life and times of Potts-Johnson, as the small band of immigrants of which he was the vibrant spark, attempted to establish a permanent presence in an area that was surrounded by a congeries of minority ethnic groups, in frenzied competition one with the other. It is to Potts-Johnson, high school tutor of the future Nigerian nationalist, Nnamdi Azikiwe, that we turn for the earliest stirrings of a local proto-nationalist consciousness, that was, at once, socio-economic and political. Spokesman for his group as well as the indigenous majority, Potts-Johnson railed incessantly at British policy making, even as he forged his way, often with grudging official support, to undisputed local leadership of the African community in the period up to the late 1940's. Innovator in the fields of education, journalism, printing, and township politics, among others, Potts-Johnson was a commanding presence in the community up to his death, a prominence that served to further Saro elite interests, while generating profound resentment in some indigenous circles.

Saro advantage in education and familiarity with British institutions, would dictate a leading role for its leaders in township life, but the primacy of this elite would not go completely unchallenged. The many nuanced efforts of the largely indigenous petty traders of Port Harcourt and their working class associates, backed by Saro of like economic profile, to break the informal alliance between the Saro and the indigenous elites, whose hegemony held sway into the mid 1940's, is a central feature of this study. These struggles were to be rooted in confrontations over landed property. Virtual class warfare, inspired by intense competition between landlords (many of them Saro) and tenants, with the Plotholders Union being assailed by an uncompromising House Tenants Association, was the brutal outcome of the economic polarisations of this much-differentiated African community. The Saro elite was itself fractured, with patricians such as Potts-Johnson eager to make inroads into the lower classes, while others kept a social distance, evincing a clear preference for higher society.

Equally engaging in the Port Harcourt of our study, are the processes of the negotiation of ethnicity at work in the social sphere,[9] as the handful of non-Krio Saro individuals, and those of other nationalities, attempted to forge for themselves some space within the predominantly Krio cultural formation of the Saro community. Perhaps the most formidable group presence on the township's social scene, Saro society attracted many who saw social affinity to the group as a gate-way to opportunity and some preferment from the corridors of power. Members of the Saro elite were much-sought after as patrons of the ambitious.

This is also a social history of a people away from home—their dreams, aspirations, travails, and diverse vicissitudes of fortune. We survey the challenges of efforts at cultural retention, reinforced through periodic travel, by the well-to-do, to nodal centres such as Freetown, Lagos, and Calabar. For the vast majority, the pursuit of Kriodom would, of necessity, reside exclusively in a linguistic attachment to Krio, and an unwavering involvement with Krio values, mores, observances and institutions, mostly acquired by secondary transmission. This would in itself present a major challenge to a community that was of some economic differentiation, while in pursuit of a socially communal corporate existence. Identification with Sierra Leone would bring reprisals, and some censure, from the indigenous community, and the Nigerian government, and this, in the short term, would be met by a stoic defiance, buoyed by expectations of protection from consular officials from Sierra Leone, based in Lagos. That these hopes of compatriotic support were not always to be gratified, nor protection readily conferred, would be a matter of great distress for the beleaguered Saro.

It is our concern also in this study to review the lines of social class that passed through Saro society, and to observe their careful mediation through the agency of the ethnic Union, that social leaven that made a community out of individuals of diverse means and a host of proclivities. These bonds would be at their most vital from the late 1940's, when, with the progressive erosion of Saro dominance, indigenous forces rose to crowd the Saro off the political stage, and consign them to the social margins. These developments would usher in a most trying period for the immigrant group, as, with independence, it sought to carve a niche for itself within a demographically dense eastern Nigeria (soon to be gripped by the ravages of civil war), while retaining cultural, and in some cases, nationality ties to Sierra Leone. The Nigerian government and a number of its citizens would regard with extreme impatience the professed twin loyalties of the Saro community. The group's publicly demonstrated attachment to Krio cultural observances, and its passion for matters Sierra Leonean, would engender much cynicism and attract some discriminatory treatment from the Nigerian populace. This, in turn, would cause a few Saro to seek security in a political retreat into Nigerian citizenship, and a less ostentatious involvement with the culture of the "homeland". In this immigrant experience of some crisis, the Saro denouement in Port Harcourt was not unlike the frustrated political expectations of the Saro of Lagos, or those of the Krio of Freetown—minority ethnic formations with unrealistic hopes of abiding group influence and some superordination, that were rooted in a fleeting colonial preference, but generally indulged in situations of profound demographic disability.

Finally, this study seeks to identify the place of the Saro in studies of the African diaspora, while also delineating the strategies for group cohesion and survival deployed by the community over the years in Port Harcourt. Studies of the African diaspora have for long been taken up with reviews of the exertions of slave communities and their descendants in the New World, the monumental challenges of adaptation to a new geographical locale, and the existential demands on the transplanted of life in western capitalist society.[10] These studies have reviewed within the context of a burgeoning pan-African consciousness the many seminal contributions of W.E.B. Du Bois, Edward Blyden, Marcus Garvey, C.L.R. James, George Padmore, Sylvester Williams, and other luminaries, whose efforts were geared toward restoring pride and dignity to the black race. A people long traduced by slavery confronted the challenge of either opting for continued assimilation into the western society of their emasculation, or pursuing a more militant identification with the Africa of their ancestors. Allied to the latter impulse, and of cardinal significance for our purposes, has been the quest for a return to Africa. The nostalgic yearnings of Garvey's Universal Negro Improvement Association, the cultural irredentism of the Rastafarian, the insistent demands for repatriation of Trinidad's Mandingos, and the Freetown experience of the Krio, all belong to this relentless search for ancestral moorings.[11]

Migratory desire would not, however, end with the return to Africa. Wyse has stressed the need for further review of the African diaspora within the African continent, those wanderings to far-off places, in some instances, from home bases of happy memories, in others, from centres of unfulfilled aspiration and much frustration.[12] The Saro experience in Nigeria belongs to both shades of this experience, the extension along the west African coast of that peripatetic impulse that would not be stilled in those who yet must wander.

But what do we know of the reception that awaited the "Stranger" in the lands around the Niger where kinship ties of the sort enjoyed in Yorubaland were not generally available? What challenges would he face, and to what survival strategies would his community resort? Perhaps, even more significantly, we need to establish how his experience approximates that of such minority groups as the Dahomians of the Ivory Coast and Niger, the Ghanaians of Nigeria, the Lebanese of West Africa, and the Asians of Uganda. Minority communities under threat from indifferent host societies have been known to adopt a range of initiatives to improve their situation. These could range from inter-marriage with their hosts and peripheral political involvement, to substantial but discrete gift-giving to those in authority, as well as the varied pursuit of social goodwill within the ranks of the indigenous society, often the prime source of the immigrant's unease. Drawing on Georg Simmel's concept of "Der Fremde" ("The Stranger", 1908), William Shack has observed that immigrant groups though "inorganically" appendages to their host societies, are often "organically" a part of them as a result of the peculiar attributes and values they often contribute to their adopted communities. This explains why, in the long term, the immigrant's assimilation into the host community becomes possible, should circumstances favor it. At his advent, the stranger is neither "alien" nor "citizen". His existence is modulated by the local social organisation ("societas") and the political authority ("civitas"), and he occupies a liminal position "betwixt and between" the poles of "alien" and "citizen". Under colonialism in Africa, the strangers immigrant status was often secure and free from violation, for as long as he operated within the law. Colonialism seldom differentiated between hosts and strangers. Both groups attracted similar treatment, and laboured under the same disabilities. With the end of colonialism, however, the stranger could find his immigrant status much compromised by positions adopted by the new government. Though he could still proceed to citizenship, the likelihood of his becoming an alien, subject to harassment, sundry victimisation, even deportation, significantly increases.[13]

The travails of the Saro of Port Harcourt, in the years after Nigeria secured political independence from British colonialism, are of prime concern to the concluding sections of this study. We confront here, in stark relief, the changing fortunes of the immigrant community, and review the many imperatives of communal solidarity in the face of some social ostracism and state-directed discrimination, even as frustration bred flagging morale and disillusion in some immigrant circles caught up in an obdurate attachment to old ways.

1

THE FORMATIVE YEARS, 1912–30

The Sierra Leoneans of Port Harcourt (the Saro) are an ethnic formation that was predominantly Krio, with token representation from some of Sierra Leone's other ethnic groups. These immigrants were attracted to this Niger Delta township for a variety of reasons at the beginning of the 20th century. Freetown, on the Sierra Leone peninsula, their spiritual home, had been established in the 18th century, by British humanitarians, as a settlement for liberated slaves, Maroons, and other ex-slave returnees from North America and the Caribbean. A number of these ex-slaves had come to England from Nova Scotia, following their unsuccessful participation in the American War of Independence on the side of the defeated British. The Freetown social experiment would in time, produce the highly differentiated community that evolved into Krio society, of which much has been written.[1] The resettlement effort was pioneered in 1787 by various philanthropic, trading, and enlightenment-oriented interests in Britain, that were out to atone for the many wrongs of the slave trade. These individuals were motivated by the vision of a "Province of Freedom" where ex-slaves, inspired by European values of Christianity, commerce, and entrepreneurship, would evolve into a self-governing black community, that would be an object lesson for others on the African continent. As beacons of light to their unlettered neighbours, it was hoped that these returnees would serve as purveyors of western civilisation, and thus further the cause of British penetration of West Africa. The settlers who were now being repatriated to Freetown from London, Nova Scotia, and Jamaica, had thus been socialised into European values through many years of foreign residence, and this was amply reflected in their Christianity, European names, political aspirations, fondness for the English language and European forms of dress, their rugged individualism, and, above all, the immense pride they took in their extra-continental provenance and connections. In 1807, the British moved to abolish the slave trade, and naval patrols based in Freetown would now have the task of apprehending illegal slave ships, and presenting their crew before courts of Vice-Admiralty, and Mixed Commission. The rescued captives, the "Liberated Africans", became a part of the evolving Krio society of Freetown, and, initially, the object of much derision at the hands of the returnees/settlers who believed themselves superior to these unfortunates who had never really left continental waters. In time, however, settlers and Liberated Africans would come into greater identification, a process much assisted by the latter's edge in commerce and entrepreneurship. Krio society would promote elements of its Africanity alongside its western cultural filiations, but generally at a social distance from its indigenous hosts.

With the imposition of colonial rule by the British over, first, the Sierra Leone peninsula in the early nineteenth century, and then, later in the century, over the hinterland territory which took the peninsula's name, the Krio community, mainly settled in Freetown, became the prime beneficiaries of the educational opportunities provided by the various missionary societies. These efforts would culminate, in 1827, in the establishment of Fourah Bay College, the crowning point of the regime of elementary and secondary schools that had been introduced over the years. By the turn of the 19th century, the Krio had produced West Africa's earliest colonial *literati*, a group that, with official encouragement, would serve in a sub-imperial role within the colony of Sierra Leone, and in other British dependencies along the West African coast. Nigeria, to which a host of Liberated Africans traced their ethnic roots, would be a prime attraction for this nascent Krio diaspora, where, before long, they became the "Saro", or "Saro people".

Early Constitutional Developments in Sierra Leone

Some initial discussion of constitutional change in Sierra Leone becomes necessary at this point. Although as we will soon see, the proud Saro of Port Harcourt, by the 1930's, would take considerable umbrage at the suggestion that Port Harcourt developed in the shadow of Freetown, Lagos, and Calabar, there is considerable evidence to suggest that colonial policy-making and local reactions in those cities would constantly be monitored in Port Harcourt Saro circles over the years. This was, perhaps, not wholly unexpected for a number of reasons. Firstly, without quite admitting it, the Saro of Port Harcourt would regard these centres of Krio life as beacons to guide their progress in this new outpost of Krio endeavour, and they invariably judged their advance by the concessions granted in those communities. Secondly, as we will soon discover, some of the Saro travelled regularly to Lagos, Freetown, and Calabar, and, in turn, they played host on many occasions to relatives and friends visiting Port Harcourt from those centres. They thus kept in touch with the motivations of their principal political actors, and garnered ideas that could be utilised in their interactions with the British. Finally, from the earliest days of settlement, the Port Harcourt Saro were avid readers of the Freetown and Lagos press, and such papers as the Weekly News, the Sierra Leone Guardian, and the irreverent Aurora, added much spice to local conversation.

Knowledge of early constitutional change in Freetown and the methods of its procurement were most instructive to this fledgling band of pioneers in Port Harcourt. For largely as a result of the pressure exerted on them by the Krio, and in some grudging acknowledgment of British dependence on educated Krio personnel for the staffing of some positions in the colonial bureaucracy, the British, by the 1860's, had recognised the need to grant some political participation to the subject population of Freetown. Krio pressure groups such as the Sierra Leone Bar Association, the Rate Payers Association, the African Civil Servants Association, and the African Progress Union, led this challenge of early political mobilisation. By 1863, Britain had allowed a nominated legislative Council, and a municipality, controlled by the Krio, was in place in Freetown by 1893.[2] These were major political developments that allowed some scope for the politics of lobbying and pamphleteering which appealed greatly to the Krio middle class of lawyers, doctors, newspaper editors, and other deeply political professionals. While acknowledging British magnanimity in these actions, Krio leaders such as T.C. Bishop, J.J. Thomas, A.J. Shorunkeh-Sawyer, and E.H. Cummings, among others, would initiate the debate on elective representation which Dr. H.C. Bankole-Bright, a medical practitioner, and other future leaders would continue in the years ahead under the aegis of the regional organisation, the National Congress of British West Africa (NCBWA).[3]

Britain and Nigeria

The British occupation of Nigeria has to be seen within the context of the abolition of slavery, the European scramble for Africa, and the securing of trading and other economic interests in the area. By 1861, Britain had declared a colony in Lagos, and she proceeded thereafter, by force of arms to subjugate the Yoruba peoples of the surrounding hinterland. By 1885, she had imposed claims of protection on the "Oil Rivers" further to the south-east, an area of great potential for trade, but with African leaders such as Jaja of Opobo, who jealously guarded local sovereignty, and profits. Britain would move swiftly against such local potentates, in Benin, among the Itsekiri, and elsewhere, on the pretext of safeguarding freedom of trade. The overthrow of "the Long Juju" resistance of the acephalous Igbo in 1902 brought these local reverses for the imperial march in southern Nigeria to a point that gave some meaning to the Protectorate of Southern Nigeria that had been declared in 1900. The occupation of northern Nigeria demanded the collective genius and exploits of Sir George Goldie, the monopoly capitalist on the Niger, Lord Lugard, the father of Indirect Rule in Northern Nigeria, and Joseph Chamberlain, Colonial Secretary in the Salisbury cabinet of the 1890's. A deft combination of sharp trade practices, numerous treaty signings with African leaders, and well-appointed pacification raids against northern Emirates, gave the British a protectorate in Northern Nigeria by 1 January 1900. Lugard became its High Commissioner, and the business of securing outstanding areas such as Nupe and Sokoto, was promptly taken in hand in measures interchangeably of force and diplomacy. In 1906, the Colony and Protectorate of Lagos were united with the protectorate of Southern Nigeria, and in 1914, the vast northern and southern enclaves were amalgamated as the Colony and Protectorate of Nigeria. Governors and Lieutenant-Governors were appointed to head a civil service constituted in two principal sectors, viz., a political branch made up of Residents, District Commissioners, etc., with responsibility for the provinces, districts, and the central secretariat, and a technical branch of professionals to preside over education, public works, post and telegraphs, and other departments of government. In Northern Nigeria, the British allowed the indigenous rulers much sway in governance under the system of indirect rule, with special protections of Islamic institutions and observance. In the south, imperial officials had more direct responsibility.[4]

The emigration movement from Sierra Leone to Nigeria, commencing in the 19th century, has received far too much scholarly attention to bear recounting in detail here.[5] The Saro performed pioneering work in Lagos, Ibadan, and other principal centres, in the church, in education, commercial enterprise, the British colonial bureaucracy, and allied fields of endeavour. Drawn to Nigeria by the cultural pull of natal roots, some of the Yoruba in the evolving Krio population of Freetown had longed for a return to the homeland. By April, 1839, some sixty Liberated Africans had sailed for Badagry with various trade goods. They returned, delighted at the reception they had received, but failed to convince the British to start a Badagry colony.[6] Undaunted, however, they would continue to travel to Nigeria in ships owned by wealthy Liberated Africans. In time, these Saro became active members of communities in Lagos, Abeokuta, and other outlying towns. They served in the professions, but also as traders of local produce, and in the import and export sectors. Wyse has documented the many exploits and contributions of J.P.L. Davies, Henry Robbin, J.J. Thomas, R.B. Blaize, and others,[7] pioneers in diverse fields of endeavour. Wherever they went, they took with them the Christian gospel, and elements of western civilization of which they believed themselves worthy exemplars. Their socialisation, not always painless, was greatly facilitated by the fact that they were often returning to the warm embrace of family members, and this partly explains the ease with which some of their number became active players in chieftaincy and local politics shortly after their re-incorporation into Yoruba society.[8] This was a luxury not to be enjoyed by the vast majority of the Saro that came to Port Harcourt. They generally had no kinsmen in the Niger delta, and would have to make their way largely unaided by the indigenous population.

Early Constitutional Developments in Nigeria

Constitutional developments in Nigeria, with initial concentration on Lagos, would feature a great deal of Saro involvement. On annexing Lagos in 1861, the British introduced a Legislative Council of nominated African representatives and a majority of British officials. This body was dissolved in 1922 by the Governor, Frederick Lugard, who already had a reputation for despotism and some negrophobia,[9] to be replaced by a larger assembly, the Nigerian Council. African representation was still by nomination, with the six representatives being two Emirs from Northern Nigeria, the Alafin of Oyo, and a representative each from Lagos, Calabar, and Benin-Warri.[10] The Saro of Lagos, led by a lawyer from the Gold Coast, J.E. Caseley-Hayford, soon found this arrangement to be rather limiting of African political involvement, and plans to launch a regional organisation to represent the four British colonies of Sierra Leone, Nigeria, Gold Coast and Gambia, were promptly taken in hand, the outcome being the aforementioned National Congress of British West Africa (NCBWA). In 1920, the NCBWA sent a deputation to London to demand, among other things, Legislative

Councils in the British colonies where half of the members would be elected Africans, and the other half, nominees. They also called for greater involvement in taxation policy-making as well as the expenditure of revenues, and requested the introduction of a West African University.[11]

Lord Milner, the Secretary of State, was outraged at these suggestions, and the Governor of Nigeria, Hugh Clifford, condemned the presumption of the educated African middle class to speak on behalf of the African majority, of whom, in his view, they could be hardly representative. The aristocratic Clifford had served in Malaysia, and was believed to be somewhat of an expert on native policy.[12] Clifford, it turned out, was also an enlightened, liberal, and far-seeing administrator, and a substantial improvement on his predecessors, Lugard and Sir Graeme Thomson.[13] His *volte-face* in 1922 thus becomes more understandable. For though in a much-quoted address in 1920, Clifford had reiterated his opposition to educated African claims based on notions of "self-government, patriotism, nationality, and nation",[14] he saw the wisdom, two years later, of introducing a Legislative Council in Nigeria with elective representation. Under the 1922 Constitution, the Legislative Council of Nigeria was allowed 46 members, with 27 as officials, and 19 as unofficials. Of the African unofficials, 4 were to be elected, three from Lagos, and one from Calabar.[15] The people of Calabar, with a very vocal Saro population,[16] revelled in the national elevation that had come to their south-eastern town which had strong ties to Port Harcourt. Clifford's gesture would unleash a political rivalry of a sort between these two towns, and one that would shape many aspects of the political culture of Port Harcourt in the years to come.

Early Days in the Niger Delta

Long before a Port Harcourt existed, the Church Missionary Society (CMS) had sponsored the work of Saro clergy in various communities of the Niger delta, and the adjacent lands of the Igbo. From tentative beginnings in the 1860's at Bonny, much quickened by the consecration in June 1864 of the Saro, Samuel Ajayi Crowther as Bishop of the Niger Delta, the gospel and its educational endeavours had reached Brass, Kalabari, Okrika, Opobo, and other riverine communities.[17] These pioneering forays were, of course, not free of controversy. Ayandele has chronicled, in fair detail, the convulsions that gripped the early Anglican Church in the delta in the second half of the 19th century.[18] The Niger Mission crisis, generated by accusations of racism levelled against the European clergy, featured prominent Saro cultural nationalists such as the Rev. James ("Holy") Johnson. Saro clergy were in turn excoriated by their white adversaries, who dismissed them as ambitious "swarms of ragamuffins."[19] Before passions cooled, Bishop Crowther would himself be disgraced by Church authorities, a circumstance that drove him reluctantly towards religious independency, and an involvement with the virtually autonomous experiment, begun in April 1892, of the Niger Delta Pastorate.[20] Holy Johnson would pay a dear price for crossing swords with the superiors of his church. When a much-chastened Niger Delta Pastorate returned to the CMS fold in 1897, Johnson had to content himself with an Assistant Bishopric ("Half Bishop"), when general lore regarded his erudition and sundry accomplishments as richly deserving of the episcopate.[21] Though much vilified by their white colleagues, the Saro had served as the rock of the Niger Mission, and it was often grudgingly conceded that, but for their service, the Mission would have collapsed completely.[22]

If the Saro ran foul of their European adversaries, they were no more secure with the Ijaw of the delta congregations, who came often to regard them as foreigners, out to retain monopoly control of the church, and much indifferent to aboriginal aspirations. This disenchantment greatly undermined the church's progress, and would ultimately receive powerful expression, with significant indigenous support, at the turn of the century, in the prophetic Garrick Braide movement.[23]

Life in Early Port Harcourt

Activity in the early days of settlement in 1912 was dominated by the infrastructural concerns of port construction and the introduction of railway facilities into the area. Governor Lugard personally supervised the selection of the port site after reviewing locations in Calabar, Itu, Okrika, Oron, Onitsha, Sapele, and Warri. Okrika clearly offered the best prospects for an entrepot for produce and mineral evacuation, as well as the handling of trade goods, even though its lands adjoined a terrain of mangrove swamps. It possessed the required deep water levels that were vital for harbour construction, and its creek on the Bonny river offered attractive promise of adequate storage facilities for in-coming ships. Construction work on the Port Harcourt site began in November 1913 as materials and men were moved in for work on the projected Eastern Nigeria railway. By 1914, a temporary wharf for the off-loading of materials had been completed, and with the construction of the Port Harcourt to Aba line by January 1916, the terminus began to show signs of more regular activity. The first consignment of coal came by rail from Udi in 1916, for shipment to Lagos by obviously proud harbour officials at the beginning of June.[24]

A Growing Racism in British Society

Port Harcourt's emergence must been seen against the background of a growing tide of racism in British colonial policy-making. From about the 1860's, British official attitudes in West Africa appear to have been increasingly influenced by the writings of Richard Burton and other European negrophobes,[25] who resented African middle-class acculturation into European values as seen in their education, forms of dress, social deportment, and general orientation. The Krio were a major target of this opprobrium.[26] Outstanding achievements in education had brought rewards to the Krio and the Nigerian Saro, as could be seen from the positions they held both in private practice and in the colonial bureaucracy. In Freetown of the 1850's, education in the sciences, the arts, medicine, the law, and engineering, among others, had brought appointments to the colonial service as doctors, surgeons, and officials in various departments.[27] In Lagos, the Saro had similarly prospered. Samuel Ajayi Crowther and James Johnson rose to positions of prominence in the church.[28] In 1885, Charles Pike acted as deputy Governor, after successful tours of the Customs and Treasury departments. A.C. Willoughby, in 1881, became Assistant Inspector and Deputy Sheriff of the Police; J.A.O. Payne was appointed Chief Registrar of the Supreme Court.[29] By the turn of the century, however, these halcyon days were over, swept convulsively in overwhelming official British resentment of the Krio and the Saro, and reflected publicly in an unwillingness to recognise them for appointment to the Colonial Service. By 1900, in Lagos, only the conservative, Henry Carr, commanded a position, as Inspector of schools and Assistant Colonial Secretary, that was comparable to a European appointment.[30] Discrimination in the health service was even more startling, as we will soon discover.

In Freetown, of the same period, not only had the Krio been dropped from the cocktail and other social circuits, dismissed contemptuously as caricatures and "savvy niggers", few could come by any meaningful position in the civil service.[31] By 1904, the British, ostensibly for health reasons and a concern over malarial infestations, had introduced residential segregation to Freetown, as Europeans moved to Hill Station, abandoning the local population to the valleys of the peninsular.[32]

The Hill Station episode is instructive for our review of early Port Harcourt, for residential separation of the races was the preferred option in the Niger delta township *ab initio*. Europeans were to occupy a special reservation in the western plains, to be separated by a neutral zone from the African settlement to the east. This was the residential policy that was in place as railway construction workers and other forms of labor arrived on the site in 1912, recruited largely through local chiefs who were induced by gifts and, at times, other less welcome coercive measures, to send their able-bodied into the job market. District officers established recruiting networks with communities in Aba, Bende, Degema, Owerri and Uyo districts, and, by September 1914, some 7403 largely unskilled workers were employed in railway construction alone.[33]

Responsibility for the physical development of Port Harcourt in the opening years was entrusted to the Railway department. It presided over the segregated residential zoning programme, the demarcation of building sites, drainage lines, and streets, with the District Engineer in a supervisory role. In time, however, other departments of the administration would progressively relieve the railway department of various functions for which they were better suited, and this process of administrative transfer was almost completed by the early 1920's, with the Public Works Department, for instance, taking control of the maintenance of all township roads by 1921.[34]

As functioning departments became a part of the routine of Port Harcourt, more jobs were generated and many economic opportunities created for those with an education, traders, European firms, and sundry adventurers, who now progressively moved into the township. Firms such as the African Traders Company, Elder Dempster, John Holt, G.B. Ollivant, and the African Oil Nuts Company, among others, had secured sites by 1920, providing clerical and other jobs to new residents, and farm income to the surrounding palm-producing peasant households. These operations also attracted small-scale traders, artisans, and domestic workers into residence. The vast pool of unskilled labor was largely recruited locally, but for skilled jobs (clerks, teachers, clergy, artisans, etc.), Port Harcourt had to rely initially on neighbouring riverine communities such as Bonny and Opobo. Schools established by missionaries in those communities had produced some educated indigenes. Their numbers were, however, augmented by skilled recruits from Calabar, Lagos, Onitsha, and other West African territories, such as the Gold Coast and Sierra Leone. While a large proportion of the skilled newcomers, including the Saro, found clerical work with the colonial government or in the import and export firms, banks, and other finance houses, some set up private artisanal operations as masons, carpenters, and plumbers.[35] Contract work as suppliers of food and various goods to the government was particularly attractive for the handful of Saro, Igbo (with palm-produce funds), and other residents that could raise the required capital.

Port Harcourt's emergence hastened the decline of Bonny, for many years a home to some Saro, and an area of British Consular operations since the signing of the anti-slave trade treaty with King Pepple in 1839.[36] Bonny now lost its prominence as a centre of trade and administration as the colonial government progressively moved its structures and personnel from the riverine town to the new township. When the Marine and Customs departments left Bonny, more European firms in the produce and merchandise business left for Port Harcourt to occupy strategic locations closer to the new railway. By 1926, a newly constructed Residency in Port Harcourt had replaced the old consulate at Bonny, and with it came more traders, several long-standing Bonny residents, and a number of immigrant civil servants, among them a number of Saro.[37]

Port Harcourt's commercial opportunities would attract into permanent or semi-permanent residence a number of peasant producers from the neighbouring Igbo, Ijaw, Efik and Ibibio-speaking communities. For the first time, many of these farmers could trade directly with the European merchants, thus by-passing the extortionate middle-men who had routinely creamed off a fair part of their profits. Travel to Port Harcourt for short stays during which trading negotiations were conducted became a regular part of the production cycle for many peasant households. The more affluent producers took to establishing business residences in Port Harcourt, and progressively, some took to spending as much time in the township as in their home areas. Representatives of the Hausa, Fulani, and Yoruba communities soon joined the Saro, Togolese and Gold Coasters as permanent residents by 1920. Unfortunately, the official records do not shed much light on the demographic impact of these immigrants. Their presence clearly added a cosmopolitan dimension to township life, as will be later reviewed, and they expanded the market for the goods traded by resident Indian, Syrian, and Lebanese traders, who also set up shop in Port Harcourt in these pioneering years. Trading on a much smaller scale than the European firms, for whom they sometimes doubled as agents, these Indians and Levantines would present African entrepreneurship with its stoutest challenge before World War II, a matter to which we shall later return.

The Challenge of Urbanisation

Pauline Baker's excellent study of Lagos has mirrored some of the difficulties encountered as settlement progressed in Port Harcourt.[38] As a community of newcomers, some indigenes, others immigrant, early Port Harcourt society would face the multifarious demands and pressures of urbanisation. That these tribulations were being encountered on the eve of war, and in the midst of parlous economic conditions, exacerbated the scale of difficulty. Away from their home locations, the residents would need to develop the support structures and processes that would ensure security of life, while affording some opportunity for wholesome interaction with other individuals who were often complete strangers. Such social institutions as churches, schools, mosques, and various organs of social recreation (Clubs, unions, etc.) would have to be created if life outside work was to have any meaning.

Urban life affords freedom from the traditional restraints imposed by kinship obligations, and with its many opportunities, it holds out immense possibilities of social mobility within a structurally differentiated environment. The possession of material resources and some education was often crucial to success, but equally significant were personal endowments of charisma and outstanding abilities at geniality. Life in cities could also be anxiety generating. The heterogeneity of the environment, its many unexpected requirements of acculturation, the general absence of familiar kinship restraints and supports, and the wanton individualism it fosters, have often been known to ensnare the unwary. Paradoxically, the desire for freedom which often dictates migration into the city often leads inexorably to a search for mechanisms of corporate support that would replicate those safety-net institutions left behind in traditional society. Little has written of the migrant's recourse to ethnic unions, benevolent thrift societies, and various cultural and voluntary associations, as he seeks to bring some order and stability to life in his new location.[39] From tentative steps in homogenous ethnic unions, the more emboldened drift into multi-ethnic groupings, an index of a growing confidence, as well as a readiness to take on more risks in a bid for greater opportunity.

Women also migrate into towns, sometimes as wives, but often as unaccompanied adventurers, eager to shake off patriarchal bonds, and to avail themselves of the many freedoms that only towns can offer.[40] Usually less well educated than the menfolk, and largely unskilled, women often take to trading activity and domestic labour, and at times in desperation, prostitution.[41] Educated women were themselves also often at a disadvantage, as the colonial state reserved most jobs for men, leaving teaching and nursing as the most common options for this class of women.[42] Even more than the men, therefore, women in towns would develop a great need for the voluntary association or union.

Saro Experience

In the years leading up to World War I, the Saro of Port Harcourt toiled daily with the hardships of an inflation-ridden environment. Conditions were austere, and social amenities were few. There was no school in the township before 1914,[43] and when efforts were made to introduce one, it should hardly surprise us that this was the by-product of Christian activity. Nduka has written of Ambrose Hart, originally of Bonny, whose home housed the first church in Port Harcourt in 1914. Hart's efforts soon came to the notice of the Saro, Archdeacon D.C. Crowther (son of the distinguished Bishop), who was head of the Niger Delta Pastorate, based at Bonny. Crowther's intervention would lead to the establishment of St. Cyprian's Church in Port Harcourt, under the guidance of the Okrika Parish, then under the Rev. Cole. It was the church house that served as St. Cyprian's Day School, introduced in 1916, the first school in Port Harcourt.[44] By 1921, Port Harcourt, with a population of 7185 residents had 5 schools, with 378 pupils and a complement of 8 teachers.[45] Banham Memorial School was established in 1928 with the blessing of the Methodist Church.

With educational facilities so limited, Port Harcourt depended heavily on the Saro and other West African residents as well as the aforementioned indigenes from Lagos and Onitsha predominantly. The Saro slowly embarked on the process of forging social ties with these educated indigenes. Material conditions for these clerks, teachers, artisans, and clergy were extremely precarious in the pre-World War I period, and after, as will shortly be reviewed. This may well explain the small size of the Saro population by 1914, approximately between 15 and 20 households.[46] Unfortunately official records do not help us to be more precise on population figures. Their material difficulties apart, the Saro were poised as the most prominent immigrant group with the requisite preparation to take advantage of new opportunities should conditions improve. They were strategically situated for leadership positions in education, the clerical services, the church, and in the multi-ethnic voluntary associations that would inevitably come with more prosperous conditions. In the short term, however, difficult economic times had first to be weathered, and it is to these challenges that we now turn in closer review.

Early Economic Conditions

As already indicated, economic conditions in the early days of settlement as the eastern railway was being constructed, were trying in the extreme. The boom conditions generated by the doubling of Nigeria's export volume index between 1900 and 1912[47] brought inflationary conditions to newly emerging areas such as Port Harcourt. A further doubling between 1912 and 1924[48] would greatly complicate the township's economic woes. Export crops constituted some 80% of these receipts, and the expansion in railway construction had given a major boost to agricultural production. The local oil-palm industry of the Niger Delta, recovering from the stagnation of the last three decades of the 19th century,[49] was a major contributor to this success. Unfortunately, a fledgling Port Harcourt was in no position to benefit from this expansion in agricultural scale. The exigencies of the period ran wantonly across racial lines, and drew a number of petitions to London from the local white employees, not up to fifty in these pioneering years.[50] In October 1915, Lord Lugard, now the Governor-General of Nigeria, noted that "owing to the extremely high cost of living at Port Harcourt, the clerks sent from Lagos or Zungeru were suffering considerable hardship".[51] He expressed the hope that eventually "supplies would get cheap as the line reached new markets."[52]

Conditions did not show much improvement with the end of the war. In April 1919, as deterioration continued, European members of the Nigerian Civil Service based in Port Harcourt, reiterated their earlier plea of December 1917 for supplementary remuneration. In a petition to the Secretary of State, they noted "the severe pecuniary disadvantage" under which they laboured. The officers drew attention to the support their case had received in 1916 from A.S. Cooper, the late General Manger of the Railway, and from M.Y. Grant, his successor. They requested "a special Port Harcourt allowance at the rate of £60 per annum to date back to January, 1917", and attached a list comparing goods prices in Port Harcourt to those of Lagos, Nigeria's capital city,[53] as is shown in Table 1-1. It was hoped that this desperate plea would convey to senior officials the gravity of the economic situation.

The local administration was not much impressed by the case the officers had made, and, in a minute accompanying the petition to Viscount Milner, A.G. Boyle, the Acting Governor, made the following comments:

> "I regret that I am unable to recommend . . . that this be granted. I do not consider that the cost of living at Port Harcourt is any greater than at Forcados,

Table 1-1

Comparative Statement of Prices
Lagos and Port Harcourt (April, 1919)

Native Produce

	Lagos	Port Harcourt
Yams each	3d to 4d	8d to 1/2
Chickens each	1/6 to 1/9	3/- to 4/-
Eggs each	1d	2d to 3d
Onions each	1 1/2d to 2d	4d to 9d
Oranges each	1/2d	1d
Pineapples each	1d	4d
Avocado Pears	1d	2d
Ground Nut oil (per bottle)	1/6	3/-
Beef per lb	8d	1/-
Bones for soup	1d	3d
Fish per lb	1/6	2/6
Bread	6 ozs. 3d	4½ ozs. 3d
2 days	6d	P.H. Allowance 13
		½ ozs. 2 days= 9d

Imported Goods

	Lagos	Port Harcourt
Lard per lb	1/4	1/9 At French Co. Their supply now finished. Miller Bros. price 2/4d
Sugar	10d	1/-

Kerosene for drying purposes at least 1/2 gallon per week @ 10/6 per 4 gallons

Cold Storage

	Lagos	Port Harcourt
Imported Lamb per lb	2/-	3/3 to 3/6
Sausages	2/-	4/-
Cheese	2/6	3/-
Butter	4/6	4/8

Source: CO 583/75, PRO.

Calabar, Bonny, and stations similarly situated. . . . officers who were in Africa in the pioneer days would have indeed fared badly had they not shown initiative in arranging to obtain from other sources food supplies not brought to their doors for sale, and I . . . believe that a similar initiative (sic.) shown by the residents of Port Harcourt would have equally beneficial results."[54]

An administration raised on parsimony, unflinchingly committed to defraying expenses exclusively from local revenue sources, and eager to advertise its constancy, was not about to cave in to pressure, even if this emanated from its expatriate personnel. This *tour de force* was ample warning to the African lobby.

The Saro and the Early Economy

Early observers often commented on the solidarity of the Saro community, a bonding not least dictated by the indigency and sundry privations that came with the economic difficulties of early settlement. The Station Magistrate at Port Harcourt observed in November 1919, "the many occasions when a Sierra Leonean man has been arrested on a criminal charge [and] his countrymen have invariably tried to influence the Police in the accused's favour . . . ".[55] Immigrant experience reinforced primordial communal tendencies, and this was often manifest in the zeal with which the Saro supported each other, particularly in periods of stress.

The more economically devastated of the Saro, such as the unemployed, often had recourse to official favour in their efforts to supplement communal hand-outs. When all else failed, they would plead for repatriation to Freetown. In October 1919, J.M. Metzger, once of the Printing Departments in Freetown and Zungeru (Northern Nigeria), now resident in Port Harcourt since 1914, petitioned the Governor, Sir Hugh Clifford. He complained that he had "never . . . been offered any privilege of further work in the government or a compensation of (sic.) the 22 long years service in both the Sierra Leone and Nigerian governments, nor any passage to return home . . . ". He wrote of being "stranded in the port penniless", with a family of four.[56] In July 1922, another Saro, J.B. Macaulay, clerk of the Nigerian Railway, died with no relatives in the township, and efforts had to be made to locate his mother in Freetown.[57] Such instances of deprivation were not uncommon in Saro experience in the Port Harcourt of the pioneering years. They would inevitably set a tone for the configuring of the group's social relations in the years that lay ahead.

Material conditions, extremely difficult for the poor in the early years, were worsened by the rather dilatory process of the official demarcation of the African residential quarters in what became the "native town". This made housing highly problematic, and introduced slum conditions. Even government officials often despaired of the likelihood of attracting more residents to Port Harcourt, with accomodation being so limited, and so prohibitively expensive.[58] Not surprisingly, Port Harcourt's early appearance was far from prepossessing, and Governor Hugh Clifford himself, painted a picture of a place forlorn when he visited in October 1919. Clifford noted: "The roads are unmetalled, except for a few yards immediately in front of the Railway offices . . . The whole settlement is overgrown and unkempt to an extraordinary degree".[59] The depressing environment was reflected in the foul mood of the township's residents. In conveying his impressions to the Secretary of State, Clifford added: " . . . men with letters in their hands assailed me and my private Secretary at every turn, and the unanimity of the complaints leads me to think that the affairs of the Station have not of late been managed in a very satisfactory manner".[60]

Conditions were only fractionally better for those in business at this time, for official contract awards, on which may had come to depend, were intermittent and unreliable. The Saro, I.R. Benjamin, who for 18 years had served as a contractor in Calabar, Opobo, and Port Harcourt, petitioned Governor Clifford in October 1919, in some desperation. He wrote: " . . . there are many permanent contracts here such as the clearing of refuse in the native town and in the clerk's settlement . . . ". He, however, complained that those jobs were being scheduled to prisoners. He requested that he be recommended to the Senior Medical Officer "for a permanent contract", as he was a man "of families here and at (sic.) Sierra Leone", and had to provide for them.[61]

The material insecurity of the period, relieved sporadically by communal group support, was pointing ineluctably to the need for the institutionalisation of such group mechanisms as had made life in Yorubaland and Freetown infinitely more tolerable. Such organisations included the Church, the ethnic Union, and thrift and loan societies, those invaluable aids of urbanisation that were inestimable in their significance in difficult times. Some of these already existed in the indigenous communities around Port Harcourt, but few Saro seemed willing, in the early years, to proceed beyond informal friendships and closet concubinage to the formal marital unions that would have guaranteed access to these avenues of material succor. Most Saro were strictly endogamous in these opening years, and the social reserve of Freetown still largely characterised their relations with local society. Moreover, this was a season of economic difficulty for locals too. The Saro population of Port Harcourt, up to the late 1920's, was small, and far short of a hundred residents; few of its members, it would appear, had fully committed themselves to permanent residence. Most were eager for further assurance of the township's viability. Thrown together by common economic problems, immigrants and indigenes were "amicably disposed towards each other", and the administration often celebrated the absence of political strife in these challenging times.[62] The Saro kept up their connections with relatives and friends in Freetown, Lagos, and Calabar, as much for emotional as for economic reasons. Letters were more frequently exchanged as the expense of home visits reduced the latter's regularity.

The Early Church

Conditions did not improve much as Port Harcourt entered the global depression of the late 1920's. The Church now emerged as the cardinal social institution in Saro life. Although the Anglican communion had preached its gospel assiduously throughout the delta for a longer period, and with some success, the Methodists were not to be easily deterred from also seeking to establish congregations in the area. Many a Saro would become devoted members of the Methodist Church of Port Harcourt. Unlike the Methodist experience, much has been written of early Anglican activity in the township; from the establishment of the St. Cyprian congregation around 1914 as part of the Okrika parish, to the introduction of an autonomous Port Harcourt District in 1924. Saro immigrants featured prominently in these activities which were accompanied invariably by some elementary educational enterprise.[63]

The Methodist advance in the area, pioneered by the Primitive Methodist Society of London, would come to the Niger Delta from the neighboring Cross River/Ibibio field of the Oron and Ebukhu Circuits, effectively opened up from about 1893 with the pioneering work of the Revds. R. Fairley and F. Pickering.[64] The Wesleyan Methodists were also in search of converts in the Niger Delta, and, as will be reviewed presently, Saro instrumentality in introducing this segment of the Methodist Church into Opobo and Egwanga, from about 1913, is a matter of copious record.[65] In 1916, officials of a Wesley Methodist congregation, Port Harcourt, applied to the District Officer for a plot of land on which to construct a chapel and a mission house.[66] Some records indicate that the early Methodist church was called "Zion" at this stage, and only became "Wesley" in 1930.[67] This church became the central body for the social reproduction of its Saro membership, a venue for interaction and group identification in the difficult pioneering years. Wesley's membership was much ravaged by the economic conditions of the time, and only some 17 years later would the congregation act on its land grant with a ground-breaking ceremony, preliminary to construction,[68] a building fund having, by this time, been established.[69]

Port Harcourt's dismal fortunes began to change in the late 1920's even as the global depression, soon to be reviewed, appeared on the horizon. A major addition to the community at this time was the Saro, Dr. I.G. Cummings, who joined the colonial service as an African Medical Officer in 1925.[70] Cummings' arrival immediately sparked off a major controversy over the site of his official residence, and must be examined within the context of an increasing racial intolerance in British colonialism since the 1890's. The British had adopted a policy of residential segregation for the races in West Africa, but had been slow in its implementation in some of the territories under their rule. In June 1914, Sir Frederick Lugard, the Governor-General, had expressed some exasperation over this delay. In official correspondence, he noted: "Although the policy of segregating Europeans and of locating their residence at a distance of at least 400 yards (when possible) from those of natives, has, I believe, for some years been accepted in West Africa, I found, on my return to Nigeria, that no definite steps appeared to have been taken to define the areas which should be assigned for European and native dwellings respectively, and applications for leases were constantly submitted which violate this principle".[71] Lugard was eager to end this ambiguity, and new towns, such as Port Harcourt, were to be the testing grounds of his resolve. By April 1916, Lugard could confidently inform London that "the principle of segregation between Europeans and Natives and various other sanitary precautions have been given effect . . . ".[72]

It was into this segregated environment that Cummings was plunged through his posting to Port Harcourt. Tom Gale has written of the discriminatory treatment meted out to qualified African doctors by the British in West Africa during the second half of the 19th century.[73] In 1902, when a West African Staff unit was commissioned, all African doctors were denied access to it. Even though some European officials themselves privately preferred African medical personnel when they were ill, prejudiced officials were generally allowed to hound African doctors out of colonial positions on the pretext that they were either incompetent (a charge clearly not borne out by most records) or that they inspired no confidence in the white clientele. Cummings' victimisation was of a slightly different order. He had attracted consistently favourable official reviews, over the years, in his work, and his official conduct had been almost unimpeachable. In 1917, he was said to be of "quite respectable ability", and judged to be "regular and accurate in the work of his district", and "very punctual". The Principal Medical Officer considered Cummings "quite European in manners", and neither "aggressive nor objectionable". He was said, in all, to be "hardworking, unobtrusive, and a favourite with Europeans in his district".[74]

Though ostensibly highly regarded for his education and general deportment, official policy in Port Harcourt precluded Cummings from residing in the same neighborhood as his white counterparts of the civil service. Cummings was assigned a house in an area that would later be described as "insanitary".[75] When this proved to be an embarrassment to the administration, and a threat to the officer's health, he was subsequently moved into a "bush rest house", which was re-roofed and provided with a cement floor and screens for his benefit. It was subsequently suggested that Cummings be assigned No. 97 of the European Reservation, but the members of the all-white Port Harcourt Township Advisory Board, (an Institution we shall soon review) denied the request. They described it as "ultra vires", and instructed the Resident to secure another site on which to construct quarters for the African doctor. This site was subsequently obtained "in the vicinity of the female prisoner's lines".[76] The problem of racism, which would feature prominently in township debate in the coming years, had made its official debut into the Port Harcourt scene. In time, its corrosive impact would imperil relations between the administration and the people of Port Harcourt, engender charges of African elite collaboration with a racist officialdom, and fracture the lines of social cooperation between the different segments of the African population.

There was, however, a slightly more promising dimension to the Cummings debacle. His presence in Port Harcourt served as a catalyst for expanded Saro immigration into the township. In the late 1920's and 1930's, more Sierra Leoneans with a higher level of education (a few college graduates, but mostly high school, with some technical training) took up residence in the township, even as the tightening noose of the depression began to be felt in the progressive immiseration of the township's residents. In February 1930, Nathaniel Vincent, a Saro, called on the local Station Magistrate to provide him with material relief. He explained that he had come to Nigeria as a missionary with the Delta Pastorate in 1906, and that after 3½ years of service, his wife, who had left for Sierra Leone to fetch their daughter, had decided not to return. "I was asked to resign", he continued, "as according to English Church rules, I can't re-marry, my wife being alive". At 63, he could find no work, was down with "acute rheumatism", and had now been unemployed for a year. His friend and compatriot, E.C. Taylor, of Imo River, into whose home he had moved for shelter and food, had died in February. "I am obliged to appeal and petition the Resident through you . . . ", he wrote, "that government should [send] me to my country, Sierra Leone". The Sierra Leone government, on being approached, declared Vincent destitute, and having secured from him an undertaking to refund his passage to Freetown of £ 5.9s., had him repatriated to Freetown.[77] The miserable circumstances in which the more hapless immigrants found themselves were certainly not about to abate.

The case of Alicia Williams is similarly instructive, and directs us to the peculiar difficulties experienced by unprotected women in difficult urban situations. She had arrived in Nigeria in 1911 with her husband who was an engineer for John Holt. At his death in 1919, she became a "washer woman", as she could not afford the passage to Freetown. She confessed to living off her Saro compatriots, "who I could now say are tired of my visits to ask for help". In her plea to the administration, she continued: "Instead of dying of starvation, I am compelled to ask you kindly for repatriation to my country Sierra Leone. . . . I am on (sic.) my 65th year".[78] Even as they explored foreign lands, the Saro never lost sight of Freetown's potential as a sanctuary for returnees, a haven where the distressed could seek solace. Over the years of sojourn in Nigeria, an embarrassing return to the protective embrace of kin was always judged a more prudent outcome compared to enforced misery in the adopted country.

The Effects of the Global Depression

The depression that started in the late 1920's was to have a crippling impact on the economy of the Niger Delta, and that of eastern Nigeria in general. An economy long ravaged by inflation and some unemployment was about to receive further hammering. The oil-palm industry which was at the heart of the local economy was savaged by the slump. It was this industry that generated capital for trading activity and other related forms of enterprise, and it was a major source of income for the payment of colonial taxes. The configurations of oil-palm production had long been a matter of official discussion, and by 1914, the colonial government had decided against allowing expatriate-owned plantations in Nigeria. This proved to be a major disincentive to British capitalists, for without access to land, investment in oil-palm processing appeared to be too risky an undertaking.[79] For a British administration now intent on promoting African-owned plantations, policy making in the years before the depression revealed a bewildering lack of foresight and imagination. Scarcely any research into the oil-palm industry was undertaken in the 1920's and 1930's. In 1929, the agriculture departments of the British West African colonies rejected calls for an oil-palm research station, stressing instead greater concentration on "economics, land tenure, meteorology, behaviour of soils, plant pests and diseases, [and] the behaviour of new crops".[80] Research on improved oil extraction techniques through the use of more efficient presses had recommended the adoption of more efficient devices in 1923, but not until 1932 were Duchscher presses finally introduced.[81] The new presses would, however, greatly compound the work-load of the average producer; it was thus highly unlikely that they would be adopted widely in a period of declining prices. Very few Africans purchased presses between 1932 and 1938. With the onset of the Depression in the late 1920's, African producers did not therefore operate in a psychological environment that would have buoyed their spirits in a season of economic decline. Whereas Nigeria supplied 61 per cent of the world's oil-palm exports in 1926, her tally would drop to 22 per cent by 1938. In 1926, palm products constituted 49 per cent of total Nigerian exports, but only 34 per cent in 1938. Meredith has chronicled the disastrous plunge in prices in these difficult years.

> "The f.o.b. price of palm oil fell from £23.14s per ton in 1929 to a low point of £4 per ton in 1934, rising to £12 in 1937, and dropping to £5.2s in 1938. Kernels were £13 per ton in 1929, £3.12s in 1934, £9.4s in 1937, and £5. 10s in 1938. The average f.o.b. price of palm oil in 1921-9 was £22. 10s; between 1930 and 1938 it was £9. 3s. The average for kernels was £13. 10s and £6.14s".[82]

Nigeria's principal European buyers of palm produce were generally suffering from contracting markets, at a time when local production in areas like the Niger delta was expanding.

The economic difficulties of this period of settlement, were, undoubtedly, a factor in the decision to form a Sierra Leone Union (SLU). This became imperative as numbers grew, with the entry of more Saro workers, businessmen, preachers, and bureaucrats into Port Harcourt, in the late 1920's. The immigrant of these years who was destined to be the most prominent Saro of the coming period was, unquestionably, the Rev. Lionel Randal Potts-Johnson. Let us now embark on a review of the early exploits of Potts-Johnson.

The Rev. L.R. Potts-Johnson

We know little of Potts-Johnson's early life in Sierra Leone.[83] He was born on 5 February, 1886 in Freetown to Madeline Margaret Johnson (nee Potts), and her husband, whose identity is also a mystery.[84] The young Potts-Johnson attended the Methodist Boys High School, in Freetown, and later left for Lagos, Nigeria, where he was initially attached to the Colonial Secretariat. Not much enamored of colonial service, he next tried his hand at some teaching when he joined the tutorial staff of the local Kings College. Before long, however, Potts-Johnson was in training for the Christian ministry,[85] and we know more of his activities from this point on. He was ordained into probationary ministerial status in the Wesleyan Church in 1912,[86] and would spend the next six years in a course of study in the Lagos Church, leading to full ordination as a Methodist Minister. This was normally a four-year programme, but Potts-Johnson was deliberately set back two years in 1914 as disciplinary action by the church for his having "dishonorably broken an engagement of marriage . . . ".[87] Somewhat of a ladies' man, and prone to some indiscretion in matters of the heart, Potts-Johnson would be the subject of many a peccadillo over the years. This particular brush with the authorities of his church, was perhaps, one of the earliest. The sanction of 1914 was merely the prelude to further acrimonious disagreement in conjugal matters between the Church and its often rebellious charge.

This infraction apart, Potts-Johnson served his probationary period with distinction, often emerging at the top of his class in annual examinations. In the Probationer's examination of 1912, he scored the highest, with a 74.7% average. W.T. Balmer, the programme's director observed: "Potts-Johnson has begun well, but I would like him to write more clearly. His words are at times difficult to make out". The examining board judged Potts-Johnson's reading list for the examinations "satisfactory".[88]

While on probation, Potts-Johnson served on the staff of the Wesleyan Church's Lagos District, and was assigned initially to the "Educational Department", under Rev. Oliver Griffin, the District Chairman.[89] It was at this time that developments that would take the young Potts-Johnson into the Niger delta sector began to unfold. In 1913, the Wesleyans reported that "a number of African christians from Lagos and the Gold Coast have formed a church at Opobo (Egwanga) where they reside as government clerks and employees of various firms . . . ".[90] Potts-Johnson was now despatched, by the Lagos Synod, to Opobo to preside over this fledgling Wesleyan congregation.[91] He appeared to have taken to his new responsibilities with considerable zeal, and moved swiftly to make a mark the authorities would perforce observe. In 1915, the Church reported with much satisfaction on Opobo: "With the appointment of the Rev. L.R. Potts-Johnson, the work rapidly extended (sic.) into the surrounding country", providing "an entirely new field of wonderful potentialities . . . ". It noted that "over sixty people were baptized during the war".[92] The authorities were fulsome in their praise of their appointee's efforts. In 1915, they wrote: "Mr. Potts-Johnson has done excellent work at Opobo as the reports and statistics will show. We have a membership of 111 and over 100 scholars in the Day School".[93] The financial realities of a new station would, however, soon becloud this euphoric prospect. By 1917, the work at Opobo was becoming a major burden on the slender resources of the Church, and the Wesleyans began to consider the possibility of handing over their responsibilities to the Primitive Methodists who had preceded them in the neighbourhood.[94]

In 1918, it was "unanimously recommended" that Potts-Johnson "be received into the full connexion with the conference" as an African minister.[95] Though financially problematic, Potts-Johnson's service at Opobo had expanded the mission's outreach, and delighted the authorities, not least for its dramatic conversion exercises which were often a matter of graphic reportage. One such ran:

> "At Opobo . . . after one Sunday morning service during which the sacrament of baptism was administered, some fetish worshippers, belonging to a neighbouring compound, invited us to their compound, and three made a public renunciation of their fetish faith, and as a proof of their sincerity and earnestness asked us to put into the fire all the paraphernalia and instruments of the fetish worship . . . . Subsequently, the great fetish priest of the town, the last of the old stock, offered himself for baptism, and is now a regular attendant on the means of grace".[96]

Such scenes of the public disavowal of traditional religion were the stuff of which missionary dreams were made, and encomiums flowed liberally over those who made redemptive forays of this magnitude possible.

There were, by 1920, "over one hundred adult baptisms in Opobo Town alone", and the church had grown from four to seven local societies, "with fourteen other preaching places", all of which had "their own places of worship", and kept "a healthy spiritual tone".[97] As word spread of the church's reputation, more requests for pastoral support came from surrounding communities. In 1920, the Wesleyan Synod of Eastern Nigeria was approached by the people of Port Harcourt for a resident Catechist who would provide "pastoral oversight" to their township.[98] The church responded by assigning Potts-Johnson to Port Harcourt.[99] By 1921, Potts-Johnson was also in charge of Wesleyans in Calabar, alongside his Opobo duties.[100] In addition, he trained local agents in Opobo. In 1921, Joshua Epelle, Isaac Green, R.G. Mfon, Dick J. Jaja, and G.S. Campbell, were some of the agents under his instruction. A difficult grader, Potts-Johnson scored only two of these candidates over 40% in that year's examinations. He found their work generally "disappointing", and complained that they failed to address "themselves seriously to the work set". He found in them "an absence of careful and systematic study".[101]

By the early 1920's, Potts-Johnson had obviously found his mission duties limiting, and he hankered after new experience, and some further study. In 1922, without official permission from church authorities in Nigeria or London, he left Nigeria, and arrived in England for further studies in the sciences. With great indignation and scarcely-veiled embarrassment, the Missionary committee in London reported Potts-Johnson's unexpected arrival to the Synod in Nigeria, as well as his request to enroll at Manchester University: "We had no certain information from you as to whether he had your sanction or not for such an undertaking, and the committee was in some embarrassment as to the course it should take in his case. Having regard to the fact that he was here, and that in his bearing and statement he commended himself to the committee, it was decided to permit him to enter on his studies and remain in this country until your Synod could reach a decision in his case, and communicate with us".[102] The London authorities saw no possibility of Potts-Johnson embarking on the desired degree programme, and on the advice of M.F. Houlton of Didsbury, they decided to recommend instead a period of "special training as a teacher".[103]

The Lagos Synod graciously allowed the absent Potts-Johnson a "dispensation", enabling him to proceed with his studies.[104] This, it was hoped, would allow him time to matriculate, and commence his teacher training programme.[105] To help with Potts-Johnson's duties in Opobo, the Synod assigned Rev. Fred Platt to the community.[106] Unfortunately, the mission's work in Opobo now began to decline dramatically. The educational work suffered greatly in Potts-Johnson's absence. The Egwanga school was said to be "under-staffed and inadequately furnished", with "only one Third Class certified teacher", and "seven to nine pupil teachers".[107] The Opobo churches proved incapable of governing themselves as Wesleyan Methodists, and it was noted that "the absence of the Minister-in-charge has greatly contributed to this great draw back".[108] The finances of the church were equally in poor shape for proper records had not been kept. Potts-Johnson was himself said to be in possession of the sum of £15 belonging to the local church's Ete group. The latter's members were withholding financial donations until this amount was refunded.[109]

Meanwhile, in England, the Missionary Committee had made arrangements for Potts-Johnson to study at Kingsmead after his matriculation at Manchester University, to pursue a diploma in teaching.[110] To enter for the diploma, Potts-Johnson had to pass the intermediate examinations which were slated for June 1923. As if the authorities' misery were not already sufficiently compounded, Potts-Johnson now requested permission to further extend his stay into December 1923, when he could attempt the diploma examinations as well.[111] London continued to remonstrate with the Nigerian Synod over the irregularity of Potts-Johnson's case, and expressed much concern over his chosen field of study. The authorities threatened that they could not promise like consideration in the future should this problem recur: "In the case of Mr. Potts-Johnson it was not at all clear what advantage to his ministry it would be to take a science degree, and while we are prepared to give permission for him to proceed further in his study of science, we do not consider that it is the most suitable course for a minister in his position to take".[112]

As though to worsen London's discomfiture, the Synod in Nigeria next reported that it "heartily recommends that Rev. L.R. Potts-Johnson be permitted to remain in England to pursue his studies until December 1923".[113] Had London any suspicions of local complicity in Potts-Johnson's bravado, these must have received great reinforcement from this communication. Potts-Johnson's dogged persistence, and his contempt for rules that worked to the African's disfavour, had obviously impressed some members of the Nigerian Church. Few of his peers were willing to join London in its displeasure over his conduct.

In the event, Potts-Johnson failed to secure a pass at the intermediate examinations of London University in June 1923, and the London Missionary Committee, now reluctant to order his summary return to Nigeria, made arrangements for him to enter Westminster College, where he would have "every facility for the pursuit of his scientific studies".[114] Yet, even as the authorities were proving to be more accommodating of this nagging problem, they communicated to Nigeria their rejection of two new African applications for further study in Europe. In December 1923, the Missionary Committee advised the Nigerian Synod that "it did not feel able to accede at the present stage to [the] request that Mr. Ajibola and M.T. Aguiah should be permitted to visit Europe to take special courses of study". "We are glad", it noted, "that in this case you followed the procedure which we should like you to follow in dealing with all such cases. The application of the individual should be considered in the Synod, and your recommendation upon it should be forwarded to the Missionary Committee with a clear indication of the nature of the work for which special training is desired".[115] Potts-Johnson may well, perhaps, have anticipated the fate that might befall his application had he approached London from Nigeria for leave of study. Presenting the authorities with a *fait accompli* may not have been such an unreasoned approach after all.

It was reported in December 1924 that after a three-year stay in England, Potts-Johnson had returned to Nigeria.[116] It is not clear from the records what qualification he obtained in his studies, but the London Committee, obviously relieved, was generous in its commendation of his efforts. It wrote: "He won everywhere for himself a good name by his preaching and in his course of study, particularly at Westminster College both staff and students were impressed by his diligence and glad of his fellowship".[117] The Committee expressed the hope that the Nigerian Synod would find for Potts-Johnson "within the district some appointment in which he will be able to use to the full the educational knowledge and experience which he has gained by his residence and his work in England".[118]

The Lagos District Synod minutes of 1925 reported Potts-Johnson in service as an African minister in Lagos.[119] It would appear that he did not return to Opobo after his sojourn in England. The decline in Opobo had meanwhile continued, and had occasioned the appointment, by the Wesleyans, of a "Special Commission" to visit the area, and make recommendations to the authorities.[120] Among his duties in Lagos, Potts-Johnson now served, in 1926 and 1927, as "Temperance and Young People's Secretary", an office designed ostensibly to promote abstinence from alcohol and related vices in the laity.[121] In 1928, he was reported to be the African Minister in Calabar.[122] It was also about this time that the Wesleyan authorities in London received word from Nigeria that certain "lay representatives sent to the Synod in previous years", were not "living consistent Christian lives, and should not have been in good standing as church members".[123] The principal infraction under consideration appeared to have been adultery and a reluctance to whole-heartedly embrace monogamy, matters in which, as will be evident later, Potts-Johnson held a line that was contrary to official thinking in his church. London stated its position in the matter without equivocation, and there was no hint of compromise in its tone: "We wish to assure you of our sympathy and our support in your endeavours to purify the church, and to maintain that ideal of the home and of marriage which we derive from the Lord himself . . . . Monogamy is not according to the doctrine and practice of the Wesleyan Methodist Church an institution belonging to European civilisation; it is an institution of our Lord and master himself, and the observation of it is an indispensable part of the New Testament morality".[124] London called on the Synod "to maintain social purity and fidelity to the christian marriage bond", and ruled that "men who trespass against these are not eligible for membership or for office within the church".[125]

It is clear from the records that Potts-Johnson was already formally married to his wife, Nancy Eniton, by this time. The correspondence with London did not refer to adulterous complications with ordained members of the church. The developments that followed London's ruling on this sensitive matter would, however, suggest that Potts-Johnson was much exercised on the issue, largely through his rejection of the position his superiors were wont to follow. For barely two months after London pronounced on the subject, it was reported that "Brother Potts-Johnson" had "intimated his intention to resign as from the end of the present month".[126] Potts-Johnson would make good on this expectation. By December 1929, his resignation from the active ministry had been accepted by the London conference.[127] He would retain his status of an ordained minister, and, in the coming years would occasionally deliver sermons from the pulpits of Port Harcourt's churches, even though he persisted in his controversial views on Christian marriage, and openly championed polygamy.[128] We see in Potts-Johnson's thinking and attitude to westernisation, shades of those African Personality concerns that had characterised the public pronouncements of Edward Blyden and Mojola Agbebi.[129] For these earlier thinkers, the supreme challenge faced by the African elite was the dialectical fusion of western forms with African cultural belief in a bid to nurture individuals that were models of unimpeachable Africanity. Indifference to African culture was not to be regarded as a mark of refinement, but as a retreat from cultural responsibility. Such cultural reflection in the face of European rejection and a growing official racism in Freetown had produced similar reactions. Although such Krio anglophiles as H.C. Bankole-Bright and C.D. Hotobah-During had generally been unaffected culturally by the contemptible conduct of their European peers, others, more sensitive, had called for the adoption of cultural values that were more distinctly African. In 1887, a Dress Reform Society had been established to popularise African designs in Freetown. A number of Krio also took to adopting African names. A.E. Metzger became Tubuku-Metzger, and E.N. Jones now preferred to be Lamina Sankoh.[130] With his resignation, Potts-Johnson was clearly now set to embark on a decidedly more secular path of advance, with minimal involvement in the official councils of the Methodist Church.[131] He now took up permanent residence in Port Harcourt, and would make the township his home for the rest of his life.

Of all the Saro, Potts-Johnson was destined arguably to have the greatest individual impact on the fortunes of Port Harcourt in the period up to the early 1950's. His vision for the township made him the self-appointed spokesman of the African community, as he pronounced almost weekly on a whole range of controversial issues. On 4 January 1930, Potts-Johnson gave Port Harcourt its first newspaper, and embarked on an adventure that would be strikingly reminiscent of that very lively Freetown press of an earlier period.[132] We know nothing of Potts-Johnson's background in journalism, nor are we informed, in any detail, as to his intellectual interests outside his London odyssey. Besides some familiarity with the pan-Africanist ideas of Edward Blyden, and the Gold Coaster, Kweggyir Aggrey, we know little of what he read, or how he came to these intellectual wellsprings. What is not in doubt is his boldness of vision, his rather combative temperament, and a familiarity with the tenor of debate that had made such Freetown papers as the Weekly News and the Aurora, such potent vehicles of Krio anti-colonial opinion. As Proprietor and Managing Editor of the Nigerian Observer, a weekly, Potts-Johnson adopted as the paper's motto, "For God, our Country, and our Race'.[133] The paper, he explained, would be "devoted to the interests of education, religion, commerce, race problems, and various other problems affecting British West Africa".[134] He further noted: "We have left out politics. In our opinion, politics in West Africa have been so muddled that it is like a muddy pool, and none can drink of it with safety. . . . when the political sky is clear and the atmosphere less humid, we shall come out for occasional airings".[135]

These were prophetic words, for throughout the 1930's and 1940's, the Nigerian Observer, like the contemporary and largely Saro-run press of Lagos, would editorialise on a host of incendiary issues confronting the generality of the African population. The local colonial administration would experience many an awkward moment from these "occasional airings", and it would vent its displeasure accordingly, limited only by its perception of the need for African elite support at that material moment. Published in English (except for a column in the vernacular during the great war), and aimed particularly at the reading public of Port Harcourt, the Nigerian Observer quickly became daily fare for many. Copies of the paper occasionally found their way into the riverine communities, but we know of no efforts to promote sales in those regions. Riverine concerns were seldom presented in its pages. Port Harcourt township matters were its cardinal pre-occupation, and Potts-Johnson was unrelenting in their discussion.

The Sierra Leone Union (SLU)

The aforementioned economic difficulties of the depression years called for even greater solidarity among the Saro as they came to grips with the many demands of urbanisation in the Niger delta. The indigent had to be supported, the retrenched, consoled. The time seemed opportune to institutionalise the group's social welfare instincts in an organisation dedicated to supporting all Sierra Leoneans. By 1930, though still experiencing difficult economic conditions, the Saro had started to more frequently observe the Krio cultural practices that were such an integral part of the group's cosmology. Though Christians and Muslims, the Krio had generally retained those African cultural beliefs that celebrated man's passage from birth, through marriage, to death. Most of these ideas were derivatives of Yoruba culture. The birth of a child was often the occasion for a *Komojade*; a young couple's engagement was celebrated at a *Put Stop*; and the dead were sent on their way, and periodically memorialised, in elaborate *awujoh* feasts.[136] It was at the *komojade* that a new born child was introduced to its neighborhood, and given a name. At a *Put Stop*, relatives of the groom-to-be formally requested, in elaborate pageantry, the hand of the "intended" bride in marriage. This ceremony combined Christian and African religious elements. Among the gifts presented by the future groom's representatives was a calabash, kola nuts, various domestic items a wife would use (such as needles and some thread) but also a Bible, a ring, and some money. *Awujoh* commemorations of the dead were mandatory on the third, seventh, and fortieth days after the death, and on any other future occasions (usually anniversaries, or periods of stress in the surviving family) deemed appropriate. *Awujoh* feasts featured much Yoruba/Krio cuisine, and beans, *agidi*, jollof rice, *furrah*, fufu, ginger beer, and vegetable soups were staple fare. The *awujoh* was held in acknowledgement of Krio belief in the cult of the ancestors, and in supplication of ancestral protection for those left behind by the departed. The funeral wake held before burial, the *awujoh* celebrations, and the memorial church services held periodically in conjunction with feasting, were all designed to publicly demonstrate the esteem in which the deceased was held, and, as social occasions that brought relatives and friends together, they served to promote cohesion through the reinforcing of social ties.

In a Port Harcourt of so many strangers, it comes as no surpsise that the Saro felt a great need to maintain communal solidarity. Ethnic cooperation would not only reinforce common values, it would offer protection to the vulnerable, and advertise to all the community's resolve to stand firmly by its members. The Saro of Lagos and Calabar had blazed the trail in these cultural matters through their punctilious observance of Krio/Yoruba customs and traditions. Their periodic social gatherings had also served to mediate their members into the wider community.[137] Given the material means, the Saro of Port Harcourt would do no less. By the end of the 1920's, their thoughts were already turning to the matters of a Sierra Leone Union.

Early social mobilisation among the Saro ought also to be seen within the larger context of communal group activities within the territory as ethnic communities responded to the demands of urbanisation. From about the late 1920's, various ethnic and kinship unions emerged in the principal urban centres of Nigeria. The Owerri Divisional Union, the Calabar Improvement League, the Urhobo Renascent Convention, among others, were established to give identity to specific groups away from home, and to maintain the lines of cultural and material support to the village communities.[138] A vital point of distinction between early Saro union experience in Port Harcourt and that of Saro groups in Yorubaland ought, however, to be established at this point. The efforts that led to the formation of Port Harcourt's Sierra Leone Union reflected the homogeneous character of this immigrant community. Bound by common experience, and with no significant local kinship ties in the Niger delta, the group was easily drawn to a central cultural experience in Krio culture. The Yoruba experience, as Kopytoff has demonstrated, was much more differentiated. In Fyfe's memorable phrase, "only in Sierra Leone were all the children of Oduduwa, the Yoruba ancestor-God united".[139] While Badagry and its neighbourhood met the requirements of some of the emigrants to western Nigeria, others found their roots in Abeokuta and other Yoruba towns. For many, the object was to blend into local culture, not to carve and celebrate a distinctive niche of foreign provenance. Henry Robbin who supervised the Church Missionary Society's cotton interests in the 1850's was always emphatically Egba. And Thomas Babington Macaulay who ran the Christian Institution in Abeokuta left no one in doubt of his Oyo parentage.[140] The Lagos Saro drew great hostility from the local population because of their arrogance and superior airs, their affinity to the British, and the economic competition they posed.[141] It was not therefore in their interest to stress their Sierra Leone connections in spirited Union activity in the early years. Only with the approach of World War II, with greater confidence in their cultural situation, would most Saro in Yorubaland embrace with zeal the Saro unions that had been around for some time.

There were no official ethnic unions in Port Harcourt at the end of the 1920's. A previous attempt to get a Sierra Leone Union (SLU) started, had ended in failure. In March 1930, Potts-Johnson addressed the subject in his paper, and deplored the absence of unity within the African population. He lamented: "Owing to this lack of unity . . . several important and in some cases irrevocable administrative and executive acts have been allowed to stand. . . . the Jekris, Ibos, Efiks, Yorubas, Fantes, and Sierra Leoneans etc. should have separate associations of their own, and then there could be formed a central committee of various tribes . . . to make representation to the proper quarters". Such representation, he continued, could not "fail eventually, if not immediately to produce good results". In his accustomed hortatory style, he asked: "Should we continue to live in our congenial atmosphere of individualism? Will not the leaders of each tribe seriously take the matter to heart and summon a meeting of their people . . . why should we not in our little world of Port Harcourt practice the principles of cooperation and self help"?[142]

Addressing his own people, the Saro, more specifically, Potts-Johnson called for a Union of Sierra Leoneans, referring to one such society of the past which was now moribund. He criticised the new individualism to which Sierra Leoneans were succumbing, dismissing it as counter to the group's primordial communal instincts. He observed: "Sierra Leoneans in Port Harcourt are very partisan in temperament which they invariably take into society. However, be it said, to their credit, that only a moment's notice is required whenever there is a case of distress with one of their member, and the whole (sic.) of them would rally round, and do him a good turn . . . . they have the germ of cooperation in them, and they can unite when there is need for it". He drew attention to the SLU already in existence in Enugu, and challenged local leaders to like initiative. By April 1930, Potts-Johnson had issued a circular inviting all Sierra Leoneans to a meeting at the schoolroom of St. Cyprian's Church in Port Harcourt. He promptly secured the support of the Ven. Archdeacon D. C. Crowther, another prominent local Saro resident.[143] Crowther, son of the late Bishop, was in charge of St. Cyprian's at this time.[144] By May 1930, the SLU was said to be in the process of formation, and Dr. I.G. Cummings had been appointed its first President, with S.M. Reffell as Secretary. Monthly meetings, often held at St. Cyprian's, were organised, at which Saro of all social classes interacted freely, blurring for a time, the obvious class fissures that defined their various occupational pursuits. Often, at meetings, a leader of the group was invited to give a talk. In October 1930, Cummings addressed the members on the importance of "Self Education". The affairs of the Union were handled by an elected executive and, in the first elections, the following members joined Cummings and Reffell on the board:

L.R. Potts-Johnson–Vice President
A.W. Roland Porter &
E.A. Brown Davies–Joint Assistant Secretaries
I. Babington-Johnson–Treasurer
Other board members of the period included J.S.D. Thompson, Athan J. Boyle, I.R. Benjamin, V. Lionel Smith, and Mesdames T.E. Williams, G. Gouch Johnson, Efusion Johnson and Lydia Mccarthy. Over one hundred members were in the initial enrollment, and a book of rules and regulations was to be drafted.[145]

By February 1931, the Union had further expanded its membership and scope of activities. Arch. Crowther gave a lecture in which he reviewed the efforts of the early Sierra Leoneans and Gold Coasters of Onitsha at Union activity. The SLU was reported as having raised £900 for the construction of a church, refusing the "financial support from the Church Missionary Society. . . . [and] wanting to do it all themselves". The Church was subsequently built and named Bishop Crowther Memorial in memory of an illustrious compatriot.[146] Union meetings were often a blend of recreation, re-union with relatives and friends, and the staple admonition to avoid vices and the errors of the past. At a meeting in February, 1931, Arch. Crowther told the group: "God has a purpose in view hence he allowed this Union to be formed . . . I beseech you, let not jealousy or timidity, or the love of gossip break it".[147]

The SLU celebrated its first anniversary in April 1931, at a thanksgiving service at St. Cyprian's, with Arch. Crowther delivering the sermon. Other activities included "a grand picnic" on the grounds of the Okrika Masonic Temple, for which "huge preparations" were made. The Union bade farewell to its founding President, I.G. Cummings, who was retiring to Sierra Leone, in May 1931. A send-off gathering was organised in his honour, with Potts-Johnson as chairman. The Christian character of the SLU was very much in evidence throughout the proceedings, as was its more educated membership's penchant for the classics and florid oratory. The function commenced with the singing of "O God of Bethel by Whose hand Thy People Still are Fed". In an address presented to Cummings, the SLU members generously noted his efforts in getting the organization started: "And now our frail bark has hardly put to sea when by a stroke of circumstance over which we have no control, those fond hopes and expectations have been blasted by your severance from us—by your leaving these shores for the homeland which boasted citizens we are". In his reply, Cummings promised to retain his membership, and return to Port Harcourt periodically. A Mr. G. Olumide of the Lands Office entertained the group with "lively music" until 10:00 p.m., when the ceremony drew to a close with "God Be With You Till We Meet Again". Cummings received souvenir gifts of an "Indian table cloth in rich silk with fancy floral design, and an artistic piano top cover". He left Port Harcourt by sea the next day for Freetown on the Abinsi.[148]

The Union did not confine its activities to the immediate concerns of its membership. Periodically, it ventured into the public realm, reaching out to officials of the government. When the Governor, Sir J. Aloysius Byrne left on transfer for Kenya in November, 1930, the SLU addressed the following cablegram to his Excellency: "Greetings and congratulations appointment Governorship, Kenya. Also appreciation practical interest manifested people's welfare. Deplores official change but wish self and lady Byrne health, long life, prosperity new sphere". Obviously touched by the sentiments of his immigrant subjects, the Governor promptly cabled back: "Sorry to leave West Africa".[149]

When after much factional wrangling in Lagos that greatly undermined Saro unity in that city, the deposed and exiled Oba of Lagos, Eshugbayi Eleko, was restored to his throne in 1931, the SLU sent its congratulations. Lagos events were a matter of constant review in Port Harcourt's Saro circles, and the rivalry between those Saro titans, Herbert Macaulay, leader of the Nigerian National Democratic Party (NNDP), and Henry Rawlinson Carr, Inspector of Schools and Assistant Colonial Secretary, during the 1920's, had been monitored with great interest. S.M. Reffell, Secretary of the SLU, wrote: "I was requested to convey to the committee members of the Prince Eshugbayi Eleko's celebrations their very sincere and genuine congratulations on the happy return of the Prince from his enforced exile at Oyo".[150] Ties with the Saro of Lagos were close, and their patient cultivation was a matter never to be ignored.

Activities involving the larger public were also organised. On August 1930, a "social" was held by the Union at St. Cyprian's to mark the Bank holiday. The program included a concert, with games and refreshments. Mrs. Leighton Johnson, a Saro, whose husband worked for the Nigerian Cold Storage Company, addressed the gathering, which did not disperse till midnight. Anniversaries of the Union were celebrated with services at churches frequented by the Saro, such as Wesley, St. Cyprian's, Banham, Archbishop Crowther Memorial, and the Salvation Army. Funds raised at these services often went principally toward church related projects. To mark its second anniversary, Union members attended Wesley Church, Bonny Street, with the Saro, Rev. H.H. Macaulay, officiating, and Arch. Crowther in attendance. The offering went towards the church's building fund.[151]

With the formation of the SLU, the Saro had now established a framework for the periodic review of their multifarious concerns, and the proferring of solutions that may secure suitable remedies. In opening up membership to all Sierra Leoneans, the SLU had given an earnest of its intention to transcend the particularities of class, ethnicity, and social location as indulged in the parent Sierra Leone society. Herein lay the alluring prospect of Saro success in avoiding the cleavages that had bedeviled inter-ethnic cooperation in Sierra Leone. That Krio culture was to be the staple fare of the SLU, the Saro being predominantly of that ethnic formation, was a challenge to be confronted by non-krio aspirants to membership; the choices made by the few non-Krio Saro that resided in Port Harcourt would afford rich insights into the possibilities of inter-ethnic empathy in diasporic environments.

Early Government in Port Harcourt

As the African population of the township increased, it was inevitable that the colonial government would come under pressure to provide some representation for the African viewpoint on official policy. In Freetown, this lobbying function, as earlier remarked, had been performed by the Krio middle class through their numerous pressure groups.[152] The issue of elective representation was one of the major reasons for the formation of the National Congress of British West Africa (NCBWA). Though initially rebuffed in Nigeria, NCBWA advocacy had certainly played a part in the introduction of the 1922 constitution, which brought Calabar elective representation in the Legislative Council. In the years after World War I, Port Harcourt seemed poised to make its political requirements known. Its population would grow by 1921 to between 7000 and 8000 residents, with the

European population at 135,[153] up from 44 in 1916.[154] The land question was becoming a central point of discussion, as African residents attempted to acquire plots for the construction of dwellings in the township. Unlike the situation in Freetown, the British administration of Port Harcourt allowed no African freeholding of land. Leaseholds were the preferred option, a matter that would generate much acrimony in the future, when, invariably, local conditions came to be compared with those that obtained in Freetown. Plots were demarcated by the office of the Commissioner of Lands, and annual land rents were charged at the rate of £1 for 5000 sq. feet. The plots were generally of three specifications, viz., 100 x 50, 60 x 30, and 70 x 30. The rents collected in 1917 for the three were £1, 7/6, and 8/6 respectively.[155] The local administration undoubtedly saw land rents as a major revenue source, as well as a tool with which to control demographic expansion in the township. Rents paid by the plot owners ultimately determined the amounts they in turn assessed their tenants as house rents. Not surprisingly, house rent rates became a major issue of controversy in the early years of Port Harcourt's existence. The African population never considered them fair, and, with only a few Africans affluent enough to be plot owners, landlords attracted much obloquy. The African majority, living in rented accommodation, saw their landlords as callous profiteers, which a number obviously were.

In 1918, a Township Advisory Board (TAB) had been inaugurated to assist the Local Authority and the Resident (political heads of the local colonial administration) in administering the second-class township. Over its thirty-one year existence, the TAB would come progressively to attract, as official nominees, local educated Africans and businessmen, predominantly from such groups as the Ijaw, the Yoruba, and the Saro. Only rarely was an Igbo representative appointed to the board, even though this community was well represented in the township's population. The ethnic rivalry between the indigenes of the communities around Port Harcourt, and their Igbo neighbours, has a long and harrowing pedigree. The British were not unaware of this circumstance, and they appear to have brought an unusual sensitivity to potentially explosive issues that could have widened the rift between the two sides. In the infancy of her colonial experience, Port Harcourt was to be shielded from the tensions that could result from wranglings between ethnic constituencies.[156]

Besides the Igbo, another group would come under much official circumspection in the early years when nominees to the TAB were being discussed. This was the African lawyers, mostly Yoruba. The Nigerian colonial administration had developed some apprehension over the work of lawyers in the Eastern and Central provinces, and between 1910 and 1914, it had reduced the jurisdiction of the Supreme Court, thus curtailing the professional activities of the lawyers. These restrictions were not lifted till 1933.[157] The lawyers' reputation in Western Nigeria for controversy and contumacious conduct in defence of African interests, was legendary, and it preceded them into Port Harcourt. At a TAB meeting of May 1925 where African representation on the Board was discussed by the Local Authority and other European officials, it was decided that "none of the lawyers should be considered as candidates".[158] The Board was less troubled by the two African nominees it finally selected, viz., J.F. Ikiroma-Owiye,[159] and the Saro, I.B. Johnson. Ikiroma-Owiye was the proprietor of the local Custodian Stores, and an aspirant to a chieftaincy title.[160] He belonged to that select group of indigenes that was beginning to make its mark in trade, and which, generally, was on very good terms with the local Saro elite of Potts-Johnson, other professionals, and businessmen. I.B. Johnson was born in Freetown in 1883, where he had his early education. In 1903, he was in clerical work in Freetown, and served for a time as Army pay clerk in the colonial government. By 1905, he had left for Nigeria, and would serve in the Nigerian Treasury in Calabar, Opobo, and Port Harcourt up to 1921, before retiring to private life in Port Harcourt. His wife was the former Rosamond Taylor, a woman of great industry. Johnson had taken courses in photography in England, and, in his retirement, he was a contractor to the Prisons Department, an auctioneer, a photographer, and a transport proprietor.[161] Even in these early years, there was much speculation on Johnson's material assets, and many regarded him as the wealthiest African in the township. His appointment to the TAB gave him a public prominence akin to Potts-Johnson's, and together, they would emerge in the years leading to the 1950's as the two most dominant Saro in the community. Port Harcourt society was progressively becoming more differentiated in its class composition. The activities and ambitions of the more affluent of the Saro conjured images of the Lagos of the 1880's where, like Victorian gentlemen, local Saro had revelled in soirees, balls, and concerts.[162] The vast majority of local residents in Port Harcourt were outside this select band, and their expectations were of the speedy improvement of material conditions through the creation of more and better paying jobs. Africans on the TAB were expected to pursue these objectives aggressively. Their performance would come under the closest scrutiny in the years ahead.

The TAB came quickly under pressure from the African community to address its many problems. These ranged from issues of work conditions, unemployment, and African housing, to the more general matters of

township infrastructure, centering on roads, drainage, and recreational facilities. At its meeting of March 1927, Ikiroma-Owiye, supported by
Johnson, moved the following motion: "That in view of the conditions
under which plots are given out to natives, and the disastrous effect the
multiplication of European shops in the native town will have upon the
native traders in particular, and the trade in general, the Board is of the
opinion that the sale of the plots by natives to Europeans (sic.) commercial
houses is irregular, and consequently no new leases must be recommended".[163] Although the European officials on the Board defeated this
motion, arguing that it was "unfair to those firms who (sic) had not hith-
erto acquired a trading plot but might wish to do so in the future"[164] it
served notice of the gnawing concerns in the African community over prevailing official commercial policy. White applicants were being favoured in
allocations, and this was fuelling resentment as African residents squared
up to the challenges of land law in a township that was growing at a phe-
nomenal pace. At the same meeting, the African members demanded that
whenever plots became vacant in the native town, preference in leasing
should go to Africans. Weir, a white official on the Board, rejected this idea
in an amendment in which he called for vacant plots to be put up for
auction, and "granted to the highest bidder". His amendment in defence of
white traders who were already making major commercial inroads into the
core areas of African residence, ultimately failed, and the African members
prevailed.[165] European insistence on free trade was being increasingly perceived by the African community as unfair competition, condoned by
officialdom's indifference.

A major area of concern in the mid-1920's was that of local infrastructure, especially the public latrine, the water supply, and local drainage.
Motions on these subjects were filed repeatedly in the TAB by the African
representatives who were obviously under great pressure from their constituents, as will be evident shortly. I.B. Johnson served notice of his concern over the dilapidated state of the township's roads at a meeting of June
1926. In the following month, he moved "that the construction of the new
public latrine at the corner of the clerks recreation grounds be suspended
pending consideration at the next meeting, as a latrine at this particular
point would prove offensive and unsightly".[166] Ikiroma-Owiye backed him
in this motion, which was subsequently carried. The African members would,
however, soon realise that the passage of motions did not necessarily guar-
antee their swift implementation as policy. Not much was accomplished by
these lobbying efforts, and, in the interim, African residents were growing
ever more impatient, and complained of the ineffectiveness of their repre-

sentatives. In January 1928, Johnson raised the vexed issue of the local water supply. He argued that the people were willing to pay for a supply that was reliable, and called for services to be extended beyond 6:00 p.m.[167] The Local Authority proved to be adamant on the subject of an extended water supply, and the patrician Johnson, never one for a sustained confrontation with the authorities, easily backed down.[168]

General African living conditions not having much improved by January 1919, the Africans on the TAB again petitioned the administration through the Board. Johnson reported "the harassment of Africans in the township by sanitary officers who denied them access to water stand-pipes on the pretext that those facilities had been reserved for [the] flushing of the drains". This constituted great hardship for an African community without installed individual household access to the water supply, which made communal stand-pipes a much sought-after facility. The Senior Sanitary Officer knew of no such instruction, and promised to investigate.[169]

In a residentially segregated Port Harcourt, the nuisance factor of the public latrine, designed for African use, continued to elude official attention. I.B. Johnson, though relatively more affluent than most African residents, also had his home in the African residential zone, and he could not ignore the menaces of this facility. He complained of the stench it generated throughout the African section of the town. The Senior Sanitary Officer promised "to mitigate the nuisance by having the pans emptied later in the morning; he pointed out that the pans could not be emptied more frequently owing to the cost of the labour involved, and that, . . . it was not always easy to recruit labour for the work".[170] Requests for concrete steps "from the fish market to the creek" similarly received short shrift. It was increasingly obvious, by the mid 1920's, that the drawing-room manner of the TAB's African representatives had failed to influence official thinking, and procure meaningful alleviation of African grievances. Port Harcourt was now on the verge of a major change in its political mood as, in dire frustration, the working classes and the small-scale African traders embraced the more rumbustious politics of confrontation.

The African Progress Union (APU)

Political developments in Port Harcourt in the mid-1920's were greatly influenced by the currents of mobilisation in Lagos. We have already remarked the close connections between the two societies. Lagos had a rich history of political agitation, from the house and land tax protests of 1895, through opposition to a proposed water rate levy in 1908, to the challenge of the West African Lands Commission in 1912, which attempted to introduce the land tenure policy of Northern Nigeria to the south.[171] In 1908, two Saro doctors in Lagos had formed the Peoples Union to oppose unpopular colonial measures. The passage in 1909 of the Seditious Offenses Ordinances reflected official impatience at these protests and the accompanying barrage of newspaper criticism of its rule. Sapara Williams, a Saro in the Legislative Council, had challenged these restrictions on the press, but as Coleman has indicated, African opposition in the Lagos of the period up to 1923 had been generally sporadic, lacking in sustained commitment, and initiated, for the most part, by the unimaginative fringe of the educated elite.[172] Society had not progressed much beyond the moderate politics of the NCBWA.

With the introduction of Nigeria's 1922 Constitution, a new purposefulness appeared on the political horizon. The emergence of the Saro, Herbert Macaulay, and his Nigerian National Democratic Party (NNDP) on the scene, ushered in a new activism that brought into close articulation the educated elite, the African-owned press, market women, the illiterate majority, as well as some traditional rulers, in an alliance of frightful possibilities.[173] Competition for seats to the Legislative Council would reveal the NNDP at its best in the elections of 1923, 1928, and 1933, and its "national" position on certain issues would bring the party to the notice of communities such as that in Port Harcourt. It is against this background of a new assertiveness in Lagos, many years in advance of a Freetown politics still dominated by the conservative elitism of H.C. Bankole-Bright, then leader of Krio opinion, with I.T.A. Wallace-Johnson yet to introduce a more mass-based politics, that we should review the rise of Port Harcourt's African Progressive Union (APU). Unlike the NNDP, though, the APU would be led directly from the grassroots.[174]

The African Progress Union (APU) came into existence in Port Harcourt in March 1925. Meeting in the Grand Native Club, its members, mostly small-scale traders, with some working class support, and some lower middle-class Saro representation in the leadership, decided to by-pass the TAB's African members, and take the people's grievances more directly to the colonial administration. They started off on the issue of the eviction of "squatters" in the native town "in cases of leases of plots taken up by persons other than the occupiers".[175] The APU also addressed the poor drainage situation, and the electricity problem of a rather short "lighting period".[176]

Before long, however, the APU would be ensnared by an obviously intimidated administration in a web of protocol employed to disguise official inertia in arguments of procedural irregularity. The movement's decision to approach the Governor directly brought a stinging rebuke from Port Harcourt's Station Magistrate, D.O'Connor. He dismissed the APU members as a low class of men, noting that "no one of the better class Africans—and especially the senior Africans (sic.) clerks—is a member" of the APU. He observed "more than one ex-convict on its committee . . . ", and "a large number of quite undesirable people" in its ranks. He deplored the arrogance of this "ill-chosen body of men" who had dared to address their petition ("a tissue of lies") directly to the Governor, requesting an interview. Having been instructed to meet with the APU leaders, O'Connor noted that he had "called upon the Committee to state the points which it wished to raise at the interview, but the members . . . seemed simply unwilling to state them. Eventually, they admitted that they wished to discuss [the] occupation of plots and drainage".[177] As O'Connor handed over the local Magistracy to J.M. Pollen, he counselled that the APU, which was so resource-starved as to be incapable of affording a meeting place of its own, should be kept under active surveillance.[178] These were obviously not the types of Africans of whom officials were enamored.

Undaunted, the APU addressed a petition to the Governor on behalf of its membership of over a hundred in March 1925. It protested the atrocities that were being committed in the enforcement of the administration's land rules. Africans, it maintained, were being unfairly punished for alleged violation of land laws. Citing specific cases, it identified administrative wrong-doing, and demanded redress. There was, for instance, the case of a Miss. Hester Hart, occupier of Plot No. 37E, on which she had erected a building to the value of £ 69.10s. Miss Hart was subsequently "deprived of her plot on the application of a German trader, who without any compensation destroyed the said building and is now erecting one in its place".[179] Another case of abuse cited by the APU was that of the Saro, S.B. Thomas, of Plot No. 120 E, with a house already on the site at a cost of £35. Thomas had paid his plot rent for 1925, but was evicted on 28th January, and his holding was transferred to one Joseph, "a relative of the District Clerk".[180] Similar victimisation, the APU claimed, was suffered by other Sierra Leoneans, among them, S.J. Macaulay, and A. Denson Grant, a small-scale Saro store-owner, and a thorn in the side of the Saro elite and the administration, as will be evident later. Macaulay's Plot No. 87C allocation, with a house valued at £18, had been summarily withdrawn by government for an undisclosed infraction. Denson Grant of Plot 37D was in the process of constructing his home to the value of £105 when he applied for official permission to lease the land. "He received no reply", the APU claimed, "and although he paid the annual rent for 1925, he was on the 4th March served with [an eviction] notice".[181]

The Union also condemned administrative rules that held its members in violation of building codes regarding approved design plans and official leasing permission. These had led to several arbitrary evictions. It could not accept, it argued, that its members should be victimised by a tardy bureaucracy, that failed to fully clarify its own building regulations. The APU reported the hardship its members had endured in the difficult economic circumstances of the mid-1920's. It protested "that the call upon the pecuniary resources of your Excellency's petitioners in the procuring of a plot and the erection of a permanent building thereon in a given time, and a payment of a lease deposit is most embarrassing especially under the prevailing stress . . . of the general slump in trade".[182] The APU prayed that the Governor should over-rule his officials in Port Harcourt, and restore to the deprived Africans the homes they had lost. Failing that, it demanded that adequate compensation be paid them "by the person who aspired to the possession of the land knowing it to have been occupied". The Union requested that the Governor should ensure that "similar unjust deprivation without notice and compensation" should not occur in the future, and that the petitioners, considering the harsh economic climate, be "allowed special concession to either build before leasing or vice versa upon a twelve months' notice . . . ".[183] The petition was signed by the entire executive of the APU which was a pan-ethnic coalition of Yoruba, Saro, Igbo, Hausa, and Gold Coasters.[184]

The signatories of this petition were all representatives of groups that had migrated into this Niger delta township, intent on making a new beginning in what appeared to be a most promising environment. It is instructive that the indigenous people of the area were not affected by the land allocation issues that exercised the APU leadership. Indeed, the evidence would suggest that most locals regarded APU claims with some unease, and the movement would come to be seen as representative of the predatory claims of the "strangers". This divide between indigenous and immigrant interests in land and related matters, would expand with time, and provide officials with welcome opportunities to further polarise the many fractions of the African community.

In his response to the queries raised in the petition, the Station Magistrate complained of the flagrant violation of the building codes by the

APU members and their associates. S.B. Thomas, for instance, he argued, had held his plot for three years, and had erected no structure on it. He had also failed to pay his plot rent for January 1925. His license was therefore not renewed.[185] He accused the APU of misrepresenting the case of the aforementioned Macaulay. No quit notice had been issued to him, and he had been allowed a period of grace to pay up the fees of his lease. The Station Magistrate accused the APU of making Macaulay's case without his permission. He wrote: "Mr. 'Macaulay authorises me to state that not only is this statement of the petitioners incorrect, but also it is inserted without his knowledge or permission".[186] The APU may well have exceeded its brief in stating some of these cases, but the fact remains, that as in Lagos, land policies were a perennial irritant within the African population, and a matter of much resentment of British officials. Around this discontent would coalesce a host of disruptive forces that were pernicious to the peace both of the African elite and the local colonial leadership.

By May 1925, the APU had turned to matters of foreign economic competition, an area of prime concern to its small-trader membership. It condemned administrative policy which allowed European firms to acquire trading plots in the African location for the construction of trading houses "while other established firms were compelled to purchase expensive plots and pay high rentals upon them". The Union considered this "a breach of faith", and an opportunity for "keener competition with the native traders . . . ".[187] The annual flooding of the African areas that came with the rains was also a matter of some concern to a Union with working class support. Little was being done to improve drainage facilities. The APU complained that though an estimate of projected expenditure in this connection had long been submitted, nothing had been done to effect the necessary improvements. As a result, it continued, "movement to and from work, is fast becoming an impossibility to those wearing shoes".[188]

Obviously discomfited by the APU's importunacy, local officials reacted to the movement's prodding with pique and contempt. In April 1926, the Station Magistrate at Port Harcourt scornfully dismissed the APU's executive and its membership out of hand. Although he conceded that one of its leaders was "a well established Yoruba trader", and a leasee, and another, a government pensioner, he passed off the rest as unworthy of government's attention. He noted in obvious disgust: "Of the rest of the signatories, not only are they of no particular standing but few of them do not even possess a plot, while one other is not only a debtor but is also an ex-convict. Another member of the union—who does not sign the petition—is an ex-convict two or three times over".[189] In the Port Harcourt of the mid-1920's, ex-convicts and those who held no plots of land were, in this official's view, condemned by their poverty and disrepute. Their views on land policy could therefore hold no virtue. The Station Magistrate assured the Resident at Owerri that the protestations of the APU were generally unfounded, and based on sundry misrepresentations "not calculated to serve any useful purpose".[190]

Much to official chagrin, the APU was not to be easily dismissed. In 1927, it directed its efforts to official increases in land rents. At a TAB meeting of October 1927, the Commissioner of Lands had proposed the following new land rents for the plot holders of the township:

"Class A (100 x 50 facing road) £15
Class B (100 x 50 not facing main road)£10
Class C 60 x 30 £3".

Though Commander Woodward seconded this proposal, it was later modified to £10, £7.10s, and £3 respectively, on the recommendation of the Station Magistrate and Mr. Ikiroma-Owiye.[191] The APU condemned these increases, and would later link them to the even more explosive issue of the proposed introduction of taxation into the township. Governor Graeme Thomson had decided in November 1926 to introduce direct taxation to Lagos and the six provinces of the South that had gone untaxed to date. He saw this as the only means whereby all sections of the protectorate would equitably discharge their obligations to the colonial state.[192] In a memorandum to the Governor in April 1928, on the subject of taxation, the African Progress Union requested that Port Harcourt be exempted from taxation, and that "in the event of . . . inability to do so, that the assessment rates be reduced to a minimum giving chances (sic.) for even the peasants to pay without much hardship".[193] The rural farmer had now found a spokesman for his interests, and for the first time in township history, rural claims were being articulated alongside the urban by a movement that aspired to represent all of the disadvantaged. This was a far cry from the timid advocacy of the TAB's elite African nominees.

By September 1928, the APU was assailing administration land policy which had deliberately marginalised the African pioneers of the township who, in 1914, had cleared the brush to lay out the first set of residences in Port Harcourt.[194] It observed that these hardy builders had, in turn, received only ingratitude from the authorities, for they "were pushed away . . . from their original plots and were compelled to build new plots in order to make houses for themselves".[195] It contended that this practice had gradually "driven away" the early pioneers into what had now become the native town. This had also been done without compensation for homes that had to be given up. Moreover, these earlier frustrations had been compounded by recent policy. The petition continued: "That on or about 31st July last, your petitioners were informed by the Commissioner of Lands that on or after 31st December next, unless plot owners deposited £15, £10 and £3 instead of £1 and 10s. they are paying, their license will not be renewed".[196] This the Union found unacceptable, and it demanded a policy review. The decision to impose taxation on the general public allegedly to generate funds for infrastructural improvement, and the expansion of the electricity and water supplies, was similarly excoriated. The APU called for the reconsideration of this policy alongside that of plot rent increases. "The increase of land rent from £1 to £15 and 10s to £10 and £3 calculated at 20 years purchase", it argued," will be £300, £200, and £60 respectively". This it found too great a burden for Africans to bear.[197]

Realising ultimately that the APU's case could not be wished away, the administration sought dialogue with the movement's leaders. On 25 September 1928, the APU was granted an audience with the Lieutenant-Governor. The executive members, reeling under the impact of a depressed economy, regaled this senior official with a series of problems that plagued the African community. They generally drew an adamant response, though with a hint of some compromise. On rents, for instance, the Lieutenant Governor said, *inter alia*: "The increased rents which I have already approved will remain, but I am prepared to consider any differentiation of rents if you will put that forward. The plots will be divided into 3, 4, or 5 categories in order to make the rents equitable. I have told the Station Magistrate what I have just said to you".[198]

Proceeding beyond land matters at this meeting, the Union demanded direct representation of two of its members on the TAB. The Lieutenant-Governor's response was direct and unequivocal: "No. If you ask for more African members to be appointed without reference to your union but representative of the whole community in Port Harcourt, I may consider that"![199] At this point, the Union leaders declared their lack of confidence in the TAB's current African nominees. Speaking on behalf "of almost all the various tribes in Port Harcourt" represented in the Union, the APU leaders condemned both Ikiroma-Owiye and I.B. Johnson. They "do not seek our interests", they protested to the Lieutenant Governor. Predictably, the latter rose to the defence of the African nominees who were drawn from a class-fraction with which he was obviously more comfortable. He stressed the nature of the work on the TAB which called for men of some education, who were familiar with "technical matters such as electricity, pipes, etc". Unfazed by this remark, the Union's leaders retorted that "there are others besides the members now serving on the Board who are also educated". They added in elaboration: "The present members do not keep us informed of what is going on at the meetings of the Board. For instance, the announcement of the proposed increased rents only came to our knowledge on the 31st July last. Perhaps this state of affairs is due to the fact that the members now serving were appointed by the Government and not by us".[200] This final comment touched a rather sensitive official nerve. The knotty question of elective representation, much discussed in township circles at this time, had now been raised officially. The Lieutenant-Governor promptly ended the meeting at this point.[201]

Having now cast itself in the role of unofficial watchdog of the African interest, and generally free of African elite influence, the APU would continue to diligently scrutinise government policy, demanding that its membership be regularly apprised of the direction in which the administration intended to take Port Harcourt. It had meanwhile sent its representative, a Saro, Mr. Coker, to appear before the TAB. Coker was directed to raise issues concerning the water supply, the poor location of the central latrine, the deplorable state of the roads and culverts, and the ubiquitous menace of plot rent increases.[202] Mindful of government's impatience with its activities, the Union insisted on its rights to public advocacy, and refused to be ignored. In November 1928, in a letter to the TAB, it demanded access to the Board's deliberations through copies of its minutes.[203] The Board considered this request an arrogant presumption, and the African nominees, predictably, acquiesced in this assessment, deploring the tone in which the letter had been phrased.[204] Both Johnson and Ikiroma-Owiye were obviously perturbed by the strident posturing of the APU, and they could sense the risk of redundancy to the African cause that was rapidly becoming their lot. Although their motions before the Board sometimes hearkened to the APU's concerns, they had generally failed to make common cause with the small-scale traders and their working-class associates of the APU. An almost palpable social distance separated the APU's concerns from those of the African nominees of the TAB; this clash of class interests would bedevil future relations between the African elite and the much larger working classes of Port Harcourt.[205]

The emergence of the APU raises a number of fundamental issues of significance for the development of Port Harcourt and the West African region of the late 1920's generally. Firstly, the movement's impatience with the educated African middle-class was clearly a reflection of a growing divide within African society at this time as the African elite, represented by the African nominees of the TAB, and other more affluent Africans, held on to its moderate and minimalist politics, while evincing great distrust of what it regarded as the rabble-rousing proclivities of the poorer classes. The elite distrusted strike action, and loathed the bravado of the working poor. A new set of leaders, capable of greater activism, and much more empathy with the grassroots was clearly needed, and such elite representatives of the African viewpoint as Bankole-Bright, Herbert Macaulay, and I.B. Johnson, were increasingly being perceived as of the old guard, and thus incapable of effectively representing the poor.[206]

Secondly, with the limited role played by a handful of local women in the APU,[207] but even more significantly, overwhelming female involvement in the 1929 anti-taxation protests in the neighbouring Aba, and in Herbert Macaulay's NNDP,[208] political action was becoming less a male preserve. This held significant demographic potential for future confrontations with the colonial state.

Thirdly, there was a significant difference in intellectual scale between Port Harcourt, on the one hand, and Freetown and Lagos, on the other. Unlike the latter two cities, Port Harcourt would never attract the dazzling array of *literati* that adorned those communities. This partly explains the prominence a Potts-Johnson could enjoy. The absence of a glut of professionals, however, also meant that lower middle-class individuals, uncontaminated by close contact with European officials, could emerge to put the case of the lower classes. It is in this light that the Saro, Denson Grant, should be reviewed. Local residents, like Grant, would greatly irritate the colonial administration, but they would be just as strongly resented by some members of the Saro elite who saw their thunder being stolen by these *parvenu*.

Finally, the politics of constitutionalism was even at this early stage beginning to suffer erosion at the hands of a new militancy born of the hardship of the depression in areas like Port Harcourt. The radical Youth movements of West Africa would not appear until the late 1930's, but their advent was already being presaged in the irreverence so flamboyantly displayed by groups such as the APU. Some old guard leaders of the educated elite would seek to stem the tide of their growing irrelevance by reaching out to this importunate constituency. It is to Potts-Johnson's efforts in this direction that we now turn.

2

CROSSING THE LINES OF CLASS, 1930–39

The challenge posed by the activities of the African Progress Union (APU) had raised to a position of some prominence the question of African representation in the governing of Port Harcourt. Where the British administration preferred a process of nominated representation in accord with imperial policy of political minimalism, some vocal African leaders were insisting on the right to choose leaders through the franchise. In a petition to the Governor in March 1929, the APU had stated pointedly: "We loyal British subjects of his majesty . . . firmly lay hope on British justice and fairplay in that taxation goes with representation, and to consult the welfare of the people is the first great law . . . "[1]

Not only was the principle of elective representation a matter of some debate by 1930, the desire to secure more aggressive leaders who would empathise with the aspirations of the African majority and articulate their many frustrations, was an issue of uncommon interest and general solicitude. There was a desire to identify spokesmen from within the lettered elite circles, who could be trusted to espouse the cause of the poor, even where this ran counter to elite advantage. Observers of the TAB's African nominees had recoiled in disappointment at their performance. Drawn from the indigenous as well as the immigrant (Saro) elite, they had proved themselves uniformly unequal to their charge, and their conduct had engendered the cynicism in which APU claims had flourished. There was a communal yearning for a more purposive and aggressive leadership, yet one that would be shorn of the still repulsive proletarianism that had dogged the APU's image. This climate of doubt and apprehension would ultimately provide room for the flowering of Potts-Johnson's genius. If the Sierra Leonean nominee to the Township Advisory Board (TAB), the rather aloof patrician, I.B. Johnson, could be accused of lacklustre identification with the essence of the APU, no such charge could be seriously levied against his compatriot, the Rev. L.R. Potts-Johnson.

Potts-Johnson needed little encouragement in turning the pages of the Nigerian Observer over the APU. In several editorials, he echoed the movement's economic and social concerns in the difficult days of the depression. In January 1930, the Observer reiterated its earlier call for improvement of the township's water supply,[2] and on the 22 February, it addressed the perennial drainage question. It wrote with anguished anticipation: "Within the next two or three months we shall be in the rainy season. Will the native location residents continue to suffer the inconveniences similar to those of the past rainy seasons? Will not something be done to improve the situation during the few months that lie ahead of us?" Potts-Johnson would also address the deplorable state of the native cemetery, with a stinging indictment of what he considered official racist conduct. In July 1930, he editorialised: "If such care is taken to preserve the resting place of dead Europeans, why cannot the same considerations be extended to dead Africans? Certainly the European section [of the cemetery] was improved from certain funds. If, however, part of those funds cannot be made available for the improvement of the native section, then the sooner a scheme is formulated, the better." The problem of rents, of paramount importance to the APU, also did not escape the Observer's gaze. In August 1930, Potts-Johnson called on the colonial government "to pause and think for . . . the present scale of rents is too high,and, as a matter of fact, causing hardship among the masses".[3]

That a Sierra Leonean resident of Potts-Johnson's means and status was showing such keen interest in the travails of the poorer classes, was heartening to the members of the APU. Its leaders could begin to see, in the distance, the faint outlines of an inter-class alliance with one of the notables of the township. Emboldened by these possibilities, and steadfast in its commitments, the APU kept up the pressure on the administration. In February 1930, it highlighted the case of another of the government's victims, Bakare Olashewere Ajose, who, late in January, was seen "removing his personal and household effects from his house". The APU report continued: "On enquiry, we were informed that he had been ordered by the government to vacate his plot for failure to pay last year's rent. For months, he had endeavoured to meet up (sic.) his obligations, but hard times militated against his efforts, and he together with his wife and children had no alternative but to leave the house they had occupied for years."[4] The administration was here being portrayed as a heartless leviathan, unmoved by human misery and the pain of the dispossessed.

The APU leaders felt constrained in July 1930, to approach the administration yet again on the vexed subject of land rents. They noted their earlier failure to influence official opinion, and stressed a willingness to persevere on the people's account. They called for rents to be reduced to their previous levels. Citing past experience, they recalled that when the land rent was £1 and 10s., no plot holder ever defaulted and had to be taken to court. Since the adoption of the new rates, however, "two thirds of the inhabitants are invariably being brought before the magistrate . . . and those found culpable are in some measure punished".[5] The APU stressed the aforementioned case of the Ajose family, and indicated how common such suffering had become in an African community in the throes of economic crisis. "At the present moment", it wrote, "everything is at a standstill—no work, no trade, no money—the 10s and 20s land rent originally paid is a difficulty to meet today . . . ".[6] The APU leaders explained that most Africans had had to secure loans to pay the new rates, and they wondered why Port Harcourt, a township of comparable age to the neighbouring Aba and Enugu, was demanding a higher land rent of its African population than did the administrations of those townships. The building code was criticised for requiring that "five feet square should be allowed for every building erected", and the APU pointed out the following difficulty: "Port Harcourt plots measure only 50' x 100' and 30' x 60' respectively— if 20 feet allowance be given up from these, the holders would [be entitled] to 40' x 50' and 20' x 40'. Bad for ventilation".[7] The principal solution to this land problem lay, of course, in making more land available for African occupancy. This would have allowed larger plots to leasees, indulged the stylistic preferences of the more innovative builders, while defusing the tensions that marred relations between the rulers and the ruled. Government at this time was, however, reluctant to be drawn in this direction, as it sought to control township growth, and reduce the load on public funds and facilities.

As their desperation increased, APU leaders again sought representation on the Township Advisory Board (TAB), believing this to be the only means by which they could come to influence official policy more directly. In August 1930, they recommended to the Resident, for immediate incorporation, two of their senior members. They were both Saro—the aforementioned I.R. Benjamin, a blind local contractor of sorts,[8] who was the vice-president of the APU, and that gadfly of earlier controversies, A. Denson Grant, its financial secretary. Grant, it will be recalled, had experienced land difficulties previously with the administration.[9] He was at this time the proprietor of the Liberty Store, where he reportedly sold "good champagne and other French wines . . . ". Slightly better-heeled than most of his APU peers, Grant was the sole agent and representative of Messrs. P. Roquette and A. Lauze of Benziers, France.[10] Not even established small-scale traders like Grant were spared the painful shafts of the depression. Economic hardship had thrown individuals of varying means together in the APU. Grant's business was at a low ebb, and the Union afforded sanctuary from the paroxysms of economic trauma. It was the APU's hope that Benjamin and Grant would be able to shepherd through the TAB a resolution adopted at a mass meeting held at the Africa Club in August 1930. That resolution had proposed new land rents of £2.10s for 50 x 100 plots, and £1 for those 30 x 60 feet.[11] In the end, however, the APU's nominees for the TAB, and the Union's proposed rent reduction, were summarily rejected by the colonial administration. The small-scale traders of Port Harcourt, and their working class allies were deemed too risky a proposition for the councils of state.

Their inability to influence administration policy decisively or secure representation on the TAB ultimately frustrated the APU leaders in the early 1930's. Progressively, they lost their passionate commitment to spirited advocacy, and the African population was now largely thrown on to the charity of Potts-Johnson's editorials, and the feeble preachments of the TAB's African nominees. A number of the Saro members of the APU had experienced grave hardship in their personal circumstances during the late 1920's and the early 1930's; this had drawn them even more closely into the refuge that was the Sierra Leone Union (SLU). The economic depression had shattered many lives, and leaders of the church could see the pain even in their more resilient communicants. In March 1933, the Methodist Synod commented on the amazing optimism of its African flock even in the midst of a devastating depression: "This year, more of our people find themselves retrenched from good posts in government and commerce. Work is harder to get by those who are artisans or labourers. Petty trading and marketing are less sure resources for our many women who thereby earn a livelihood, or seek to eke out the family income. Yet one is met by cheery smiles on every hand. No appeal for funds is in vain".[12] In a season of great austerity, Africans working for the Church, a good number of them Saro, were willing to make the necessary sacrifice to keep their districts viable.

Church authorities commended this spirit in the mid-1930's when they reported: "We record here also that our African ministers have without any pressure on our part, volunteered to accept a reduction of 5% in their salaries in order to save our funds. Certificated teachers, also, have loyally accepted a reduction, while catechists are foregoing increments for yet another year".[13]

Up to the end of 1936, I.B. Johnson continued to be the lone Saro representative on the TAB. His political interests continued to be of the parish-pump variety, limited in both scope and vision. His manner was, as ever, comely and non-confrontational. Undoubtedly the most prominent African businessman in the township at this time, he was comfortable in the company of his European friends, and he maintained only a casual and sporadic acquaintance with the Sierra Leone Union (SLU). Ever the martinet, he seemed attracted more naturally to issues of discipline, decorum, and propriety, than to the more mundane matters of the material condition. He may well have empathised with the plight of the African poor, but he appeared incapable of rousing himself to the passionate and sustained advocacy their interests demanded.[14] In April 1936, he invited the Commissioner of Police to do something about "the noise and hooliganism . . . in the native location" which caused residents in the area to "get no peace or quietude".[15] In a rare appeal, in September 1936, he called for increments for the African staff of the township.[16] He also took, at this time, more than usual interest in a one-month gratuity award for the next of kin of the late Francis Eze, an indigene, asking, with practised formality, that it be paid "in accordance with section 4 of cap. 13. vol. I, of the Laws of Nigeria".[17] Unlike Potts-Johnson, who had a remarkable affinity to controversy, and seemed to revel in the championing of popular causes, Johnson was the more reclusive and distant servant of the people.

Predictably, it was the more outspoken Potts-Johnson who warned of the growing tendencies to racism in the Port Harcourt of the early 1930's. He wrote in the Observer: "Truly there is something entirely uncivilised and vulgar in making colour a reason for social aloofness, and it is hoped that sooner or later men will be able to know better and endeavour to behave differently". This was a matter to which he would return on several occasions in the future, as African aspirations were frustrated by official policy that appeared to be conditioned by racial sentiment. Potts-Johnson would be unsparing in his denunciations and caricature of the prejudiced. The retrenchment of government employees in the early 1930's also drew condemnation from the Observer. Dismayed by the bulging ranks of the unemployed, Potts-Johnson wrote in July 1931: "Before serving an employee with a notice of termination . . . on the grounds of economy, the employee should be asked whether he would be willing to accept a lower rate of salary". He was convinced, he added, that "the majority of the retrenched African employees would have been too glad to agree to a reduction of wages . . . ".[18]

In welcoming the Governor, Donald Cameron, to Port Harcourt on a visit in September 1931, Potts-Johnson identified land rents as the "vexed question" of the African population. He hailed the recent official reduction of rents in some areas of the township, but questioned the manner in which those decision had been made: "We do not know whether government sought the opinion or advice of some prominent natives before arriving at the figures embodied in the reduction scheme. If they omitted to do so, it is a mistake". He further maintained that "Europeans however experienced they may be cannot know everything about native affairs".[19]

In May 1932, Potts-Johnson demanded an end to the harassment of plot rent defaulters, and called for all rents to be scaled back. In an editorial, he wrote: " . . . during the last few weeks, the officers of court have been very busy executing numerous [writs] of *Fifa* on the properties of defaulters. It is certainly clear that the rents . . . are far above what the average lessee can afford. We know of several cases where the seals remained in the properties several days while the unfortunate people concerned were making strenuous efforts to raise loans, and several cases also came to our knowledge where the rents were actually paid from money thus received on loan". Potts-Johnson called on government not to over-estimate the return that came from plot ownership in the township. To dispel notions of excessive profit from all rented real estate, he noted: "There are, it must be admitted, some plots yielding very profitable yearly returns, but the number of such plots, unfortunately, is limited and confined to a definite area".[20]

Potts-Johnson had become a major force in articulating popular frustration by 1932. Though firmly of the patrician mould, and, like Edward Blyden, hardly living the life of the regular African resident,[21] he had reached across class lines to reflect the frustrations that wracked the more disadvantaged segments of the African community. As a member of the African elite who openly identified consistently with grassroot issues, Potts-Johnson stood alone. There were few elite imitators (indigene or immigrant) of this conduct which projected an inter-class vision of the township's political possibilities. This was risky behaviour that could place individual preferments in considerable jeopardy. Potts-Johnson's innate irreverence, and the security that came from independent means, fostered this brazen contempt for conventions that muzzled elite opinion. We should not, however, over-state the ideological framework within which these remonstrances were being made. The Potts-Johnson of this period was no radical nationalist, seeking an end to British control of Port Harcourt. He spoke to this himself in an editorial of November 1932, when he wrote: "We are anxious for progress and we desire any measure of self government in any sphere provided we are fit for it, but at the moment, assumption of self government . . . is nothing different from putting the cart before the horse". Potts-Johnson believed in a longer period of colonial tutelage, which would prepare the African for that ultimate responsibility of self government. "Before we can be ripe for self government", he wrote, "in matters political, educational, religious, and economic, there must be widespread education of the best type".[22] These were the politics of gradualism, common to the West African educated elite at this time.[23] Like his peers in Lagos, Freetown, and Accra, he believed liberation would come of patient preparation, in the not too distant future. To adopt revolutionary tactics would be precipitate, and subversive of the cause. On a number of occasions, he would commend his creed of *festina lente* to his readers. Potts-Johnson was certainly not about to read the riot act to the British Raj, and he was not firmly committed to the radicalism represented by such groups as the African Progress Union (APU) of Port Harcourt. The early to mid-1930's were a period of great disillusionment for the educated elite in West Africa generally. The demands of the National Congress of British West Africa (NCBWA) had been instrumental in securing limited elective political representation in Sierra Leone, Nigeria, and the Gold Coast, but the much-touted rewards were yet to be realised. Elective African representation had done more for municipal than national politics. Herbert Macaulay's NNDP for all its vaunted militancy and refreshing iconoclasm was little more than a Lagos party. African leaders by their willingness to sit in territorial Legislative Councils had scuttled the idea of a united British West Africa. Their inability to make any lasting impression on colonial policy further underscored their redundancy, and deepened apathy in the fledgling electorate. Britain had no intention of sharing decision-making authority, and the despondency of the West African electorate was promptly seized on as an index of the premature pursuit of elective representation by the educated middle class.[24] While Herbert Macaulay's NNDP was being ravaged by "personal jealousies and quarrels over the spoils of office", official reports in Freetown were describing his counterpart, H.C. Bankole-Bright as "a fire-brand . . . rapidly flickering to extinction."[25] These were difficult times for established Krio and Saro leaders, but Potts-Johnson did not succumb to despondency.

His advocacy of local and territorial issues persisted, and officials in Port Harcourt were constantly reminded of their many short-comings.

When next Potts-Johnson returned to the anguished issue of inflated rents, he would juxtapose Port Harcourt's situation to that of neighbouring British colonies. He identified disparities in land tenure systems as central to Port Harcourt's dilemma. In highlighting the inequity of the Niger delta experience, he opined: "The difference between our local landlords and those of the other colonies that we know is that in Port Harcourt, house holders build on Crown land for which privilege they pay a yearly rental, while householders of our sister colonies, for example Sierra Leone, build on lands acquired either by purchase or inheritance, and are freehold . . . ". He argued that " . . . the inflation . . . on house rents is the direct result of the increase on land rents. An expeditious decrease on land rental . . . would . . . inevitably hasten a decrease in house rents". Potts-Johnson called on landlords to reduce their rents, and invited tenants to "work hand in hand with their landlords by paying their rents . . . "[26] This was a partnership that would be painfully slow in coming to a Port Harcourt where class lines were beginning to be sharply drawn, with resultant antagonisms that were exacerbated by economic crisis, and the absence of creative policy initiatives.

As 1933 drew to a close, the Saro of Port Harcourt received the good news of the appointment of their compatriot of the neighbouring township of Aba, S.B. Rhodes, to the Legislative Council of the territory. This led Potts-Johnson to reflect further on the matter of African political representation, an issue never distant in Saro conversation since Calabar's earlier elevation. He called for an increase in the number of elected African members in the Legislative council, and criticised "the preponderance of [the] official majority . . . " in the House. He contended, in a fashion typical of the African elite, that franchise rights should not be limited, as was the case, to the Africans of Lagos and Calabar, but that they should be extended "to the provinces giving a vote to literate and educated members of the coast towns for the time being, thus enabling each province to elect provincial members". In further elaboration of his highly selective political thinking, Potts-Johnson wrote:

"This right is the least return an educated tax payer and householder could and should enjoy in recognition of his having performed his political civic duties. He who pays the piper must call the tune. . . . If the ends of the high aims of government to train the people to future self government are to be justified by the means, we submit that the present literate or educated section of the country, should begin this training now in modern and progressive methods of citizenship. If the country and people must be developed on modern lines and after the manner of civilised peoples, we say let it be all round. Half measures will not do".[27]

The chords of a proto-nationalist awakening were now being sounded in Port Harcourt, and the demand for expanded representation would not abate until some official concession was granted. A new level of political debate was being engaged, and it would demand more creative forms of African political organisation. Concern would continue to be expressed over the more basic issues such as overcrowded rented accommodation (a major fire hazard), the need for a maternity hospital, and the poor water supply.[28] These customary matters would now, however, have to compete for articulation with the more politically salient issues of an expanded and elevated political representation for Port Harcourt. New leaders would be required for this task, and more durable coalitions would have to be forged. The Saro would participate vigorously in these new initiatives, sharing the saddle with some members of the indigenous elite of chiefs, budding entrepreneurs, civil servants, and other notables. The inability to pull the indigenous working classes and their allies along in these political forays, would, however, engender suspicion and breed resentment. The immigrant wing of the African elite would pay dearly for such insensitivity.

The African Community League (ACL)

As already indicated, the mid-1930's were a time of great frustration in African educated circles in British West Africa. The proto-nationalist activities of the National Congress of British West Africa (NCBWA) were still a feature of the political landscape, but morale was generally low. The Freetown branch of the congress organised a major conference in 1936 to revitalise the movement and engender some sorely-needed optimism. For some fifty-four days, delegates took up various issues of national concern— agricultural improvement, the national health, legislative reform to improve judicial access in the areas outside Freetown occupied by the majority of the indigenous (non-Krio) population, and the matter of promoting closer cooperation between the Krio and that aboriginal enclave.[29] The local British officials were not impressed. The Saro of Lagos were in similar despair. Their dominance of the upper ranks of African employment in the colonial bureaucracy and in the mercantile houses rankled deeply in those sections of local society that still considered them "native foreigners". Coleman reports that "as late as 1936, outward remittances by native foreigners totalled £545,875 a year, which exceeded Nigeria's average pre-war annual expenditure on education".[30] Such conduct could not have inspired much local confidence in the emigre community.

Rivalry between indigene and immigrant communities was also present in Port Harcourt, and a rare public dispute between the two sides, in 1935, would lead to the formation of a new political organisation to give voice to African claims. In that year, the jubilee of King George V was celebrated. To mark the occasion, the Resident of the Owerri Province suggested that a congratulatory message be drafted by the African community of Port Harcourt. The Resident invited Potts-Johnson to carry out the assignment, and he, in turn, promptly enlisted the penmanship of the Rev. E.K. Williams, a local Saro who was renowned for his erudition and his florid prose. Etheldred Kenicson Ikudaisi Williams had come to Port Harcourt on loan from the Methodist Church of Sierra Leone.[31] Born in Allen Town, outside Freetown, in 1890, he had taught in several elementary schools, and at the Methodist Boys High School in Freetown. In 1923, he was ordained, and served the Methodist church among the Limba before coming to Nigeria.[32] In Port Harcourt, Williams would rise to the positions of Senior African pastor, Superintendent, and Manager of Methodist schools.[33]

Rev. Williams did a draft of the letter as Potts-Johnson requested, but word of the exercise soon reached Z.C. Obi and other prominent indigenes "who were all very . . . annoyed over the fact that the aborigines were not informed before such a message . . . was sent to the king of England".[34] To arrest a fast deteriorating situation, Rev. Williams proposed the inauguration of an African Community League (ACL), "with a view to disseminating public opinion and sentiment in such and other matters".[35] The League drew its members from all of Port Harcourt's ethnic groups, and its mission was to supplement the efforts of the APU in presenting the people's grievances and viewpoints to the administration. Rev. E.K. Williams was appointed its first president. The ACL got down to work immediately. There were pressing issues of the African material condition to be addressed, and a multi-ethnic ACL seemed a perfect organ for the championing of such causes. In October 1935, the new body addressed a petition to the Lieutenant-Governor, requesting that "in the light of the depression . . . Government should re-consider the market stalls rent", and that "provision be made for an adequate supply of water" in the township.[36]

In February 1936, the ACL, in a memorandum to the Resident, called for rent reductions, especially on the Hospital Road. It requested that private block 50 x 100 rentals on that road be reduced from £10 to £5 since, contrary to the administration's viewpoint, this was not a "commercial street", and there was "nothing attractive [there] for any commercial enterprise".[37] The League also addressed the subject of the Palladium, a fast-growing public recreational facility in the township, once used as a cinema hall. It argued that with the cinema no longer a functioning enterprise, the building had "ceased to be a profit making business . . . ". It thus requested that the Palladium's annual rent be reduced from £30 to £10.[38]

The ACL would also attempt to secure rent reductions by supplying the government with up-dated information on the commercial possibilities of various sections of the township. This was data Africans were better placed to generate, it argued, since it flowed naturally from their lived experience. For the Aggrey road, "the leading commercial area in the native settlement", it recommended that rents be reduced from £15 to £10. It saw the real hub of commerce as the area between Market Road and Kano Street, even though it had taken a heavy toll from the depression, which made recent land rent hikes, from £1 to £15, on its plots, unrealistic. The ACL protested that "though the rents collectible from tenants have decreased from between £120 and £150 to £60 and £30, and even . . . lower as books can testify, . . . government rents still remain at £15." This was unacceptable. It argued that "owing to the repeated rise and fall in trade, some shops would remain unoccupied for a period", thus making rents from tenants irregular.[39] The League called for land rents on the Creek Road to be reduced to a flat rate of £4, commerce in that section of the township having dramatically declined. In glaring detail, it traced the contours of economic collapse in the area: "A few years ago, 4 European firms, GBO, UAC, H.B.W. Russell, and J.W. Jackel established there. The first was closed down. The second is actually struggling for existence . . . as the contents of the shop indicate plainly . . . The third is no longer carrying on business at (sic.) Port Harcourt, the fourth has removed (sic.) to Aggrey Road. Thus only one of the four is still marking time on this road".[40] On the whole, the ACL appears to have had much greater success in its less confrontational approach with government than the aforementioned APU. That its leadership was African-elite based certainly enhanced its credentials with a class-conscious administration. This would work to its benefit in the short term, but, with the years, its fragile base in plebeian circles would be used against it by officials as well as African critics, as will be reviewed presently. When, however, in September 1936, the administration announced further rent reductions, the ACL appeared to its delighted members to be playing a winning hand.[41]

Much encouraged by the modest victories it had scored, the ACL leaders next invited the Resident to a meeting in September 1936 at the Banham Memorial school. They compiled an agenda which reviewed "the matter of the water supply, improvement of the streets, and the bringing of the electric light [system] into line with a place like Lagos . . . ".[42] Port Harcourt never failed to pattern its ambitions on the Lagos model with which many Saro had first-hand experience. The League also wanted a discussion of the possibility of the government issuing electric utility meters to the households of its employees who desired them, as well as a review of the inadequacies of the local police force.[43] Another matter was also raised that affected most homes in the township, viz., the domestic use of firewood, and its growing inavailability. The African leaders demanded to know "what provision under the forest ordinance is made for people who would want to cut their own firewood for their domestic purposes". They requested information on the licensing of wood cutters, and called for such a system if one did not already exist. The Resident was urged to restrain the local Hausa chief, who was about to move his people away from the native town to the newly opened lands of the neighbouring Diobu. The ACL expressed the hope that "government could find a way to prevent this", as the chief was acting purely to escape rising plot rents. Landlords within the ACL were obviously nervous at the possibility of losing their house tenants and the business they brought to their shops. Finally, in a concern reminiscent of the APU's exertions, the ACL requested an increase in African representation to the TAB.[44]

By October 1936, the ACL was requesting reductions in the electricity tariff to a flat rate of 1/6[d] per month for each light, a meter system of 9[d] per unit, and a 1[d] for "every unit above assessment". The League could not, yet again, resist the temptation to compare local conditions with those of Lagos, where, it maintained, electricity tariffs were of the order of the League's proposal in a city "with all its other privileges . . . ".[45] To ease the township's postal difficulties, the ACL called for an up-graded postal system, with the provision of a stamp selling office and a pillar box in the native town.[46]

In his comments on the ACL's representations, the Local Authority questioned the League's claim to speak on behalf of all the African people. He noted, with some mischief, that "Ibo representation on the League . . . did not appear to be a fair proportion of the population of Port Harcourt".[47] The Authority was, of course, being disingenuous here for the tensions that had often frustrated efforts at the incorporation of the Igbo were a matter of public record. The ACL's request for an African representation of eight on the TAB[48] was not, of course, conceded, but in January 1937, contrary to official reservations regarding Igbo under-representation, the administration appointed two more Saro to the TAB in a group of three new nominees. Presented by the Local Authority as nominees of the ACL, they were the Rev. E.K. Williams, and F.O. Lucas, a lawyer;[49] the third nominee was S.N. Obi, an indigene, who was the assistant chief Clerk of the Treasury. Ikiroma-Owiye had, by this time, lost interest in the rather ineffective TAB, as evidenced by his reluctance to respond to meeting invitations.[50] On the assumption that he had relinquished his appointment, the administration now appointed Potts-Johnson to be his replacement. With I.B. Johnson still a serving member, the Saro dominance of African representation was now overwhelming. By this appointment, Potts-Johnson had now secured another public platform for the articulation of his views. This was timely, for with the approach of war, the African population would face an array of vexing issues that required sustained advocacy. Potts-Johnson's public utterances had, to date, been largely confined to the pages of the Nigerian Observer. For the first time, he now had a forum where administration policy could be taken up directly in debate, and officials pressed to account for choices they had made. Given the circumstances, the possibilities for an acrimonious outcome in spirited exchanges were immense.

Other Pre-War Activities of the TAB and ACL

The anguished appeals of the African community to the colonial administration for the improvement of local infrastructure appeared to be yielding some positive result early in 1937. In March, the Nigerian Observer commented on the general improvements that were taking place. It noted that "new drains, construction of good roads and additional pumps for [the] water supply" were proof of this township renewal. With obvious relief, it exulted: "Port Harcourt is really becoming what is expected of her".[51]

This is not to suggest, however, that the pressures exerted on officialdom were about to abate. If anything, they increased in relative intensity. By May 1937, E.K. Williams was plying the TAB with requests for a shed for food sellers at Okrika, and for the construction of a bus shelter at the local car park.[52] Both requests met the usual official skepticism as to funding, but Williams was encouraged to submit his proposal with details as to site and design.[53]

On the more political front, the ACL expressed its disappointment over the government's decision to admit only three of the League's six nominees to the TAB; this it took as an index of continued official indifference to matters of African representation. It also called on the administration to allow "native contractors" to construct official buildings, roads, and water supply facilities, which would empower African entrepreneurs, and expand job creation. These contracts were being monopolised by European firms, and the ACL demanded an end to this discrimination. It invited the administration to open up more opportunities for budding contractors as was "being done at other places in Nigeria . . . "[54]

The calm of the TAB was shattered on 2nd August 1937 by the sudden death of its member, Rev. E.K. Williams, after a residence of just over three years in Port Harcourt. This plunged the Saro into grief over a compatriot so widely respected. Eloquent tribute was paid to his memory by officials[55] and members of the African community. At the time of his death, Williams was President of both the Port Harcourt Christian Council and the ACL, and "patron of several clubs".[56] He had died suddenly after making a speech at a reception at St. Cyprian's Church in honour of the newly consecrated Bishop A.C. Onyeabo. F.W. Dodds, Chairman of the Eastern Nigerian District of the Methodist Church, who had worked closely with Williams had this to say:

> "Of Mr. Williams it is difficult to speak too highly. He was, quite unequivocally, a tremendous worker, more full of energy and fire and enterprise than any African I know in any mission . . . To me he has been a right hand man, and I shall miss him sorely. One can hardly hope for a more helpful African colleague, so willing at all times to do what he could to assist. The position, as far as I am concerned, is that I have none whom I can [now] call upon . . . ."[57]

Williams was laid out at the Banham memorial schoolroom. In attendance at his funeral were choristers, representatives of the Women's Guild, the Boys Brigade, the Boys Scouts, alumni of his *alma mater*, the Methodist Boys High School of Sierra Leone, and many others.[58]

Having paid glowing tribute to the late E.K. Williams,[59] the TAB returned to its customary pre-occupations. In August 1937, Potts-Johnson and Lucas demanded acceleration of work on the drainage "out fall" on the Creek road, estimated to cost £550, and suggested that the government should bear half of the cost of construction as this was part of the officially approved drainage plan for Port Harcourt.[60] Official reluctance to fund local projects rankled deeply, and African nominees demanded a change of attitude if the burden on the taxpayer was to be relieved. Potts-Johnson also requested that the public latrines be removed from the Creek road, and that the beach be converted into a marina. This latter proposal, which would involve the re-siting of the local fish and wood markets, was shelved on the advice of the Local Authority.[61]

Port Harcourt welcomed the Governor on a visit in September 1937. He was honoured with a reception by the ACL at the Palladium. There is no evidence that the League used this occasion to take its case on various troubling issues to the highest official in the land, surely a missed opportunity, and one of which the leaders of the working classes of Port Harcourt would remind the elite in the years ahead. The ACL also played host to W.E. Hunt, the Chief Commissioner of the Southern Provinces, when he visited Port Harcourt. During his stay, Hunt unveiled the silver jubilee fountain on the Crowther road.[62]

By August 1937, the late Rev. E.K. Williams had been succeeded in the presidency of the ACL by George Spiff, who also now joined the TAB. We do not know much about Spiff, but he was of Sierra Leonean descent, being of a Saro mother. We also know that he had attended the Sierra Leone Grammar School in Freetown.[63] Spiff's surname reflected the growing tendencies to inter-marriage between the Sierra Leoneans and their indigenous hosts from the 1930's onwards, a matter to be reviewed more closely later, and one that would be of cardinal social significance in the trying years ahead.

With most of the TAB's African members now being also actively involved in the ACL, there was a cross-fertilisation of ideas and agenda between the two bodies. Issues generated in one invariably received articulation and some reinforcement in the other by the late 1930's. In January 1938, I.B. Johnson brought before the TAB the matter of the rising incidence of indigency in the African sections of the township.[64] The Board also reviewed the situation in the adjacent lands of Diobu, which were attracting a lot of "unauthorised building and squatting" activity, and drawing tenants away from the main African location.[65] This threatened the rent receipts of African elite landlords, and was thus a matter of grave concern. The TAB sent a delegation of Potts-Johnson, I.B. Johnson, Spiff, May, and Edmondson, to walk through the Diobu lay-out, and advise on the delineation of plots for the area, in a bid to regulate its expansion. It was the general view that a new settlement should be allowed to develop in Diobu, "to relieve the congestion in the existing native location", but this was not to be allowed to proceed without the controls that would ensure a smooth transition, which secured elite interests.[66]

Although African representation on the TAB had been increased, there was yet some concern over the effectiveness of some of the nominees. The desire to end the nominative process, and to introduce instead one of election, was receiving much attention in the township. In April 1938, the Nigerian Observer's editorial called for Port Harcourt, "a no man's land", to be run on the same lines as Lagos. It demanded representation by the popular vote of all tax payers. Only this, it contended, would curb the indifference of some of the African nominees of the TAB, and weed out the "yes men", "mere ornaments" who contributed nothing to the debates. The Board's advisory status was also questioned. "This may be good for such townships as Aba or Opobo, but not for Port Harcourt", it concluded.[67]

The earlier controversy over escalating firewood prices also reached a new intensity at this time, and it engaged the attention of African leaders in both the ACL and the TAB. Potts-Johnson condemned the inflationary trend,[68] and this provoked an angry retort from the forestry department, one of many such confrontations to be played out in the coming years. Nicholls, its senior assistant conservator wrote the following response:

> "I have to say . . . this is a mischievous, irresponsible statement in direct contradiction of the facts, which I have personally verified. In the first place, a rise in the price of fuel was not anticipated by myself or others in direct touch with these matters. Far from the price being increased by 50%, it has actually decreased by 29-50%. Two months ago, a 100 foot cord of mangrove billets . . . cost 14s, and it can now be obtained for 10s. The interests of the consumer in this case are subject to the same influence as bear on those related to any other staple commodity—that is, they are affected by the law of supply and demand, and are not entitled to any special government protection.[69]

Potts-Johnson had touched a rather sensitive nerve, as he reflected popular concern on a matter that deeply affected most households. That Nicholls took umbrage at his remonstrance would scarcely preempt future observations of the same vein. Capitulation on an argument of township interest did not come easily to this Saro leader.

Another troubling issue of this period, and one that touched the subject of immigration at the core, was that of local Syrian representation on the TAB. The Syrians were involved in local wholesale and retail trading, and although they generally enjoyed good relations with the African business community, their success inspired some jealously, fuelled by the official protection they were believed to enjoy. Syrian leaders in the late 1930's were believed to desire representation of one of their number on the TAB. When this matter came up for review, the Board agonised inconclusively on the subject for a considerable while. In its report on the matter, the Nigerian Observer noted: "It was decided that the question of Syrian representation on the Board be left over until such time as a desire for such representation arises".[70] Saro experience of Syrian and Lebanese traders in Sierra Leone would greatly condition the community's views on this matter. Most took these Levantines to be unscrupulous exploiters, who should receive no encouragement whatsoever. Local memory was still fresh on the anti-Syrian riots that had occurred in Sierra Leone in 1919, when the Syrians/Lebanese were accused by the Krio and others of various hoarding practices that were disruptive of trade, and constituted the prime source of local inflation. Demands for the expulsion of the Syrians from the territory had accompanied those protests, and it looked ominously as though Port Harcourt was headed in the same direction.[71]

Like his colleagues on the TAB and the ACL's executive, Potts-Johnson took a dim view of the bureaucratic delays that still surrounded official land policy. He criticised the "red tapism" governing the allocation of plots in the township, a perennial irritant to those with plans to take up permanent residence in Port Harcourt, as well as others who merely wanted a second home in the area. The latter was a reference to the more affluent inhabitants of "Abonnema, Buguma, Okrika, Bonny, Bakana, Brass, [and] Opobo", riverine communities of the Niger delta. For the most part, these individuals were chiefs or traders in search of vacation homes in Port Harcourt, where, according to Potts-Johnson, they could "spend a comparatively quiet time", and "mix with the different people from almost every part of the world, exchange ideas with them, and widen their own outlook on various subjects". The paper demanded an end to the frustrating delay in such plot allocations.[72]

As in previous years, administrative tardiness in responding to the numerous appeals for African improvement from the more moderate flanks of African opinion, invariably engendered the emergence of more radical claimants. The APU had been born of such frustration. On the eve of World War II, Port Harcourt witnessed, for a brief while, yet another eruption; this time, the rise of a local branch of the Nigerian Youth Movement (NYM), with ties to the parent organisation in Lagos. The NYM had emerged, in part, on a wave of anti-immigrant hysteria in western Nigeria, directed at the local Saro. Between 1936 and 1938, it had developed as the principal nationalist group in Lagos, with an agenda that transcended the more domestic, Lagos-bound politics of the rival Nigerian National Democratic Party (NNDP) of Herbert Macaulay, a prominent Saro. The NYM demanded franchise reform that would accelerate the move to self-government, judicial improvements, equality of economic opportunity for all, a programme of free and compulsory primary education, and greater scope for Africans in the civil service.[73] The NYM must also be seen in its wider West African context. It reflected the aforementioned discontent of the poor and the disadvantaged with the largely elitist pre-occupations of the African leadership.[74] Its roots lay in the Lagos Youth Movement, formed in 1934 by the Nigerians, Samuel Akinsanya, H.O. Davis, Dr. J.C. Vaughan, and Ernest Ikoli. This organisation sought to challenge the colonial government's discriminatory education policy which was crippling the local Yaba Higher College. In 1936, the group changed its name to the Nigerian Youth Movement (NYM), and soon became, in the words of Ezera, "Nigeria's first genuine nationalist movement."[75] The NYM should also be reviewed alongside the meteoric rise to prominence in Nigeria of Nnamdi Azikiwe, soon to be the most dominant Igbo on the national scene. In 1937, Azikiwe returned to Lagos from the Gold Coast where he had edited the African Morning Post. He subsequently pioneered a new trail in Nigerian journalism through the introduction of the West African Pilot and other newspapers, which circulated in the other cities of the territory, such as Port Harcourt. The young and dynamic Azikiwe, former pupil in Lagos of Potts-Johnson in his teaching days,[76] now came to symbolise that youthful quest for change in Nigerian politics that had been present for several years. Although Azikiwe's education in the United States did not commend him to his British overlords, it would be used to devastating effect in his editorials and other columns that pilloried colonial officials on a wide range of issues. Azikiwe's militant rhetoric led naturally to the NYM, and he became a member in 1938. The Youth movement, now embarked on a major challenge of Herbert Macaulay's fifteen year dominance of Lagos politics through the National Democratic Party (NNDP), and in subsequent Legislative Council elections, the NYM easily prevailed over the NNDP.[77] This was the beginning of the end for Herbert Macaulay.

In Freetown, H.C. Bankole-Bright and his conservative fraction of the Krio elite was similarly imperilled. In 1938, the socialist-oriented Krio, I.T.A. Wallace-Johnson, whose marxist credentials as a trade unionist included a period of study in Moscow, and many years of activism in the Gold Coast and Nigeria,[78] formed the West African Youth League (WAYL). Wallace-Johnson's objective was to develop a more mass-centered politics that would bring the Krio and indigenous protectorate groups into closer empathy and some anti-colonial cooperation. Even more than the infinitely more resilient Herbert Macaulay, Bankole-Bright would recoil at the ferocity of these youthful ideas. He resented Wallace-Johnson passionately, and his outrage increased as he saw his political fortunes plummet in the late 1930's. By December 1938, Bright's support of the colonial government's measures to curb Wallace-Johnson's activities had made him so unpopular that the membership demanded his resignation from the Vice-Presidency of the local NCBWA branch.[79]

The Nigerian Youth Movement (NYM) of Port Harcourt

Meanwhile, by July 1938, the radical presence of the NYM had begun to be felt in Port Harcourt, as, predictably, local developments mirrored activities in Freetown and Lagos. Counting some Saro in its executive,[80] the Port Harcourt NYM was equally impatient of the older generation of Africans, especially those in the political elite. It saw the latter as thoroughly incapable of resolving the many economic contradictions that confronted the youth of Port Harcourt. The elite was judged to be too moderate, and much too timid to procure the desired alleviation of African misery. The Nigerian Observer, true to the minimalist politics of its proprietor, Potts-Johnson, appealed to the youths for patience, and the eschewing of immoderation. The paper called on the younger population to "make haste slowly", and it counselled inter-generational cooperation, if success against unfair politics was to be achieved. It criticised the NYM's policy which denied membership to those over fifty, allowing them only the role of patrons. "The fathers of today, are the sons of yesterday . . . ", it admonished. The paper called on the NYM to make room even for the "illiterates", and the members of the township' existing unions, who can constitute branches of the organisation.

Though mildly condemnatory of their exuberance, Potts-Johnson realised that, ultimately, the restlessness of the youth could only be stilled by improved economic conditions. By July 1938, Port Harcourt had experienced more than a year of an acute trade depression. Local produce prices had collapsed, and the cost of imported items, such as building materials, had soared astronomically. The Observer called for a detailed country by country review of the nuances of the economic crisis, to be conducted by the metropolitan power. "Perhaps by so doing", it noted, "some means may be discovered whereby local difficulties may to some extent be surmounted and . . . sufferings (sic.) alleviated".[81]

While appealing to the NYM for moderation, Potts-Johnson kept up the pressure for the up-grading of the local infrastructure, an exercise that would itself generate some employment opportunity. He was unrelenting on the drainage front, demanding in September 1938, the "construction of a drain on the west side of the Barracks road to connect with the new out-fall".[82] I.B. Johnson was also unusually active as 1938 drew to a close. With talk of the possible outbreak of global conflict already in the air, Johnson pressed the administration on the subject of gas masks, demanding to know if they would be "available for issue to the public in the event of an emergency".[83] The African elite was out to prove to the youth that it had not abandoned its obligations to the community.

In November 1938, the Nigerian Observer again addressed the NYM in the aftermath of elections in Lagos in which its parent branch had defeated the NNDP of the Saro stalwart, Herbert Macaulay. A major issue in the acrimonious political campaign had been that of nationality. The use of the slogan "Nigeria for the Nigerians" in political rallies, caused a stir in immigrant Port Harcourt, and the Saro widely discussed its troubling implications. The NYM had opposed the election of immigrants to the Lagos Council, and, the rebuffed immigrants, in their turn, had charged their hosts with callous ingratitude over past immigrant contributions. The Nigerian Observer entered the fray, condemning immigrant comment on their earlier indispensability. It blamed the defeat of the Lagos NNDP on Herbert Macaulay's autocratic pursuit of a personality cult, and invited the public to drop the nationality discussion. "The less we talk of this question . . . the better it will be for the general welfare of West Africa", it concluded with obvious unease.[84]

Potts-Johnson's efforts and entreaties may well have struck a chord in the local NYM, for when in November 1938, it organised a public meeting at the palladium in Port Harcourt, it invited Potts-Johnson to take the chair.[85] The Saro members of the NYM executive, A. Pratt, a dispenser in government service, and L.A. John, a cashier at the local Barclays Bank, were in attendance, with other leading officials. The meeting addressed the rumour that Nigeria could soon be handed over to the Germans, like its neighbour, Cameroon. Potts-Johnson confessed to dismissing the rumor initially, until its persistence caused him to review it more closely. He lamented the tendency to treat Africans "as a young race with no prospect of rising", stressing "what a shame it would be" should Nigeria be "sold to another nation who (sic.) will ask us to begin everything anew". He reviewed the legal, economic, and social ramifications of such a transfer, and commended the NYM for convening a public forum on the subject. When, however during the meeting, an assistant chief clerk in the Resident's office, E.O. Wey, suggested the addition, to a resolution to be drafted, of the words "our individual loyalty to the throne", he was "cried down by a section of the audience". Potts-Johnson requested the inclusion of the phrase, but his motion was defeated. As the crowd grew more restless, Potts-Johnson "raised the song 'God Save the King'". Although some joined him in singing, "others walked away". The meeting ended inconclusively, a portent of the abiding mass disenchantment with both the African elite and the colonial administration.[86] In its response to this incident, the Resident expressed his grave disappointment. He was particularly disturbed at the group's rejection of Wey's amendment which had read in full: "That this assembly place on record its unflinching and traditional loyalty to the British government". Although the amendment was seconded, the house had voted it down.[87]

The youth of Port Harcourt had openly demonstrated their chagrin over prevailing conditions, and their disappointment in the seeming collusion of the local African elite (of which the Saro were a prominent fraction) with an unpopular colonial administration. They had indicated that their tolerance of Potts-Johnson was not unqualified. He was himself somewhat compromised by association, and could not be totally free of blemish. The administration, in its embarrassment, would turn to the discredited African elite for help in shoring up its flagging fortunes, and, hopefully, assuaging the hostility of the poor and the aggrieved. This would be a major challenge for the older generation of African leaders.

In December 1938, the NYM organised Youth Day Celebrations. It held a Thanksgiving service at Wesley Church, with the Revds. H.L. Forde and M.D. Showers officiating. The choir was drawn from all the protestant churches of Port Harcourt. At the service, it was reported, there were "more than 120 comrades in white attire, emblem of a pure and simple heart". A "Comrade D.A. Olubi" read the lesson. Islamic observance was also a feature of these celebrations. We have no evidence of practising Saro muslims in Port Harcourt, and such muslims as there were appear to have been predominantly Yoruba. Some of them were very active in the NYM. Like their Christian comrades, Islamic members of the movement also organised a similar service at the Central Mosque at this time, where they were joined by Christian representatives of the group. The Chief Imam addressed the gathering on the subject of unity. The NYM also organised a public lecture at the schoolroom of St. Cyprian's Church. Comrade J.K. Trezise chaired the occasion, and he was supported by Comrade Dr. S.A. Awoliyi, Daddy Ajagbe, F.C. Obi, Mrs. Savage, Mrs. Antus Williams, and Mrs. V.O. Ekpene. The lecture was delivered by Comrade D.A. Olubi of the medical department. Communist literature had obviously found favour in some youth circles in Port Harcourt, as the generous use of "comrade", as in contemporary Freetown,[88] would suggest. The NYM, however, never appeared to have progressed much beyond casual acquaintance with the ideology, to more systematic study, and local advocacy of its philosophy. Its identification with Russia was more youthful exuberance than informed and committed political activism. To round up its celebrations, the NYM held a garden party at the Jubilee Memorial Park. Representatives from Aba, Abonnema, Opobo, and Ikot Ekpene were expected at this and other functions.[89]

Faced with a new militancy, with obvious Russian pretensions, the administration turned yet again to it proven allies. In its annual report for 1938, the government, eager for African elite support, paid a rare public compliment to the ACL which it addressed as a "useful body" of men.[90] In turn, a loyal Potts-Johnson[91] expressed his delight over the "categorical denial" of the rumour "of a possible transfer of Nigeria to Germany, not only by His Excellency, the Governor, but also the Under-Secretary of the State for the Colonies". He appealed to Germany, Spain, and Italy, to put an end to war-mongering, and pursue the path of peace. He wrote in conclusion: "If all the nations are sincere in their efforts, we may face the future with calm and confidence. Let us all resolve—there be no more war".[92] On the domestic front, it would appear that Potts-Johnson entered 1939 believing that he could keep his friends both in government and in the more radical fringes such as the NYM. This tendency to run with the hare and hunt with the hounds, was the cornerstone of his gradualist politics. He was the consummate middle-roader, out to meld the disparate segments of society into a coherence that would secure the African welfare, while also preserving elite gains. The developments of the coming years would severely test the wisdom of this centrist approach.

Other Pre-War Economic Issues: Potts-Johnson and Economic Nationalism

If the National Congress of British West Africa had registered few successes on the political front, its record on economic matters was even more dismal, for it came to these activities with even less preparation. The inter-war years were a time of great economic decline in the West African region, following on a preceding period of prosperity. Although the educated elite desired a programme of industrial expansion, Britain had no intention of jeopardising its manufacturing exports. From about 1920, the prices of West Africa's export crops had declined sharply while those of imported manufactures escalated amidst declining wages and increasing competition for African traders from European firms, as well as Indian and Levantine entrepreneurship. African liquidity was generally low, and bank loans went increasingly to Indians, Syrians, and Lebanese, not to the African store-owner who could hardly raise the collateral now routinely demanded. The middleman stranglehold of the European export firm was depleting the profit margins of the African farmer, but efforts to break free by establishing autonomous farmers unions with direct export access to Europe met little success. The efforts of the NCBWA to introduce a West African Cooperative Association in charge of the direct shipment of produce also failed for want of capital and economic initiative on the part of the Congress' leaders.[93]

By the early 1930's, with the NCBWA in decline, Winifred Tete-Ansa, a produce dealer, and others, attempted to pool farmers unions in the Gold Coast and Nigeria toward securing higher produce prices that would sustain an African bank, and reduce dependence on white capital. Because these schemes were generally under-capitalised, they failed miserably. By 1930, cocoa farmers in the Gold Coast were involved in a holdup of produce, as they refused to part with their crops unless prices improved. These boycotts would continue into the late 1930's, sustained by opposition to the "Cocoa Pool", a cartel of European firms established in 1938.[94] The Nigerian Youth Movement opposed the cartel, but such a challenge of economic policy, mounted territorially, stood little chance of procuring effective reform. A more concerted effort from all the West African colonies was required, and Britain would not allow its emergence.

Potts-Johnson's economic reflections on the African material condition had begun with the global depression. In an editorial of the 25 January 1930, he had raised the contentious issue of African access to the means of production, and their control of resources throughout the continent. He had asked: "How then can the African eliminate once and for all, the commercial inequality of which they complain so much.[95] This was a question on which he was much exercised throughout his public life, and the search for answers to it became, for him, almost an obsession which greatly influenced the business decisions he would make over the years. In raising the subject of African economic self-sufficiency in 1930, Potts-Johnson re-echoed the concerns that were often expressed in a Freetown of a much earlier period—the avid interest evinced in agricultural matters in the late 19th and early 20th centuries by such Krio pioneers as Samuel Lewis, "Independent" Grant, Abayomi Cole, and S.B. (Abuke) Thomas.[96] For the Niger delta, however, these reflections would anticipate by a number of years the later ruminations of Nnamdi Azikiwe.[97] In this sense, Potts-Johnson's sustained disquisitions on matters economic could be said to have opened up an area of discourse not much in evidence in earlier delta debate.

In attempting an answer to the question he had himself posed, Potts-Johnson found the path to African economic salvation in self reliance, pan-African economic cooperation, and the independent mobilisation of economic resources. He urged the African people to a greater economic resolve: "Let them float companies of their own; let them cease to distrust themselves; let their leaders be imbued with the moral stamina which is so common among more progressive nations; and finally, let them act more and complain less". Should this approach be adopted, he averred, Africans will be in a position "to dictate prices for the produce of their land. No Combination of trading firms, however collosal, will usurp their natural right from them". Africans could then squarely confront the specious arguments, often encountered, regarding the prices the world market could offer for their produce. In elaboration, he noted: "If any merchants were to say that he is guided by prices in the home markets, Africans could then tell him that if there is demand in the home markets for African produce, prices fixed by Africans must prevail".[98]

This was unusually passionate economic nationalism for the Niger Delta of the 1930's, and it bespoke Potts-Johnson's budding entrepreneurial instincts, as will soon be evident. He was an avid believer in efficiency in the work place, and in the need to engage, for any position, the best qualified personnel available, irrespective of their creed or colour. Having himself received training in the sciences in England, he was particularly keen on promoting the interests of the European-educated African. He wanted to see more of their number in senior positions in the colonial bureaucracy. In April 1930, he addressed this subject in his paper, arguing that the time had "come for government to begin to think seriously about Africans who received their education and professional training in Europe". He called on government to engage such people more rapidly in "higher appointments" which were "being invariably filled by Europeans". As already indicated, he was particularly sensitive on the issue of race, and addressed it publicly at every favourable opportunity. When word reached Port Harcourt, in August 1930, of discriminatory treatment suffered by Africans on the high seas on board the R.M.V. Accra, Potts-Johnson reacted instantly. "Whose fault" is it, he asked, "that one man was made White and another Black. It is all a matter of accident. It was not a question of choice. No option was given to either to choose . . . why should one man be made to suffer eternally on account of the hue of his skin? Why?"[99]

Having for long perceived the link between race and the African's economic deprivation in the colonial calculus, Potts-Johnson averred that racism could only be dethroned through the attainment of economic independence. Such freedom would be elusive unless Africans pursued economic enterprise relentlessly. Somewhat of a visionary, Potts-Johnson called on the people of Nigeria, in October 1931, to re-dedicate themselves to economic emancipation. He wrote: "We should . . . one and all begin now to encourage African enterprise so that during the next decade our country can boost not of one but of five or more banks, owned, financed, and controlled entirely by Africans". In addition to African-owned banks, and other finance houses, Potts-Johnson stressed the importance of "cooperative institutions of different kinds". He called for local ownership of Insurance Companies, and other financial instruments "that will make us feel that as Africans we have a destiny". The African population was urged to review and emulate the African-American experience, where "our kith and kin . . . can boast of several institutions owned and controlled by themselves . . . ", in spite of past failures and set-backs along the way. "They were not discouraged—therefore, Nigerians, be ye not discouraged", he exhorted.[100]

For African economic enterprise to thrive, Potts-Johnson emphasised the need for prudence in the conservation of individual material resources. The avoidance of wasteful social expenditure was a cardinal imperative. He deplored the wanton mis-use of resources in traditional social observances in the Niger Delta, a matter of much sensitivity. He wrote: "The Coast Town people usually adopt a peculiar attitude where money is concerned. They are prepared to waste their money on useless things, like coral beads, massive gold rings, studs, . . . dowry, funerals, and the like, but where the interest of their own children is involved, they pretend that they are the poorest people in existence". Potts-Johnson considered it "disgraceful" that local children were generally not well provisioned in basic clothing, as several parents saw investment in their children as hazardous in the light of the prevailing high levels of child mortality. This had to change, if the future was to be secured. By November 1931, in the depths of the economic depression, Potts-Johnson was reviewing Nigeria's worsening terms of trade, which had produced low export prices, and a highly inflationary import regime. He saw the answer to this problem, which might well persist for some time, in the African pursuit of local manufacturing. Raw materials had to be processed into manufactured goods of the sort that had become expensive imports. "What we want", he wrote, "is manufacture (sic.) on a very large scale, organised, financed, and controlled by strong and important native combines. Then and only then shall we be able to protect our own interests". He saw economic self-sufficiency, and the prudent husbanding of individual resources as the key to dignity and corporate material security. On this, he noted: "If we are determined to assert ourselves within the limits allowed by law, we shall command respect, and shall be able to effect radical changes in our present deplorable economic relations with the outside world".[101]

As he pressed on with the formulation and refining of his economic ideas during the depression, Potts-Johnson came increasingly to assign some primacy to the effective control of agricultural production by the African community. He called for "a Nigerian or West African Union of Producers", with branches throughout the region. He projected that such a union would generate its own data "as to the uses to which [African] products are put in foreign countries, to ascertain the prices of all the finished articles made from or containing" African material. Such information would be invaluable in pricing negotiations. His hope was to see prices revert to their 1913-18 and 1930-31 levels, when they were judged to be fair, and African producers enjoyed a reasonable return. Potts-Johnson demanded that current pricing policy be guided by the statistics of those favourable years, for only then would African producers receive an equitable return on their output.[102]

Of all the leaders of the township, Potts-Johnson was the most consistently forth-coming on the subject of African unemployment during the depression. With his sights on European firms, which were reluctant to engage African personnel in senior positions, he editorialised repeatedly on the need for a change of attitude. He called on the management of those firms to recognise the substantial African contribution to the huge stocks of capital they had amassed after only some two or three years of operation in West Africa. He asked: "Is the African then not reasonably entitled to some appreciable share of these profits even by way of good wages and sufficient commissions?" The time had come, he argued, for the progressive replacement, by Africans, of the more expensive European personnel, who were a major drain on the "annual recurrent and non-recurrent expenditure of firms".[103]

Though directing his critique at European employment practices for the most part, Potts-Johnson did not wholly exonerate his own African people. He demanded that the unemployed and the retrenched be more creative, and suggested that they explore the relatively undeveloped poultry sector. He admitted that this area might not be as lucrative as cocoa or palm produce farming, but recognised that it did possess much untapped potential. Besides, it required little capital outlay: "A few pounds, a few labourers, a few chickens, and a little care and attention are all that is needed", he reasoned. For African enterprise to succeed, Potts-Johnson cautioned against the mindless and "ruinous competition indulged in between African traders". He deplored the "buy and sell at all cost" mentality, putting this down to a growing tendency to individualism, and the resultant failure to properly assess economic variables before embarking on a particular line of business. He condemned a circumstance where "as soon as one man starts a new venture, scores of others immediately embark on the same business, and very often to the detriment of their former line of business . . . ". Potts-Johnson criticised the general neglect of farming, in preference of trade, except for "the poorest class", and poured scorn on African retail purchases that only enriched the Levantines and Asians: "The Indians and Syrians have entered on the scene, and are making huge profits from their exceptionally large sales, and all we do is . . . help them to clear their stocks by making barely sufficient to cover the expenses of carrying their goods about without anything to lay by".[104]

He urged a greater respect for goods produced by Africans, and called for "new native industries", if Africans were not to remain perpetually "hewers of wood and drawers of water". The dire straits of the African economy, he argued, were partly the consequence of a local inability to appreciate things African. He held up the Hausa of northern Nigeria as a group worthy of some emulation. It was the Hausa who were taking to producing most of their basic requirements, though southern Nigeria gave them scant credit, and dismissed their group as of less than average intelligence. The Niger Delta was lagging behind the northern and western communities of Nigeria, he argued, being overly dependent on palm produce and monoculture. He portrayed the Hausa and Yoruba as more inclined to varied industrial pursuits, and more adaptable to new environments. On the need for expanded citrus production, Potts-Johnson called on the local African population to use its surplus lands more wisely in the cultivation of "pineapples, bananas, paw-paw, oranges, pears, and other fruits much in demand in Europe". In conclusion, he demanded of the local population a greater openness to economic innovation. Of this he wrote: "Let us be up and doing, and travel . . . to gain experience from other parts of the country, so that we may not entirely be left behind in the struggle for existence . . . Unity and cooperation will help us a great way if only we can be sincere and true to each other".[105]

Much as he criticised his people for their apathy, indolence, and lack of vision, Potts-Johnson was always prompt in their defence when their precarious material state was further assailed by external agency. In April

1933, the government, under pressure of the depression, announced its intention to reduce the salaries of some of its African employees. This elicited a stern rebuke from Potts-Johnson. He called for the cuts to "be reasonable and fair", and urged that the "burden will fall lightly on the poorly paid members of the service who do not enjoy such privileges as free quarters, seniority allowance, free passages to and from their country, full pay (sic.) leave, and the like". This was a scarcely-veiled attack on the government's European employees, who, along with their compatriots in the metropole, were regarded, by Potts-Johnson, as indifferent to the plight of the Nigerian people. He accused Britain of being taken more with the affairs of Australia, South Africa, and Canada, with their sizable white populations, than with the people of Nigeria, which had "no existence on their map". The British people, he believed, were generally indifferent to "the outposts of the Empire".[106]

By April 1933, Potts-Johnson's economic ruminations had lighted on the possibilities in the local export of frozen dairy products and beef. This was "one out of several ways out of the present danger" of economic collapse, he averred.[107] Another way, perhaps, was to insist on Britain deriving her imports from within the Empire, and to the economic benefit of the colonised. When, in the 1930's, the British took to the importation of whale oil from Norway,[108] an enraged Potts-Johnson sounded the alarm. Britain's argument was that she had not taken full advantage of all the whale oil available to her on free entry terms, and had grossly under-utilised her own capacity as producer of 52 per cent of the world's whale oil. She further averred that she was not in the business of subsidising Nigeria's oil-palm producers at the expense of the British whale oil industry. This was basic economics, but callous outrage in the ears of the African colonised. In an editorial, Potts-Johnson demanded: "Will the mother country continue to watch with apparent indifference the death by a slow but sure process of strangulation of the staple trade industry of an important part of the Empire, while non-members . . . continue to thrive . . . ". He saw as a double standard British recourse to non-Empire markets when the colonised of Nigeria were being barred from "cheaper Japanese goods".[109] In 1934, Britain had imposed quotas limiting the import into Nigeria of Japanese textiles and footwear.[110] This had been done to protect British manufacturers, but it had forced prices upwards in Nigeria. Potts-Johnson demanded an end to such attempts to aid British industry at the expense of the colonised territories, admonishing the metropole to a more just conduct. In a tone of undisguised sarcasm, he added: "We are sure that much as the mother country is desirous of protecting the interest of Lancashire, the cries of our own poor people who can ill afford to buy expensive goods will not be lost on her . . . "[111]

In the quest for better palm produce prices, Potts-Johnson enjoined the producers of Port Harcourt to emulate the persistence of the African farmers of the Gold Coast, who had sent "a deputation to attend the cocoa conference . . . in England" in the summer of 1934. Potts-Johnson was no doubt familiar with the incidence of economic nationalism in that territory in reaction to the aforementioned "Cocoa Pool" cartel of European firms which had led to the cocoa hold-ups of 1908-1938.[112] Nigerian farmers, he intoned, could not afford to "sit idle and look on". The situation in the Gold Coast had spawned several salutary lessons, and Nigerians were being urged to review them urgently. When palm produce prices improved marginally in October 1934, a much relieved Potts-Johnson welcomed the development, and the impetus it gave to trading activity. He wrote of the need to maintain the price level through the production of a high quality crop. Only this would see Nigeria through foreign competition, enabling local producers "to demand the highest marketable price". As producers of the finest crop, Nigerians could then demand the best price "or refuse to sell".[113]

In June 1935, Potts-Johnson addressed the reluctance of the Royal West African Frontier Force (WAFF) to absorb more of the educated unemployed. He called for their recruitment as junior officers, and raised the question of advancement criteria within the WAFF. He demanded to know why "when a native has distinguished himself in the force and has attained to a certain rank, he is transferred to the police force either as a sergeant-major or an inspector? . . . " He further noted pointedly: "We know that it will be felt in certain quarters that we are attempting to introduce an innovation. But why should there be no innovations?"[114] Potts-Johnson cited the experience of India where locals had enjoyed the benefits of elevation in the service, and had become military officers, and had fought with distinction in European wars. He saw no reason why similar recognition should be denied the African soldier, who seemed in no way less equipped for higher responsibility.

The palm produce price did not hold up for long, and by July 1935, it was back to its fluctuating ways. Potts-Johnson criticised the slump, and expressed despair over the many speculations as to its cause. "Some there are", he wrote, in some impatience, "who think that over-production the world over is responsible for the unprecedented situation; others are of the opinion that tariff walls . . . play a very important part in the matter. Whatever may be the explanation, we do not think much time . . . need be wasted on it when once expert opinion favours it. The one thing needed is the cure . . . ".[115]

The township's unemployment problem worsened as the depression progressed. In September 1935, Potts-Johnson remarked that in the past, a school leaver never stayed unengaged six months after graduation. He lamented that a young man who now found a job after a three-year search was "very fortunate indeed", for many were jobless onward of four or five years after leaving school. The older educated African residents of the township were faring no better, particularly in the upper echelons of the civil service. He wondered rightly whether it was official policy to keep educated Africans out of such senior positions, and noted in frustration: "The more the country is advancing, the more it seems those whose education, standing and professional training entitle them to leadership of their people and to higher appointments are, with a very few exceptions, discouraged".[116]

By August 1936, it appeared that the worst of the depression in falling produce prices, unemployment, and general economic misery, was coming to an end. A new mood of optimism in Saro and other African circles was about, and Potts-Johnson captured this in an editorial of the period. He commented on the improvement in trade, and invited the authorities to commence the review of "economy measures" that no longer seemed appropriate. He referred to depression activity which had led to the closure of government-run schools, the retrenchment of teachers, the withdrawal of financial support to schools, and the consequent lowering of standards in such institutions. Calling for the "gradual restoration of the former conditions", and the recognition of changed economic circumstances, he advocated remedial measures, such as a lowering of the electricity tariff, that would bring some instant relief. Potts-Johnson appealed for official review of the electricity meter rate, assuring the government that "the cheaper the unit or lamp rate . . . the greater will be the demand". When, much later in the economic recovery, government proposed to answer the appeals for an increase in the water supply by raising the water rate, Potts-Johnson again spear-headed the outraged African lobby. Claiming to speak on behalf of the "proletariat", he demanded "a sense of fair play".[117]

Though forever mindful of the government's responsibility to protect the citizenry, and provide equitable economic conditions, Potts-Johnson's ultimate expectations of African economic fulfillment appear to have resided in his faith in self reliance, and the expanded African ownership and control of the means of production. As already outlined, this was the theme to which he always returned with an almost homiletic insistence. Not even improving economic conditions could change this orientation. In September

1938, he called for the establishment of a Nigerian Fruit Company for the export of bananas to the rest of the world in which Africans would play a leading role. When in July 1939, a local African entrepreneur, E.A. Koku of Barracks road, recently retired from government service, established the township's first brick-making business, Potts-Johnson was ecstatic. He had in the past referred to the inordinate cost of imported building materials, and called for alternatives. Here, at last, was some evidence of a response to his entreaties. Potts-Johnson praised Koku's foresight, and hailed him as an exemplar of African industry and dedication to economic liberation. He wrote in exhortation:

> "If we are to become economically emancipated, we must begin right now capitalising business ventures of our own, which would be able to employ a large number of our people, and help relieve unemployment in the country. Those . . . who have money in hand can best render service to the race by investing in some reasonable commercial ventures, as by financing native institutions. Only by releasing tied up capital can we hope to usher in political and economic emancipation".[118]

Potts-Johnson would himself live by this creed. Besides providing Port Harcourt with its first newspaper, he established, with his own funds, its first secondary school, and would be involved in various other pioneering efforts, as will be reviewed presently.

On the Eve of War

Port Harcourt started 1939 on an optimistic note. Work on improving the water supply to the native town was reported to be in progress, with pipes being laid in several areas.[119] Rent reduction proposals were being entertained by the TAB.[120] This halcyon phase did not, however, last very long. The alarums of war were soon on the horizon, and the Nigerian Observer noticed the growing bewilderment in African circles as the realisation of impending conflict dawned. It referred, in April, to the "large proportion of the inhabitants of Port Harcourt" who were "disturbed in mind as to their safety". The mood in the township was not much relieved by increases in rail fares in July, by the Nigerian Railways. All were agreed that the hike in rates came "at the most inopportune time". The Nigerian Observer appealed to the administration for a review. It demanded: "Will government take our plea on behalf of this struggling class and allow the reduced rates to continue"?[121]

In an effort to address the perennial problem of rising prices, the Local Authority, in September 1939, appointed a committee to make recommendations on the matter. Its brief was to investigate the problem thoroughly and report on "any necessary measures regarding the control of foodstuffs, and for the purpose of disseminating information and government regulations among the public . . . ".[122] The members of the committee were three Saro, Potts-Johnson, F.O. Lucas, and I.B. Johnson, as well as the medical officer, Dr. Nunns. The ACL was requested to send two representatives, the Syrian and Lebanese communities, two, the Indians, one, and the Hausa group, one. The committee also had representation from the market traders, and the Motor Transport Union.[123]

The work of the committee would, however, soon be overshadowed by the grim specter of war. On 9 September, the Nigerian Observer responded to Governor Bernard Bourdillon's announcement of the declaration of war against the Germans. The editorial cautioned against "the temptation of profiteering and inflating the price of necessary articles of food . . . ". It called for "coolheads" on "shoulders already weighted by anxiety". It was unequivocal in its support of the Allies: "Our empire and the cause she has espoused and is out to defend is the cause of liberty, and each man, woman, child, is to pray for her success and the cause of democracy . . . God Save the King". The paper, which had been a weekly up to this point at 3[d] a copy, now became a daily, at a penny, starting 14 September. It began to carry a war news column, first in English, and then, under *Akuko Agha*, in the vernacular, to reach a wider readership. The matter of war relief was now also taken in hand, and paradoxically, war would provide the opportunity for the blossoming of the arts and social talent in Port Harcourt's African population. One of the earliest fund-raising activities was sponsored in November 1939 by the Nigerian Youth Movement (NYM), and the newly established Women's Emergency Committee, in which Saro women held key positions. This was a film shown at the Africa Club, which was followed by a dance at the Palladium. The Resident, E.N. Mylius, was himself, Chief Patron, with many indigenes and Saro in attendance. All proceeds went to the war relief fund.[124]

In its annual report for 1939, the local colonial administration was fulsome in its praise of the efforts and support of the "educated business and professional Africans" who were members of the Township Advisory Board. It commended them for their having shown "considerable public spirit", and for making "the Local Authority's duties pleasanter (sic.) and less difficult".[125] The support of this group would be crucial during the war, as Saro and indigenous members of the African elite interacted more closely in official as well as civic society. Both sides would come into greater empathy, and lasting bonds of friendship would, in some cases, be forged. Elite cooperation, and the seeming propinquity of these more advantaged Africans (immigrant and indigene) to the local colonial administration, would deepen suspicion in grassroot circles, and engender further alienation. Many would distrust an elite that enjoyed some official favour, and appeared to operate often on terms of mutual confidence with white society.

On the eve of the war, the Saro had established a commanding presence on the economic and political platforms of township life. Though beneficiaries of official appointments and sundry preferments, they had (in the case of Potts-Johnson, principally) emerged in a watchdog role that demanded transparency in government conduct. Although their leaders were generally perceived to be of a station that set them above the common run of township society, they had also manifested some concern over the many privations that afflicted most households. Would this be enough to calm the restive torrents of working-class discontent? Was there room for genuine inter-class cooperation with immigrant participation? These are issues to which we shall return later. It is to matters of a social order that we now turn.

3

ESTABLISHING A GROUP PRESENCE, 1930—49

The regime of Saro social activities in Port Harcourt appears to have been conditioned over the years by three major objectives. These largely determined the scope of the community's social outreach, and the risks it was willing to take in an urban situation where African immigrants from outside Nigeria constituted a very small fraction of the total population. Firstly, the Saro desired to maintain the corporate cultural identity of their group while protecting its members from sundry violations that might emanate from the colonial government or the indigenous population. This appears to have dictated the need for strict discipline within the Sierra Leone Union, and other communal structures, with enforcement responsibility being assigned to a largely male elder category, dedicated to ensuring continued patriarchal control. Secondly, while maintaining the group's identity, there was a concern to secure its progressive articulation with the larger society by a process of lateral incorporation that might require some limited exogamy to procure social access into select segments of local society. Thirdly, the Saro community greatly desired the continued cultivation of ties with Freetown, the "homeland", and with such Saro enclaves as were to be found in such cities as Lagos and Calabar. This was central to cultural affirmation and group identity. In the pursuit of these objectives, the contradiction between lateral integration into the larger society, and the cultural pursuit of ethnic particularity was not always obvious to some of the group's members. Nor did sufficient thought go into the wider political implications of ethnic exclusivity in a territory already celebrated, by the 1930's, for its potent indigenous cultural nationalism. Under colonialism, these contradictions could easily be sustained. In an environment of political independence from British rule, however, they could greatly threaten the peace of the immigrant community.

Saro social endeavour will be reviewed in the following five principal areas of major activity—education, the church, general social commentary, the Sierra Leone Union as well as Saro involvement in other multi-ethnic associational groupings, and those perennial "socials" and *awujoh*,[1] marking various highlights on the group's calendar, that brought the Saro and their local associates together in what seems to have been, in good times, perennial merrymaking. To highlight also the disparities in life-style between the more affluent Saro and the rest of the community, we propose to examine closely the social activities of the Potts-Johnsons and the I.B. Johnsons. This should not only provide a glimpse into the domestic circumstances of these leading patriarchs of the Saro community, but, through such a review, we may well begin to understand the factors behind their highly contrasting approaches to the public realm.

As we discuss the social exploits of the Saro, it is also essential to begin to determine the group's success in transplanting to Port Harcourt the cultural ethos of the Freetown Krio, and the Lagos and Calabar Saro, the principal social formations from which they hailed, and by whose standards and values they would be constantly assessed. An attempt also needs to be made to determine the reach of Saro social activities, and the degree to which it transcended elite confines to touch the lives of the poorer sections of society, acknowledging, of course, that the Saro were themselves highly differentiated economically, with some on the margins of subsistence. Unfortunately, we have no accurate figures for the Saro population as at 1930-40, but it would appear that it continued to be generally small, and in the region of some 30-40 households in these years, with a total population below 200.[2] There was, of course, always a floating population of Krio and Saro visitors (relatives, friends, old secondary school mates, etc.) from Freetown, Lagos, Calabar, and other centres. Total population numbers therefore tended to fluctuate somewhat, and were clearly much augmented in periods of Christian celebration such as Christmas, Easter, and Whitsuntide.

Education

Saro residents in Port Harcourt had close affiliations with such Freetown schools as the Methodist Boys High School (MBHS), the Sierra Leone

Grammar School (SLGS), the Annie Walsh Memorial School (AWMS), and the Methodist Girls High School (MGHS). These were among the finest schools in Freetown, and there were thus certain parallel educational expectations within the Saro community resident in Port Harcourt. Saro involvement in the early educational work of the Niger delta which was provided principally by British missionaries, was significant and not always free of controversy.[3] By 1930, Port Harcourt itself was in the midst of an education debate, which stemmed from certain racist comments on colonial education policy. The official at the centre of this controversy was T.S.W. Thomas, one-time chief secretary to the colonial government of Nigeria, now Governor of Nyasaland (Malawi). Thomas was reported as having said during his inauguration as Governor at a luncheon given by the Town Councils of Blantyre and Limbe, that he "preferred East . . . to West Africa", for the latter was "going too fast in the matter of education." This comment, reported in the Nigerian Daily Times, was promptly taken up by the one-time teacher, Potts-Johnson. He saw it as a challenge and an affront to the people of Port Harcourt, and left his readers in no doubt as to the group response it should elicit. He opined: "If there is still any responsible servant of the crown in West Africa who entertains such as Mr. Thomas is alleged to have expressed, let the Coast Town people of Owerri Province . . . and the rest of West Africa answer by formulating schemes for more national schools . . . ".[4] In this observation, Potts-Johnson was not only rejecting limits on African educational advancement, he was calling for an educational curriculum with greater national cultural relevance as will soon be evident. Moreover, he demanded greater emphasis on the education of women, an area of great neglect.[5] Colonialism had greatly increased the marginalisation of African women, a point to which we will soon return.[6] Potts-Johnson's observations on official education policy generated much debate in local African circles, and the search for more educational opportunity crystallised around the subject of the absence of secondary school facilities in Port Harcourt. Up to 1930, local parents had sent their children to Lagos and Calabar for secondary education, and many now considered this no longer acceptable. In October 1930, Potts-Johnson called on the Chiefs and other local leaders to consider the establishing of a secondary school in the township. He condemned government policy on the matter, deploring the absence of a government school in the township, and the transfer of the burden of education to the missionaries, whom he commended for their excellent performance against innumerable odds.[7]

Potts-Johnson's appeal did not rouse the government to action, and local conditions for secondary education remained unchanged. Having despaired of officialdom's indifference, Potts-Johnson, in February 1931, introduced the Enitonna Tutorial Course in English and Arithmetic.[8] He named the programme after his wife, Nancy Eniton, daughter of Joseph Lewis Williams, a Saro of Lagos.[9] Instruction of secondary school quality, was provided by carefully selected tutors, and it was hoped that this would be the prelude to a more formalised system of training. He next appealed to the government to introduce a system of compulsory education, and suggested that, should depression conditions render it impolitic to embark on what could be a matter of some expense, the business of "enquiry, estimates, and general propaganda" be taken in hand immediately as an exploratory step.[10]

Potts-Johnson unveiled for his readers, in January 1932, his vision for the future education of the youth of Port Harcourt. This was an arena in which he was about to have great impact. His reflections on the educational emphasis West Africa should pursue examined a debate of long standing, and one that had caused some division in the West African elite over the years. For whereas such luminaries as the Krio, James Africanus Horton, saw the path to African independence in a mastery of the classics and other rudiments of European education, others had favoured the "National School" concept that was modelled on Booker T. Washington's Tuskegee Institute.[11] The latter approach would emphasise agricultural and industrial training alongside the more academic components, and it was believed that this would better prepare the African for his environment. In an age of predominantly Grammar Schools, the future seemed to be greatly in need of more artisans, and the expansion of vocational training.[12] The West African educated elite did not generally appreciate this need for diversification, and not many had been impressed by the introduction, in 1895, of the Presbyterian's Hope Waddell Institute in Calabar, which combined literary and industrial training.[13] Potts-Johnson was much influenced by Edward Blyden's concept of the African personality, and he believed in the urgent need to avoid further social corruption through the indiscriminate embrace of European values. Like Blyden, he was skeptical of some of Christianity's cultural prescriptions, and he inclined himself to a more accommodating view of polygyny and related aspects of traditional culture that had been generally dismissed by some European observers as repugnant.[14] He desired an educational system that would inculcate a greater cultural sensitivity. He found Sierra Leone's pre-occupation with Grammar schools an unimaginative choice, and advocated instead a curriculum that would make of the African an "industrial asset", through an emphasis on training in the sciences, but with premium being placed on Africa's requirements. The influence on Potts-Johnson's thinking of another of his mentors, Kweggyir Aggrey, was unmistakable in these comments.[15]

By March 1932, Potts-Johnson had established the Enitonna Printing Press, with the Saro, S.J.E. Bright, as Head printer. He next approached the government for permission to start a secondary school of his own in the township, the proposed Enitonna High School (EHS). Government gave its consent on the understanding that staffing arrangements would be satisfactory.[16] Potts-Johnson released the prospectus of the EHS on 6 April 1932 under the motto, "Pro Deo, pro patriae, pro genere vivimus". It indicated that there would be no boarding facilities initially, but that this would be introduced once the school moved into more permanent premises. Pupils of the school would be prepared for all major examinations such as the Oxford and Cambridge locals (senior and junior), those of the College of Preceptors, and London matriculation. Students from outside the township were welcome, and, in the absence of a boarding department, the school undertook to lodge them in local homes personally selected and approved by the Principal. The school was to be non-sectarian, and it ran classes from standards III to VI. Students were required to pay the following fees:

Middle forms (stds, V & VI)–£1.8s per term
Lower forms (std. IV)–£1.5s. per term
Lower forms (std. III)–£1.10s. per term

All fees had to be paid in advance, and a tuition discount of 10% was allowed to siblings.[17]

The EHS was formally opened on 2 May 1932, with prayers from the Rev. Dodds, Superintendent of the Methodist church, an address by the Principal, Potts-Johnson, and the introduction of the foundation tutors, A. Jaja of Opobo, and E. Fila Nabribere. Five boys and two girls were the foundation pupils. A cross-section of the township's elite, several Saro, and a number of indigenes, attended the ceremony.[18] By August 1932, the school had moved to a new site at Ilorin Street, off the Aggrey Road, and it had introduced a small boarding department. An Enitonna bookshop was fully operational by November 1932, and an advert of the period proclaimed its many and varied offerings: "sells all kinds of school books, stationery, and exercise books at prices that defy competition. Gramophones, gramophone records, copies of negro spirituals, with music, music pieces, office requisites, etc. are also stocked."[19] Potts-Johnson, the entrepreneur, was now putting theory into practice, and pointing the way to African improvement and self-sufficiency. The EHS celebrated its first anniversary with great fanfare in May 1932, and at thanksgiving services at St. Cyprian's, with the Ven. Arch. Crowther delivering the sermon. The Superintendent of Education, C.T. Quinn-Young, was invited to deliver an address, at the palladium, on "The Aims of Education in Nigeria". Funds raised during the celebrations were devoted to a school library fund. An ecstatic Potts-Johnson celebrated his handiwork in an editorial, with much elan: " . . . and how can the people be blamed for fixing their attention on her? Is she not the first school of her kind in Port Harcourt, the premier town of the division? Let us all hope that she will prove herself worthy of her existence . . . "[20]

Having come this far on a major project, one can, perhaps, understand Potts-Johnson's outrage, in April 1933, during the economic depression, when word emerged of the government's intention to limit African secondary education to standard IV in a bid to ease the unemployment situation. This rumour appears to have confirmed his earlier fears, and validated African views on European unease over local educational advancement. Potts-Johnson's angry reaction is cited *in extenso*:

> "If the idea is to save us from unemployment among clerks, can the government assert whether there is no unemployment outside the ranks of clerks? Are (sic.) the government aware of the number of carpenters, masons, etc. who are unemployed? If there is abnormal tendency to become clerks, should the proper remedy be a lowering of the standard of education of the majority? Would it not have been better, and more paternal if government were to encourage men of superior education to become mechanics, etc. by offering better wages, facilities . . . than at present obtains? . . . As far as we are concerned . . . the present policy cannot reduce unemployment among clerks, and until government give (*sic.*) . . . a better reason, doubts will still remain in our minds".[21]

The African community would tolerate no discriminatory educational policy, and Potts-Johnson was determined to have progress at any cost. By September 1933, the EHS had unveiled its new library, and with 65 pupils on it rolls by May 1934, with an average daily attendance of 60, there was great optimism. Plans to erect a permanent home for the school moved a step closer to fruition in December 1934, when O.W. Firth, the senior Resident, was invited by Potts-Johnson to lay the foundation stone of a new building.[22]

Seven of the nine pupils entered by the school for the Junior Cambridge examinations held at Onitsha in March 1935, passed the test, and were much celebrated in the township.[23] Work on the new EHS building on the barracks Road was completed by April 1935, and Potts-Johnson organised a formal opening ceremony, with the senior Resident, H.C. Stevenson, in attendance. The programme included a reunion of alumni and present pupils, a procession around the township, and a football match. Perhaps the item on the programme which commanded the most interest was the public debate between the aforementioned Rev. E. K. Williams, and "Professor" Algerine Kelfallah Sankoh,[24] both Saro, on the subject "School or Church—which is of more value to the community?" The school was featuring here two of the township's most prominent luminaries, men of great erudition who were highly regarded for their learning and their oratory. Sankoh was the former Isaac Augustus Johnson, who had been very active in the 1880's in the Dress Reform Society of Freetown. That movement had represented Krio efforts to reclaim lost African identity through name changes, and the flamboyant use of distinctively African dress.[25] The festivities of the EHS ended with a "grand fete" on the school grounds.[26] By September 1935, the EHS had its own brass band as it marked its third anniversary. After Thanksgiving services at Banham, it celebrated Speech Day, with prizes being handed out by Mrs. F.W. Dodds, wife of the Superintendent of the Methodist church. Several dignitaries were present, including the prominent Saro resident of the neighbouring Aba and Legislative Council member, the Hon. S.B. Rhodes. An alumni association of the EHS was formally inaugurated in April 1936, and it was immediately mobilised for various fund-raising activities in connection with projects of improvement at the school. During its anniversary celebrations of 1937, the school oganised an operata in three Acts entitled, "Pearl, the Fishermaiden". Funds raised during the various activities went toward the construction of a science laboratory, and a dormitory for boarders.[27]

By January 1938, Potts-Johnson had appointed the aforementioned Saro, A. Kelfallah Sankoh, to the position of Vice-Principal of the EHS. Sankoh, much celebrated for his intellection, had spent the last six years in an editorial capacity at the Nigerian Observer.[28] As of November, 1938, the EHS had 152 pupils on its rolls, thirty of them in the boarding department. New student additions since 1935 had been a follows:

1935	—	44 pupils
1936	—	63 pupils
1937	—	73 pupils
1938	—	85 pupils

Two students were now on scholarship, one of the bursaries, for three years, being funded by a local barrister from Yorubaland, O.A. Alakija, a close associate of the Saro. The second award went to any promising student whose parents could keep him in school until he had passed the Senior Cambridge examinations, and joined the school's teaching staff. The school's star pupil in 1938 was, undoubtedly, G.D. Okpara, who had just successfully completed the London matriculation examinations. A foundation pupil, Okpara had already passed the Junior Cambridge exams, as well as those set for the Nigerian Higher Elementary Teacher award. By November 1938, he was preparing himself, at the EHS, "for the Intermediate Bachelor of Arts [degree] . . . of London University",[29] a remarkable feat in a secondary school setting. Enitonna High School unveiled a new building housing its science laboratories in 1939. Two Saro members of the local clergy, Revds. M.D. Showers and H. Forde, were on hand to bless the new structure, and a cross-section of the Saro community attended the dedication ceremony.[30]

Potts-Johnson's vision for secondary education in Port Harcourt had enjoyed much actualisation by the late 1930's.[31] He had invested capital and time in an independent, African-controlled project of the type he had repeatedly advocated, and had thus provided an object lesson in African entrepreneurship. His stock rose considerably with his EHS venture, and Enitonna's success continued into the period of World War II, although the school could never raise sufficient capital to implement some of the more significant industrial ideas of its founder. This flagship of Saro educational endeavour continued to be a testament of Potts-Johnson's commitment to African entrepreneurship, and an achievement that brought much pride to the immigrant community. In May 1942, the school marked its 10th anniversary, with a Foundation Day service, and thanksgiving observances at St. Cyprian's. A football match, a grand bazaar, a reunion of present pupils and alumni, speech day celebrations, and a concert at the Roxy, were the other highlights of the programme.[32] Throughout the war, the school's appeal to the government for financial assistance in the form of a grant-in-aid met with no success. Potts-Johnson would be commended on the eve of the 13th anniversary of the EHS for soldiering on "without a penny . . . from any source whatsoever".[33] Although plagued by financial difficulty, Enitonna continued to be seen as the local beacon of light for the Saro. Like their Lagos and Freetown counterparts who had pursued similar projects, they believed that through this premier institution, they were making a lasting contribution to the region's educational development. The community participated actively in the public functions of the school, and discussed its achievements with immense pride.

The Saro in the Growing Church

We have already noted early Saro involvement in the religious life of Port Harcourt. This would increase significantly as of the 1930's. Saro religious affiliation went principally to five local churches in the early years. These were Wesley Church, St. Cyprian's, Banham Memorial, Bishop Crowther Memorial, and Christ Church, reflecting the much greater preponderance of Anglicans in the immigrant community. Alongside indigenous parishioners, Saro lay members played very active roles in church ceremonial, and in various aspects of committee work and church governance. Like their compatriots in Freetown of whom Steady has written,[34] Saro women were prominent in these activities. Being mostly housewives in the early years, they found in the church one of the few public openings for the enjoyment of equal status with the men, and thus eagerly availed themselves of this exposure.[35] Wesley Church had a functioning Women's Guild by 1931, and this brought Saro and indigenous women together in regular fellowship. The Guild organised regular anniversary celebrations and public meetings to which members of the Saro and indigenous elites were always invited.[36] Saro women came to fulfill the role of mentors and guides to their local counterparts, and their advice was frequently sought on domestic matters of proper home management, cuisine, and child-care.

Saro leadership was crucial to the early development of Wesley Methodist Church, and the community supplied a significant part of its funds, as seen, for instance, in donations toward a new organ in January 1932. The Sierra Leone Union celebrated its second anniversary with divine services at Wesley in May 1932, and offered a special collection to Wesley's building fund.[37] Plans for a new Wesley church facility had reached a decisive stage by May 1933, and a "turning of the first sod" ceremony was organised at the building site. The church had a sabbath school by 1933, with Mrs. N.E. Potts-Johnson and another Saro, Mrs. J.M. Johnson, actively involved in its operations. The General Superintendent of the Methodist Mission, Rev. F.W. Dodds, and Rev. Potts-Johnson presided at the foundation-stone laying ceremony in August 1933, with donations of £60 toward the building, which was completed early in 1934.[38] Young men of the Saro community were very prominent in youth and other activities at the church in these years—S.J.E. Bright and A.M. Samuels were church secretaries in the mid-1930's, and L.A. John directed the Sabbath School and the Boys Brigade, with D. Scotland Cole as assistant superintendent of all sabbath school affairs. Beyond the regular Bible study and related activities, the youth were encouraged to explore and develop their oratorical and dramatic talents. The staging of "The Resurrected Prodigal" was the highlight of Sabbath School anniversary celebrations in July 1934.[39]

We are not as informed on detailed parallel activities involving Saro Anglicans of the premier St. Cyprian's church.[40] We know, however, that the Saro, inspired by the earlier example of the Crowthers, were similarly active in that congregation. The Saro carpenter and contractor, E.Odu Thomas, supervised the construction of the church from the late 1920's into the mid 1930's. From his *Owo O Ni Ran* workshop, he embarked on the project in 1929, at a time when the congregation could raise only £300 for a building estimated to cost 2-3 thousand pounds. Thomas had just built the new St. Cyprian's schoolroom, with Arch. Crowther's encouragement. The church had entered into negotiations with the European firm of Messrs. H.E.B. Green and Company, but it had asked for £10,000 in 1923 for the project. In desperation, the congregation decided to turn to Thomas. Thomas would complete work on the building in time for unveiling celebrations which occurred between 24 March and 6 May 1934. Various groups in the church were assigned celebratory days during the ensuing festivities, and "Yoruba Associations' Day", "Women's Day", and "Delta Pastorate Anniversary Day", were just some of the group observances that lauded Thomas' handiwork.[41]

This section of our review will be incomplete without some discussion of Potts-Johnson's involvement in the growing church after his resignation of 1929. Surprisingly for a Methodist church that was known to enforce its service codes punctiliously, though no longer in the active ministry, Potts-Johnson was allowed to deliver sermons on invitation, officiate at special church gatherings, and serve in other areas of church life after his resignation. In April 1930, shortly after severing official ties, he took the pulpit at an evening service at Wesley, and was back on 27 April. He addressed the congregation at Banham Memorial in October 1930, and was guest preacher at Mother's Union anniversary celebrations at St. Cyprian's in December 1933. Before the arrival on loan from Sierra Leone of the aforementioned Rev. E.K. Williams, Potts-Johnson gave supernumerary service at Wesley.[42] By April 1934, he was Steward of the Port Harcourt Circuit. When the 13 year old Saro pupil, Priscilla Boyle, died in July 1934, Potts-Johnson was one of the officiating clergy at her funeral. On the invitation of the Sunday School authorities at Wesley, he delivered their anniversary sermon in July 1935, and was guest preacher at Wesley's choir day celebrations of September 1935. An active alumnus of the Methodist Boys High School, Freetown, he delivered the sermon at the 63rd anniversary celebrations of the schools' existence to other alumni in Port Harcourt, in April 1937.[43] This involvement with the church would continue into the 1940's. We cannot explain the Methodist Church's unusual conduct here in allowing Potts-Johnson, who was no longer in its employ, such official access to its facilities. Informants in Port Harcourt attributed these developments to the force of Potts-Johnson's personality, his cordial relations with the local church hierarchy, and the many requests for his services from local parishioners who considered his resignation rather premature.[44] An unwillingness to enter into a public debate in the pages of the Nigerian Observer, and elsewhere, of Potts-Johnson's eligibility for these roles might also have been a factor in the church's acquiescence.

Saro involvement in the local churches continued throughout World War II (soon to be reviewed), and even the Methodists seemed increasingly to be moving in a more high-church, conservative direction. When, in June 1940, in the enervating climes of a humid Port Harcourt, a European sailor-preacher, J.S.C. Lindsay, took the pulpit at Wesley, without a jacket, his congregation was astounded. The Nigerian Observer conveyed the group's revulsion: "No one could believe he was a preacher, but a sailor who had missed his way. . . . one wonders whether there was any backbone in the officers of the church who were present, including Rev. H.L. Forde, the superintendent of the circuit, to say to this sailor clergy [that his appearance] was irregular and intrinsically incompatible with the tradition of Methodism".[45] Sartorial propriety was a cardinal plank in Saro church attendance, and no concessions would be allowed to those who wandered away from the approved codes.

Potts-Johnson's preaching activities appear to have continued, but with fewer public engagements in the war years. One such occasion was the harvest celebrations of the local Baptist Church in October 1942, when, on invitation, he delivered the sermon. Predictably, he kept up his critique of church policy as seen, for instance, in the authorities' attitude towards bachelor African clergy. Whereas European bachelor missionaries were tolerated by the church, their African counterparts faced constant pressure to take a wife. Potts-Johnson found this unacceptable. His crusade in defence of polygamy was also maintained, and he poured scorn repeatedly on those that would criticise the institution. In September 1943, he opined: "Those who say that monogamy has come to stay in Africa, and polygamy must go, are capable of believing that the sun would rise from the west and set in the east. The African is essentially a polygamist and will so remain indefinitely." Rather scornfully, he recommended monogamy for races that had attained to "a high standard in spiritual life", and ended defiantly: "why worry to be monogamous when some African monogamists are worse than polygamists?"[46]

The Saro in Social Advocacy and Public Comment

With enormous presumption, the patriarchs of the Saro of Port Harcourt, over the years, came to arrogate to themselves the role of natural guardians of the township's moral economy. They appear to have assumed that their educational and other accomplishments had won them the right to pronounce periodically on issues of social moment. Surprisingly, not many indigenes questioned this effrontery in the stranger community in the period up to the mid-1940's. The evidence would, in fact, suggest considerable local willingness to be guided and counseled on matters of urban social decorum by those believed to be most familiar with European values.

Throughout the 1930's, Potts-Johnson and Kelfallah Sankoh reflected patrician opinion in the pages of the Nigerian Observer. Their almost weekly commentaries were a barometer of township debate, and in their prescriptions could be discerned an undisguised claim to chart the path of social advance. Paradoxically, the much-westernised Saro would also use these opportunities to defend the African cultural charter as already evidenced in Potts-Johnson's views on polygyny. Treasured elements of cultural practice had to be protected from violation by European notions of progress and reform. This was a responsibility some members of the Saro elite did not take lightly.

We will now review some of the recurring themes in Saro social commentary. The subject of illegitimacy, much valorised by missionary preachments, was one such subject on which Potts-Johnson's cultural sensibilities were much exercised. In January 1930, in his characteristic iconoclasm, Potts-Johnson, whose differences with the church authorities were a matter of public knowledge, wondered why the church refused to baptise children born out of wedlock, when "these infants were born through no fault of theirs".[47] The rising hem-line of women's dresses also caught the Observer's gaze. As guardian of the public decorum in a patriarchal Port Harcourt, the paper noticed that "the skirt is getting shorter and shorter: instead of 8 inches below the knee, it is at the knee, and sometimes above it".[48] It called on seamstresses to advise their clients accordingly, for standards of modesty had to be upheld, even as new fashion frontiers were explored.

In May 1930, the paper invited African medical practitioners to "wander off the beaten track", study indigenous methods of the treatment of disease, and publish books on the subject. It similarly admonished "experienced lawyers whose forensic achievements do not compare unfavourably with those of their learned friends in more advanced territories", to codify the traditional laws of the land. The paper stressed the professional's greater responsibility to society to pass on the fruits of knowledge. It observed: "If they too like the rest of human beings simply worked for their living and died without conferring on their fellow men benefits in the form of published works, our opinion is that they led a life of selfishness".[49] The gambling practices of the young also came in for some review. In February 1931, Potts-Johnson railed against its rising incidence in a depression-ravaged Port Harcourt. He warned that if the vice was not quickly arrested, it would "bring ruin to many youthful lives and untold misery to many homes".[50]

In this, as in other subjects, Potts-Johnson directed the message at all of Port Harcourt's residents, not just his own Saro people. He saw the township as an ethnic melting pot, and felt it incumbent on all to strive for its common well being. He preached pan-ethnic unity ceaselessly calling for "unity and cooperation among the Ibos as a whole, the Sierra Leoneans . . . the Gold Coast people . . . the Yoruba . . . the Jekris . . . all the different tribes existing in Port Harcourt". He was confident that once this was achieved, "unity and cooperation in the larger sense, and among all the African sections . . . which is the need of the hour will not be difficult to obtain".[51]

As Port Harcourt ushered in the new year in December 1931, Potts-Johnson appealed for a greater sobriety in the usual end-of-year festivities. He cautioned against the "demon that seems to be let loose as soon as the hour of twelve ushers in the new year", and the "pandemonium" that ensues, with "the ceaseless beating of kerosene tins and the like". Elaborating on this, he continued: "We do not say that people should not enjoy themselves but there are limits to everything. We would therefore ask our police authorities to endeavour . . . to see that everything is done in a moderate and orderly manner". He added, rather scornfully, and with the contempt and the condescension the African elite often reserved for their unlettered neighbours: "In a place like Port Harcourt where the ignorant predominate one can say with confidence that only a very small fractional part of the people really understand the true meaning of the season". Though highly gregarious, Potts-Johnson obviously had a limited threshold for common deviancy. Like others of his class, he despaired easily of the social excesses of the more exuberant of the grassroots.[52]

Perhaps because of his own personal circumstances of childlessness in marriage, and the known liaisons he had with Saro as well as indigenous women in the township,[53] Potts-Johnson was a stout defender of polygamy. He first addressed the subject, in some detail, in February 1932, when he wrote: "Our own matrimonial problems . . . are not on all fours with those of the more advanced parts of the world. In our own case, there is now a sort of struggle between the imported form of marriage, and our own form. There are many of us who pass through the forms of marriage prescribed by the state and the church, and yet find it difficult to disregard the native form. Herein lies our difficulty". He added pointedly, that "the African has from time immemorial been a polygamist". The church had generated "a clash of cultures" in this area, in his view, and the African had experienced difficulty in abandoning "the age long practice of his ancestors."[54] This could very well have been an attempt to rationalise, even justify,his own personal conduct in relations with women. There obviously were several observers in the church who held this position. Some Saro were also not persuaded that Potts-Johnson was at his most objective in this matter.[55] This is one area of Potts-Johnson's life that will always remain in the realm of conjecture. His hedonism, on the other hand, leaves no room for doubt. Potts-Johnson, the archetypal patrician epicure, always enjoined the people of Port Harcourt to live their lives to the fullest. In commending to them the new Saro management of the Palladium, a recreational facility in the township, in May 1932, he wrote of the African as "a jolly creature", and a lover of pleasure: "Life after all is too short, and it behooves all sensible men to make the best of it . . . . We must find time for enjoying pleasures of some sort . . . to have the proverbial good time".[56]

Potts-Johnson's interests in local African medicine and the traditional legal codes, was complemented by a fascination for indigenous African music. In July 1932, he welcomed Messrs. Ballanta and Colingwoode-Williams, both reputable Sierra Leonean musicians, to Port Harcourt. He congratulated them on their virtuosity in the performance of Bach, Handel, Mozart, Chopin, and others. He, however, suggested that it was time " . . . to interpret . . . native African minds". He called on Ballanta to produce "African musical works" that would compare favourably with such masterpieces as Handel's Messiah, and the Dead March in Saul. He appealed to African composers for some emulation of the example of Ekundayo Phillips, organist of the Christ church Cathedral, Lagos, who had set various Yoruba dirges to classical music.[57]

Potts-Johnson was equally impatient of Africans who arbitrarily copied the values of whites, and saw themselves as the equivalent of black Europeans. His admiration of Aggrey and Edward Blyden came through poignantly in these observations.[58] To him, the Japanese were a people who had done brilliantly in preserving their cultural and "racial individuality", and he urged that Africans should acquire from Europeans the best of "their moral and social codes", without sacrificing loyalty to African culture.[59] In a piece entitled "The parables of Salvio", the Observer extended its review of cultural eclecticism and adaptation. In obvious reference to residually conservative and disparaging British and Saro attitudes toward local Nigerian culture, it wrote in an appeal for cultural empathy: "I thought too how wise it is to adapt yourself to your surroundings, and the people among whom you live. For impatience will never stir them from the habits of their age and generation. And it is but foolishness to seek to change the manners of men in a moment".[60]

Returning to the subject of evolving women's fashions in February 1933, the Nigerian Observer displayed its facility with contemporary *haute couture*. In a light-hearted piece, it reviewed the range of current designs, and the peculiar names by which they went. It mentioned the "Bishop sleeve, Squeeze power, Dry sleeve, Mutton leg, Short sleeve, Sleeveless, Low neck, High neck, Medium, Polly tail skirt, Umbrella skirt, Kiss-kee-dee" and the "Empire". It found the "Empire" the most graceful design, and commented on the more titillating efforts in blouses that went with loose dresses: " . . . they cut the neck of this so wide, that however much the garment is adjusted, one shoulder and a large portion of an arm must be left loose. They christened this style "show boby".[61]

Social comment during the depression was, at times, rather pointed, as when it assailed some of the extravagant cultural practices of the day. One such area was the customary over-expenditure on local funerals. The Nigerian Observer noted sternly that to observe an all-night wake during which food was always served, and then to provide "sumptuous refreshment after the memorial service is something bordering on madness". It advised that a wake be held only "when a corpse is kept overnight",[62] to keep expenses at a minimum. This was very much in keeping with Potts-Johnson's views on the need to husband local resources with prudence so as to make meaningful investments possible.

The Saro would also wade into the controversial waters of the Osu institution. The Osu were cult slaves among the Igbo, and though slavery had long been abolished officially in Nigeria, the innate prejudice of the system could still be observed in the discriminatory treatment meted out to some individuals believed to be of Osu descent in the Owerri province, of which Port Harcourt was a part. In August 1933, the Observer called on those concerned to release the "bonds that fetter human beings . . . ", and to discard customs that did not elevate the African people. The indictment of the Osu practice would anticipate by a few years the public protests over their treatment by the Osu themselves in Igbo society, of which Ekechi has written. In 1936, representatives of the Osu condemned the manner in which the freeborn (Diala) victimised those of Osu descent in denying them basic economic and political rights in the colonial state. They criticised their exclusion from the ruling councils, and, like Potts-Johnson, called on the British to end this outrage, failing which, they threatened to withhold their taxes.[63]

In an equally unrestrained and stunning critique, this time of the township's social scene, the Nigerian Observer, in March 1934, described a depression-ravaged Port Harcourt as "the quagmire of iniquity, the cesspool of prostitutes, the dumping ground of renegades, the battlefield of strife, the theatre of hypocrites, and a hell below . . . "[64] No elaboration accompanied this acerbic characterisation, but it appears to have reflected the social pressures that came with economic devastation. This was obviously a township of many difficulties that required urgent attention. By highlighting these conditions, the Observer was serving notice on government as to the people's expectations.

Concern was also expressed over the utility of the provincial courts in the Nigerian judicial system, where litigants apparently faced the law as interpreted by largely uneducated Chiefs and Elders, and without the benefit of access to legal representation. Saro leaders dismissed these institutions as anachronistic legacies of the Lugardian system of Northern Nigeria, designed to frustrate judicial reform in the south, while curtailing access to the Supreme Court. The Nigerian Observer condemned the record of some Nigerian Governors on this matter, commending only Governor Cameron, who had supported reform, thus sounding "the death knell of the provincial courts", and providing litigants with greater access to legal counsel.[65]

The economic difficulties that came with World War II would expand the scale of prostitution in Port Harcourt as unemployment disrupted family life, and more single women took up residence in the township. In these circumstances, it was not unusual for arbitrary accusations of involvement in prostitution to be levelled against the innocent. In May 1944, Potts-Johnson came to the defence of those whose reputations were being besmirched by these false charges. He referred to current efforts to rid the township of prostitutes, and while condemning prostitution and its disturbing increase, he rose to the defence of the innocent. There were in the township, he claimed, several women without husbands who were leading industrious lives as fish traders, garri makers and sellers, market women, cement block moulders, and seamstresses, who would never "stoop to the indignity of becoming the playthings of men . . . ". He cautioned that it would be "a sin, and a shame to say that because [they] are without husbands . . . they are living a life of prostitution".[66]

Potts-Johnson's earlier reflections on pan-Africanism received a boost in January 1945, with the arrival of two African-Americans in Port Harcourt. He was enthusiastic in welcoming them to the township, and stressed the need to cultivate diaspora ties in the cause of black unity. He urged: "A programme of national unification should be undertaken here to give evidence of our desire to embrace our brothers over the seas".[67]

The Activities of the Sierra Leone Union (SLU)

We have reviewed the origins of the Sierra Leone Union (SLU), and the role played by Potts-Johnson and other Saro patricians in convening this organisation to promote group solidarity. We now discuss some of the Union's activities in the 1930's and 1940's, when it entered fully into the role of social clearing-house for visiting Krio and Saro friends and relatives, beacon of Krio tradition and ceremonial, and arbiter of disputes and disagreements within the Saro family. In this, it was not unlike the Parapos societies of the immigrant Yoruba residents of the Gold Coast/Ghana in this century.[68] In April 1933, the SLU celebrated its third anniversary with divine services at St. Cyprian's at which a member, the Rev. S.S. Williams delivered the sermon. A picnic was also organised on the grounds of the Okrika Masonic Temple, in addition to a grand parade around the town, and a torchlight procession at nightfall.[69] The Union's activities in the mid-1930's were guided by an executive committee headed by I.A. Williams, with Potts-Johnson as his assistant. It was in these years that the Saro elite began to forge very close social ties with the elite fraction of the indigenous community, with whom it served in the colonial bureaucracy, the church, the local finance and mercantile houses, and in local business. These elite members received regular invitations to SLU activities, and they, in turn, got their Saro associates to participate in their social circuit. The less advantaged members of the indigenous community observed these social proceedings mostly from the side-lines, with some curiosity, and, as would be evident later, with the smouldering resentment that is often born of social marginalisation. They could see the growth of an inter-elite alliance, with little scope for the involvement of the poorer classes.

This social cross-identification was now progressively being reflected in a Saro reconsideration of earlier endogamous practice, a development that initially divided the SLU, but later came increasingly to be accepted as inevitable. The Saro elite began to play prominent roles in the nuptials of their indigenous associates, and to feature, as celebrants, in those activities themselves. When, in July 1934, J. Douglas-Jenewari, of New Calabar married Sarah Peterside of Opobo, the Saro, Rev. S.S. Williams was one of the officiating clergy. Kelfallah Sankoh gave the bride away, and I.B. Johnson, Potts-Johnson, and other notables of the SLU attended the reception.[70]

For reasons that are largely unexplained, though perhaps not unconnected with the global economic depression, SLU meetings and activities appear to have tapered off somewhat from the mid-1930's into the early 1940's. The outbreak of war, which spawned a new set of challenges (with Win-the-War fund-raising at the core) involving the energies of the Saro, must have been a factor in this development. By August 1940, however, Union members were again active as they marked the tenth anniversary of the SLU. The Saro, Rev. M.D. Showers officiated at thanksgiving service at St. Cyprian's, a cinema show and dance were organised at the Rex, and Max George, a leading social organiser among the Saro, supervised the activities. The band of the Enitonna High School (EHS) featured prominently in these celebrations.[71]

During annual Union festivities in 1943, the Rev. D.D. Coker of St. Michael's Church, Aba, a Saro, referred to the community as "Niger-Sierra leoneans" (sic.), an affirmation of their twin loyalties and obvious pride in a dual heritage.[72] Coker's remark, though innocuous at the time, would be of immense political significance in the coming years. Under colonial rule, strangers like the Saro were not differentiated from the locals by the British Raj, and twin loyalties of the sort that was being entertained by the Saro went largely unremarked. With political independence, they would not go unchallenged.

A major highlight on the Union's calendar in 1944 was the transfer of Rev. and Mrs. M.D. Showers from Port Harcourt to Umuahia. Potts-Johnson and the Saro, joined by the Ven. Arch. E.T. and Mrs. Dimieari, and others, organised a farewell reception at the EHS hall to recognise the Showers' contributions to the Saro and the wider community.[73] The Union similarly celebrated the arrival,in January 1945, in Port Harcourt of Bishop T.S. Johnson of Freetown. Potts-Johnson was effusive in his praise of the Bishop's "brilliant scholastic achievements". Potts-Johnson had now assumed the presidency of the SLU, and coordinated the Union's 16th anniversary activities in June 1945. This was a twin celebration for the Saro office manager of the local branch of the United Africa company (UAC), N.J.C. Cline, had just received another promotion, and was also marking his transfer to

Abonnema, in the riverine areas of the delta.[74] When shortly thereafter, the Saro's compatriot, one-time member of the Legislative council, and prominent resident of the neighbouring township of Aba, S.B. Rhodes, was elevated to the office of a Puisne Judge, the SLU had cause for further celebration.[75]

Saro "Socials", their Female Organisers, and Related Group Activities

Saro social life in Port Harcourt in the 1930's and 1940's reflected, in many ways, the social pre-occupations of Freetown, Lagos, and Calabar. Child-naming ceremonies, christenings, engagements, weddings, birthday and farewell occasions, and memorial observances for the dead, were all opportunities for members of the community and their indigenous associates to come together in festivity. These activities were invariably accompanied by the elaborate preparation of traditional krio dishes[76] and they provided the opportunity for Saro hosts to advertise their munificence, and display exquisite culinary ability. In a Saro group of some class differentiation, the celebrations of the affluent were often the most elaborate, and they were a prime attraction for the poorer Saro, and invaluable supplements of domestic cuisine in difficult economic times. Memorial services and the unveiling of tombstones were major social highlights on the community's calendar, as were the society weddings which, increasingly, featured unions between Saro families and some from within the indigenous population. Not all Saro, of course, approved of marriage to locals, as we will see later in the case of the wealthy I.B. Johnsons. Most, however, accepted the growing and compelling inevitability of the trend.

The Saro took great pride in Krio culture, and it was to their cultural advantage that Port Harcourt attracted very few non-Krio Saro permanent residents in the period up to independence in 1960. Only three such families (the Meyers, Mansarays, and Kallays) were known to the SLU by the early 1970's,[77] and their members had allowed themselves some incorporation into the cultural idiosyncracies of the majority Krio formation, but without sacrificing primary affiliation to their respective ethnic communities.[78] The porous nature of ethnic boundaries in Sierra Leone has been much remarked in the literature.[79] This fluidity which was very much in evidence up to the 19th century as seen for instance, among the Krio, is believed to have given way to a greater rigidity in the 20th century.[80] This purported departure should not, however, be greatly exaggerated. Enculturation into Krio society has continued in the present century on an obviously smaller scale, and it was clearly a possibility for those non-Krio Saro who came to Port Harcourt. In the event, the latter chose not to exercise this option, evincing a marked preference for accommodating those elements of Krio culture that were crucial to social reproduction, while retaining primordial ties to natal roots.

In a social circuit, in good times, of much activity, the Saro marked their joys and sorrows in a perennial flow of reciprocal home visits, church and Union gatherings, cemetery activities,and the like. News of family bereavements or weddings in Freetown, Lagos, Calabar, and other centres, conveyed by letter, or relayed by visiting friends or relatives, drew fitting responses from the community's members. They were also often carried on the pages of the Nigerian Observer. Appropriate rites and obligations were expected to be performed, and individuals who failed to mark these ceremonials, either through financial inability, or worse, through negligence, lost face within the group, and became the subject of much local gossip.[81]

Although the Krio of Freetown were acknowledged as the parent community, the Saro relished the opportunity to prove their superiority over Freetown, whenever there was such occasion. When, for instance, in the late 1930's, the diocese of Port Harcourt was approached by the Freetown church for support in generating greater religious fervour in the homeland, delta Christians celebrated their approaching pre-eminence! Potts-Johnson could not conceal his delight. He wrote: "We have nothing but surprise to express at this. For we have been accustomed to look upon Sierra Leone as the most enlightened spot of all British West Africa, and for things to come to such a pass as to make it necessary for Bishop Horstead to send a Macedonian cry to Nigeria for help cannot but fill us with wonder . . . . Perhaps some day . . . the Archbishop of Canterbury may consider it necessary to send to Nigeria for missionary volunteers . . . ".[82]

As already indicated in this study, the Saro came of all social classes, and some of their number lived on the economic margins, a distant remove from the affluence of the I.B. Johnsons and the Potts-Johnsons. They worked in a range of employments, in various departments in the civil service, but also in local finance houses, and in European companies such as the United Africa Company (UAC), and George Bernard Ollivant (GBO). Some were privately employed as petty traders, artisans and craftsmen. (See Table 3-1). Status was often reflected in residential accommodation, with the vast majority living in regular township dwellings in the neighbourhood of the Aggrey Road, and Victoria, Accra, Freetown, and adjacent streets. Wealthier members of the group occupied so called "convenient garrets" of two or

Table 3-1

A Cross-Section of the Occupational Involvements of the Saro in the Period up to 1939

L.A. Barnes	Marine Department
J.S. Benjamin	Barrister-at-Law
A.G. Boyle	Contractor and Transport Operator.
Edward Browne	Clock/watch repairer
C.P. Coker	Carpenter and contractor
J.W. Cole	Poultry farmer
E. Davies	Engineer, Marine department
V.A. Davies	Public Works department
Max George	Sportswriter
Mrs. L. Hamilton-Leigh	Seamstress
C.W. Hunter	Cashier, Public Works department
Ladipo John	Cashier, Barclays Bank
A. Leighton-Johnson	Cold Storage Company (Supervisor)
T.L. Johnson	Tanned leather dealer
J.S. Macaulay	Marine department (clerical)
T.J. Macaulay	Baker
J.S. Meheux	Post and Telegraphs department (technical)
Felix Meyer	Chief Clerk, Nigerian Railways
Jonathan Nicol	Dispenser and Optician (Government service)
F.J. Phillips	Funeral Undertaker
D. Atanda Pratt	Dispenser (Government service)
J.E. Stober	Education department (clerical)
E. Odu-Thomas	Carpenter, vegetable gardener, and contractor
J.S.D. Thomas	Chief Clerk, Nigerian Railways
Montacute Thompson	Barrister-at-Law
Arthur Williams	Employee of the Crown Bird
Israel Williams	Post-master and surveyor
P.G. Williams	Tailor and draper
A.C. Willoughby	Inspector of Police

Source: Riv. Prof files (NAE), and entries in the Nigerian Observer, the Eastern Nigerian Guardian, and the Nigerian Eastern Mail.

three storied homes, but in the same neighbourhoods.[83] All aspired to owning their own homes, and many would move from rented accommodation to home ownership with the years. Entering one's own home was always cause for a "social", and many were elaborately celebrated, with the appropriate traditional house-warming observances.

As in most colonial societies of the time, the women of Port Harcourt were greatly disadvantaged, and the Saro were no exception. On a relative scale, Saro wives generally enjoyed a higher standard of living as compared to the majority of their indigenous counterparts, and often their class positions were rightly defined by that occupied by their husbands. Most wives had a high school education, but they had generally married hypergamously in an endeavour to improve their economic fortunes.[84] As such, even where their education was comparable to their husband's, his favoured access to further training in a colonial state that had greatly undermined the pre-colonial gains of women,[85] made marriage a major economic decision for all but the rare materially independent women. Saro and other women operating under conditions of some material dependence, could also therefore be said to have lived within an urban variant of those relations which Stichter and Parpart have described as the patriarchal mode, characterised by the unequal access of women to productive resources.[86] This is not, however, to suggest that these Saro women were completely helpless.[87] The vulnerability of their position led many to seek a measure of economic autonomy even under marriage through the raising of capital, often from husbands, for investment in petty commodity production. Wives as traders of home-made goods, and as bakers, were a common feature of Saro life into the 1950's. Another mark of female initiative, and one with lasting group significance as will be evident in our concluding chapters, was the initiation and the dogged pursuit of marital relations with locals by some of the Saro women. Saro fathers were often reluctant to have their daughters married into local families, but a number of women saw this outlet as both an escape from domestic patriarchal bonds, and a stepping stone to greater economic opportunity. At considerable personal risk, and amidst accusations of dragging the family name in the mud, a number would exercise this option as their only salvation.

If, on the whole, however, in spite of the marginalisation of women, the incidence of divorce among the Saro in the years up to World War II was low,[88] it was certainly not for want of cause. It reflected more the risk-avoidance choices of the Saro women, and the economic imperative to stay attached even if this called for ignoring the many peccadillos of the more notorious husbands in the Saro community.[89] In the Port Harcourt of the period, where official preferment often depended on the government's favourable perception of the individuals' marital environment, it was important to keep up appearances.

With the Saro men being generally distant from basic hearth-hold concerns, the preparations and arrangements that went with "socials" and like activities fell heavily on the women. They were always in charge of culinary matters, decor, and related activities, and the frequency of these events imposed a heavy toll in time and effort. This, it appears, was not always acknowledged by the menfolk, and, but for a few exceptions, women generally enjoyed little recognition outside their home environments. This is a matter to which we shall return later.

Table 3-2 summarises some of the social occasions that brought the Saro and their indigenous friends together periodically. These events deserve close review for they address directly the subject of the peculiar ethos within which the stranger community procured its social reproduction. One strives in vain for knowledge of the roots of Saro resilience in the face of later xenophobia if these activities are not fully contextualised to reveal the informal networks and arrangements that sustained a sense of community even in the most embattled periods of immigrant experience. Home visits, Union gatherings, weddings, funerals, house-warming parties, and other such occasions provided the opportunity to share experience, and evolve the survival strategies that would be vital in the coming years. Visits to Freetown, Lagos, Calabar, and other centres, and the periodic hosting of distinguished guests (such as the Sierra Leone Legislative Council member, J.A. Songo-Davies, and the Judge, Roland Awunor Renner),[90] relatives, and friends from those communities, afforded the Saro many networking opportunities to compare colonial experience and discuss strategies for addressing new problems, while up-dating information on the personal circumstances of loved ones far away. Attendance at social gatherings organised by indigenous friends was also crucial to the immigrant community's wellbeing. When G.T. Don Pedro of the United African Company (UAC) hosted a traditional *Iria* ceremony for his wife, Virginia, in September 1937, Saro guests included J.P.A. Cole, M.O. Davies, C. Taylor, and Theo Francis. There was an even bigger Saro elite turn-out when S.N. Obi opened his new home to the public in October 1939.[91]

On occasion, Saro assembly was dictated by developments of some gravity. One such was the arraignment and conviction, in March 1940, of the Saro, Ladipo Ade John, a cashier of the local Barclays Bank. Justice Ivor Brace sentenced John to a term of 2¼ years imprisonment for "fraudulent false accounting and stealing." This was a major blow to the local Saro

Table 3-2

A Cross-Section of Saro Domestic Social Activities (outside SLU Functions) in the 1930's and 1940's

Date	Event	Source
April 1930	Meheuxs travel to Freetown	Nigerian Observer (hereafter NO) 26 Apr. 1930
June 1930	J.S. Macaulay returns from Freetown	NO 31 May 1930
June 1930	Wedding of Modupe Coker and Claude B. Jones	NO 28 Jun 1930
August 1930	Death of the mother of Postmaster/Surveyor, Israel Williams in Freetown	NO 9 Aug. 1930
October-November 1930	Death of sister of A.W. Porter in Freetown	NO 1 Nov. 1930
November 1930	Death of the sister-in-law of one-time resident Dr. I.G. Cummings, in Freetown	NO 15 Nov. 1930
May 1931	Death of S. Everton Cole (SLU procession to the cemetery)	NO 23 May 1931
June 1931	Mrs. L.M. Showers returns from Freetown on the "abinsi".	NO 27 Jun 1931
October 1931	Death "in mysterious circumstances" at the foot of a cliff of S.M. Reffell, Secretary of the SLU	NO 17 Oct. 1931
Jan. 1932	Installation of L.R. Potts-Johnson as Master-Elect of the Okrika Masonic Lodge, with J. Stanley Benjamin, presiding, F.O. Allagoa as Potts-Johnson's Senior Warden, and I.B. Johnson as his Junior Warden	NO 30 Jan. 1932
March 1932	W.S. "Driver" Johnson and Mrs. Stella Davies leave for Freetown on the "Adda"	NO 19 Mar. 1932
April 1932	Bans of marriage of Arthur Williams and Annette Songo Davies published in Port Harcourt. Wedding to be held at the Holy Trinity Church, Freetown.	NO 16 Apr. 1932

Table 3-2, cont'd.

Date	Event	Source
April 1932	Mrs. Lydia Leighton Johnson dies in Lagos en route to Freetown on the "Appam".	NO 14 May 1932
July 1934	Saro mark death in Freetown of Ven. Arch. E.T. Cole	NO 14 Jul 1934
September 1934	Wedding of Harriet John and Johnnie Fowell Boston, with reception at Bishop's Court, Aba.	NO 8 Sept. 1934
June 1935	Visit of J.A. Songo-Davies, member of the Legislative Council of Sierra Leone	NO 8 June 1935
October 1935	Death of Ethelbert Davies of the Marine Department	NO 5 Oct. 1935
August 1936	60th birthday celebrations of Mrs. L.E. Macarthy	NO 8 Aug. 1936
September 1936	Wedding of Enitonna Head printer, S.J.E. Bright and Ophelia Pratt	NO 26 Sept. 1936
December 1936	C.W. Hunter marries the indigene, Patience Pepple	NO 19 Dec. 1936
January 1938	Mackinson Johnson elevated to Worshipful Master of the Okrika Masonic Temple	NO 29 Jan. 1938
May 1939	Potts-Johnsons host the B.A. Q. Taylors of Opobo in a two-day celebration	NO 6 May 1939
June 1939	Rev. M.D. Showers celebrates 25 years in the ministry	NO 1 July 1939
October 1939	Saro mark award of Certificate of Honour to J. S. Macaulay of the Marine department	NO 24 Oct. 1939
April 1940	Thomas Jacob Manly-Rollings marries the indigene, Clementina M'Bashu	NO 4 May 1940
March 1941	D. Atanda Pratt, government dispenser, proceeds to Lagos on leave; V.A. Davies of the Public Works Department leaves for Lagos on transfer	NO 1 Mar. 1941
June 1942	A.W. Cokers hold memorial services for the late Marion Coker who died in Freetown	NO 12 June 1942
April 1946	The Ira Brights organise house-warming for new home on the Aggrey road	NO 3 May 1946
June 1949	Awnjob by the Manly-Rollings' in memory of the late T.J. Manly-Rollings	NO 17 Jun. 1949

image, although it was not the first recorded incarceration of a Saro in Port Harcourt.[92] Equally tragic, and with suspected elements of some xenophobia, was the death in February 1944 of another Saro, and a clock repairer, Edward Brown. Brown's death at Niger Street, opposite the Ayambo Villa, came at the hands of Onya Ngele, a man from the riverine community of Nembe. Ngele, who may well have suffered from a mental condition, employed a machete, and wounded two more people before he was finally overpowered. The immediate motive behind the attack could not be easily determined, but it left the Saro greatly traumatised, and some seemed visibly shaken in the retelling of it to the author some forty years after it occurred.[93]

Another significant development of the early 1940's, this time, with major cultural implications, was Saro celebration, in August 1942, of the engagement of Betty Meyer to Daniel Abadoo. The ceremony was performed in the traditional Krio style even though Betty's father, Felix Meyer, was a Mende immigrant from Sierra Leone. With his Efik wife, Alice, Felix had entered fully into the cultural values of his Krio compatriots. Saro elders conducted the ceremony, and it featured the traditional speech-making and the presentation of a tray of approved items, both traditional and western.[94]

There was much celebration in December 1948 when the Saro welcomed to Port Harcourt the Rev. J.A. Babington Johnson, M.A., B.D., Mrs. Johnson, and their five children from the USA. The new arrival was the brother of I.B. Johnson, and he had recently been appointed General Superintendent, and Supervisor of Schools, of the African Methodist Episcopal (AME) Zion mission. Johnson had attended the Methodist Boys High School, Freetown, and had gone to the United States initially in 1916. On his return to West Africa, he had served at the Liberian University College, where, for six years, he was in charge of the Education and Psychology departments. He later became the Vice-President of that College. In 1930, he had returned to the United States, and was given charge of the First Providence church, in Rhode Island, while also serving as "Presiding Elder" of over 35 other congregations. Mrs. Johnson had also trained in the field of education.[95]

Rev. Johnson took to the social circuit with great passion and commitment soon after his arrival, and, before long, he was actively involved with the Price Fellowship Society of Port Harcourt. Under the group's auspices, he gave a lecture , in March 1949, at the Roxy, on the topic, "Africa and her Needs". Johnson called for more industrial education, identifying Japan as an exemplar of modern industrialisation. He enjoined his audience to be less critical of Nigeria's colonial power, Britain, as the nation moved towards independence, and emphasised the need to educate more of Africa's women.[96]

The Saro in Early Clubs and Associations

The task of convening Port Harcourt's earliest social organisations appears to have devolved largely on its African civil servants, the employees of various European firms, and local small-scale traders. Away from their home communities, these individuals were out to create social welfare mechanisms that cut across ethnic categories, and afforded some solace from the tedium and stress of township employment. The Saro took a keen interest in these activities, and were often founder members of some of these organisations. In 1920, a Grand native Club was inaugurated. It later became the Africa Club, and I.B. Johnson was among its earliest presidents. Dublin Green, an Ijaw with Saro connections, also served in the presidency in later years.[97] Members were closely vetted on admission to preserve the Club's exclusive character. Such tendencies did, however, reinforce the impression that the more successful members of the African community were at pains to distance themselves from the less well-to-do. Indigenous associates of such clubs left many with the unsettling feeling that they preferred the company of the immigrant members of their class to that of poorer Nigerians. These impressions would feed anti-immigrant sentiment over the years, and they would invariably explode to further exacerbate intra-African tensions.

By August 1930, dramatic performances in which the Saro took leading roles, had begun in Port Harcourt. Shakespeare's Merchant of Venice was one such production, with Maggie Butcher as Portia, and Clarence Garrick, another Saro, as the Duke. The Nigerian Observer made its debut as theater critic in that production.[98] There was a Minstrel Society in operation by December 1930. The aforementioned, Felix Meyer, a Saro of the Mende ethnic group, who came to Port Harcourt directly from Freetown, and later became Chief Clerk in the Nigerian Railways, was a leading member of the group. His wife, Alice, an Efik from Calabar,[99] whom he met in Nigeria, was also a member. Together, they were once described as the Minstrel's "moving spirits".[100] In February 1931, the Minstrels organised a performance in which an African dance, the Uqua, was conducted by Mrs. Meyer, with Felix Meyer doing the song "My Blue Heaven", and the members of the group staging the play, "Divorce Case".[101] By August 1932, another society, the Port Harcourt Social Octet had been formed. Felix

Meyer was its director, with Max George, (pianist), S. Dakin Davis (Secretary), and Messrs. Rigsby Elliott, Burnley, George Uranta, Wilcox, and D. Williams, as members.[102] Uranta and Wilcox were the only non-Saro in this founding body. The Minstrel Society dedicated its new brass band in May 1933, by which time Alice Meyer was the group's president. The ceremony was held in the great hall of the Enitonna High School, and Potts-Johnson conducted the band.[103]

In the 1930's, it was not unusual for Saro performers to be cast in plots built around the activities of non-Krio ethnic groups in Sierra Leone. "Professor" Ballanta, from Freetown, in September 1933, for instance, staged the play, "Bangura—King of Sandala", at the palladium with a group of Saro performers. The plot involved a King of the Susu, whose love for a young maiden brought fierce objections from his senior wife; the latter got the girl and her mother banished from their homeland, but the king was re-united with her family when, wounded in battle, she helped nurse him back to health. He, of course, ended up marrying her.[104]

By the mid-1930's, the Saro, their Yoruba associates, and some friends from the local delta communities were in the process of developing a musical group that trained on a regular basis, and held concerts periodically in the township. The leading musicians were Max George (piano), A.O. Alakija (violin, clarinet, piano), Lawrence Nicol (piano), C.A. Williams (ukelele/saxophone), A. Ola Maja (trumpet/cornet/banjo), J.B.S. Hart (piano/jazz sets), and C. Jones (banjo). Felix Meyer was the group's principal convener, and its repertoire ranged widely from negro spirituals to maringa music. Maja also directed the Okrika Dance band; there was much demand for the services of these budding musicians.[105]

The hand of the rising middle-class of the Saro and indigenes could also be seen in a Port Harcourt Literary and Dramatic Society that was being revitalised by September 1935, "with a view [to] animating the social and literary tendencies of the community for the promotion of such interests among the schools . . . and . . . for the regeneration of scholastic ideals and activities . . . ". Membership was open only to those with a secondary school education, or its equivalent. Applicants also had to be "of good character". Women were welcome, but they had to have passed Standard VI in secondary school.[106] As society became more differentiated, the educated were closing their ranks, and devising recreational pursuits that complemented their training. The new Diamond Club that was inaugurated in March 1937, also proceeded along these lines. Besides L. Ade John, its vice-president, and J.P.A. Cole, its auditor, both Saro, most of its officers and members were indigenes, an index of the inter-cultural, class-based cooperation of these years. The club organised ballroom dances, and was closely affiliated with the Optimists, a sister organisation formed in 1938. A. O. Alakija was president of the latter body, with the Saro organist, Max George, as Secretary and musical director, and Felix Meyer as Vice-President. The Optimists celebrated their talents in musical comedy and dance, and the Resident, N. Mylius, often graced their performances.[107]

Multi-ethnic organisations of this type would maintain their membership and activities even in the difficult years of World War II, organising various performances to generate funds for war relief. The township's most popular recreational facilities, the Roxy and the Rex, were often the venues of these activities, but some were also held at the local Africa Club, which had a predominantly indigenous leadership by 1945, but with some Saro in the membership. The shift in local influence from the Saro elite to a group composed more directly of indigenes, both Igbo and Ijaw, was clearly evident in this organisation as the war progressed. It presaged the political *volte face* that would come with the peace of 1945, as we will soon discover in this review. The writing was clearly on the wall by 1944, as more educated non-Saro rose to occupy major social roles in township life, with an accompanying prominence in local debate on ever more controversial issues. The results of elections to the Africa Club's executive in January 1944, were most instructive in this regard.

The following officers were returned:

President	Dr. O. Ajibade
Vice-President	M.A. Equgoo
Secretary	A.E. Allagoa
Assistant-Secretary	F.U. Achikeh
Treasurer	S.K. Agboh
Financial-Secretary	C.S.O. Orakwue
Auditors	R.O. Nzimiro & S.G. deSouza
Bar Manager	G.C. Ikokwu
Tennis Captain	J.C. Roberts
Cricket Captain	A.G.K. Abalo
Others	Z.C. Obi, A.M. Coker, F.E. Johnson, D.A. Pratt, G.O. Akomas, S.N. Kalu, I. Abacheta, and Mbukpa.[108]

The indigenes were rallying to occupy the centre state of township life, and the days of uncontested Saro dominance were clearly drawing to a close.

The Alumni of the Methodist Boys High School (MBHS), Freetown

Although, as earlier remarked, other prominent secondary schools in Freetown were represented in the Saro community, undoubtedly the largest and most active contingent was drawn from the Methodist Boys High School (MBHS). Potts-Johnson was himself an "old boy", and a much-driven organiser of alumni activities in Port Harcourt. Not surprisingly, a rivalry developed between the alumni of the various schools, and they competed fiercely through their public activities for the attention and the purse of local residents. The MBHS alumni marked the school's 59th anniversary in 1933, and alumnae of the sister Methodist Girls High School (MGHS), Freetown, were invited to participate in the festivities.[109] For its 60th anniversary, they launched a "Tregaskis and J.C. May Memorial Fund", to commemorate two of their more distinguished Principals.[110] Potts-Johnson was the honoured preacher at divine services at Wesley Church to mark the 63th anniversary,[111] and not even World War II would disrupt these activities.

For their 66th year, in April 1940, a procession of alumni, in school colours, took to the streets of Port Harcourt, with the Rev. H.L. Forde and B.J. George, both alumni, officiating at the accustomed thanksgiving service. Latunde Sapara, a recently deceased alumnus, was also memorialised.[112] Glowing tribute would also be paid by the alumni, in April 1943, to the memory of three illustrious "old boys" that had served Port Harcourt well: R.R. Elliott, who died in September, 1940; "Professor" A. Kelfallah Sankoh, who passed away in October 1940; and Leighton Johnson, who succumbed in May 1942. Resident Saro alumni of the Sierra Leone Grammar School (SLGS), Freetown, among them F.G. Spiff, A.J. Boyle, and O.S. Thomas, also participated in these activities.[113] Anniversary celebrations in April 1944 featured a concert and dance, with the Rev. E.J.T. Harris, alumnus and resident of Calabar, delivering the annual sermon.[114]

Social Activities of the I.B. Johnsons and Potts-Johnsons

The Potts-Johnsons and the I.B. Johnsons, undoubtedly, offered the most elaborate entertainment of all the township's Saro. Unfortunately for many, these did not come very often. The patricians were skillful managers of their assets, and public demonstrations of their largesse were scrupulously regulated and sparingly offered. The I.B. Johnsons also travelled with a facility that was generally unmatched,and these trips sometimes took them out of the continent. In this section, we will briefly review aspects of the social itineraries of these dominant Saro families in the years up to World War II, to underline the social scope and privilege that only a few Saro enjoyed, a situation strikingly reminiscent of the differentiation among the Freetown Krio and the Gold Coast Saro, among others.[115] The social record of Saro exploits in the period under survey would be incomplete and lacking in credibility without this review.

With resources generated from the EHS, the printing business, a postal agency,[116] the newspaper, agricultural interests in Okrika, and some investments in leather tanning,[117] among others, the Potts-Johnsons were comfortable. We have already reviewed their involvements in the arts, the Masonic Lodge, and the Sierra Leone Union. These went alongside various political activities. With such a demanding schedule, it appears that domestic celebrations were not a priority for the childless couple. In the early years, unlike others of their class, they rarely held birthday celebrations.[118] They were no better at wedding anniversaries. In a rare observance of February 1937, they reportedly celebrated 21 years together, at home with friends.[119] By this time, Mrs. Potts-Johnson had generally acquired a reputation for unapproachability and some indifference to matters of a convivial nature, a viewpoint scarcely improved by her childlessness, and her pique over Potts-Johnson's much talked about dalliances in local society. She was not given to much entertaining, and her spouse, perhaps wisely, did not insist.[120]

Vacations away from Port Harcourt, often taken separately, were seldom pursued before 1939, but they came less infrequently in the later years. Some Saro of the middle class travelled much more frequently than the wealthier Potts-Johnsons. Surprisingly, Rev. Potts-Johnson paid no visit to Freetown throughout the 1930's and most of the 1940's. It was only on the eve of his death, on doctor's orders, that he broke this habit, as will be reviewed later. In October 1932, he went to Calabar for Methodist Union celebrations, and was in Lagos and Accra, in 1933, on the S/S Wadai. In 1938, he attended the Methodist Synod at Uzuakoli.[121] There may well have been some undocumented trips, but informants stressed the irregularity of Potts-Johnson's travels away from Port Harcourt in these years. With the outbreak of war, it would be the early 1940's before Potts-Johnson ventured out again after his Uzuakoli meeting. In August 1941, he left on a northern tour of Jos, Zaria, and Kaduna.[122] We are not informed on the purpose of these visits. He was also reported as spending a weekend in

Abonnema, in July 1943, "in connection with the reception organised by the Kalabari Central Union in honour of . . . Morgan Bob-Manuel, retired collector of customs".[123] Bob-Manuel was known to be a close personal friend, but in the then prevailing social conditions of Port Harcourt, this could well have also been another effort to consolidate local social ties in a season of a growing xenophobia. By April 1944, Potts-Johnson was in Barking Ladi, in Benue Province, on a short vacation. True to form, the Potts-Johnsons organised no celebrations to mark the silver jubilee of their marriage.[124]

The I.B. Johnsons, perhaps materially even more provisioned than the Potts-Johnsons, had two children. The couple appear to have devoted a lot of time to family relaxation and recreation, in these years, with casual involvement in the SLU, a greater commitment to Masonic Affairs, and a lot of stay-at-home evenings. In February 1930, they unveiled a tennis court at their residence, the only such private facility in the township. According to the report, "several ladies and gentlemen were present, many sets were played, refreshments served, and a very enjoyable evening was spent . . ."[125] For a time, the Johnsons held a liquor license at the Palladium of which they were proprietors in the early 1930's, while also operating a cinema in partnership with S.B. Rhodes, member of the Legislative Council, and their compatriot of Aba. Birthday celebrations were much more frequent in the Johnson household.[126]

The Johnsons were also avid travellers. In June 1930, Mr. Johnson left town on the Abinsi for Europe, via Freetown, where he made arrangements for his daughter's education. In Europe, he was to visit France, England, and Germany, and other parts of the continent before returning to Port Harcourt the following October. There are no recorded reports of any other Saro travelling to Europe at this time.[127] In January, 1932, the Nigerian Observer reported Mrs. Rosalind Johnson's return to Port Harcourt from Freetown. Barely two months later, she was off again, this time, by the Ajasa, to join the Apapa for London, with a brief stop in Freetown to get her daughter, who was proceeding to Europe for further studies. Mrs. Johnson would spend the next 2½ years away from Port Harcourt, visiting "the UK, Germany, and France".[128]

I.B. Johnson travelled to Freetown in September 1933 to get his son, who was about to enroll at the EHS. By this time, he had invited his mother-in-law, Mrs. Esther Taylor of Freetown, to visit the family in Port Harcourt. Mrs. Taylor actually died in Port Harcourt in April 1938, as she was about to return to Freetown. Her funeral, at St. Cyprian's, with Revds. M.D. Showers and E.T. Dimeari officiating, attracted a large Saro turn-out, with some coming from as far afield as Calabar. Syrian and Indian merchant associates of the Johnsons were also present.[129] When they hosted a send-off party, in October 1934, for the J. Fowell Kojo Bostons, the Johnsons put up a splendid show. The party was preceded by sets of tennis, and a group photograph. For dancing on the tennis court, music was supplied by a "grand gramophone". A cross-section of Saro society, and their Nigerian friends, attended the occasion.[130]

In July 1937, the Johnsons, travelling together, left Port Harcourt, on the Apapa, for Lagos, where they were joined by their son, for a visit to England, where the younger Johnson was to commence further studies. When in February 1939, they marked their 21st wedding anniversary, the Johnsons invited "a few of their friends till late in the evening". The Observer reported "a very enjoyable time . . . ".[131] The Johnsons would maintain this active, though select, social schedule into the 1940's. In April 1940, Mrs. Rosamond Johnson became the first African woman in Port Harcourt to travel by air. She flew from London to Kano, where she was warmly received by her husband, and Mrs. Potts-Johnson. The Nigerian Observer invited others to "take a leaf out of Mrs. Johnson's book".[132]

A close-knit family, the Johnsons always had their son home from his King's College, Lagos, base for vacations. In January 1943, the couple celebrated their silver wedding anniversary. Although it was described as "a very quiet affair", the Johnsons invited some friends and associates to their home to mark the day, and "all who were fortunate . . . to be present had a really good time".[133] The Saro would turn out in full force, in June 1948, to welcome back to the fold, Dr. Amicitia Rosalind Babington Johnson, LRCP, LRCSI, LM (Rotundor), daughter of the I.B. Johnsons. Arriving on the M.V. Calumet from Southport, England, she was hailed as only the third woman in West Africa to qualify as a medical doctor. This was an outstanding achievement in a Saro community where a college education was rare. The Johnson's son, "I.B. Jr". was also studying medicine at the time, and he was said to be expected home soon to "join forces with her".[134]

By the end of the 1940's, the Saro had emerged as a cultural force on the social stage of Port Harcourt. A community of predominantly Krio descendants, but open to non-Krio Saro, it exemplified, in a limited way, some of the possibilities of corporate pan-ethnicity in the diaspora. The Saro had become a recognisable social presence in the township, particularly in the circles of the rising middle-class of civil servants, teachers, clerks, pastors, local businessmen, employees of local finance and mercantile firms, and the like. This was the constellation within which the Saro principally operated. In the church, the Masonic Lodge, the clubs, and other associations, they interacted freely with their middle-class indigenous hosts, some of whom had become relatives through marriage. How successful the Saro would be in maintaining the social dualism of identification with both Nigeria and Sierra Leone, becomes the principal challenge of the coming years. Saro ability to transcend the common perception that the group represented favoured immigrants, in alliance with the indigenous elite for the fat of the land, would also be crucial.

Another significant challenge, and one that Fyfe has remarked for colonial Freetown,[135] was the tendency in these years for Saro ranks to be depleted by premature morbidity. Between March 1944 and July 1948, the Saro would lose some of their most resourceful and outspoken men and women. The dedicated contractor and administration critic, I.R. Benjamin, died in March 1944,[136] to be followed in January 1945 by Archibald Denson Grant, for long an activist, and the gadfly of a host of causes. Grant who had long retired from government service, was from Wilberforce, just outside Freetown. On coming to Nigeria in 1908, he had served in the customs department, the medical service, and the legal department, before retiring in 1919. He arrived in Port Harcourt in 1920, and soon established himself as a small-scale trader of wines and hardware. He was still actively engaged in his business three months to his death. A stout defender of the rights of the people, and without the diplomatic skills of Potts-Johnson and I.B. Johnson, the combative Grant had been prominent in the African Progress Union (APU), and the Rate Payers Association. For many years, he had waged war relentlessly against local landlords over high rents. The Nigerian Observer remembered him as "a man of inflexible will, [who] was always prepared to fight an issue to the bitter end . . . [and for which] he was gravely misunderstood".[137]

In September 1947, the much respected Saro matriarch of Bonny Street, Mrs. Ella Horton died, to be followed in December by the very talented Alice Meyer, a veritable pioneer of pan-ethnic possibility in Saro ranks.[138] It would next be the turn, at 55, in July 1948, of Lucius Arthur Barnes, once of the Marine department, and the Treasury, and for several years, a successful copra dealer. W.S. Pratt of Victoria Street followed Barnes in the same month.[139] The leaders of the Saro were passing off the stage with an amazing rapidity, and often, at a comparatively young age. Local political action would certainly not be the only threat to Saro interests in the coming years.

4

POLITICAL AND ECONOMIC CHANGE IN THE WAR YEARS AND AFTER, 1939—49

The 1940's were a most eventful decade for Potts-Johnson and the Saro of Port Harcourt. Not only did the immigrant community witness a major global conflict with significant ramifications for township life, it began also to experience major transformations in its station as strangers in a Nigerian territory soon to be engulfed in major nationalist activity. Stranger status came under increasing assault and intense scrutiny, and profound questions regarding the long-term residence of non-Nigerians in a politically independent territory began to be raised with a disturbing regularity. Before we review these significant developments, we must, however, set the Port Harcourt scene within the larger territorial context of the 1940's.

World War II was indeed a transformative experience of radical proportions for the people of Nigeria, and relations between the educated elite and the British officials would be profoundly altered by the territorial developments of these years. In West Africa generally, the aforementioned Youth Movements would progressively yield space to much larger and more diversified political groupings, which became the nationalist parties that led the challenge for independence.[1] By 1941, the Nigerian Youth Movement (NYM) was swamped in a crisis of ethnic competition over the replacement of Dr. K.A. Abayomi, who had recently resigned from the Legislative Council. Ijaw and Yoruba factions, and their respective allies within the movement, were sharply polarised by this debate. The eventual selection of Ernest Ikoli, an Ijaw, as Abayomi's successor, led ultimately to the collapse of the NYM.[2] The seeds of ethnic competition which would bedevil Nigeria's political development in the future were clearly being sown in these activities. Now unencumbered by NYM politics, Nnamdi Azikiwe would exploit the conditions of austerity generated by the war, and the resultant general worker's strike of 1945, to further advance his national political credentials. The strike by employees demanding higher cost of living allowances in an inflation-ravaged Lagos, had come precisely two months after the publication of Governor Richard's constitutional proposals for the territory, and the introduction of the so-called "obnoxious ordinances" into the statutes. With scarcely any consultation with the African leadership, the Richards constitution was peremptorily introduced in 1947. It had the principal effect of incorporating Northern Nigeria into the Legislative Council, and instituting a system of regional advisory councils for the northern, eastern, and western provinces, under a very limited franchise that was certain to draw the ire of the educated elite.[3]

Nnamdi Azikiwe, whose support for the 1945 strike had drawn official criticism, and led to the banning of his two Lagos newspapers (the West African Pilot and the Comet), now claimed knowledge of an official plot to assassinate him. This acrimonious atmosphere provided the backdrop for the first major territorial outing of the National Council of Nigeria and the Cameroons (NCNC), a political party, which had been formed in August 1944, with Herbert Macaulay as president, and Azikiwe as general secretary. Although lacking northern support, the NCNC had attracted a large following in the south, and one of its earliest campaigns had been against the Richards constitutional proposals, which it deemed most inadequate in its franchise provisions and its obvious preference of the chiefs and other traditional leaders over the educated elite. The NCNC had also condemned the "obnoxious ordinances". The latter refers to four new provisions in respect of mineral resources, public and Crown lands, and the tenure of chiefs.[4] In sum, the minerals ordinance vested all control of precious metals and related materials in the British Crown; the lands ordinances increased Crown control of vast areas of local territory; and the ordinance on chiefs greatly inflated the Governor's territory-wide powers over their appointment and removal from office. The NCNC launched an eight-month country-wide campaign to protest these laws, and despatched a delegation to London in June 1947, which was snubbed by the Secretary of State.[5]

Port Harcourt's war experience, and subsequent developments of the 1940's, have to be reviewed against this national background for, during these years, we see in this township, at a microcosmic level, many of the salient elements that accompanied the nationalist struggle against British colonialism—the arrogance and heavy-handedness of a colonial officialdom much given to racist practice even though greatly in need of African elite support, which it courts periodically through national honours and other such awards; an African educated elite that greatly resents this conduct, but is desirous of co-optation unto government boards, and keen on demonstrating its loyalty by raising funds for war relief; and an inchoate indigenous nationalist lobby eager to dismantle immigrant control of the local productive forces and the related political process. It is to the war and these factors that we now turn.

War Fund Activities

As war appeared imminent, security arrangements, reminiscent of local efforts in the 1920's to contain Bolshevism, Ethiopianism, Pan-Islamism, and Pan-Africanism,[6] were put in place in Port Harcourt. The public utterances of African leaders and newspaper editors came under close surveillance.[7] In 1939, the Nigerian Observer was directed to cease its coverage of news on Italy and Abyssinia (Ethiopia).[8] When the Observer's sister paper, the Nigerian Eastern Mail, in September 1939, speculated on a possible gas attack during the war to which Africans would be vulnerable, E.N. Mylius, the Resident, was furious. He denied that Europeans had already received gas masks for their protection as was being insinuated, and called on Potts-Johnson and other editors to avoid such scurrilous reporting.[9]

The Saro elite featured prominently in the fund-raising activities toward war relief, and they seemed particularly keen on proving their loyalty against the background of a 1939 intelligence report that had questioned the commitment to the Allied cause of some Saro workers. The report had noted: "Several informal talks have been had with the masters of ships in Port Harcourt, and in two cases, the question of loyalty of the Sierra Leonian (sic.) fireman was brought up. In both cases, the opinion was expressed that trouble would have to be expected of them as there were indications that they were not prepared to fire their ship during a state of war."[10] When the author put the contents of this rather cryptic note to informants in Port Harcourt, they acknowledged the existence of the rumour at the time, but added that it reflected more the then prevalent discontent with work conditions, than the perceived indifference to the Allied cause.[11]

Potts-Johnson was very supportive of the emergency war measures. These comprised the mandatory curtailing of the electric power supply, the introduction of a local defence unit, and the appointment of special police personnel to shore up local security.[12] In July 1940, a Win-the-War Fund committee, drawn from the Saro and indigenous elites, was inaugurated, and although one of its members, the Saro, Max George, was disinclined to admit Syrians unto the board, reflecting long-held resentments, all racial groups were invited to join the fund's activities.[13] Throughout the war, these programmes would take the form of dances, raffles, film shows, cabaret, fetes, and related activities.[14] Potts-Johnson, in August, 1940, invoking hyperbole, warned of the dreadful problems that would beset the British colonies should the allies be defeated: " . . . all that the church stands for will be trampled over, and all schools, bookshops [and] printing establishments will be scrapped. All government offices will be closed, and the workers disgraced and turned out . . . all pension (sic.) lost and other privileges enjoyed under the British rule abolished . . . ."[15] This was very effective propaganda, and obviously music in officialdom's ear. As a rallying call to the faithful, it certainly got the loyalty juices flowing. Fund raising activity in the township and in the neighbouring Aba increased significantly in the early 1940's.[16]

By December 1940, Potts-Johnson, who was the president of the Win-the-War Fund, reported that £600 raised by the fund and the Women's Emergency Committee, which had substantial Saro representation, had been despatched to Lagos. I.B. Johnson was himself a dedicated fund-raiser.[17] The drive for donations was, however, suspended briefly between March and June 1942 when £90 6s., allegedly raised by some Igbo traders, failed to reach Mr. Leys, the fund's financial secretary. The amount had apparently been diverted by some individuals.[18] Potts-Johnson was empowered during the suspension period to re-organise the Fund's machinery with a view to greater efficiency.[19] With the resumption of activities in June 1942, a comic soccer match between immigrant Saro players, appropriately named the Wanderers, and an indigenous side, the Nigerian Rovers, was a huge success. Potts-Johnson and other patricians lost 0-7 to their local hosts.[20] As the war drew to a close, 30 September to 7 October was declared War Relief Fund week throughout the Eastern province. The Chief Commissioner set the entire province a target sum of £2,500. Port Harcourt easily exceeded its target allocation of £750, raising a grand total of £1257. 7s. 3d.[21]

Local Economic and Political Developments

Port Harcourt's population had grown significantly by the early 1940's. Its non-African component as at 1940 was as follows:

British	118
American	3
Other European	21
Syrians and Lebanese	80
Indians	11

The Lebanese population had doubled in a year, perhaps an index of some of the anxiety and resentment in Saro circles.[22] We have no figures for the African population at this time, but, by 1945, it was estimated at 33,700.[23] There are also no official records of the Saro population at this stage of Port Harcourt's growth, but there is little to suggest that it had grown much beyond 30-50 households. This would have amounted to between 100 and 200 permanent residents, not accounting for the usual stream of visitors to Saro homes.[24] Of the impact of the war on the township's population, officials had the following impressions as at 1940:

> "It cannot be said that Port Harcourt has suffered very much on account of the European War. There has been some restriction of trade; some articles such as stockfish are no longer imported and others especially building materials have been short and expensive. The trade of middlemen in palm produce has no doubt also declined, but Port Harcourt is not a producing area, and the fact that the number of ships visiting the port has been 294 as against 345 in 1939 may perhaps be taken as an index of the degree to which its entrepot trade had declined".[25]

This positive assessment was not, however, shared by all. The agenda of the Township Advisory Board (TAB) and the African Community League (ACL) during the war years, clearly reflected the dissonance in perception of African difficulty between the government and the African leadership. With painful regularity, concerns of the pre-war years continued to recur in the ACL and TAB debates of the 1940's.[26] Potts-Johnson was President of the ACL by April 1940, and that body and the TAB continued to confront the austerity issues of local taxation (introduced in June 1940),[27] and soaring utility rates for the local electricity and water supplies.[28]

These economic difficulties appear to have been exacerbated by increasing Lebanese and Syrian immigration into the township, and the resultant increase in competition from the operations they introduced. Small-scale African traders, active in the local Nigerian Youth Movement (NYM) branch in the 1940s, among them some Saro, were particularly incensed at these developments. Two members of the Saro community served in the NYM executive in the early 1940's. S. Atanda Pratt was vice-president, and C.A. Williams was the financial secretary.[29] Long-held Saro fears of Levantine economic domination, rooted in Freetown experience,[30] were now fed by a Daily Service editorial of August 1941, which discussed the appointment of a Syrian, G. Calil, to the newly established Starch Marketing Board. In tones that strikingly resonated the Saro attitude to these immigrants from the middle-east, the paper reacted: "Syrians are foreigners in this country. . . . In a free, progressive, and independent Nigeria . . . there will be no room for a single Syrian. We cannot understand the Syrians. Their methods of trading and of living are completely strange to us . . . so un-British and so un-Nigerian are they . . . ." Raising the spectre of foreign economic domination, it continued: "We do not want the economic strangulation of Sierra Leoneans and of people in other places where the Syrians have managed to establish themselves to be repeated here . . . we will endeavour to tolerate their presence so long as we fall short of dominion status. When that goal of our ambition is reached, they themselves, we suppose, realise already that there is not enough room for us and for them."[31] This passionate rejection of Levantine strangers was being made in unequivocal terms, and the Saro immigrants saw in it their group's immunity, and the protection of its interests. It convinced them of their social acceptance by the host society, and this was no mean comfort in the 1940s.[32] The Resident moved swiftly to stem this xenophobic outburst with an apology from the paper to E. Haddad and the other local Syrians. But much harm to local relations had already been done, and Port Harcourt's potential for the rejection of strangers perceived as exploiters had once again been revealed.

Land Issues, Rents, the Building Codes, and Related Matters

A plethora of land related matters emerged during the 1940's that would impose great strain on the already fragile relations between the African community and the local British officials. Many charges of insensitivity to the economic plight of the African people would flow from these developments, but they would also reveal the gulf that separated the more affluent African residents from the poorer majority. The class polarisations of Port

Harcourt would unfold in their stark enormity in these controversies, and the Saro elite of property owners came increasingly to be seen as an integral part of the people's problems.

It all began in August 1942 when the township's African leaders accused the Local Authority, R.K. Floyer, of insensitivity to the economic hardships and frustrations of the African majority. Floyer was subsequently transferred out of Port Harcourt to dam the tide of protest, and this victory over an official believed to be "obsessed with pre-conceived notions", would set the scene for future confrontations with the local administration. As Floyer left for Degema, the Nigerian Observer taunted that it was its hope that "the climate of Kalabari [would] suit him better." Of his successor, C.H.S.R. Palmer, the editor noted menacingly: "I am just beginning to study him, and it may be necessary soon to draw a pen picture of him."[33] Under Palmer, relations between the government and the African community would suffer profound deterioration, and land-related matters were central to this decay.

Arbitrary rent increases by local landlords, and demands for advanced quarterly, rather than monthly rent payments, had compounded the economic burdens of the working poor. Rent increases, in the 1940's, of the order of 33$\frac{1}{3}$ per cent were not uncommon, and Potts-Johnson had called for a Rent Assessment Board of the type that operated in Lagos to address this anomaly.[34] Under Local Authority, Palmer, landlords would also have their frustrations. These came principally from the administration's building codes, a hold-over of the 1930's when the African Progress Union (APU) had faced similar difficulties.[35] Landlords that contravened the building codes were now having their plots re-possessed, and the buildings on them demolished. Potts-Johnson found such official conduct "sound in point of justice, but unsound in . . . equity".[36] Palmer's office was at the centre of this unpleasantness, and before long, charges of racism were being hurled against it by the Saro and other leaders. When during the visit to Port Harcourt, in November 1942, of Governor and Lady Bourdillon, no African leader was invited by the local administration to dine with the visitors, relations sank to a new low. Potts-Johnson wrote of "a class of European officials who either think the Governor's visit was intended only for Europeans, or who imagine there is no class of Africans . . . qualified to sit at dinner with His Excellency". The Local Authority, Palmer, was accused of snobbery. An indignant Potts-Johnson wrote: "We consider it a definite affront to us as a race. . . . we find it difficult to understand why in a place like Port Harcourt and Aba (sic.), where there are African Magistrates, members of the professions, and other eminent Africans, not one of them was thought good enough to be honoured with an invitation. . . . There is no room for racial segregation in this country". He warned that Europeans who practised discrimination were "a hindrance to progress", and "will not be tolerated here". Palmer subsequently responded with the explanation that he had not compiled the disputed guest list. Although this brought him some exoneration from the Nigerian Observer, it was evident that relations had not been repaired,[37] and more was to come from an African elite that yielded no quarter on matters of its station and privilege.

A resolution tabled and passed at the TAB meeting of 8 October 1942, further widened the rift between the government and the African leadership on land matters. Proposed by officials of the administration, it called on the government to "take steps to re-enter plots held under build-ing leases in cases where the leasees have failed to comply with their build-ing covenants after due notice and warning, with a view to establishing a pool of vacant plots for leasing to suitable persons after the war". African members on the TAB, condemned this policy as oppressive and unmindful of the prevailing high cost of building materials which often made it im-possible for defaulters to comply with the law. They called for leniency, and an extension of the grace period which would allow those in the wrong to come into compliance after the war.[38]

When the Local Authority, Palmer, seemed unmoved by these ap-peals, the African Community League (ACL) turned to E.N. Mylius, the Resident. Potts-Johnson led the delegation, with Dr. Ajibade as its spokes-man. The ACL critised Palmer's attitude, and condemned his wanton demo-lition of defaulters' homes. Palmer's defence was direct and uncompromis-ing. He saw Port Harcourt as "a town of back houses", and emphasised that whenever residents "took plots which they were unable to build in confor-mity with the building covenants, it was his duty to relieve them of such plots, war or no war . . . ". He was clearly unwilling to yield on this matter. After several exchanges, the meeting reportedly ended, surprisingly, on a note of cordiality, with the Resident undertaking to review each case on its merits and with sympathy.[39] This obviously exceeded the African leaders' wildest expectations. Although they had scored no more than a hollow victory, the members of the delegation were commended by the Nigerian Observer for their resolve against Palmer. The paper claimed that African leaders had proved they had "backbones", and could "hold their own if elected to represent rate payers on a Municipal Board should Port Harcourt be fortunate to have one."[40] Small gains were being celebrated from the roof-tops, in eager anticipation of future political reforms from a grudging official benefactor.

Persistent pressure on the rent front, and repeated demands for official controls yielded some dividends as 1942 drew to a close. The Local Authority announced the pegging of all rents at their June 1941 levels, and threatened legal action against landlords who exceeded the set limits, or evicted tenants who owed less than six weeks of rent. A Rent Assessment Board was also to be convened with the Local Authority at its head.[41] These measures brought some relief and encouragement to Potts-Johnson and the African leadership generally. At last, it seemed they could present tangible evidence of some achievement to their rather impatient constituents. This was, however, the deceptive calm before the storm that had long been looming for some time. Port Harcourt was about to be engulfed in a major crisis between the Local Authority and the African leadership. It came early in October 1943, when the African members of the TAB decided to invoke an earlier resolution of that body. It had provided as follows: " . . . when a house which is ordered to be broken down is inspected by a member of the Board, and the member is satisfied that the house can be repaired, the Medical Officer of Health and the Executive Engineer should be requested to re-inspect the house concerned for re-considering their opinion".[42] This move was obviously designed to undermine the power of the Local Authority. It was crafted in the same spirit as a subsequent editorial of the Nigerian Observer which accused Palmer of retroactive application of the demolition law to buildings under construction before 4th March 1943, the date the law took effect.[43] Palmer fiercely disputed this imputation. He wrote: "This office has not refused to issue a certificate of fitness for occupation in respect of any building begun before the 4 March 1943, on the grounds that it does not comply with the new building regulations. The . . . Regulations No. 4 of 1943 came into force on the 4th March 1943. . . . I would suggest that [you] verify your information before criticising in print".[44] The Nigerian Observer stood its ground, demanding an explanation of the Local Authority's retroactive review of construction sites, which, in its view, was tantamount to a witch-hunt. It queried further: "In view of the continued and relentless demolition of houses, and its consequent dire result on the health and convenience of a large percentage of the people of this community, the public is naturally anxious to know why certain newly completed buildings are shut up. . . . we hope we are not asking too much if we asked Mr. Palmer for a press statement on the matter".[45]

When Palmer failed to respond, Potts-Johnson went on the offensive. He called the Local Authority a dictator, and admitted his readiness to face "the full force of Palmer's wrath", for he would not be prevented "from speaking . . . the truth". He accused Palmer of chicanery, and supplied evidence of a case where construction work on a home begun in June 1942, had been halted on the Local Authority's orders. Palmer was accused of over-reaching himself, and of acting *ultra vires*. Potts-Johnson blamed Palmer's conceit on a vote of confidence he had recently received from the TAB. He also condemned Palmer's insistence on 125 sq. ft. floor space for African homes, when the law called for 120 sq. ft. Palmer was taken to task for forcing residents to build on 2400 sq. ft. plots when the law allowed 2500 sq. ft. "If this were all", Potts-Johnson opined, "we might have been tempted to plead in extenuation that Mr. Palmer is unable to read the law correctly. But these are not all. When we say that he has been doing everything possible to make things hard for the people, we are not exaggerating". Potts-Johnson wondered whether Palmer may be out of his depths in his present position: "It may be that the work is too much for him. Port Harcourt is a large and growing township, and Mr. Palmer has never before worked in such a large town. We therefore suggest that a change to a less arduous town will do him no harm".[46]

The administration finally decided to resolve the impasse over Local Authority, Palmer, in May 1944. It ordered Palmer's transfer out of Port Harcourt to the delight of his African critics. On the day of his departure, a crowd gathered at the railway station, chanting "goodbye Mr. Palmer; Mr. Palmer must go".[47] As Palmer left town, there were appeals for reconciliation between the "dissentients" and the "champions". Both sides were invited to address the outstanding issues in a spirit of "common agreement".[48] Palmer joined the Lands department in Lagos, and was replaced by a Mr. Bryant. In a final comment on Palmer, the Guardian had this to say: "There should be a vast difference between a criminal lawyer who has to match all his legal wits against the ingenuity of hardened crooks, and an administrator of civil laws. . . . we have no doubt that Mr. Palmer will have ample rooms (sic.) for the display of his wide knowledge of laws in his new office whilst the people of Port Harcourt have a more understanding Local Authority in Mr. Bryant".[49] The African lobby had won another significant victory, and Potts-Johnson's remonstrances had created yet more embarrassment for the local administration.

Housing issues were again in the forefront of the African agenda in the early post-war years, and the African leaders kept up the pressure on government to improve conditions, and maintain the ceiling on plot rents. They also emphasised the need to open up the adjacent Diobu area to housing projects that would relieve the pressure on the central township. A post-war municipal development sub-committee was formed in 1945, and it made detailed recommendations to government for a housing scheme at

Diobu. It called for "three storied tenement buildings, each containing 20-30 quarters". Each quarter was to have two living rooms of not less than 150 sq. ft. each, and a store. Although latrines and bathrooms could be communal, it provided for individual kitchens. The committee, of which the Saro, C. Egerton Shyngle, was a member, recommended that monthly rents for a quarter, to be affordable, should not exceed 12s.6^d, and it called for an initial investment in a block of 24 quarters at a projected cost of £4,500.[50]

Working Class Reactions to the Land Controversy

The controversy over building codes and their enforcement by the Local Authority, C.H.S.R. Palmer, which we have just reviewed, sharply polarised the social classes within the African community of Port Harcourt. In developments that were strikingly reminiscent of the advocacy of the African Progress Union (APU) of the 1930's, working class residents and their associates began, once again, to publicly vilify what they perceived as African elite collaboration with the colonial authorities. At a meeting of the African Community League (ACL) held at the St. Cyprian's schoolroom in October 1943, these tensions re-surfaced in a very dramatic form. A Mr. Yoko, an indigene, who claimed to speak on behalf of a "special committee" condemned the African nominees of the Township Advisory Board (TAB) for the vote of confidence they had given Palmer shortly before the confrontation of October 1943 over his building code policy.[51] This was public censure, by an indigene, of a representative group that was predominantly Saro. Yoko demanded that the League and the African community dissociate themselves from this vote that had come from the elite, and that a request be made for Palmer's removal from office. Potts-Johnson was present at the meeting, and, along with another TAB member, Dr. Ajibade, he apologised for their poor judgment in assessing Palmer. He spoke of the embarrassment of the TAB's African members when they discovered, after the vote, that "Palmer had resumed his activities by throwing the palm wine vendors and market women from their stalls without notice to the Board." The ACL meeting voted to dissociate the League from the confidence vote, and when Potts-Johnson suggested that a letter be drafted outlining the hardships that had come of Palmer's actions, that move was judged too tame a response. There were calls for a delegation to see the Chief Commissioner in Enugu, and for the convening of a committee of twelve to document Palmer's activities.[52] The rift between the African elite and its constituents had widened dramatically.

The formation of a House Tenants Union in January 1945 was, perhaps, the logical culmination of this divide in social class relations. At a meeting held at the Enitonna High School (EHS), 267 tenants met to organise for the defence of their interests. Potts-Johnson had called for such a Union in May 1944, to help tenants "withstand the wiles of plotholders", whom he considered increasingly "rapacious" in their rent assessments. The Union's principal leaders were N.D. Godswille-Hart and W. Osika, both indigenes, and B.J. George, a Saro.[53] The Union pledged itself to protecting the "suffering tenants" of Port Harcourt, inviting responsible citizens to become its patrons, and providing material support for tenant members in difficulty.[54] At its meeting of November, 1946, it elected a new executive that would raise, in a manner previously unknown in the township, fundamental questions of class and nationality in Port Harcourt. As we will soon discover, the Saro elite would be the target of much of this controversy. The officers returned at those elections were as follows:

N.D. Godswille Hart	President
I.A. Lawal	Vice-President
I.W. Osika	Secretary
J.N. Bassey	Financial Secretary
James O. Hart	Treasurer
A. Meyer and J.O. Ogobi	Joint Auditors

Other executive members were: T.K. Abara, Alex O. Stowe, S.E. Peters, M.K. Owunka, and Madam Amadasu.[55] Like that earlier mentioned executive committee elected to preside over the Africa Club in January 1944,[56] this executive grouping of the HTU was made up predominantly of indigenes. The once seamless Saro dominance of local township organisations was being progressively eroded, and lower-middle and working class indigenous aspirants were moving in to occupy positions of influence in local society. This was a radical departure from earlier tendencies.

By the end of 1946, the HTU had some 300 members.[57] Its existence had called forth a rival Plotholders Union, a movement of the landlords about which, unfortunately, we know very little. Port Harcourt seemed inexorably bound on a course of class warfare. The colonial government assured the HTU of its full support, and stressed its determination to check tendencies to rent profiteering. Plotholders, for their part, rejected any attempt to curb their powers of periodic rent review. The administration acknowledged that these class tensions would only be relieved through "the provision of new plots in new layouts."[58] Translating this thoughtful observation into concrete policy was, of course, another matter altogether in the tangled bureaucratic skein of ambivalent policy making which called for running with the hare, while hunting with the hounds.

The cauldron of indigenous working class discontent that had been seething for some time in Port Harcourt exploded with some force in November 1947. The House Tenants Union (HTU) addressed a petition to the government on the vexed matter of township plots, and the official procedures for their allocation. The Union found the policy "highly questionable, partial, discriminatory, and tending to give the impression of keeping the tenants section of the community ever and for all time a plotless and houseless people".[59] The Union's protests identified the area of the Hospital Road as the most disputed zone, for it had observed that land allocations there had gone "to some . . . who already own from two to three plots . . . without . . . regard for the feelings and the demands . . . of other people without a single plot". Elite gains at the expense of the masses were clearly being addressed here by a rather irate HTU membership. In a stinging indictment of official policy, the Union condemned the plot allocation procedure, and exposed its patent inequity. The members wrote indignantly: "It is a fallacious argument that the basis of distribution should be on the taxable income of the persons to whom any commercial plot is allocated. Those now holding plots in the commercial centres especially Hospital and Aggrey Roads, and who are said to be paying higher taxes were also formerly of the class of the common and ordinary man . . . ".[60] This was a direct challenge to the economic hegemony of the township's African elite, the principal plotholders, of whom the Saro were a prominent fraction. Potts-Johnson, and other Saro plotholders, may well have been acceptable to the indigenous elite, their economic co-evals. They were, however, increasingly *personae non gratae* to the poorer indigenes, who were themselves eager to end the era of political tutelage under the Saro, so as to emerge as autonomous political practitioners and economic agents in their own right. Potts-Johnson was, perhaps, more acceptable than some of the more aloof patricians of his class; but this made him no less an immigrant exploiter.

The debate over immigrant and indigene rights was increasingly being aired in a township whose population was some 40,000 by November 1947.[61] Of this number, some 6000 were said to be "unauthorised squatters" in the Diobu area, and 275 were non-Africans, of whom 84 were Asiatics. The township was still plagued by a shortage of affordable accommodation at the end of 1947, and this was reflected in astronomic increases in house rents. The Tenants Union had to engage a lawyer to challenge the more flagrant cases of profiteering. Although the Local Authority would comment on "a definite lessening of political tension" in the township in November 1947, on his return after an absence of some eleven months,[62] this reflected more a shift in the political calculus of Port Harcourt's discontent, than a general political thaw. New battle lines were being drawn. Intra-African class competition was becoming as significant as the more common inter-racial struggles. The housing problem had polarised the African community, and the Local Authority himself marvelled at the restraint that was being displayed in circumstances that would have generated riots in towns of less cohesion.[63] With unusual candor, he blamed his own government for allowing this situation to develop. He wrote: "The responsibility for delivering the tenants tied and bound into the jaws of these sharks must rest on the shoulders of the government, which in ten years, with the best will in the world, has only succeeded in making two additional plots available for leasing in the African town."[64] Unfortunately, these pronouncements would not be accompanied by the desired review of the land question. Landlords generally continued to have their way with exorbitant rent increases, and tenants would increasingly have recourse to anti-elite protestations as their frustrations mounted.

Potts-Johnson in Other Economic and Political Debates

Soaring rents and callous landlords were by no means the only economic challenges confronted by the poor in the Port Harcourt of the 1940's. Equally significant were problems of profiteering traders (often involved in the adulteration of the goods they sold),[65] rampant inflation, and expanding unemployment. Potts-Johnson came to the defence of employees of the Electric Power House who faced a pay-cut in December 1941, and he repeatedly condemned the "fancy prices" of unscrupulous local traders, who persistently ignored official attempts at price control.[66] In October 1942, the local administration had imposed the following rates:

> "Rice 18s. per cwt. wholesale; garri 3s.1[d] per 95 lb. bag, 1[d] per 3 salmon tins and 1[d] per 6 cigarette tins; meat (beef, mutton, pork) 6[d], 7½[d] and 9[d] per lb. respectively; edible palm oil at 4s. per 4 gallon petrol tin and 2½ per beer, whisky or gin bottle".

Traders in the local markets generally ignored these recommended prices, and many indulged in the adulteration of their goods.[67] While calling on the government to rein in offenders, Potts-Johnson and other African leaders demanded local political reform that would increase the ability of African leaders to address these difficulties. The Township Advisory Board (TAB), for instance, was judged long overdue for a radical overhaul that would end the virtual life tenure of its African nominees, who were mostly pawns in the hands of the Local Authority and the Resident. Potts-Johnson condemned the nonchalant attitude of some of these nominees, and the contempt with which the largely advisory TAB was being treated by local officials. He demanded legislative powers for the body, as well as the up-grading of Port Harcourt into a municipality, like Lagos.[68] Throughout the 1940's, various representations on municipal government would be made to the central administration, alongside requests for greater funding from London of the post-war recovery.[69] Potts-Johnson called on the local community to pursue African interests more aggressively and he denounced the apathy that still existed in some circles. He queried: "The [TAB], the ACL, the Conference of Chiefs . . . these are political bodies consisting of men who are leaders of opinion in this area. What are these bodies doing? Are they satisfied with their economic, social, and political conditions? Unless we are ready with plans and suggestions, broadcast to the world and not hidden in our bosom, we shall certainly be left behind . . . ."[70] More African representation was required on all official bodies dealing with the welfare of the African community, and the African leaders called repeatedly for their inclusion in these councils.[71]

For most officials, however, these requests were sheer humbug, emanating from the ranks of the educated owners of property who claimed to speak on behalf of the majority.[72] Government responded, in November 1943, by barring the press from meetings of the TAB, and E.N. Mylius, the Resident, accused newspaper editors of "fostering inter-racial antagonism."[73] This censorship brought a stinging rebuke from Potts-Johnson who saw in it attempts to reinforce the "deep line of demarcation" that had always separated the races. He criticised the condescension of the European officials, and called on Mylius himself to lead the way in inter-racial empathy.[74] Elite demands for reform were generally receiving short shrift, and these failings were increasingly being interpreted by the majority as reflective of a lack of will and a general incapacity in those who represented the African people. There was a growing impatience with the Saro and other elite leaders, and the latter's inability to effectively communicate their difficulty with officialdom would deepen suspicions of their collaboration with the British Raj in the exploitation of the African poor.

Potts-Johnson and National Politics: The Legislative Council and the Eastern House of Representatives

The Saro residents of Port Harcourt had followed the activities of the Legislative Council with some interest over the years, since Calabar's admission into that body in the 1920's. The tenure of S. Bankole Rhodes, the Saro's compatriot of the neighbouring Aba, in that body had also sustained this fascination over time. As discussion of expanded African political representation progressed during World War II, it was, perhaps, inevitable that the Legislative Council would feature prominently in the debates.

In the early months of 1943, Saro circles were agog with excitement over the rumour that Potts-Johnson was being considered as the successor to S.B. Rhodes in the Legislative Council. Often described as "a strong link between black and white", many regarded Potts-Johnson as ideally suited to represent the Rivers Division.[75] The name of I.B. Johnson was also making the rounds, and, inevitably, the two Saro leaders were now being compared publicly, in indigene and Saro circles, as to their suitability for the exalted office. The Nigerian Eastern Mail, which saw Dr. Ajibade also as a contender, had this to say, and we cite the comment *in extenso*:

"Although there is nothing in particular against Mr. I.B. Johnson, no one seems to favour his candidature. It is said that he has not in the past evinced any particular interest in the affairs of Port Harcourt. The sufferings of the people . . . do not seem to interest him one bit. In the [TAB] where he has held his seat longer than anyone else, he has not shown any desire to watch the interests of the people, and above all, he is not so easily accessible. On the other hand, . . . Johnson is *persona grata* in official circles, where he is held in high esteem. He has recently donated £1500 to the government, free of interest, and this fact together with his friendship with . . . Mylius, Resident, Owerri Province, seems to mark him out as the likely government nominee. If he is nominated by the government, it is said that he would be representing officialdom and not [the] Port Harcourt community. . . . The Rev. . . . Potts-Johnson, if elections were to take place would score the highest votes. He has always shown very keen interest in the affairs of Port Harcourt; he is easily accessible, and any poor man or woman can see him at any time. He is always ready to help those in distress, and if satisfied that the cause is a just one, he is always prepared to take up the people's case. His popularity . . . is testified to by the fact that he is the chairman for almost every important function, social or political. He is a valuable member of the [TAB],. and chairman of the . . . [ACL]. He is the President of the Sierra Leone Union, and the President and organiser of the Win-the-War fund committee . . . On the other hand, he appears to be *persona non grata* . . . with the Resident, . . .

Mylius, on account of his activities against Mr. Palmer, the unpopular Local Authority. So far as is known, there is nothing against him officially, and his movements against . . . Palmer should not be allowed to overshadow the commendable help he has rendered . . . between the government and the governed".[76]

Comments such as this from the indigene-owned press, would throw Potts-Johnson's contributions into sharper relief, introduce some unease into an otherwise unified Saro leadership, and inspire much political ambition in the ranks of those who regarded themselves as being marginalised by immigrant elite dominance of the political process. The repercussions were to be far-reaching, and indigenes were beginning to organise politically to challenge for control of local structures.

In December 1943, a Rivers Division People's League (RDPL) was formed. Its aim was political aggregation, and it advertised the following objectives: "To work towards a common understanding among all the peoples of the Rivers Division, wherever they may be, who have natural affinity, common problems, identical cultures, and mutual sympathies, with the ultimate aim of being placed in one Administrative Division as soon as practicable".[77] The emphasis on peoples of "identical cultures" was no fortuition, and it held out little promise of Saro incorporation. The League held its inaugural meeting at the Enitonna High School, with over a thousand present, among them a wide assemblage of the indigenous elite.[78] This was a sign of things to come, for Saro dominance of the political process had engendered a growing cynicism, and members of the indigenous elite were beginning to respond to this by progressively distancing themselves from the politically unpopular strangers, tainted allies who now had to be cast off.

The replacement of S.B. Rhodes in the Legislative Council became a matter of much debate in the township in the opening months of 1944. Saro and other leaders were eager to know the government's position on the issue, at a time when indigenous political forces were massing to assert their interests. The Nigerian Observer framed the matter thus: "Will Port Harcourt be represented in the Legislative Council or not? If not, why not? If so, how soon? Is it going to be representation by election or . . . by nomination. If Port Harcourt's vested interests could be represented, why should the community itself be ignored?"[79] These were weighty matters, of some delicacy. They spoke to a growing impatience with colonial restrictions. But they also reflected prevailing political anxieties in the Saro leadership.

A response finally came in February 1944, with the nomination of the indigenes, Arch. E.T. Dimieari and Ernest Egbuna to the Legislative Council for a term of three years. The much-fancied Potts-Johnson had been passed over. Saro political fortunes had suffered a major official snub.[80] Much encouraged by these appointments, the Rivers Division Peoples League (RDPL), on 4th March, organised a reception in honour of Dimieari's elevation. As President of the ACL, Potts-Johnson addressed the gathering, and he "stressed the oneness of the people's ambition, aspirations, and problems". He again appealed for unity, and the "eradication and obliteration of the tendency to tribal discrimination".[81] The disappointment of the Saro over this outcome could not, however, be disguised. The British had chosen indigenes over the more politically celebrated Saro emigre. A Saro community that was profoundly lacking in introspection did not, however, regard this development as a harbinger of their impending political marginalisation. Like the Freetown Krio in similar circumstances, the Port Harcourt Saro believed that they could control the political stakes in the future, their vulnerability as strangers notwithstanding. Britain's ambivalent conduct in playing off immigrants against indigenes as suited its purpose in these years, clearly encouraged this disillusion.

As the second world war drew to a close, Potts-Johnson and the executive of the African Community League (ACL) addressed the subject of future constitutional change in Nigeria. At a public meeting attended by representatives of all the major ethnic groups in the township, in April 1945, the ACL petitioned the Secretary of State for the Colonies directly. It condemned the proposed Richards constitution for Nigeria, in forthright terms:

"This meeting is of the definite opinion that a Legislative Council, to to meet the present day needs must consist of a number of members elected by a popular ballot to represent the people throughout the country, and that the present qualifications which make voting the privilege of a favoured few be scrapped so that voting may become the right of the common man in Nigeria . . . [in] triumph over dictatorship, oligarchy and all other forms of repression of the many by the privileged few . . . ".[82]

Port Harcourt shared the revulsion of Nnamdi Azikiwe and the NCNC, and its educated elite was eager to see Africans assuming greater political responsibility for the conduct of the affairs of the territory. Azikiwe (destined to become Nigeria's first President at political independence from Britain in 1960), was no stranger to Potts-Johnson. He had been one of his pupils when he taught at the Wesleyan Boys High School, Lagos.[83] Their acquaintance had since been renewed with Azikiwe's return from his studies in the United States. In June 1946, the ACL held a reception, at the Roxy, in honour of a delegation of the NCNC. Potts-Johnson chaired the occasion. In his speech, he commended the programme of the party, noting that Edward Blyden would himself have endorsed their efforts at African unity and the recognition of talent, had he been alive. The secretary of the NCNC, which had a large Igbo following, addressed the gathering on the 137 organisations that constituted the party. Azikiwe, the "acting President of the delegation", used the occasion to condemn the aforementioned Richards constitution for Nigeria. He excoriated the "various anomalies . . . in the Land acquisition and Minerals Bill ordinances", dismissing them as undemocratic and "contrary to the principles of trusteeship". Another NCNC stalwart, Nwafor Orizu, also spoke at the function.[84] We do not know if Potts-Johnson ever became a member of the NCNC. His presence at this reception, and the support he gave to the party's program, however, indicate some willingness to participate at the level of national politics. Potts-Johnson never regarded his immigrant status as a disqualification for political involvement of any sort. If anything, he seems to have considered himself one of the best prepared for these endeavors, a matter in which he yielded pride of place to no one.

An editorial of the Nigerian Observer attempted to crystallise Potts-Johnson's thoughts on national politics in September 1946. Under the evocative title, "What Does Nigeria Want?", Potts-Johnson condemned oppression, exploitation, and discrimination. While commending the British for their efforts in Nigeria, he stressed the unequal nature of the colonial relationship, as seen in the inordinate economic contributions the colony had made to the British exchequer. In an unequivocal note, he opined: "Just now Nigeria is a subject race. But she should not be a subject race for a longer time than is necessary or consistent with honest intentions". He called for freedom of trade, and the lifting of import and export restrictions that frustrated trade with countries outside the British Empire. He described the existing European cartels as "the commercial vampire" that preys on Nigeria's "economic lifeblood", and, therefore, had to be destroyed.[85] Potts-Johnson's old mantra of economic nationalism was now skirting the more decidedly political borders of de-colonisation. Port Harcourt had joined the nationalist bandwagon, and the local Saro elite still believed it could make a contribution to the debate, and even secure a place at the settlement.

Potts-Johnson did not limit himself to irreverent entrepreneurial pronouncements, nor was his vision of Nigeria's future confined to British options exclusively. He called for more scholarship awards for the African community, "to be tenable in places other than Great Britain", and derided the substance and the object of past bursary awards, which had generally offered training in the more mundane areas of experience. He demanded "scholarships not for six months spent in England for the acquisition of the knowledge of the correct way to lace a shoe or spend money. We want scholarships . . . to places like America, Russia, France, Switzerland, and Germany". He called for awards that would produce more "lawyers, doctors, mining engineers, manufacturing chemists, and mechanical and electrical experts". Citing the "obnoxious ordinances", Potts-Johnson condemned metropolitan exploitation of Nigeria's minerals, a matter that demoralised the African population; he denounced the payment of "mineral royalties to persons who are in no way natives of the country". In unequivocal tones, he concluded: "Nigeria wants her colonial status abolished".[86] By the end of 1946, the NCNC had established a branch in Port Harcourt. The Zikist movement of youthful NCNC associates, had also found a local presence in the township, with John Umolu, a local Edo storekeeper, as its leader.[87] The Zikists were opposed to the local political dominance of the wealthy African patricians, and this would make for uneasy class relations in the years ahead. It was, perhaps, a measure of Potts-Johnson's political sagacity that he managed to maintain a close working relationship with the Zikist's and the youth generally, even presiding at some of their rallies.[88] His ability to cross generational lines, and identify with those of other social classes was truly remarkable.

Though obviously disappointed in his Legislative Council ambitions, Potts-Johnson was to fare better in the stakes for the Eastern House of Representatives. In December 1946, the Saro received, with pride, the news of his nomination, by the government, to the Eastern Assembly. His brief was "to represent the Urban aspect of life in Port Harcourt".[89] The unofficial leader of the Saro now had yet another platform from which to proclaim his increasingly controversial views and varied concerns. Potts-Johnson was obviously delighted at this recognition, and he was warmly applauded by the ACL when that body received the joyful news.[90] The Eastern Nigerian Guardian extolled the virtues of the "popular reverend gentlemen", recounting his activities as "religious preacher, principal and founder of the self-supporting, non-secretarian secondary school, President of the Community League, Chairman of the Win-the-War Fund Committee . . . and local Secretary of Cambridge University". It admonished Potts-Johnson on the "sacred responsibility" of representing Port Harcourt, and counselled that "the welfare of the greatest majority" should be both provided and protected. Over-concentration on issues pertaining to the African elite would be a breach of faith. Potts-Johnson was urged to persist in his opposition to the proposed Richards constitution, and enjoined to support the programme of the NCNC.[91]

In January 1947, Potts-Johnson delivered his maiden speech at the Eastern House. As would be expected, this was a wide-ranging presentation, in which he attempted to identify the principal issues that faced the residents of Port Harcourt. He stressed the township's uniqueness, being an autonomous creation, free of provincial leanings, and unencumbered of specific ethnic affiliation. He saw Port Harcourt as destined to lead the Eastern Province, and speculated, with eager anticipation, on the day when the township would boast as many as four representatives in the Legislative Council. He spoke proudly of Port Harcourt's financial contributions to the war effort, and opined, in conclusion, that the township, "a little child," shall lead the rest of the eastern region.[92]

He developed these issues at greater length in August 1947. Potts-Johnson called for the up-grading of Port Harcourt to a first class township, a matter he claimed to have reviewed previously with the government's Financial Secretary in Lagos, and confessed to disappointment and frustration "over the tardy and dilatory way in which the affairs of Port Harcourt" were being handled. He demanded greater despatch to enable the township's leaders to convene mass meetings where details of the transition could be reviewed with the people. He also requested greater official promotion of agriculture, and highlighted the Nigerian Agriculture and Fishing Company which had been formed at Okrika, and of which he was a shareholder. This company had excited much local interest, and Okrika Chiefs had willingly supplied it "communal land". The Company's requests for technical advice from the Director of Agriculture and his department had, however, gone unanswered. Overtures to the Fisheries department had been similarly unsuccessful. Potts-Johnson saw this indifference of the government to African initiatives as partly the cause of apathy in the youth of Port Harcourt. He spoke of a role also for local companies and firms in agricultural expansion, and issued the following challenge to them: "The firms and trading houses who get out motor cars, motor lorries, guns, and gun powder could be induced to get us also ploughs and tractors, and other mechanical instruments".[93]

Potts-Johnson demanded a greater efficiency of the postal services. He noted the poor performance of some postal workers and reported to the House his findings on investigating their work schedule: "Upon enquiry, I was made to understand that it was mainly due to shortage of staff, and also to employment of some ex-servicemen who have not proved to be so efficient in the work as they might have been". Potts-Johnson complained of mail routinely mis-directed to his home, and of telegrams that never got delivered in the expected 24 hours.[94] In his final speech for 1947 before the Eastern House, Potts-Johnson would return to the subject of the municipality. He expressed his joy at the prospect of Port Harcourt becoming only the second township in Nigeria to enjoy municipal status, and called for "a fat grant" from the government to bring meaning to this historic transition. The representative for Port Harcourt also called for additional revenues for road and drainage construction, if the vision of Port Harcourt as "a big garden city" was to be realised, and her dominance over Enugu affirmed! He requested that the government should provide a Community Centre for Port Harcourt at the earliest opportunity. On trade, he demanded that barriers introduced during the war on transactions between northern and southern Nigeria be lifted, and called for the free circulation in the south of the groundnut oil and potatoes of the north, and the reverse flow to the north of the South's palm oil and garri produce.[95]

In a reference to employment conditions, Potts-Johnson recommended that Africans in the service of the township should enjoy the same facilities as civil servants, particularly in matters of leave arrangements, and salary levels. He deplored the government's delay in responding to worker's petitions on these subjects. Finally, he requested grants-in-aid for private schools, such as his Enitonna High School, which were forced to operate solely on fees paid by the pupils. On this, he noted: "We, as private school proprietors, are doing all we can . . . to help our people; we are doing all we can to satisfy the growing thirst for education . . . and I think and firmly believe that we deserve every encouragement and sympathy from the government".[96]

Potts-Johnson's views on the timing of Nigerian independence had not, however, undergone much change by December 1948.[97] He still regarded independence as a very distant objective, and was content with a power-sharing arrangement in the interim. In an address to the Eastern House, he noted: "Why fight for self government when it is already here . . . If those who died 15 years ago could come back and see things as they are today with Africans in the positions they now hold, they would gasp with wonder". Those remarks were strikingly reminiscent of the Potts-Johnson of January 1932, who had cautioned the Indian leader, Mohandas Gandhi, against political action that could lead to his incarceration.[98] In the political conservatism of the closing years of his public life, Potts-Johnson would invest municipal status for Port Harcourt with far more political significance than it really justified. A believer in the politics of incrementalism, he came to see revolutionary political struggle as inherently disruptive, and subversive of desired objectives. In this speech before the House, he told his colleagues: "If we fight, we will only retard the day [of liberation], and that is also the opinion of the Port Harcourt people".[99] This may well have been the position of Port Harcourt's African elite. The township's lower classes, however, may not have been as persuaded. Potts-Johnson elaborated on this theme when he reviewed the impending elevation of Port Harcourt. Speaking on self-government, he declared: "Some give a time limit of 15 years . . . some ten, some five, and some even say now. . . . Well, I say that Port Harcourt is having self government on January 1, 1949, and we shall not disappoint our onlookers".[100] Potts-Johnson's reassuring political cadences may well have brought some comfort to officialdom. They, however, did not capture the temper of the popular will in Port Harcourt, as future events were to indicate.

Potts-Johnson in Other Developments of the 1940's

While playing a leading role in African political representation in Port Harcourt in the 1940's, Potts-Johnson was also involved in a wide range of other activities. He remained active in his business ventures, and devoted much time to providing adequate housing for his employees.[101] He supported efforts to keep the public apprised of national developments through the provision of public loudspeakers which relayed the daily news bulletins at the local King George V Jubilee Park.[102] By April 1947, he was on the township's Library Committee, and he had also taken on himself the role of clarifying publicly local rumour on various issues that could further undermine relations between the government and the African community. When, for instance, the Public Works Department was accused, in May 1947, of the mis-use of £20,000 of tax payer's funds, Potts-Johnson investigated the allegation. He reported that the amount involved was more in the region of £3,750, expended on three buildings, but he condemned the wastage nonetheless.[103] Potts-Johnson had also become a mediator of local ethnic conflicts. When a dispute pitted local Igbo fishermen against their Kalabari competition, in August 1947, it was Potts-Johnson that was invited by the two sides to arbitrate. He is reported to have settled the disagreements (of which we have no details) amicably.[104] Potts-Johnson also participated actively in the campaign to introduce cinema shows on Sunday to Port Harcourt, a move much opposed by the church.[105]

   It came as no great surprise, therefore, when in the New Year's Honours list for 1949, released by Buckingham Palace, the Rev. L.R. Potts-Johnson was awarded the MBE for meritorious service to Port Harcourt and Nigeria.

This brought great joy to the Saro community, and the honour was warmly received by Port Harcourt's elite. It was seen as "a richly deserved recognition" of which the entire population of the township could be justly proud.[106] The Governor, Sir John Macpherson, and the Chief Commissioner, Pyke-Nott, sent their congratulations, and Potts-Johnson's life and contribution were much remarked in the local press. A lot was said of his pioneering efforts in education, journalism, and the press, political organisation, war relief, public librarianship, and prison work, among others.[107] The African Community League (ACL) celebrated Potts-Johnson's achievement at a grand reception, and he was toasted as "champion, leader, and architect of several measures" that had transformed Port Harcourt. In his response, Potts-Johnson humourously described his MBE as signifying "More Battles to be Encountered", and he paid generous tribute to his wife, Eniton: "It is true", he remarked, "that without her active cooperation and assistance, I would not have been what I am today. For the last 33 years, we have been struggling together, and she has proved to be a very valuable partner . . . loyal, true, devoted, and affectionate . . . ".[108]

The Saro community and their friends also marked the award of the MBE to Potts-Johnson. At the Roxy, in February 1949, they organised a reception in his honour and composed a song, "What say you about Potts-Johnson" for the occasion. The programme featured choruses and songs by the Kallays, violin scores, and a congratulatory address read by C.U.M. Gardner, and presented by Mrs. Effusion Johnson. The Resident was in attendance, and he spoke glowingly of the honoree.[109]

Indigenes React to the Political Prominence of the Saro

Potts-Johnson's far-flung activities did not delight some of Port Harcourt's indigenous Igbo and Ijaw residents, and we must review the mounting opposition to his political dominance of township life in the 1940's. Although the Saro were aware of some resentment in the indigenous ranks even before the war,[110] by March 1944, disapproval was being voiced more publicly. In an anonymous letter to the Eastern Nigerian Guardian, Potts-Johnson was accused of failing to effectively represent the African viewpoint at a recent appearance before the Elliott Commission on Higher Education. His performance was characterised as lacklustre, and unbecoming of the people's representative. Obviously unaccustomed to such close scrutiny from within the African community, Potts-Johnson countered that he had only been interviewed privately, and, unlike Dr. Ajibade (who addressed the commission), was not allowed to formally appear before the body. He tried to deflect the charge by appealing for greater African unity in Port Harcourt, and presented this as a pre-requisite of self government. Uncharacteristically, however, he also threatened to sue the writer for damages of £500.[111] This was uncommon sensitivity for the usually large-hearted and tolerant Potts-Johnson.

The growing tendencies to subject elite performance and conduct to close review, and the demands for greater accountability that were proceeding from the lower echelons of the African community, were not entirely lost on the administration. It realised the need for greater attention to non-elite views, if it was to escape charges of partisanship. When, for instance, in August 1946, the Resident discussed the possibility of establishing a Planning Authority to oversee the infrastructural development of a post-war Port Harcourt, he underlined the need to look beyond the "gentlemen of independent means" in constituting the body. An indigene, S.D. Akambo, 2nd class clerk of the Public Works Department, was called upon to serve and represent the "viewpoint of the salaried working classes."[112] Such moves would not, however, easily mollify some sections of local opinion, nor would the re-naming of local streets to celebrate indigenous heroes of the African people arrest the growing unease amongst the disaffected.[113]

By March 1948, Potts-Johnson was in another public controversy over remarks he had previously made in the Eastern House about inefficient ex-servicemen in the postal department.[114] The predominantly indigene-based Ex-Servicemen's Union took umbrage at his views, passed a vote of no-confidence on him, and accused him of tactlessness and provocative conduct. In another unprecedented rebuttal, Pots-Johnson defended his position in both the Nigerian Eastern Mail and the Nigerian Observer, and he demanded a suitable and prompt apology from the Union.[115] There is no record of such an apology being tendered by these veterans of World War II who were, in this instance, perhaps, reflecting some of the heightened political consciousness that came of war experience.[116]

This incident was of minor significance, however, when compared with that which unfolded later in June 1948. Potts-Johnson was again the principal target. In a letter to the Eastern Nigerian Guardian, E.N. Godswille-Hart (brother of N.D. Godswille Hart, President of the House Tenants Union)[117], an indigene, raised fundamental questions of a very disturbing nature. He demanded the immediate convening of the ACL for the purpose of electing a new executive, and described most of the current members of the ACL's executive as "Yes men", who were of the "old brigade", and were generally "foreign" and "little-minded". He inveighed against what he regarded as an autocratic atmosphere at ACL meetings, stating that "progressive Nigerians" would have no truck with such dictatorship. On the highly emotive subject of township rents, he queried: "What have the officers . . . done to come to the aid of the tenants who have been bled white by the commercial house owners? . . . what have they done to see to it that the streets and roads . . . are macadamised? What steps have they taken to see to it that more fly-proof meat stalls are provided . . . " He called Potts-Johnson a "would-be Life president" of the ACL, and accused him and his officers of an inability "to bring about practical unity among the various tribes . . . ". In conclusion, he demanded: "The idea of Life President and officers must be scrapped immediately . . . autocratic officers must step down . . . ".[118] This was a major challenge of African elite claims to represent the community, but it indicated even more fundamentally the revulsion for the Saro stranger leadership that existed in some local quarters. Port Harcourt was now experiencing a political exuberance and an irreverence, the likes of which it had never known before. The indigenous resurgence was clearly on the move—the days of Saro dominance was now truly numbered.

As often happened on these occasions, it was an official of the government who sought publicly to restore Potts-Johnson's battered dignity. When Sir Frederick Bernard Carr, Chief Commissioner, Eastern Provinces, proceeded on retirement, in September 1948, the ACL organised a reception in his honour. Carr used the occasion to salute Potts-Johnson's contributions to the growth of Port Harcourt. He commended his pluck in the Eastern House debates on the township's political future, and praised his dedicated service as the people's representative.[119] Official support of this type for the beleaguered Saro leader would not, however, silence the critics completely. In January 1949, N.D. Godswille-Hart, the local leader of the House Tenants Union (HTU) went on the offensive in a renewed attack on the Saro patricians. He denounced I.B. Johnson for too long a tenure on the Township Advisory Board (TAB), and described him as "non-political-minded". (sic.). Godswille-Hart claimed to have "not the slightest grudge against . . . Potts-Johnson". He in fact commended Potts-Johnson's entrepreneurial contributions to Port Harcourt, comparing them to those of the NCNC leader, Nnamdi Azikiwe. He praised Potts-Johnson's efforts in providing employment for over 20 local residents since May 1932. Godswille-Hart, however, demanded to know why the ACL had held no elections in 1947. Pointedly, he asked: "Who is responsible for it? Who is the Hitleric (sic.) director behind the screen? Is Rev. L.R. Potts-Johnson Life President of the League?"[120]

He criticised Potts-Johnson for his unwillingness to serve as a patron of the House Tenants Union, an invitation to which position he never answered. This was obviously a snub from the patrician that had rankled deeply in non-elite circles, and it reflected Potts-Johnson's own contradictions, as well as the widening chasm between the social classes in an increasingly politicised Port Harcourt. In a direct challenge to the other members of the ACL whom he obviously considered weak and indecisive, Godswille-Hart demanded that he be contradicted publicly if any of the members of the League were in disagreement with his views. While conceding that "the ten-year long President" would continue to be "a notable humourist", he wondered whether this gift for mirth justified his protracted tenure. Without equivocation, he queried: "Is Rev . . . Potts-Johnson, the would-be Life President of the . . . League indispensable? Why then have the representatives of the various tribes . . . allowed dictatorship and autocracy to reign supreme in the League in these days when the cry for democracy is loudest? If . . . Potts-Johnson made the final exit into the great beyond, will the . . . League be dissolved?" In an obvious reference to the recent MBE award, Godswille-Hart condemned "all West Africans who [were] foreign title minded", and called for them to be "ostracised in all respects". He dismissed such individuals as having "not the slightest economic and social interest of Nigeria at heart . . . ", and called on the ACL to organise emergency elections immediately, stressing that it was time "a new President was elected".[121] Port Harcourt's stranger community of the Saro was clearly being served notice in this confrontation of the strong antipathy its leaders provoked in some indigenous quarters. Their seeming divorce from the mundane concerns of the township's embattled tenants was being underscored, and, implicitly, their material comfort and political dominance impugned by restive elements that had found their voice in the aftermath of war. The public criticism of I.B. Johnson and Potts-Johnson, their leaders, left the Saro disconsolate and much traumatised.[122] Increasingly, conversation would now turn around strategies for group survival in an increasingly inhospitable environment. Some comfort, however, came from the public defence of Potts-Johnson mounted by the other ACL leaders in February 1949. At a League reception to celebrate his MBE, the congratulatory address noted, *inter alia*: "The Presidentship (sic.) of the League is an enviable position, and you have won the election for 10 years under the supreme policy of popular ballot, and that noble success in itself . . . is strong evidence of your efficiency of character to satisfy the wishes of the people whom you serve".[123] Yet again, the elite had closed ranks to defend its own. This would not, however, deflect the opprobrium born of deep resentment of stranger gains and successes in this Niger delta township.

End of World War II, Municipal Status, and the Death of Potts-Johnson

Port Harcourt was in a jubilant mood in May 1945 when Nazi Germany surrendered. Potts-Johnson celebrated VE day in an editorial in which he recounted the blessings of membership of the British Commonwealth, and demanded "united mass bombing" to "obliterate Japan . . . from the face of the earth".[124] In October 1945, Port Harcourt held its victory parade, with Potts-Johnson and his compatriot, D. Atanda Pratt, welcoming local officials to the celebrations. Certificates of Honour, and medals, were awarded to deserving recipients, and a fund was launched to raise £3000 for the construction of a local community hall.[125]

With the end of the war, local thoughts turned quickly to the subject of Port Harcourt's elevation from a second-class township to a municipality, like Lagos. Local officials came under renewed pressure to effect the change, and some interpreted these demands for the greater devolution of authority as elite desire for greater access to taxpayers' funds, inspired by ulterior motives. With studied paternalism, the administration, at the end of 1945, commended the contributions of the township's more "detribalised" African leaders, "the more intelligent members of the community", and expressed the hope that, with continued tutelage, they would increasingly realise their potential as future leaders.[126] By August 1946, the Resident of the Owerri Province, appeared himself to have been persuaded that Port Harcourt's 34,000 residents deserved municipal status, not least for the township's prominence as a major commercial nerve centre in the Eastern Province.[127] Although first-class township status would mean higher taxation, an issue of some concern, for a time, for both the Igbo Federal Union and the Plotholders Union, Potts-Johnson, Dr. Ajibade and other TAB leaders, by September 1947, had persuaded many of the need for some sacrifice as the community progressed.[128]

It was Potts-Johnson that tabled the formal motion on the municipality in October 1947 at a meeting of the Township Advisory Board. The motion passed the Board unanimously.[129] By January 1949, these discussions were far advanced, and outstanding issues of expanded taxation[130] had been generally resolved as plans for Town Council elections were taken in hand. Voters Information Bureaux were set up by the administration, and individuals drawn largely from the African elite were appointed to them, and charged with preparing the electorate on voting procedure. Potts-Johnson was assigned to the "B" ward, alongside the indigene and fellow Creek Road resident, C.E. J. Egi.[131] When the TAB discussed the design for a township seal, Potts-Johnson recommended one portraying a man, a ship and a palm tree.[132]

In May 1949, Potts-Johnson, acting on the advice of his doctors, left Port Harcourt on a short vacation. Although he had not visited Sierra Leone in over two decades, he now headed for Freetown, via Lagos and Takoradi. We know nothing of his activities in Sierra Leone, but he was back in Port Harcourt after only a brief absence. Though not in good health, he promptly joined a party of the unofficial members of the Eastern House of Assembly, who were then on a tour of the Eastern Province, to collect data on proposed local government reforms.[133] As the elections approached, in June 1949, Potts-Johnson broadcast a message on the local radio to the people of Port Harcourt. He urged them to vote wisely so as to provide the township with a Council of "intelligent men and women of sound commonsense", who could be counted upon to make the necessary "sacrifices for the good of their country". He called for leaders of integrity, who would eschew bribery and corruption. He also referred to his failure to qualify as a candidate for the "B" Ward in the impending elections. He had had to withdraw his candidacy "for some technical reasons", which he did not elaborate. He urged the electorate in a final plea: "When the day for the election comes, nobody will be more zealous than I in trying to see that the right men are chosen to fill their right places. . . . may we . . . make this venture a great success, and bring great credit to this our enviable town of Port Harcourt".[134]

Election day brought success to the Zikist movement. The published results were as follows:

The Zikists	7 seats
The Nigerian Republic Party	6 seats
The Port Harcourt Secret Society	5 seats

The following individuals were now sworn in as the new Councilors of a township about to be up-graded to first class status: V.K. Onyeri, M.D. Okechukwu, Chief M.I. Asinobi, A.O. Akuwuike, C.U. Dibia, G.C. Nnonyelu, B.L., B.O.N. Eluwah, S. Macebuh, Mrs. E. Adeshigbin, P. Okirigwe, and R. Madueme. No Saro made it into the new Council. The political rout of the immigrants was now complete at the level of popular representation.

Potts-Johnson would not witness the inauguration of Port Harcourt's new council. As already indicated, he had been in failing health for some time, and his itinerary had been much curtailed in the early months of 1949 on the orders of his doctors. On the 17 June, 1949, it was reported that the Rev. L.R. Potts-Johnson had died at his Creek Road residence, at about 9:00 p.m. He was only 62. The news stunned the Saro, and Port Harcourt was plunged into a period of mourning. Tributes came from various sources, for, though an immigrant stranger, Potts-Johnson had touched the lives of many, and his efforts had not been limited to those of his social class or his immediate community. The Eastern Nigerian Guardian recounted the many highlights of Potts-Johnson's life. The paper celebrated his contributions in the fields of education, the press, the leather-tanning industry, and in agriculture. It referred to Potts-Johnson's diligence in matters of religion, where he was "devout, earnest, and zealous", even after his resignation from the active ministry. It described him as "the main live wire" in civic matters, and one who "lived for Port Harcourt and . . . died for Port Harcourt". It quoted a statement Potts-Johnson had made recently in which he had said the following about himself: "It has always been my principle in life that wherever I live, I should create a definite impression, and leave a definite mark behind, which, when others see, would know that Potts-Johnson had lived there". This, the paper thought, summed up his glowing contribution to the township's progress.[135] Ironically, Potts-Johnson had died on the eve of the declaration of Port Harcourt as a municipality and a First Class Township, issues he had long pursued. Commentators described him as a Moses "who saw the promised land but did not set his foot on it".[136]

R.K. Floyer, President of the Port Harcourt Town Council, paid generous tribute to the late Potts-Johnson. He referred to the experience of working with him for ten years, and saluted his knack for chairing meetings and public functions. He had found Potts-Johnson's leadership skills particularly invaluable in the following situations: "When there were a lot of people . . . all wanting to do much the same thing, but all wanting to do it in different ways, of finding some compromise, or some turn of words to which everyone could in the end agree, so that the matter went forward, and did not remain as such in a mass of argument". Floyer considered Potts-Johnson "one of the few real Port Harcourt men".[137]

Charles Ndaguba, an indigene, in his tribute on radio, described Potts-Johnson as a personal friend, who "overworked himself and allowed death to snatch away his life before his time".[138] Letters of condolence were addressed to Mrs. Potts-Johnson by the Resident, L.T. Chubb, and by other leading officials of the government, among them R.K. Floyer, Paris Jones, R. Bushell, and G.M. Rushmore. The Igbo Union also wrote to express its shock and regret. Telegrams came from the Chief Commissioner, Eastern Provinces, and from the Resident of Calabar, Mr. Mayne. Many Saro, in Port Harcourt, and beyond, sent their condolences in telegrams, as did a number of prominent indigenes. In his letter to Mrs. N.E. Potts-Johnson, submitted on his behalf by the Resident, Rivers Province, the Acting Governor consoled the widow with the thought that Potts-Johnson had "had the satisfaction of seeing his efforts towards the recognition of Port Harcourt as a municipality crowned with success".[139]

News of Potts-Johnson's death came as a surprise to most residents of the township. It was reported that "people stood dazed at the calamity that had befallen (sic.), and others doubted the news for many had not known that he . . . had been ill". Observers noted that "weeping was everywhere evident".[140] The corpse was laid out at the schoolroom of the EHS, and it was reported that thousands filed past to pay their last respects. Before the funeral service, the Freemasons cleared the hall, and performed "the secret rites" of their fraternity, under the direction of the Master of the Lodge, A. Adesigbin, who would also later officiate at the graveside. The funeral service was at Wesley church, and a detachment of the Boys Brigade under Lieutenant J. Osho and Sergeant E.O. Adeyemi, was on hand to receive the coffin. Members of the Okrika Lodge, led by the Saro, Banke Johnson, with sword in hand, and George Spiff, the Standard bearer, formed a guard of honour. Rev. P. Kingston, Chairman of the Methodist Church, Eastern Provinces, conducted the service, assisted by Rev. B.C.U. Onubogu of the St. Peter's CMS Church. In his address, Kingston reviewed Potts-Johnson's contributions to the church before his resignation, and saluted his dedication.[141] Among officials at the service were L.T. Chubb, the Resident, R.K. Floyer, G.M. Rushmore (Town Clerk), C.H. Brown (Development Officer), R. Gibson (Sub-Treasurer), and M.K. Millet (Superintendent of Police). Potts-Johnson's former pupil, and now the leader of the NCNC, Nnamdi Azikiwe, was also present.[142]

Pupils and alumni of the Enitonna High School (EHS), also mourned their founder and principal. The Headmaster, Mr. Inyang, conducted religious devotions at the school on 20th June, with the singing of hymns, and a five-minute period of silence. The school was then closed for a week in Potts-Johnson's memory. In his tribute, R.E. Ezekiel Hart, an alumnus of the EHS, recounted his late Principal's dedication, charity, and compassion: He wrote: "He cared for each student alike no matter the parentage, and was a symbol to both students and tutors. That all hands are not equal, he knew, and throughout, he tempered his regulations with mercy. For though the normal time [for] expelling debtor students was a week, he would extend it four-fold to allow the poor ones [to] make up their differences (sic.)". Hart emphasised Potts-Johnson's approachability, and his willingness to assist those in need. In conclusion, he observed: "He has fought like a hero, and inspite of his shortcomings, and who has none, he has done such things that all who knew him should be proud . . . ".[143]

In its memorial to its proprietor and founding editor, "the second oldest newspaper in Nigeria", [144] the Nigerian Observer, celebrated Potts-Johnson's "ideal of service", and his penchant for public duty. Now under the Saro, J.C. Roberts, the paper took pride in Potts-Johnson's many contributions, and declared proudly: "His name will remain indelible in the minds of many . . . . In religion, in politics, in education, he contributed much. He was a man—when comes such another".[145]

Memorial services for Potts-Johnson were later held at Banham Memorial Church, with Rev. Babington Johnson delivering the address. After the service, Potts-Johnson's Saro heirs and other mourners, went in procession to the cemetery, where, as was the custom, Babington Johnson delivered a grave-side tribute. The party then left for the Potts-Johnson home, where the usual refreshments were served, and rites observed.[146]

In July 1949, the congregation of the A.M.E. Zion Church held a memorial service for the late Potts-Johnson. Among the mourners was Miss Caroline Mary Johnson, sister of the deceased, who had learned of his death while at Takoradi, en route to Port Harcourt. Several tributes were delivered by the Saro, and their associates in the indigenous population. Among the speakers were several local dignitaries—the Rev. Theo Aderin, Messrs. J.A. Okoro, N.A. Dublin Green, I. Warrior Osika, Councillor S. Mac Ebuh, Dr. O. Ajibade, A.C. Nwapa, J.C. Roberts, and Rev. M.U. Harry.[147] Potts-Johnson's death brought a significant chapter of Port Harcourt's evolution to a close. The Saro had lost their unofficial leader, but many an indigene would also miss Potts-Johnson's advocacy of diverse causes pertaining to the interests of the poorer sections of the society. The Saro were now clearly at their most vulnerable as strangers in a Port Harcourt increasingly given to nationalist pursuits. No one among Potts-Johnson's Saro heirs seemed capable at this time of the dogged persistence, irreverence, wit, and good humour that he had demonstrated so consistently over the years. Measures to secure immigrant group interests would progressively dominate Sierra Leone Union activity in the coming years. Many new challenges now awaited the once confident emigre society, and it would need to be at its most resourceful as political independence approached.

5

THE GATHERING CLOUDS:
INDEPENDENCE, THE CIVIL WAR,
AND ITS AFTERMATH, 1950—75

With the death of Potts-Johnson, his Saro heirs in Port Harcourt lost their prominence on the political stage, and their lives came to be increasingly dominated by issues of group survival as Nigeria moved toward political independence, with a growing xenophobia directed at resident strangers in some quarters. In scenes reminiscent of Herbert Macaulay's retreat before Youth Movement forces in Yorubaland, and foreshadowing the much later Krio capitulation before overwhelming indigenous forces in the Sierra Leone of 1961, the Port Harcourt Saro bowed to the compelling logic of their demographic incapacity as they left the centre stage of local political activism, resorting only periodically to such political overtures as seemed likely to protect the community's interests. As the territory approached political independence in 1960, no local Saro resident would feature prominently in the party-political stakes that were played out in the township. The stage was mostly dominated by the Igbo, and their Ijaw associates. The most immediate challenge that the Saro now faced was one of nationality. The first generation of Saro residents was dying out, and at a relatively young age, and their progeny, the majority of whom had never been to Sierra Leone, would now have to carve a niche for themselves within the coming independent state, if they were not to return to the Sierra Leone from whence their parents had come. Those without local marriage ties would generally seek to hold on to a wholly Krio life-style and value system. The minority who had conjugal links in local society, attempted to retain twin cultural ties to both the Krio social formation, and the indigenous ethnic community of their affiliation. Nigerian and other non-Sierra Leonean spouses of the Saro would also be very active in the group's socio-economic orbit after 1950, and, as mediators often between the immigrant and the indigenous communities, they would play significant social roles particularly in periods of tension. A few would seek to pursue their incorporation to its logical conclusion, by volunteering for Sierra Leonean citizenship. Other Sierra Leoneans who were not of Krio stock, but had always functioned within the essentially Krio matrix of the Saro community, would continue to be a part of the social melange of the post-1950's. One thus comes to observe in these social interactions, an on-going process of the negotiation of ethnicity, in which natal ethnic roots were generally being retained, while new Krio-like identities were forged and manipulated for diverse existential purposes. The Felix Meyers, Mende husband and Efik wife, had blazed the trail in this area of social accommodation in the preceding period. A few imitators would now continue to pursue like social incorporation.

With independence, the Saro who were the progeny of Saro/indigene unions would come easily into the option of Nigerian citizenship, through the legal processes of naturalisation. The path was much more problematic for those who were wholly immigrant. Most of the first and second generation Saro of Port Harcourt would choose not to exercise the local citizenship option of pursuing naturalisation. They showed a distinct preference for retaining an immigrant status which they considered pristine, and generally opted for twin affiliations to Sierra Leone and Nigeria. Even those who became Nigerians appear to have accorded greater premium to their Sierra Leonean heritage, immersing themselves to a far greater degree in Saro cultural observance, than in those of their Nigerian option.

It is necessary at this stage to attempt a review of the circumstances of the Saro within the context of the increasing accentuation of their "stranger" status, which, with independence, becomes that of "alien" for those without Nigerian citizenship. Like a host of immigrant communities, such as the Lebanese in West Africa, the Asians of Uganda, the Chinese in Southeast Asia,[1] among others, most Saro had held on to their primordial cultural traditions while living in their adopted country. Although, inevitably, there had been some cultural borrowing into the community from local society, this had been of relatively minor significance for the vast majority of Saro. With independence, operating conditions in Port Harcourt were about to change dramatically. Various studies have shown that host communities that demonstrated remarkable tolerance of the cultural particularity of "stranger" formations under colonial rule have sometimes exhibited far less charity to such groups once independence was won. "Strangers" came swiftly to be branded as "aliens", and they have often been subject to considerable victimisation, even mass deportation, as has been the case in recent Ugandan and Ghanaian experience, to mention but two.[2]

The Saro community in Port Harcourt as constituted in the early 1950's, belongs to that category of "outsiders" of West Africa of whom Elliott Skinner has written.[3] These are African groups that had left their original home areas to reside for very long periods of time in the lands of their adopted communities. Such groups, Skinner observes, were often characterised by their frenzied pursuit of opportunity, which made some of their number far more successful than their hosts. In time, as Georg Simmel has also observed of such communities, relations between the "stranger" and his "host" come to be characterised by simultaneous elements of affinity and remoteness; the stranger is close, yet distant—he is involved in his new society and adds his peculiar attributes to it, while also appearing to be indifferent to its basic values.[4] This stranger is not, however, to be confused, Skinner argues, with the European invader of Africa, who comes, for instance, as colonist, or settler. For such immigrants, Skinner employs the term "estranger", for they had the power to direct the lives of the autochthonous society, and could even consign its members to the status of "aliens" in their own land.[5]

The Saro have been reviewed up to this point in our study in their twin relations with the African host community of Port Harcourt, and the European estranger colonial administration. The Saro elite had developed close ties with their indigenous counterparts over the years, and both groups had monopolised African political representation in colonial Port Harcourt. It was, however, the Saro fraction of this elite that generated the most revulsion in the poorer sections of the indigenous community.[6] Under colonial rule, the Saro immigrant had lived as a British subject under the estranger's protection, which accorded him many opportunities for personal economic and political development that were not generally open to most indigenes. This had created much ill-will. With independence and the departure of the estranger, this resentment of the privileged "stranger", now often "alien", would progressively dominate relations between the two communities.

Political Change

Before we review the protective arrangements to which the beleaguered Saro resorted after independence, we must assess some elements of local political change in the immediate aftermath of Potts-Johnson's death. By December 1949, G.C. Nonyelu had succeeded to Potts-Johnson's position in the Eastern House of Assembly, ushering in a new era of Igbo dominance of Port Harcourt's politics that would largely feature Owerri and Onitsha factions in fierce competition for the spoils.[7] Port Harcourt's new Town Council was, before long, a matter of much official regret and profound disappointment. Faced with the more importunate and strident claims of the aggressive nationalists who now made up the new Council, the government longed for a return to the tame and desultory politics of the I.B. Johnson era. It considered the Councillors generally incompetent, and was certain that "the best men [had] not been returned at the election". It did not disguise its longing for the next poll, in 1952, when it hoped a new crop of Councillors would replace the present set, who would then "revert to obscurity, from which they should never have emerged".[8] The rising currents of nationalist consciousness had produced in Port Harcourt a new crop of indigenous leaders who appeared to be generally contemptuous of the approved patterns of deference that had regulated African conduct in the public sphere. They wanted these dispensed with, and left government officials in no doubt of their impatience.

The government accused the new Councillors of corruption, nepotism, self gratification in plot allocations, and unnecessary fastidiousness and pedestrianism in the conduct of the township's affairs. Of this it observed: "Several of the elected members have mistaken the Port Harcourt experiment in local government for a sample of self-government, and the tendency has been to regard the Council as a supreme authority unfettered in matters appertaining to Port Harcourt and its finances by any superior authority".[9] Some Councillors were denounced for resorting to "anonymous or pseudonymous contributions to the principal daily organ in order to grind their private axes", while others were excoriated for being "unduly sensitive to press criticism of their first acts as public figures". In summing up their disappointment, in 1950, government officials noted:

> " . . . it must be confessed that municipal government has not been a great success. It has been a disappointment to its officers and to the man in the street. Unfortunately, the Ordinance makes no provision for the annual retirement of one third of the members, and the election of the same propor-

tion. The majority of the present elected members are unsuited by their education, previous experience, and characters (sic.) for the weight of the responsibilities which they are now called upon to bear. It is sad . . . that such good citizens . . . as Dr. Ajibade and I.B. Johnson, to name only two, did not stand for election in 1949. There are many others like them, who, as Councillors, by reason of their integrity, could have made this . . . a real success".[10]

The legacy of the Potts-Johnson era was also a matter of some discussion in the African Community League (ACL) in the early 1950's. As already remarked, the League's officials had come under intense pressure and criticism for the scope they'd allowed the immigrant Saro elite, but they seemed quite unrepentant on this score. Still smarting from earlier repudiation of its electoral procedure, in August 1950, the ACL addressed a memorandum on the subject to the Resident. In it, the members wrote of their "traditional activities" being greatly affected by the death of Potts-Johnson. They referred to the aspersions of the recent past which were "calculated to impugn the integrity of the League . . . ", and called on the Resident to verify all allegations concerning the ACL through consultations with its officials. The members maintained that the League was "the only accredited, responsible organisation" in the township, which could serve as the "mouthpiece of public opinion", and they requested the Resident's "cooperation in terms of equal value [as] with our late President".[11] Consensus politics and inter-class alliances were certainly not priority issues for some of these African leaders.

The problems of the elite leadership of the ACL would only get worse. Working class elements were still in pursuit of accountability from those that would represent them. A meeting of the League, at the end of August 1950, was reportedly disrupted by a "large number of hooligans", with conduct "likely to cause [a] breach of the peace". The ACL had to call in police reinforcements. In its protest to the Resident, the organisation's leaders noted in obvious despair: "This is the first time in the history of Port Harcourt that the League which has won [the] respect of Governors, Chief Commissioners, members of Parliament . . . was thrown to the dust and ashes". It warned of an impending "bloodbath", if "disorderly gang" activity were not arrested.[12] On the eve of political independence, Port Harcourt's fractious inter-class competition was still being waged with undiminished intensity. This was now largely a political struggle between indigenous Nigerians, but the prominence of some Saro in the local economy, and their perceived cultural exclusivity,[13] would cause their interests to be featured in some of these debates. The ambivalence of the Saro on the nationality question would engender greater scrutiny of their activities, and strangers perceived to be of fragile commitment to an independent Nigeria would come under a great deal of pressure from both the government and the indigenous population.

The Coming of Independence

On the eve of political independence, Port Harcourt was part of the Rivers Province of mainland and riverine communities, home of several minority ethnic groups, living on lands adjacent to those of the dominant Igbo. We will recall that the Igbo had been a major presence in township life over the years, albeit in uneasy co-existence with the locals, who took offence at the sub-imperial project, and the undisguised ambition of the Igbo in the area. Concerted Igbo attempts to fulfill a dominant economic and political role in the Rivers Province, is a matter of some documentation.[14] Such efforts caused much local resentment.

Political independence from Britain came in 1960, but civilian government in Nigeria would only endure initially for six years. The process of the overthrow of civil society by the Nigerian military in 1966, and the subsequent outbreak of armed hostilities, consequent on the attempted secession of the Igbo-dominated eastern enclave of Biafra, have been reviewed extensively elsewhere to warrant a discussion here.[15] With secession efforts, Port Harcourt would find itself in the central theater of war, as the forces of the federal Nigerian army battled those of Colonel Ojukwu's rebel regime. This was hardly unexpected, for oil resources were a major factor in the conflict, and Port Harcourt had emerged as a leading center of Nigeria's oil prospects, and thus an invaluable prize to the contending parties. Rebel forces promptly occupied the township, making a federal advance on the area a tactical certainty. The occupation, and the subsequent battle for Port Harcourt, would bring great hardship to the Saro and other "foreigner" residents of the township, including the Igbo. Many Saro abandoned their homes to seek refuge away from the hostilities, some as far afield as Lagos and Freetown. Igbo displacement was similarly widespread.

We shall return to a discussion of Saro experience during the secessionist war, but we must first identify the principal areas of activity that absorbed the energies of the Saro in the immediate post-independence period, as the community attempted to secure the interests of its members. These fall into three major categories—firstly, Saro pursuit of communal cohesion through Union and group welfare activities, accompanied by the usual regime of periodic celebration of social events (weddings, funerals, christenings, etc); these activities were pursued increasingly within a context of the disciplined regulation of the ethnic boundaries, and the negotiation of an appropriate Saro identity that would adequately project the values of the community. Secondly, Saro relations with the Sierra Leone government conducted largely through the diplomatic offices of the Sierra Leone High Commission based in Lagos; and finally, the changing role of Saro women, consequent on their increasing involvement in the work force, and the significance of this development for the real estate aspirations of the group. Before examining these factors, we must review Saro experience during the Biafran conflict.

The Saro and Biafra

As earlier indicated, the sequences of the Biafran secession have been so copiously recorded that they need no recounting in this study. Suffice it, therefore, to say that Saro sympathies in the civil war lay clearly with the federal side. In June 1969, the Saro donated £5.5ˢ to the Federal Troops Comfort Fund as an earnest of their support.[16] Like most residents of the Rivers Province, the Saro saw the Igbo as the enemy that had brought them untold suffering. Two of the author's Saro informants, W. Byron and T. Jos. Wilson, stayed on in Port Harcourt throughout the war. They were thus able to dramatically capture the tragic toll of this cruel visitation. These were some of Wilson's recollections of the conflict in Port Harcourt:

> "The war brought great confusion. I was in Port Harcourt, with Byron, and B.R. Browne throughout the fighting. There was no work. Everyone was afraid. The town was a ghostland. There was no Saro Union at the time. We had a little peace when the federal troops came. Mrs. Wilson's son, then at Kontagora, used to send us some food. Federal troops opened the stores, and made things better. The Red Cross also helped. When the federal troops came, all the Saro and the Gold Coast people gathered at 31 Aggrey Road, Pa Reffell's house, for our protection. We were guarded by federal soldiers".[17]

Wilson referred to the searches of Saro and other homes, by Biafran troops, during the occupation. These often resulted in the confiscation of goods and personal effects. He was himself sternly rebuked by a Biafran officer, during one such search, when he was caught tuned on to Radio Nigeria, voice of the federal side. Wilson recalled Biafran soldiers as being "very rude", and he spoke of the Saro's good fortune in the war period, in that only one of their number, a Mr. Taylor, died, and of natural causes. Taylor, he vaguely recalled, had once been in the employ of the Potts-Johnsons. His remains were apparently cremated by federal forces, and no Saro saw his ashes.[18]

A major outcome of the war experience, and one that would pull the Saro deeply into the orbit of the Lagos-based Sierra Leone High Commission, was the issue of abandoned property. As already indicated, the war caused many Saro and other non-Rivers residents of Port Harcourt, including the Igbo, to hurriedly escape from the township. Though these "foreigners" often left their homes in the custody of friends, members of their ethnic groups, or even well-disposed locals, this did not, in some cases, prevent irate Ijaw and others from occupying the affected homes illegally. Some members of the indigenous community saw the war, and the foreign flight, as an opportunity for settling scores with the more affluent local residents. It was in a bid to establish its *bona fides* with the federal government of Nigeria, thus paving the way to the restitution of abandoned property after the war that the Saro, in November 1969, despatched a letter to the Sierra Leone High Commissioner, and sought an audience to review its contents with the local military Governor in Port Harcourt.[19]

The letter had been written in reaction to a newspaper article published in Freetown by the journalist, Sam Metzger, who, apparently, had sympathy for the Biafran cause.[20] Metzger had insinuated in his piece that the Igbo had been victims of genocide in Nigeria, and that the Saro of Port Harcourt, deploring this circumstance, had looked with some favor at secession. The SLU denounced Metzger's suggestion, and accused him of misleading the Prime Minister of Sierra Leone, who had reacted by showing some willingness to support Biafra. It rejected claims of genocide being perpetrated on the Igbo. The SLU wrote:

> "No one intends to exterminate the Ibos. Rather . . . in their mad bid for power [they] intended to exterminate any group that opposed them. . . . this culminated in the killing of . . . Sir Ahmadu Bello, . . . Sir Abubakar Tafawa Balewa, . . . Chief Festus Okotie Eboh, and northern and Yoruba high ranking army personnel. It is significant that no Ibo leader, whether military or political was killed".[21]

The Saro accused the Igbo residents of northern Nigeria, of making light of northern frustrations during the rule of General Aguiyi Ironsi. In this connection, they observed: "You do not know the Iboman as we who lived amongst them do. They can be exasperating. They can goad you into something mad". They interpreted the northerners' violent response to the events of May and September 1966 in which they had killed a number of Igbo resident in the north, as a reaction to "extreme provocation". The photographs of their slaughtered leaders had been publicly dishonoured by a callous Igbo mob. The Saro described the Biafran leader, Ojukwu, as a Lucifer, whose credo was, "It is better to rule though in hell than to serve in heaven". They maintained that Ojukwu had been vehemently opposed to the idea of a twelve-state federation, and secession was his ploy to maintain Igbo hegemony over the neighbouring minority groups. The letter also described the anguish of the years of secession:

> "Anybody who was not of Ibo origin was looked upon as being against the Ibos. We expatriates were treated in the same way as native Nigerians of the South Eastern or Rivers States. One of our members was arrested and thoroughly beaten up by the so-called Biafran Militia, for no other reason than that he displayed the Sierra Leone emblem on his door-post".[22]

The Saro referred to various acts of intimidation during the crisis, including the ubiquitous home searches "between night fall and sun up". They accused Sam Metzger of "peddling unwholesome rumours about the Nigerian crisis", and maintained that he was obviously in the pay of the rebels. Metzger, they claimed, had also, perhaps been misled by word from "certain misguided Sierra Leoneans [of Port Harcourt] who were air-lifted home . . . by the Red Cross, at the instance of . . . the rebel High Command". In closing, the SLU berated the Sierra Leone High Commissioner's Office in Lagos, for its indifference to the plight of the Saro of Port Harcourt:

> "Sometime ago, the High Commission sent one of its Secretaries to find out whether or not there were Sierra Leoneans in Port Harcourt after the liberation. When he arrived, we all rallied round him, and made him to understand that indeed, and in fact, there are still Sierra Leoneans in Port Harcourt. We gave him a list of our names and addresses, in the hope that he would keep us informed of day to day activities in our Homeland. He was expected to send us copies of periodicals from Sierra Leone. But up till the present, nothing has happened. . . . we have now no alternative but to feel that we are a neglected people whose hopes hang in the balance".

The Union urged the government of Sierra Leone to "steer clear of the Nigerian crisis which [was] purely an internal matter", and to do nothing that would jeopardise the cordial relations that had always existed between the two countries.[23]

The abandoned property issue sometimes inflamed passions within Saro ranks, and strained relations in a community that was already much traumatised by the experience of war. Take, for instance, the case, in November 1969, of one-time Port Harcourt resident, Mrs. Victoria Pratt, now a refugee in Murray Town, just outside Freetown. Mrs. Pratt owned a home at 89 Victoria Street, Port Harcourt and the Sierra Leone Union (SLU) was seeking to represent her interests as custodian of the property; she appeared to be rather unwelcoming of this attention. She wrote from Freetown, accusing Union official, W. Byron, of scheming to appropriate her property, in the guise of protecting her interests. She maintained that an indigene, a Mr. Uzah, from Ahoada, was the preferred custodian. In a letter to Barnes, the SLU's secretary, she wrote pointedly: "You people could act for the others if they so desire, but as for me, I have appointed someone in the person of Mr. Uzah . . . and have . . . given him full power of attorney to act on my behalf on everything that pertains to . . . 89 Victoria Street. . . . I am not creating a mandate for the SLU to act for me nor to negotiate on anything as regards the said property".[24] The Union recoiled at this rebuff, and members deplored Mrs. Pratt's conduct. The SLU wrote of its many unsuccessful efforts to locate her after Port Harcourt's liberation, and its care of her property over which a number of individuals had exercised failed custodianship. The Union claimed to have no confidence in Uzah, who was believed to have designs on the property, with Byron, his principal obstacle. Uzah's alleged mis-use of the premises was itemised in flagrant detail, and his efforts to set the police on Byron, exposed, and condemned. Mrs. Pratt was accused of ingratitude to Byron, who had never acted on his own, but always on the SLU's behalf, as was also the case with other properties in the Union's custody. The Union mentioned its custodianship of the homes of other absent Saro, among them Mrs. Annet Williams, and the recently deceased, Mrs. Idowu Macaulay. It demanded to be told whether it should continue its over-sight of the Pratt property, or "hands-off" completely.[25] Disagreements of this type were not uncommon during the war and its aftermath.[26]

By November 1970, amidst recriminations over disputed custodianship and the outright failure of some returned Saro to reclaim their homes from local Ijaw installed in them, the Saro approached the Abandoned Property Authority (APA), through the Attorney General, with a detailed listing of the properties in question. In this letter, W. Byron, Secretary of the SLU, appealed for immediate relief for all the affected Saro whose homes had been designated "Abandoned property", and vested in the APA. He argued that the homes of immigrants, who had no alternative residence in Nigeria, and were now physically present in Port Harcourt, should be treated differently from cases involving such indigenes as the displaced Igbo. Byron stressed the difficulties of accommodation facing the affected Saro, who had generally fallen on the mercy of "charitable friends", and he appealed for the immediate release of these homes from the APA, to end their suffering. He appended the following names and addresses:

Mrs. Clementina Rollings	133 Aggrey Road
Mrs. P.M. Udeogu	111 Victoria Street and 59 Niger Street
Victor Johnson	121 Niger Street
Beresford Cole	10 Niger Street
H. Johnson	23 Niger Street and 26 Accra Street
Mrs. E.V. Meheux	86 Victoria Street
S.A. Cole	21 King Jaja Street[27]

By June 1973, the Saro properties question had taken an even more dramatic turn. The Rivers State government issued a statement in "cancellation of state leases on plots belonging to Sierra Leoneans resident in Port Harcourt". This was contained in the Rivers State Extraordinary Gazette No. 26, vol. 5, of 25 June, 1973. The following occupiers were listed:

Evelyn Savage	31 Aggrey Road
N.J.C. Cline	119 Aggrey Road
G.C. Wilson	125 Aggrey Road
Ajagborna Oporokum (Mrs. Thompson)	113 Victoria Street
Regina O. Olatogbin (Mrs. J.M. Johnson)	50 Kaduna Street
Cecilia S. Macaulay	194 Bonny Street
Samuel F. Cole	9 Niger Street
Joshua W. Leigh	59 Niger Street
C. Johnson	73 Niger Street.[28]

Sensing, perhaps rightly, that government was out to persecute non-Nigerians, and coerce them into naturalisation, the Saro now intensified pressure on the High Commissioner's office in Lagos, demanding that action be taken immediately to recover and protect the assets of those affected.[29] In his response, the High Commissioner, W.H. Fitzjohn, explained that he was already in communication on the matter with the Attorney-General of the Federation, Dr. Graham Douglas, and a cabinet officer, Ben Okagbue. Okagbue, an Igbo from the East Central State, he added, was himself in the process of recovering two homes in Port Harcourt from the APA. Fitzjohn called for "great restraint and patience", promising to get into the details fully during his next visit to Port Harcourt, early in 1974.[30]

Dissatisfied with this outcome, Saro leaders now approached the Governor of the Rivers State who had jurisdiction over Port Harcourt. A letter of March 1974 vividly captured the distress of a Saro people who had "lived in Port Harcourt for decades", with only loose ties to family members in Sierra Leone. They had chosen Port Harcourt as their home, and considered the affected properties the bequests from their parents, and a memorial to the group's exertions in the township over the years. They decried the government's action which was progressively consigning the affected members to "penury", and called on the Governor to remedy the situation for "foreigners" who had always lived amicably with the indigenous population, "inter-marrying and having children". The Saro described their homes as "their only hope".[31]

When Sierra Leone's High Commissioner visited Port Harcourt, in April 1975, the matter of appropriated homes was still unresolved. Although his discussions with the Saro were said to have been generally cordial, he was pressed to act more decisively on the properties issue, and he gave his hosts little encouragement by his promises of continued support. In June 1975, however, some of the acquired homes were released to their Saro owners by the government. This welcome development brought much relief to the affected residents, and the happy news was promptly relayed to the High Commissioner in Lagos.[32] The Saro had come through a chapter of their immigrant experience they would not soon forget. The properties issue had underscored an area of differentiation that time had blurred in the Saro's perception of their place in local society. For where they had come to regard their property rights as of the same order as that of the indigene, experience had taught that security in such matters did not extend to non-nationals and their associates. The path of naturalisation was being affirmed officially as the immigrant's only true recourse, and longevity of residence in Port Harcourt had purchased the Saro no reprieve.

Closely linked to the issue of abandoned property during the war was that of "displaced persons". The latter were often individuals who had lost their own homes or the rented property they had occupied, and who were now forced to be part of Port Harcourt's floating population during the war, and in the years after it ended in 1970. Some Saro found themselves in this unfortunate refugee situation, and were forced to turn to the Sierra Leone Union for assistance. Such was the plight of Union member, Sister Rollings in October 1970, when she could not prevail on the Abandoned Property Authority (APA) to release her home, nor easily identify alternative accommodation.[33] Another female member, Sis. P.M. Udeogu, was similarly afflicted at the time, and in a desperate effort to regain her Victoria

Street residence, she had to employ the services of Robert Okara, a lawyer, at great expense.[34]

The refugee problem faced by the Saro would not, however, be confined to known township residents. Sierra Leoneans displaced from other sections of the country sometimes found their way to Port Harcourt, and asked for assistance. In June 1971, a much distressed William John, who claimed to have come from the East Central State, became the charge of the SLU's welfare officers. John had been discharged from the federal army for disability during the war, and he had subsequently joined the Nigerian Railways, where he served until his recent termination. He was requesting repatriation to his Goree Street residence in Freetown. The Saro arranged his travel to Lagos, where the High Commissioner's office was expected to make plans for his journey to Freetown.[35]

Requests for assistance in tracing relatives who had been missing since the beginning of the war also came periodically to the Saro in the 1970's. In July 1972, Christine Harding, a lawyer in Freetown, contacted the Sierra Leone Union on behalf of her client, a Mrs. Leonora During, who was seeking to locate her father, Rev. Erasmus Greywoode. Last reports had placed Greywoode at Abonnema, in the riverine zone. On enquiry, the SLU established that Greywoode had died in May 1967, at Abonnema, where he was last attached to the St. Paul's Nyemoni Church.[36]

Promoting Group Cohesion

The Saro were a much transformed community by the early 1970's. Although group numbers continued to be relatively low at about 50 homesteads in the township, the structural composition of the community had undergone much change. Endogamous preference in marriage was now clearly an insistence of the past, and Saro unions with the local Igbo and Ijaw, in which Saro women had played a critical pioneering role, were now more generally accepted. More Saro women had also found their way into the workforce with the expansion of educational opportunity, and Saro female owners of property, as demonstrated in post-war representations to the Abandoned Property Authority (APA), were no longer a rare occurrence. It is worth nothing, in this connection, that a number of these female home-owners were widowed spouses of unions with indigenes. The solidarity of the Saro community, and its general cohesion, were issues of major significance following the disruptions of war.

With the Sierra Leone Union (SLU) as the hub of group activity, the Saro would now increasingly be occupied by issues of group identity and

Table 5-1

Some Social Activities of the Saro between 1950 and 1975.

Date	Event	Source
January 1950	Award of the OBE to long-time associate, Dr. O. Ajibade	Nigerian Observer (hereafter NO) 13 Jan.1950
January 1950	Celebrations to mark the acquittal of Mrs. Eniton Potts-Johnson on a charge of "stealing" books that were the property of the Enitonna Printing Press	NO, 13 Jan. 1950
May 1950	18th Anniversary celebrations of the Enitonna High School	NO, 5 May, 1950
June 1950	Anniversary service of the SLU at Wesley Church	NO, 30 June, 1950
August 1950	Mrs. Potts-Johnson receives MBE award that had been bestowed on her late husband	NO, 4 Aug. 1950
November 1950	Visit to Port Harcourt of one-time resident, Charles Egerton Shyngle	NO, 24 Nov. 1950
November 1951	Death of I.B. Johnson, ex-TAB member, wealthy businessman, and photographer, at the age of 68	NO, 16 Nov. 1951
November 1951	Death of S. Bankole Rhodes, ex-member of the Legislative Council, at 61	NO, 23 Nov. 1951
November 1951	Death of Max George, prominent Saro of the social circuit of Port Harcourt	NO, 23 Nov. 1951
January 1953	Celebration of the 24th anniversary of the Nigerian Observer newspaper	NO, 2 Jan. 1953
August 1953	Dance to raise funds toward a monument in memory of L.R. Potts-Johnson	NO, 1 Sept. 1953
July 1970	SLU group prayers for Miss. Ayo Timity prior to her departure to the USA for further studies	Executive meeting of SLU, 25 July 1970, SLDUPH
January 1971	Return to Port Harcourt of the Rev. R. Timity (son of Sis. M.K. Coker), doctoral student at Howard University, USA—arrival announced on the local radio	Executive meeting of SLU, 25 July 1970, SLDUPH
September 1975	Traditional naming ceremony (komojade) for new son of the Banke Johnsons	Minutes of general meeting of the SLU, 13 Sept. 1975, SLDUPH
September 1975	Funerary ceremonies for the late Sis. A. Marshall	Executive meeting of SLU, 11th Oct. 1975, SLDUPH
October 1975	Celebrations over the purchase of a new car by Sis. Domo-Spiff	General meeting of the SLU, 11 Oct. 1975, SLDUPH

conduct which called forth a greater insistence on the personal discipline of group members, fiscal prudence and accountability in Union matters,[37] welfare protection of the needy, and the avoidance of conflict with the law and the indigenous population. The patriarchs of the community continued to monopolise the role of the enforcer of the rules of conduct, but with some Saro women having now come into greater economic empowerment, male dominance would not go completely unchallenged. On the whole, however, female members of the group appear to have acquiesced in the fiction of an undifferentiated unity in the community, thus allowing elder males the authority that was deemed essential to group survival in an increasingly embattled environment. Let us now review some of these developments that were crucial to group cohesion.

Domestic Social Activity.

Of vital significance to group survival and corporate morale in these years was the maintenance, after the war, of the Saro's accustomed practice of group commemoration of the dead, and celebration of engagements, christenings, weddings, Enitonna High School festivities, and other such social landmarks. The pages of the *Nigerian Observer* contain copious references to these activities, some of which are presented in Table 5-1. Most of these activities had become routine, but the celebrations, in January 1950, of Mrs. Eniton Potts-Johnson's acquittal on criminal charges brought by an all-indigene party are particularly note-worthy and deserve some comment. The details of the charge of the appropriation of books that were the property of the Enitonna Printing Press are rather unclear.[38] But that the charge had in fact been brought by locals was, for the Saro, the most unsettling element. The incident indicated that the protections and immunities of the past, generously enjoyed (at times, questionably)[39] by the Saro, were now a distant memory as the nationalist movement hurtled towards independence. It left many Saro troubled, and in much greater need of the communal supports.[40]

The Sierra Leone Union.

As Nigeria approached political independence in 1960, most Saro appear to have been rather wary of the prospect, and somewhat overcome by the desire to stake a claim for themselves within the nascent independent state. Passionate cultural identification with Sierra Leonean institutions, in that environment, seemed liable to interpretation, by indigenes, as half-hearted

Table 5-2

A Cross-Section of the Occupational Involvements
of the Saro in the Early 1970's

Sis. E.E. Allagoa	Housewife
Sis. Sarian Barnes	Contractor
B.R. Browne	Electrician
G.H.S. Bucknor	Officer in the Bulk Oil Plant
J.A. Bull	Foreman, Public Works department
Sis. W.R. Cline	Trader
J.E. Davies	Accounts clerk, Post and Telecommunications Department
Sis. Domo-Spiff	Nurse, General Hospital
G.P.A. Hamilton	Assistant manager
E.O. Johnson	Store-keeper, Medical stores
Hamble Noble Johnson	Printer
Sis. E.V. Meheux	Housewife
Sis. V.E. Ogan	Baker
P.O. Potts-Johnson	Secretary, Transport Corporation
Sis. P.M. Udeogu	Housewife
Sis. C. Ulzen	Baker
A.L.O. Thompson	Trader
T. Jos. Wilson	Pensioner, from the government service

Source: List dated 30 July, 1973, SLDUPH.

involvement with Nigeria, and lukewarm support for her political goals and socio-economic aspirations. Such charges could have adverse effects on professional and occupational advancement. To be a permanent resident in Nigeria was to be seen to be undivided in one's national loyalties.[41] With most Saro opting to retain Sierra Leonean citizenship after Nigeria's independence, the group's nationality status within society became a matter of some concern, and much discussion. This inevitably attracted scarcely-veiled xenophobic pressure, as in the aforentioned abandoned properties episode.

It is difficult to estimate the extent of SLU activity between 1954 and the outbreak of the civil war in 1966. Saro memory is suspect in this area, and recollections vary widely between informants. While some claim that a normal schedule of social activities was maintained, others recall this period as one of social adjustment to new political realities, and a cautious retreat from the overtly peculiar foreign cultural observance that could attract charges of unpatriotism. The documents of the SLU for this period could well have resolved our speculations on prevailing group attitudes and behaviour. Their loss, however, during the civil war dictates a greater dependence on informant recollections. These generally suggest, for the period, more a withdrawal than an enthusiastic profession of Sierra Leonean ancestry, at least, for the first decade or so of independence. This is an area of Saro history in which more work needs to be done, if we are to proceed beyond informed surmise to more substantive determinations.

We are on much firmer ground when we review the social processes after the civil war. As post-war recovery got under way, the members of the SLU, in straitened circumstances, and desperately in need of renewed economic vigour, began to consider the possible re-introduction of the thrift and loan group practices of the period before the civil war. E.O. Johnson revived the idea, in March 1970, and members unanimously endorsed its further review after the annual April celebrations.[42] By this time, the Union had taken to organising its annual celebrations to coincide with April 27, the date of Sierra Leone's political independence from Britain.

Union activities of the 1970's were varied and unusually demanding of the time and energies of executive members. Executive and general meetings were held monthly, with provision for emergency assembly should the need arise. To emphasise the group's communalism, members were referred to as "Brother" or "Sister", and all meetings ended in an informal gathering, with refreshments, derived from member's donations. Union activities and discussions ranged from periodic group socials, the over-sight of the homes of absent members, and matters of financial management, to the arbitration of disputes within the group (some of them marital),[43] and policy formulation regarding "delinquents", i.e., members who failed in their financial and/or moral obligations to the Union. Executive members had the responsibility of enforcing the rules as laid out in the SLU's constitution,[44] and this often made for their unpopularity with offending members.

Union finances were a major impediment to the effective functioning of the community's programs after the war. Monthly dues, in June of 1970, of three shillings for males, and two for females, were not being paid regularly by some members, and this was probably a function of indifferent attendance at Union meetings.[45] By January 1973, the elders of the community, led by T. Jos. Wilson, had decided to enforce discipline in the ranks of "delinquent" members, and letters threatening expulsion were addressed to such individuals.[46] Wilson, the martinet of the SLU, saw a willingness to abide by all commitments and obligations that came with Union membership as a pre-requisite to responsible citizenship within the Saro community.[47] When to improve attendance at meetings and boost the finances, the Union adopted a group entertainment policy,[48] Wilson had to be prevailed upon not to move for the expulsion of all errant members before the policy was introduced.[49] By June 1975, Olu Potts-Johnson (to be discussed more fully presently) had become secretary of the Saro Union, and he would revitalise the finances through a membership campaign, fund-raising activities, and the re-activation of the membership dues of the older and disabled members who had up to this point being free of this obligation.[50]

Although its finances were rather precarious in the post-war years, the SLU took its welfare obligations to all Saro very seriously. As T. Jos. Wilson remarked to the author, an indigent Saro brought reproach to all Saro, and tarnished the community's image. It was thus incumbent on all Union members to assist the more disadvantaged members of the community.[51] The Union's welfare officers constantly monitored the social scene, and waited regularly on those in need. In February 1971, they rallied to the support of a much-distressed Sis. Williams of Borokiri, and when her plight seemed to demand repatriation to Freetown, the High Commission in Lagos was notified accordingly.[52] Welfare officers mediated marital disputes, visited the sick, and comforted the dying. No single case exemplified the SLU's heightened welfarist concerns after the war better than that of the Ben Williams family of Port Harcourt.

A family of two, the Williamses were in sharply reduced circumstances in the early 1970's. The Union, while providing local material support, contacted the Lagos High Commission to report their difficulty for this looked ominously like another case for repatriation. The SLU was willing to pay their fares to Lagos, and it expected the High Commission to assume responsibility thereafter. Efforts by the Lagos office to locate the relatives of the couple in Freetown would drag on for many anguished months, and by August 1973, over a year since the initial discussion, the Williamses were still marooned in Port Harcourt, and subsisting on Union charity.[53] In desperation, the SLU turned to Bishop Y. Fubara of the Niger Delta Diocese for help in September 1973. Fubara communicated the gravity of their condition to Lagos, indicating that the family's emergency travelling certificates were over a year old, and that Mrs. Williams's daughter, a Mrs. Mabel V. Marke of Brookfields, Freetown, was eager to receive them once the High Commission could arrange their passages.[54] The High Commission blamed Freetown's ministry of External Affairs for the delay in addressing the matter.[55] In the end, Mr. Ben Williams died in Port Harcourt, and, with no resources to his name, the SLU assumed full responsibility for his burial and related rites.[56] We have a glimpse in this incident of the many frustrations that often attended Saro relations with the Lagos High Commission, a matter of great disappointment for the immigrants over the years. The constancy with which the Saro fulfilled their welfare obligations to their members may well partly explain the willingness of some non-Sierra Leonean spouses of the Saro to opt for Sierra Leonean citizenship in the early 1970's.[57]

As Nigeria's independence exposed their vulnerability, the Saro developed a new appreciation of the value of local ties. A community that had once celebrated its social distance from local society now increasingly craved such connections. When the SLU was informed in February 1973 of the impending return to Port Harcourt of Olu Potts-Johnson, after successful study in the United Kingdom, the membership was in raptures of joy. Son of the deceased Saro leader, the young Potts-Johnson, whose mother was from the riverine community of Brass, was seen as a prospective interlocutor for the Saro with local society.[58] When some members of the SLU were squeamish about the propriety of inviting him to join the Union's up-coming annual celebrations, on arrival, B.R. Browne, the president of the SLU, argued that there was "absolutely nothing wrong in canvassing for new members."[59] In April 1973, Olu Potts-Johnson was formally invited to the celebrations, along with his indigenous hosts and relatives, Mr. and Mrs. George Spiff.[60] He would prove to be one of the most valuable members of the SLU, for the beleaguered Saro, in the years to come, and his presence at Union meetings still electrified the group in the 1980's, as this author observed.

The harnessing of precious local ties was pursued alongside the refining of the group's Saro image to better project the cultural particularity of the emigre community. Issues of identity came increasingly to the fore in Union discussions in the early 1970's, and some members were keen on further extending the ties with Freetown. It was decided, for instance, in April 1971 that word of all Saro deaths in Port Harcourt should be speedily transmitted to the High Commission in Lagos, and relayed in Freetown, where appropriate announcements were to be made on the local broadcasting service.[61] By October 1972, efforts were also afoot to draft a new Union constitution that would more adequately reflect the community's orientation and its elevated expectations of its membership in the areas of general deportment, collective responsibility, involvement with the homeland, and the continued promotion of Krio cultural values.[62] It was this final element that dominated Union discussions in December 1975 when Sis. E.V. Meheux passed away. Members now had to determine how true they were going to be to all the funerary components of the traditional Krio practice. It was customary for the Saro to observe seventh and fortieth day rites; some members now demanded that third day ceremonies, as performed in Freetown, Lagos, Calabar, and other centres of Krio life, be also introduced in Port Harcourt, the added expense notwithstanding.[63] This group had also been prominent in getting the Union to adopt the Krio language as the medium of expression at both general and executive meetings, even though the minutes were still to be recorded in English.[64]

Cultural identification with Freetown inevitably generated a public reaction in local society that had grave repercussions on Saro relations with some sections of the indigenous community. When in July 1972, the Saro, Mrs. Hartley Cowan, died, a major controversy with far-reaching implications began to unfold. It was a constitutional stipulation of the SLU that the Union, as a body, should not attend the funerals of Saro who were not paid-up members of the Union at the time of their deaths. Mrs. Cowan was not in good financial standing, and may not, in fact, have been an active member. Her husband, however, desired that she be honored by the Union's presence at her funeral. This was a mark of status, and one dearly treasured by the Saro. Mr. Cowan volunteered to make up all of the outstanding arrears. This show of remorse impressed the Executive of the SLU, and although it took no payments from Cowan, it recommended the Union's attendance as requested. It was at the customary wake-keeping ceremony for Mrs. Cowan that latent resentments of the Saro came to be voiced publicly. Union members were reportedly the subject of disparaging xenophobic comment by individuals of the indigenous community in the mourning party, and they responded to this provocation by walking out of the wake.[65] The author gathered from informants that the remarks in question had raised the vexed issue of African foreigners in Nigeria, who were said to be of a superior attitude, and who allegedly, looked down on indigenes. Such sentiments could perhaps not have been totally unexpected in a Port Harcourt that was recovering from the civil war, with various groups jockeying for influence, amid economic competition that was rife and unsparing. Moves by the Saro to modify the SLU's institutional image, in a bid to de-emphasise its foreign character, would date from about this incident.[66] At the SLU's general meeting of July 1972, the issue of a name change of the Union was formally tabled. An animated discussion ensued, but at its end, "no substitute names were immediately forthcoming." This was a matter of some gravity, with far-reaching implications for the community's future image, as well as its viability in an independent Nigeria. Not surprisingly, the Saro would agonise over the issue for several months.

Relations with the Sierra Leone Government through the High Commission, Lagos

We have already noted some of the frustrations that the Saro experienced in their dealings with the Sierra Leone High Commission during the years of the Biafran war, and in the matter of the repatriation of the Ben Williamses. Though much disillusioned by these encounters, the community recognised the value of maintaining a line to diplomatic officials whose intervention on their behalf could be crucial in a crisis situation. Such pressure on the abandoned property question had speeded up the release of acquired Saro homes. The Sierra Leone Union had thus maintained regular communication with the High Commission, and when, during the civil war, in November 1969, A.B. Mansaray was appointed High Commissioner, the Saro promptly extended a cordial welcome with wishes for a successful tour of office.[67]

It was through the High Commissioner's office that the Saro monitored developments in official circles in Sierra Leone. The SLU was, for instance, informed in September, 1970 of the impending visit of Sierra Leone's Prime Minister, Siaka Stevens, to Nigeria for that nation's tenth independence anniversary celebration. Although a difficult financial situation precluded the Union from despatching a delegation to Lagos to meet him, his visit brought some excitement to Port Harcourt.[68] The Saro also followed news of political unrest in Sierra Leone with close interest. The struggles between the ruling All People's Congress and the United Democratic Party, in October 1970, which led to a declaration of a State of Emergency, and Dr. John Karefa-Smart's disappearance from Freetown politics for a time, were a matter of common conversation in Saro circles.[69]

By April 1971, the High Commission had begun to make financial donations to the anniversary celebrations of the SLU.[70] The festivities that year, however, coincided with the aforementioned political crisis in Sierra Leone, and the Saro appropriately scaled back their activities in recognition of those unfortunate developments in the "homeland".[71] When news reached Port Harcourt, in August 1971, of the Sierra Leone government's efforts to rid that nation of illegal immigrants, the Saro promptly approached the High Commission for further clarification.[72] Unimpeded travel to Freetown was a matter of some priority to most Saro. Very few actually travelled outside Nigeria at this time, but the community was eager to keep the travel option open, should material circumstances improve. A response on the matter was not immediately forthcoming, for the Lagos office was in the throes of transition as H.C. Mansaray, the then High Commissioner, prepared to return to Freetown at the end of his term. The issue was finally clarified in correspondence from the High Commission in October 1971. The Union was assured that visas were not required of Sierra Leoneans entering the country, as long as they were possessed of "valid travelling documents". Members of the Union were encouraged to apply for Sierra Leone passports, and twenty copies of passport application forms were forwarded to the Union's Secretariat.[73] In November 1971, H.C. Mansaray's successor as High Commissioner, W.H. Fitzjohn, arrived in Lagos. The Sierra Leone Union was advised accordingly. With the attainment of Republican status in Sierra Leone in 1971, the High Commission in Lagos promptly reported the new constitutional development to the Saro. The community was advised that annual national celebrations in Sierra Leone would now be held on 19 April (Republic Day), not 27 April (Independence Day), as was previously the case. The Saro promptly reflected this change in their annual festivities.[74] For its celebrations of April 1972, the Executive of the SLU decided that the flag of the Republic of Sierra Leone would be flown at the residence of B.R. Browne, the Union's President.[75] Such gestures of cultural fealty would not go unnoticed by the government of Nigeria, and the indigenes of Port Harcourt. The Saro were walking the tightrope of national identification with two countries. This anomaly would increasingly be called into question as Port Harcourt's "aliens" ran the gauntlet of political ambiguity in their uncompromising cultural attachment to Krio values.

Much cherished ties to Sierra Leone were openly advertised in the highly publicised visits of Sierra Leone High Commissioners to Port Harcourt. When, for instance, in July 1973, Dr. Fitzjohn visited the Saro, this seemed a fitting opportunity to put culture on display. Union members had long discussions with the diplomat at the local Government Rest House on a wide range of issues of concern to the community. A reception was organised in his honour, with the usual emphasis on Krio cuisine and ceremonial. Officials of the Union were involved with the High Commissioner's itinerary as he toured the fibreglass boatyard, the Rivers State Newspaper Corporation, and the offices of the oil company, Agip.[76] The Saro took such opportunities of interaction with leaders from Sierra Leone very seriously, which is why they were outraged in August 1974 by what they perceived as a slight by the High Commission. The incident involved the visit to Nigeria of the Secretary of the government of Sierra Leone. Notification of his arrival from the High Commission was late in reaching the SLU because it had been routed through the office of the Governor of the Rivers State. The Saro condemned this over-sight, and remonstrated with the Lagos office over their consequent inability to avail themselves of the Secretary's presence in the country to review matters of interest to the community. They demanded more direct correspondence with the High Commission to obviate such situations in the future.[77]

Though burdened by unhealthy Union finances in the mid-1970's, the Saro would rally to the support of the homeland when calamity struck in June 1975. News reached Port Harcourt of a hurricane that had passed over Freetown leaving in its wake much damage to public and private property. President Siaka Stevens had broadcast an appeal for donations to repair the devastation which he estimated at a minimum of three million Leones. The SLU met in an emergency session to discuss its response to the appeal, and a fund-raising effort within the Saro community was immediately launched.[78] In November 1975, the Union despatched the sum of one hundred naira to the High Commission in support of Freetown's disaster relief fund. A grateful High Commissioner was prompt to report that this was the only donation to come from a Saro Union in Nigeria.[79]

Saro Women, and Group Real Estate Aspirations

This study has already noted the growing economic empowerment of women in the Saro community in the post-war period. An improved educational climate had engendered this development, as had the new freedom to marry into indigenous families, an area in which even the most conservative Saro fathers had begun to yield in recognition of its local value by the mid-1960's. When the Saro began to consider the establishment of a permanent secretariat for the Sierra Leone Union (SLU) in March 1973, Saro women with marriage ties in local society would be invaluable in representing the group's interests. Up to this point, Union meetings had been held in a house without electricity, and this had occasioned a customary run on the agenda as nightfall approached.[80] Although there were suggestions that the authorities be approached for the use of the Banham schoolroom,[81] some members began to think of acquiring real estate in the Union's name for the purpose of a permanent secretariat building. When in the Union's general elections of June 1973, female members gained unprecedented access to executive positions, among them Sisters Allagoa, Udeogu, and Ogan, all locally married, it became increasingly evident that women were coming into a new prominence in Saro society.[82] The Union now ear-marked 35 Victoria Street ("No. 35" in Saro-speak) as the desired property. This had been the home of the late Sis. P.O. Macaulay, and the Union was eager to convert its rental occupancy of the property to outright purchase.[83] Governmental approval of purchase by "aliens" would, however, be required as was now the law in the aftermath of the civil war. The Saro now began to plan for the long-term use of "No. 35", and they decided in November 1973, that the rented property would henceforth accommodate visiting Sierra Leoneans, Saro who were between jobs, as well as those that were homeless. All executive and general meetings were also to be held at the premises, as well as group "socials" and other celebratory events. Funds were voted for the proper securing of the building from intruders.[84] The Union was subsequently informed of the owner's willingness to dispose of the property, and their offer of first refusal of purchase to the SLU.[85]

By August 1975, the Union had mandated Noble Johnson, Olu Potts-Johnson, and Sis. M. Udeogu (the latter two with strong local ties), to take up the matter of the purchase of "No. 35" with the Lands Office in Port Harcourt. With Union finances at last beginning to show some improvement, members were eager to acquire the property at the earliest opportunity.[86] This would, however, be an area of great frustration for the Saro, as we will presently discover. Foreigners in Nigeria were not to be allowed easy access to landed property, and the Saro's twin affiliations to Nigeria and Sierra Leone now became a nightmare of bureaucratic entrapment from which the group would not escape unscathed.

We have reviewed in this chapter some of the initial efforts at communal group preservation of the Saro of Port Harcourt. In similar circumstances, other embattled minority communities have resorted to a host of survival strategies in addressing their vulnerability as "strangers". Some of these initiatives have clearly reflected more prudence and foresight than others. One of the most unimaginative responses surely must be that of the Dahomeyans in the colonial Ivory Coast of West Africa in the twentieth century. For while holding several elite positions in the bureaucracy and economy of that territory, due to their superior education, the Dahomeyan immigrants generally segregated themselves from the indigenous population in all spheres except politics. Their rejection by the host society even before independence was wholly predictable. The Dahomeyan emigre would fare no better in Niger.[87] Other stranger groups have been far more creative in responding to their perceived vulnerability. In Sierra Leone, some members of the Lebanese community pursued inter-marriage with locals, producing the very influential Afro-Lebanese stratum which has been very prominent in the contemporary economy and politics of that territory, especially in the area of safeguarding Lebanese gains from local economic nationalism. After independence, the Lebanese perfected their survival strategies, and their monetary donations to higher education, health-care delivery systems, community recreation, and the welfare of the poor, became the bedrock of the local donor community in difficult economic times.[88] The itinerant Ewe have been similarly creative. Under pressure of expulsion from an independent Ghana, desperate Ewe from Togo often passed themselves off as Ghanian Ewe, thus evading deportation.[89] For the Goan Asians of independent Uganda, security lay, for a time, in the manipulation of ties with their well connected middle-class African associates and friends (to whom they often gave directorships in their businesses), and in the highly publicised and well appointed invitations of President Obote and his cabinet colleagues to celebrations at the Kampala Institute.[90] In the case of Yoruba immigrants among the Asante in the colonial Gold Coast, though permitted some measure of independence of the local chiefs by the colonial British administration, the strangers saw the wisdom of addressing most of their communications with the government through the Asantehene. Such deference to a local leader of high standing was judged vital to the safeguarding of immigrant interests.[91]

For the Saro, in the period into the mid-1970's, protection was principally sought in internal group cohesion, the manipulation of social ties in the local ethnic communities, occasional demonstrations of loyalty to the federal authorities, and the patient cultivation of links with the government of Sierra Leone through its Lagos-based High Commission. This was an approach that was fraught with some risk due to its extra-territorial implications. Moreover, the Saro community, made up now of both Nigerian citizens and aliens, was itself polarised on the nationality axis, and common cultural commitment was the principal abiding unifier in group life. Tensions would inevitably result from this growing differention which received additional impetus from other developments within the community. Increasingly, Saro women were emerging (albeit painfully slowly) from their accustomed emasculation, as they received a better education, secured more rewarding jobs, and purchased their first cars.[92] A number of these women were Nigerian citizens, and thus subject to some local pressure from the ethnic groups of their affiliation. Equally significant (and a matter soon to be reviewed) was the emerging generational divide within Saro society as its youth began to chafe under the dominant and uncompromising control of the elders. The principal challenge for the Saro as they entered the 1980's was thus the imperative of staying united even as the group was caught in the throes of an expanding differentiation. The centripetal forces of cultural unity were now clearly being assailed by centrifugal tendencies emanating from issues of nationality, gender, and class. Saro success in withstanding internal group challenges, as well as the anti-alien pressures that were being generated from within governmental structures and the indigenous populace, becomes the subject of our final review.

6

THE FINAL ECLIPSE: THE RESURGENCE OF THE INDIGENES, 1976—84

In January 1975, the Nigerian Military government responded to the unremitting pressure from the Nigerian labour movement for better salaries and wages, with the Udoji pay awards. This remuneration package entailed, in some cases, pay increases to government workers of the order of 100%, plus additional bonuses for the pay inequities in increments offered in the past. The awards represented a mammoth injection of funds into many homes, and Saro employees of the public sector were among the grateful beneficiaries. The resultant improvement in material circumstances would be promptly reflected in a more spirited involvement in SLU affairs, and a greater willingness in the membership to consider the subject of the acquisition of property in the Union's name. The financial problems of the Union were now to be much assuaged, and the momentum of Saro social celebration, vital to sustaining group morale in these xenophobic times, considerably quickened.[1] Grave national problems, however, still awaited the immigrant community in its seventh decade of residence in the township of Port Harcourt. That of personal real estate would continue to be the biggest irritant, and, for some Saro, the most intractable problem of the late 1970's.

Issues of Saro Property Holders

By the start of 1976, most Saro whose homes had been acquired by the Abandoned Property Authority (APA), had resolved their problems, and recovered their assets. The Union and the Sierra Leone High Commission had been most instrumental in securing this outcome, and the gratitude of the affected Saro was to be seen in a greater commitment to the activities of the group which had been so robust in their defence. This halcyon phase was, however, dramatically altered, in June 1977, by the emergence of yet another threat to Saro owners of landed property. A.L.O. Thompson, the Union's Secretary, promptly alerted the High Commission in Lagos, to this disturbing development. He wrote of the Federal Military Government's new policy of acquiring and selling the owner-occupied homes of a number of Saro in the township. The circumstances surrounding this development are not totally clear from Thompson's initial correspondence, but he clearly conveyed the sense of renewed anxiety and angst within the affected households. The High Commissioner was urged to investigate the situation immediately, and to take up the matter with the federal government.[2]

A few days after the despatch of this correspondence, the SLU, still obviously embroiled in defining a new image that would accord more appropriately with the realities of an independent Nigeria, and the expectations of its indigenous population, approached the Abandoned Property Implementation Panel, on behalf of the "Sierra Leonean Elements" of Port Harcourt. This letter provides more background to the earlier correspondence with the Sierra Leone High Commissioner on home seizures. It made reference to a list of Saro property carried in the local paper, the Nigerian Tide, of 1 and 2 June 1977. Various homes, owned and occupied by the Saro, had been advertised for sale, apparently without the consent of their owners. The Union's petition, pleading for a stay of action, is reproduced *in extenso*:

> "These Sierra Leoneans who built these plots in Port Harcourt were mostly conscripted from school at home . . . to come and work in Nigeria, and to develop the place. They worked under the worst conditions . . . and settled here, made families, and built houses where they lived . . . and most of us had lost contact with home, and because of this, became Nigerians due to marriage. We have no second home in Nigeria. . . . these men built houses only to accommodate their families and not for commercial purposes. Our parents had these houses at their young ages (sic.), and now are very old . . ., and if pushed out . . . will live in the most unhealthy conditions that they had not been accustomed to, and may die in the process".[3]

The Union argued that some of the listed homes had, in fact, never been abandoned, and others, though once abandoned and acquired by the APA, had since been released to their owners, only to be re-acquired by government. It drew attention to the efforts of the Union and High Commission, in 1973, to rectify the situation, and their failure to secure a "permanent solution" of the problem. The Union stressed its members' material dependence on these properties, and called on the Chairman of the Panel, and the Federal Military Government, to get the homes released finally from official clutches. The following homes were listed:

Samuel F. Cole	9 Niger Street
Joshua W. Leigh	59 Niger Street
C. Johnson	73 Niger Street
Evelyn A.L. Savage	31 Aggrey Road
Nicholas J.C. Cline	119 Aggrey Road
G.C. Wilson	125 Aggrey Road
T.C. Rollings	133 Aggrey Road
Mrs. Ajagbonna Oporokun	
(Mrs. A.L.O. Thompson)	113 Victoria Street
A.L.O. Thompson	115 Victoria Street
Sarah Thomas	111 Victoria Street
Rebecca Smith	119 Victoria Street
Miss Smart	81 Aggrey Road[4]

The Nigerian government was clearly adopting a more radical position on immigrants within the territory, and pressure was being exerted on consular officials in Lagos to account more fully for their nationals resident in Nigeria. Heads of foreign missions were briefed about the government's concern over the rising number of illegal aliens in the territory, and with the recent introduction of the Economic Community of West African States (ECOWAS) in 1975,[5] the registration of all foreign nationals through their respective Embassies and High Commissions had become a national priority. The Saro were requested by the Sierra Leone High Commission to comply with these new provisions, by supplying the names, place of birth, passport numbers, "basic qualifications", occupations, employment details, and residential addresses of all adults within their community.[6] This directive caused great unease among individuals whose homes had been requisitioned. The uncertainty over property rights created much alarm as the formulation of real estate policy regarding aliens proceeded. It became painfully evident that the Saro heirs of the Rev. Potts-Johnson were not about to come fully into the protections they had expected from the Nigerian

State. In November, 1979, one of the affected Saro, F.G.T. Cole, of 9 Niger Street, addressed the President of the SLU, B.R. Browne, on his predicament. His father, S.T. Cole, had built the house in question, and had bequeathed it to him; but his ownership rights were now being contested by an indigene. A Mr. Tawari claimed he had purchased the home from the Abandoned Property Implementation Panel, and he had accused Cole of trespassing on his property, and sued for 2000 naira. Cole had to secure the services of a solicitor, and this had caused him much financial distress. He was therefore appealing to the Union for some financial support.[7]

In a related, unnamed and undated correspondence of the same period, another Saro addressed the Union also on the issue of property. The concerns expressed in this letter spoke directly to the crisis of nationality in which the Saro community was trapped in the late 1970's. The letter which came from Onitsha, but referred to property held in Port Harcourt, read:

> "When last I visited your end, I was made to understand that you have forwarded all the names of Sierra Leoneans who owned properties in Port Harcourt in order to differentiate [them] from Ibos and other tribes. For such a long time, I have submitted my deed and photostat copy to the Chief Land Officer, Port Harcourt, but up to now, not a word from the Abandoned Property committee. I will be thankful if you will be kind enough to let me know the cause of the delay . . . if they really mean to treat [the] Sierra Leone community as foreigners".[8]

The concluding section of this letter goes to the heart of the Saro dilemma at this time. Few could believe that after so many years of fruitful association with Nigeria and Port Harcourt, the government could still conceive of the Saro as "foreigners", their nationality status notwithstanding. Most Saro had come to believe that their contributions, over the years, had earned for them a place within the indigenous ranks that was unassailable, and beyond reproach. This obviously was not the government's interpretation of their status, and in this, it enjoyed the approbation of many a resentful indigene. Marriage bonds with locals may well have purchased some social acceptance. They did not, however, completely obliterate local apprehensions which were much reinforced by Saro particularism, such as cultural involvement in groups like the SLU. The personal property problems of the Saro would ultimately be resolved by the late 1980's, and mostly in their favour,[9] but frustrations in the area of real estate were by no means over. Saro efforts to acquire "No. 35" as Union secretariat would run into similar difficulty. It is this painful experience that we now examine.

Efforts to Acquire "No. 35" as Union Secretariat

We have reviewed the Saro's occupation, on rental terms, of 35 Victoria Street, Port Harcourt, and the various uses to which the Secretariat was being put. We now discuss Saro experience in their attempts to purchase the property. To raise funds towards purchase, the Union had explored the possibility of introducing a social club, open to the public, at the premises. In June 1976, a committee was established to explore the feasibility of the idea.[10] For almost three years, the Union made scarcely any progress on its purchase plans. Members discussed it periodically, especially on the occasions when some maintenance work had to be done on the property.[11] The desire to acquire the premises was, however, dealt a crushing blow in December 1979, when the Union committee in touch with the local Lands Office, was informed that the Nigerian government no longer sold property to non-indigenes. It was further explained that the Abandoned Property Authority (APA) had ended its operations in the Rivers State, the government having now purchased all unsold property for future re-sale to indigenes only.[12]

This development greatly unsettled members of the Saro Union for it was yet another painful reminder of the disabilities of immigrant status. Paradoxically, it seems also to have further concentrated Saro minds all the more in the direction of the Sierra Leone High Commission, and the homeland government. With reverses being encountered in Nigeria, the Saro now decided, for the first time, to stake a direct claim on homeland resources. They addressed correspondence to the High Commissioner in Lagos, enquiring of the possibility of Sierra Leone government-funded bursaries for the children of the Saro in school in Nigeria. They wanted the government of Sierra Leone to accord this request its "utmost consideration".[13]

Attempts to purchase "No. 35" were, however, by no means over, and the community would now call on its female members with strong indigenous connections acquired through marriage to lead the challenge.[14] By September 1981, Ebun Johnson was inviting the Union membership to make donations toward a deposit for the purchase of the property.[15] Sisters Sonny V. Joe and V. Ogan thus came to spearhead the purchase efforts, and they were empowered to negotiate on the Union's behalf.[16] In an ironic twist of fortune, female Saro, with local ties, had become invaluable intermediaries for the beleaguered immigrants. By September 1982, the support and the legal counsel of yet another locally well connected Saro, Justice Okoro-Idogu, had been secured. A committee was despatched to confer with him on the most expeditious approach to a solution of the real estate problem.[17] Okoro-Idogu suggested a petition to the Governor, to be drafted with his assistance.[18]

During the annual celebrations of April 1983, the Saro launched a Secretariat Fund.[19] They also addressed a letter to the Deputy Governor of the Rivers State, in which they recounted past Saro contributions, and called for better consideration of the community's interests by the government. The appeal read in part:

> "The ties that bind the people of this great country, Nigeria, especially the Rivers State [to Sierra Leone] are not only that of [the Ecowas] treaty, but . . . long association. The first Sierra Leoneans conscripted for colonial services entered this country as early as the nineteen (sic.) century. They helped in every field . . . Religion (Arch. Crowther, Rev. Shawors, (sic.) etc.), Engineering and carpentry (Pa. Bull, Coker, etc.), Police (Pa. Bucknor and Willoughby), Legal (Pa. Shyngle, Savage, Rhodes-Vivour etc), Education (L.R. Potts-Johnson). These ancient pioneers left footprints on the sand of time [sic.] . . . ".[20]

On the desire to acquire "No. 35", the Saro came directly to the point: We "implore his Excellency to help the Union procure a Secretariat in the State . . . ". They called on the government to treat the immigrant community as it did the indigenes, "so that our sojourn here will be of joy". The Saro commended the government of Nigeria for honouring Sierra Leone and Sierra Leoneans in the naming of streets in Port Harcourt ("I.B. Johnson", "Crowther", "Potts-Johnson", "Bishop Johnson", "Freetown"), and pledged their "sincere loyalty to the government and people of the Rivers State and Nigeria . . . ".[21]

Determined to explore all the available channels of political recourse, the Saro next approached the Governor of the Rivers State, Chief Melford Okilo, regarding 35 Victoria Street. In a letter of November, 1983, the Trustees of the SLU recounted the community's use of the premises as a Secretariat since 1960. G.H.S. Bucknor, T. Jos. Wilson, and A.L.O. Thompson, the Union's Trustees, called on the Governor to expedite the process of the purchase of the property. They submitted a brief historical sketch on the premises: "The building was originally owned by [the] late Mr. Browne (non indigene) who died before the civil war . . . his wife died . . . after the civil war. The property was being looked after by our late Vice-President, Mrs. P.O. Macaulay, till her death in June 1975, when the Union took over the maintenance of the building". The Trustees observed that the members of the Union "had applied several times" to acquire the building, "but were not attended to". They stressed the local blood ties of some of the Union's members, identifying among them, Chief G.H.S. Bucknor, (mother from Andoni), and Olu Potts-Johnson (mother from Brass), to support their claim. Local connections were now being deftly manipulated to make the case of the immigrant community, and Bucknor's pursuit of a chieftaincy title from among his maternal Andoni relations was similarly reflective of this general quest for alliances and some traditional legitimacy in local society.[22]

The Saro also began discussions on purchasing options, of which they considered the following three:

a.   Union members could deposit ¹/10 of the total cost of the property at a mortgage Bank, and raise the rest through rents levied on tenants at the premises.

b.   The well connected G.H.S. Bucknor could get a loan from his bankers for outright purchase, with the Union repaying the loan, with interest.

c.   A member of the Union with the required resources could pay the purchase price, and recover the sum through monthly rents on the property.[23]

By March 1984, the community had filed formal purchase papers,[24] but difficulties were still being encountered. Sis. V. Ogan was requested, in May 1984, to determine whether the premises were still available for sale, and report to the Union's secretary or the president.[25] Although the author found the Union utilizing "No. 35" as a Secretariat during his stay in Port Harcourt, in the late 1980's, he could not determine whether the SLDU had come into ownership of the property at the time.

Other Challenges of the 1970's and Early 1980's: From the Sierra Leone Union (SLU) to the Sierra Leone Descendants Union (SLDU)

With the non-Nigerian members of the Saro community coming under great scrutiny in these years, much effort would be devoted to maintaining good relations with the Sierra Leone High Commission, sustaining cordial ties in the indigenous society, and maintaining the cultural commitments while scrupulously avoiding the quagmire of partisan politics. For a community that was growing in its structural complexity, this would be no mean endeavour. The Saro also came to experience at this time the reality of the return to the "homeland", as one of their senior members, impelled by both frustration and nostalgia, decided to spend his final years in Freetown. The near tragic proportions of that experience would rid many Saro of their illusions of a return for good, and engender a new realism regarding permanent residence in Nigeria.

Discussions in the community in the opening months of 1977 were largely taken up with preparations to host Sierra Leone's new High Commissioner, R.E. Mondeh, who was expected to pay his first visit to Port Harcourt. Mondeh's visit had, however, to be postponed because of his involvement in the cultural jamboree, FESTAC, then being hosted by the Nigerian government. Suitable apologies were rendered, and a consignment of material including a new flag of the republic of Sierra Leone, national almanacs, and current literature, were despatched to the SLU secretariat in Port Harcourt.[26] For their annual celebrations of April 1977, the members of the SLU decided unanimously that the national anthem of both Sierra Leone and Nigeria should be employed during the thanksgiving service.[27] On republic day, traditional libations were poured at "No. 35", with the flags of Sierra Leone and Nigeria being flown until dusk. The Union membership would also decide, in May 1977, to end every general meeting with the singing of the national anthem of Sierra Leone.[28]

No effort was spared at this time in winning allies within the indigenous communities. The Saro, in May 1977, unanimously approved the introduction of honorary member status within the SLU to be open to a select group of indigenes that met the Union's requirements. Non-Saro spouses whose partners were Sierra Leoneans had long requested this option. A Mr. Yowika was the first honoree, and he was promptly followed in June 1977, by Mr. Domo-Spiff, another regular associate of the SLU. The new members were to play a very active part in the annual celebrations of April 1978, during which much emphasis was directed toward attracting more local Saro into the SLU.[29]

With mounting pressure on the immigrant population to prove its loyalty to Nigeria, and with local xenophobia in Port Harcourt headed in a similar direction, it comes as no surprise that, in June 1978, the SLU modified its name to the "Sierra Leone Descendants Union" (SLDU). Members believed that "Descendants" would sound less threatening, and would reflect more a circumstance conferred by pedigree, than a nostalgic reach for a foreign perch. They were keen on publicly proclaiming their fealty to Nigeria and her aspirations, while maintaining the cultural integrity of their community. The price of inaction on this matter was judged to be immense, and inimical of group interests. With so much at stake, the embattled Saro now opted for a public gesture that might finally calm the waters.[30]

Having now re-constituted itself as, hopefully, a less-forbidden SLDU, the Saro adopted a more aggressive line toward its Union members who failed repeatedly to discharge their obligations to the organisation. Discipline within the ranks was a matter never to be compromised. The following letter was addressed, in June 1979, to all absenting members:

> "It has been observed that you have been absent from meetings for over six months. The constitution stipulates that any member who absents himself/herself . . . for six months without permission, should be expelled. . . . Since one of our aims is to embrace every Sierra Leonian [sic.]) resident in Port Harcourt, the Union has taken a decision to be lenient. . . . unless you attend meetings on or before the one scheduled for the 11th August 1979, you should regard yourself as having been expelled . . . and your name struck off . . . the register. We hope that you will not give the Union any cause to take such action".[31]

While seeking to rein in existing members, the Union also intensified its recruiting efforts of new Saro arrivals in Port Harcourt. In June 1979, Sahrfillie and New-Year Matturi were introduced to the group by Albert Norman, a resident Saro. But for the inavailability of membership forms at that meeting, they would have been signed up as members immediately. Sahrfillie was of the Kono ethnic group, and New-Year was Mende. The SLDU, which was run on essentially Krio cultural values, but with a tradition of welcoming Sierra Leoneans of all ethnic groups into membership, was, as in the past, eager to incorporate these new residents at the earliest opportunity.[32] The commitment to a more aggressive outreach policy was also evident in February 1980. Acting on an invitation of December 1979, the SLDU made a financial donation to the Bonny Ibiminaunyo Ereogbu of Port Harcourt, a local organisation which had established a scholarship fund, and launched a fund-raising campaign. When it staged a dance, in this connection, at the Palm Garden Marina, Bonny, members of the SLDU were in attendance, to support the efforts of the society.[33] Marital and other associational ties had placed many a Saro household firmly in the vortex of indigenous social life. This imposed a social dualism that entailed much trafficking between cultures. Many Saro had become particularly skillful in combining these often mutually conflicting obligations. Amid the many uncertainties of an independent Nigeria, such social flexibility was crucial to survival in a society with some individuals that appeared to be increasingly unwelcoming of groups such as the Saro.

The place of the youth within Saro society, at this time, and that of women, deserve some comment, for we have here two groups that were vital to the future of the immigrants, though their value and significance was only being grudgingly acknowledged by the male elders of the community. By October 1980, the younger Saro had embarked on the quest for greater autonomy. Led by Jonathan Coker, they called for a Youth Wing of the Union, that would more adequately reflect their priorities. In a letter to the parent body, the desired Youth Wing was portrayed as vital to the promotion of a greater brotherhood, and the introduction of a forum for the discussion of student problems, and the value-related issues of discipline, honesty, and devotion to duty.[34] In its response, the elder dominated central executive of the SLDU demanded to know the youth's arrangements for the funding of the wing, and their projections as to total membership. This matter would be allowed to drag on for a number of years, a reflection of the misgivings of the older Saro. It was ultimately resolved against the youth's proposal, and they were directed to continue to channel their energies into the central organisation.[35] The Saro patriarchs did not surrender their hegemonic position easily, and in the generational tussle with their young, they showed little willingness for compromise over matters where their pre-eminence had always been conceded.

Saro women, though now in much greater empowerment than previously, would fare no better than the youth in the final power stakes of the SLDU. In the annual Union elections of February 1981, female members made a credible showing as they moved to occupy several prominent offices.[36] This was the first Union executive committee to fully reflect the major contributions of the Saro women to Union and community affairs. Female members had maintained a high level of involvement in matters of social organisation and welfare, and those with indigenous ties had been invaluable mediators with local society. The patriarchal ordering of the SLDU, and the rather modest education of the women, had, however, consigned female members to a largely supporting function in matters of Union governance. But for a few notable exceptions,[37] the prominence of the female membership in decision-making was in inverse proportion to its colossal social responsibility. The overwhelming dominance of male opinion in Union affairs despite recent electoral gains by the female members, would again be in evidence as 1981 drew to a close. In December, the female members of the Union, in a search for greater definition, and a boost to camaraderie, called for the adoption of a uniform dress material and design, to be worn by all females of the group on formal occasions. This was the traditional *Aso-Ebi*, common in Lagos, Freetown, Calabar, and other centres of the Krio. Sis. Bucknor was subsequently empowered to make the selection of dress material, with the approval of Sis. Comfort Ulzen.[38] When, however, the selected design was submitted to the male President of the Union for endorsement, he was unimpressed by the women's choice, and the Executive would subsequently recommend that white blouses and wrappers of choice continue to be the preferred attire for the female members.[39] Little had changed with the years in the councils of the Saro Union. The dress code for the women was still a matter ultimately to be decided by male fiat. The reaction of the women to this peremptory ruling is, however, instructive. Though obviously disappointed in the outcome of their initiative, the ideology of acquiescence in male elder pre-eminence which was judged, even at this stage, to be vital to group survival, discouraged further remonstrance. The Saro had come to operate within the fiction of an undifferentiated unity, and no one was willing to jeopardise group gains by publicly pursuing the path of dissent.[40] Patriarchal dominance would survive largely through fear of the possible ramifications of its demise.

T. Jos. Wilson: The Emigre Returns to the Homeland

T. Jos. Wilson first came to Nigeria from Sierra Leone in July 1926 to be apprenticed as a locomotive engine fitter with the Nigerian Railways in Lagos. He later served in Jos and Makurdi, arriving in Port Harcourt on transfer in 1946. Before his retirement from the railways in 1957, he worked in Enugu, but chose Port Harcourt for his final residence. In the years before and immediately after the Civil War, he took up employment again, this time with the Bulk Oil Plant in Port Harcourt.[41] We have already reviewed Wilson's experience of the Civil War,[42] and, by the late 1970's he had been in continuous residence in Port Harcourt for over 20 years. In discussions with the author, he vividly recounted the xenophobia of the years after the civil war, when the Saro were subject to the sundry victimisations we have reviewed. In some frustration, and out of a long cherished desire to rejoin relatives at the family home on Taylor Street, Kissy Village, just outside Freetown, Wilson decided, in April 1979, to return permanently to Sierra Leone. This was an unusual development, for few Saro had ever embarked on this course of action. Wilson made arrangements for the forwarding of his monthly pension to Freetown, and there were mixed feelings at his departure, particularly among the older Saro who had grave misgivings about the wisdom of re-location after such a long absence.[43]

By April 1982, Wilson, now in his third year in Freetown, began to experience difficulties in the transmission of his pension. He had been well received by his relatives, but intended to retain his financial independence. The SLDU took up the matter unsuccessfully with the Nigerian authorities, and, fearing the worst, the Union began to raise funds for Wilson's return to Port Harcourt for discussions with the pension officials.[44] In obvious financial distress, Wilson kept his situation before Union officials, and in July 1982, the SLDU despatched a ticket to Freetown for his return.[45] His arrival in Port Harcourt, in September 1982, was the occasion of much rejoicing, and the recounting of his painful experience would greatly discourage other Saro with repatriation plans.[46] Wilson's return to Port Harcourt would not, however, lead to the speedy re-instatement of his pension. In April 1984, he was still in the process of gaining access to his funds and the Sierra Leone High Commission had to intervene before the matter was finally settled, and the pension restored.[47]

Frustrations, such as that experienced by T. Jos Wilson and his family, would deepen Saro unease in post-independence Port Harcourt, and cause the community to exercise profound caution in its interactions with the wider society. When, with the resumption of civilian rule, a new National Democratic Action Party was formed in Nigeria in 1982, the Saro were invited to attend the formal launching ceremony of the political movement. In their embattled state, the Saro were eager to be seen to be above the political fray of partisan politics; the SLDU therefore politely declined the invitation.[48] The Saro who once dominated the politics of Port Harcourt, with virtual monopoly control of the Township Advisory Board, would no longer be drawn into such turbulent matters. Activities of this sort, experience had taught, were best left to the indigenes of Nigeria.[49]

For its annual festivities of 1983, the SLDU organised a twin celebration to mark the republican anniversary of Sierra Leone, and the jubilee of the Saro Union's existence. G.H.S. Bucknor, traditional chief and successful businessman, with powerful Andoni connections had now, predictably, been elected Union president as of February 1983.[50] Efforts were still afoot to further streamline Union membership procedures. A six-month probationary period for new applicants was re-introduced. Only on its successful completion would these individuals be allowed into full membership. This move, which had long been contemplated, was thought necessary to improve flagging morale and restore discipline to the Union.[51] Its final passage was, of course, aided by the return of the Union's martinet, T. Jos. Wilson, scourge of the "delinquent". In March 1983, G.H. S. Bucknor,

T. Jos. Wilson, and A.L.O. Thompson, were appointed the first Trustees of the SLDU, positions that had been much discussed over the years, but never activated.[52]

J.N. Coker chaired the Union's 12th Republican anniversary/Golden jubilee celebrations committee. An elaborate programme was outlined. The week 19-24 April 1983 was to be devoted to the twin celebrations. Other committee members were J.E. Davies, and Sisters Theresa Davies, Joyce Boyle, Lydia Williams, and S. Barnes. The programme commenced with the hoisting of the flag of Sierra Leone at the Secretariat on 19th April. This was followed by the visit of a Union delegation to the Governor of the Rivers State, a reception, and a call on the local Old People's Home, where donations were made. A representative of the Union delivered a talk on the Saro of Port Harcourt on radio and television. A soccer match was also played at the Old Recreation Stadium, and during the interval of the match, a Saro women's team took the field against a Saro Men's Team. Wreaths were subsequently laid on the graves of deceased Sierra Leoneans at the local cemetery, and the celebrations were concluded with a thanksgiving service at Wesley, followed by refreshments in the Sunday School hall.[53]

By March 1984, Nigeria had gone through another phase of cataclysmic political change. The restoration of power to civilian rulers by the military in 1979, came to an abrupt end when the army reclaimed power in 1983, ousting the regime of President Shehu Shagari.[54] The Rivers State was now assigned a new Governor, Fidelis Oyakhilome, a senior police officer. The SLDU decided to pay its respects to the new administration, and a delegation of G.H.S. Bucknor, Sis. M.C. Wilson, A.L.O. Thompson, T. Jos. Wilson, Jimmy Coker, and Sisters T. Davies and Mary Udeogu, was directed to call on his Excellency, the Governor, in April 1984. Under local siege, the Saro were keen on maintaining ties at the highest political levels, while attending to the varied affairs of their community.[55]

The concern for cultural propriety was similarly undiminished, and this was clearly in evidence, in July 1984, when Sis. Clarissa Williams passed away in Lagos. The family's plans were for funeral services in Port Harcourt, and burial in Omoku, in the Rivers State. The SLDU was informed accordingly. The Williams' intention was to get the corpse to Port Harcourt for a two-hour laying-out ceremony before the funeral service, and internment. No provision had, however, been made for the traditional wake-keeping, so dear to most Saro. The SLDU objected to this over-sight, and insisted on a wake, precedent to burial. It also called for the usual memorial service, and other observances. Its Secretary wrote: "The family should not forget our . . . custom of three, seven, and forty days celebrations. We hope to hear from you soon, so that we too [can] finalise our arrangements for the burial."[56] As guardian of tradition, the SLDU took a dim view of any breach of custom, and acts that implied indifference to cherished cultural values were not to be tolerated. Shortly thereafter, the Union's secretary, A.L.O. Thompson, demonstrated his regard for tradition and cultural propriety when, in October 1984, he hosted the SLDU at funerary rites for his mother, Sis. Nkoyo Thompson. A wake and other ceremonial were observed, and a number of Saro travelled to Calabar for these obsequies.[57]

By the end of October 1984, photographs of Nigeria's new Military Head of State, Gen. M. Buhari, and the Governor of Rivers State, Fidelis Oyakhilome, were on the walls of the SLDU secretariat. These were standard issue materials, and the Union dutifully thanked the government for making them available.[58] As the SLDU entered 1985, its thoughts turned from the temporal, to the more spiritual dimensions of life. The membership had to determine whether the customary support the Union had always reserved for the Anglican, Methodist, and Roman Catholic Communions, would now be extended to the Salvation Army as well. After long consideration, the Union members demurred, and voted for tradition, and the *status quo*.[59] Now in their seventh decade of residence in Port Harcourt, the Saro were willing to make necessary adjustments to accommodate changed circumstances. There were, however, crucial areas of cultural activity in which the community was averse to modifying group values and practice. Much buffeted by the social currents over the years, the heirs of the Rev. L.R. Potts-Johnson were proof that in some spheres of life, the more things change, the more they indeed remain the same. The price of attachment to old ways was high; but it was one many a Saro would willingly pay.

CONCLUSION

That the Saro were leading pioneers in various fields of endeavour in early Port Harcourt society could not be denied. In education, the church, the press, and African political representation, among others, their dominance was unrivalled. The community's initial freedom from local ethnic ties, which correspondingly increased its ethnic vulnerability while freeing its leaders from a host of communal pressures and obligations, and its superior educational preparation, greatly enhanced its appeal in local colonial society. Saro leaders thus came easily into official appointments, and into jobs with local mercantile firms and other employers in the public and private sectors of the colonial economy. This conclusion must, among other things, situate the expectations of those who invested confidence in these immigrants alongside Saro performance in the principal arena of opportunity, viz., public service. Port Harcourt Saro activity on the Niger needs also to be juxtaposed alongside other Saro exertions in the much better known Yorubaland context. The survival strategies of an immigrant community under siege also deserve some concluding comment.

The colonial government was Port Harcourt's largest employer, and it was arguably in the public realm that the Saro would have the most prominence, and be challenged to their more notable contributions. Through their dominance of the debate in both the Township Advisory Board and the African Community League, Saro opinion would progressively coalesce around the much-advertised views of their most prominent spokesman, the Rev. L.R. Potts-Johnson. Entrepreneur, politician, humourist, rebel churchman, and tribune and advocate of the people on a multitude of causes, Potts-Johnson was obviously on many occasions a disappointment to British officials who found their confidence in him generally unrecompensed. This study has chronicled in some detail his unrelenting critique of official policy, and we have also noted his ability to reach beyond the immediate concerns of his class to Port Harcourt's less advantaged majority, a quality that was conspicuous by its absence among Port Harcourt's patricians. Though a prime beneficiary of official preferment, and, for many years, an insider on policy discussion, Potts-Johnson maintained a discrete distance from the colonial administration, to project, at least for a time, a semblance of objectivity in his appraisal of the government's conduct. He railed incessantly at administrative foibles (a stance that could have done no violence to sales of his newspaper), and exposed official shortcomings with an unsparing regularity. Although these efforts revolved mostly around matters of local infrastructure, African welfare, and issues of fairness in the application of colonial policy, they sometimes addressed the core issue of colonialism itself, and official thoughts on the devolution of greater political responsibility to the governed. In all of his representations, however, Potts-Johnson operated within the minimalist political configurations of his class in that he was more inclined to reform than revolution—more wedded to the vision of the patient preparation of a united African community for the eventual prize, in the distant future, of self-government, than to the hasty repudiation of colonial authority. It was in this essentially teleological vision of African political possibilities that he ran foul of the more impatient of his constituents, viz., the small-scale African traders, the representatives of the working classes, and the youth, who had acquired a casual familiarity with the incendiary claims of international communism. Operating from within an alliance with the indigenous elite, founded on common business and political interests, and nurtured in perennial merry-making, the immigrant Saro leader came increasingly to be seen as an obstacle to local progress, and an unreliable advocate, for the long-term, on African misery. Potts-Johnson's dilemma was scarcely helped by his inability to proceed beyond a casual acquaintance with the House Tenants Union, as well as a penchant to view municipal government as an index of genuine African empowerment. In his problematic relations with the House Tenants Union, class contradictions had finally come home to roost, and Port Harcourt's consummate middle-roader, void of the protections of indigene status, had become the victim of his own political opportunism and expediency.

In his final years, and in declining health, Potts-Johnson was reduced to parrying the relentless attacks of an indigenous lobby that had succumbed to an almost predictable xenophobia, as it raged against its political marginalisation. To ridicule and denunciation, Potts-Johnson would oppose entreaties for local African unity, and the single-minded pursuit of self-reliant economic achievement. Faithful to the end to his creed of economic nationalism, and the championing of African values against the tide of indiscriminate westernisation, he left the stage to his Saro heirs much chastened by the gushing torrents of local political realities, and with a legacy that would ensnare his communal progeny for many years to come.

The Saro community of which Potts-Johnson was the unofficial leader was a highly differentiated assemblage of immigrants with five closely discernible major strata united by a deep commitment to Krio culture and the forging of an identity that would replicate the parent society of Freetown. These were the patricians, the lower middle class activists, the women, the non-Krio Saro, and the poor. Patrician society was characterised by its prudery and pretentiousness (which often masked gross tendencies to moral laxity), a high political profile, rarefied recreational pursuits with freemasonry at the core, and much hubris and condescension in some of the truly affluent. It was this group that bore the brunt of local political rejection, its alliance with a barely tolerated indigenous elite perhaps hastening this outcome.

The lower middle class activist stratum, of which Denson Grant was the prime exemplar, co-existed uneasily with the patricians, but generally made common cause with the indigenous small-scale traders and their working class associates with whom it shared many economic disabilities. Because of the primacy of ethnic loyalties over those of class in Port Harcourt society, however, these alliances of convenience would fail to shield even these relatively less affluent immigrants from local opprobrium in the long term for, ultimately, they were judged as "strangers", and thus of a piece with their more affluent compatriots.

The status of the Saro women qualifies, perhaps, as the most dynamic variable of our review. Clearly marginalised in the public sphere up to independence though indispensable to the community's social reproduction, they progressively emerged as the principal power brokers of the immigrant community as they expertly manipulated marital arrangements and availed themselves of educational opportunity. That they did not come into parity of status with the men was at once a reflection of the patriarchy's uncompromising tenacity, as well as female willingness to subordinate gender interests to the larger good of group harmony and survival.

Saro society also contained that handful of non-Krio Saro that had come to Nigeria largely for trading purposes, and which later immersed itself in the Krio matrix of Saro cultural observance. Because of their small numbers and cultural isolation, these families were strangers within a stranger community, a compounded vulnerability that largely explains their binary ethnicity, and the ease with which they embraced the Krio values of the SLU. Unfortunately, there is no evidence of their cultural donations into the Krio practice of the Saro, itself an ethos of much rigidity in the matter of its core values.[1]

Finally, the Saro had their poorer kinsmen of the unemployed, displaced refugees, indigent retirees, and vulnerable widows in desperate need of repatriation. The requirements of this stratum were a constant challenge for the welfarist instincts of the SLU, and in addressing their many difficulties, the Saro expanded the frontiers of community which were at the core of the group's activities, and constituted its *raison d'être*.

With Potts-Johnson's death, the Saro would commence the slide into political obscurity, and their group impact would now be more evident in their self-appointed, much-cherished, and infinitely less controversial role of guardian of the moral economy (the embarrassment of Potts-Johnson's adulterous conduct notwithstanding), exemplars of genuine pan-ethnic cooperation within their Union organisation, and passionate devotees of Krio culture. All Sierra Leoneans, irrespective of class location or ethnic affiliation, were welcome to the essentially Krio-based cultural activities of the Sierra Leone Union, a remarkable demonstration of inter-ethnic cooperation. Union activity socialised the new immigrant, hosted the visitor, courted the favour of the promising indigene, monitored the progress of other Krio/Saro formations, and projected the public face of a grossly outnumbered stranger community. In the end, Saro reluctance to embrace Nigerian citizenship after independence, coupled with the trauma of the Nigerian civil war, would generate deep resentment of the immigrants, and dictate, in their ranks, a greater social reliance on group resources, as on the rare and much-prized local connections, and the communal instincts of resilience in the face of adversity. As political and other pressures on the Saro increased, so also would the incidence of group assembly to commemorate the diverse social events (weddings, funerals, birth ceremonies, the ubiquitous "socials", etc) in the lives of the community's members. Acts of social renewal had become the balm and the sanctuary of the embattled immigrant. In their desperation, the Saro would also rely heavily on their women, especially those with marital ties in local society. Though generally marginalised, even in a relatively progressive Saro society, the women would emerge as veritable culture brokers for the beleaguered community, performing vital roles for which their menfolk were grossly ill-prepared.

Alongside communal social activity at both the domestic level and that of the SLU/SLDU, and the invaluable mediatory contributions of its women, the Saro would also employ other avenues to secure the interests of their community. A group which had prided itself on its cultural distinction and exclusivity in the 1930's would, by the 1970's, desperately crave local familial ties, connections with indigenous associations, and chieftaincy titles, in its bid for some space within indigenous society. It would also maintain close relations with the Sierra Leone government through its High Commission, and, in gestures of compatriotic outreach to the homeland, underline its faith in the protective abilities of these extra-territorial structures.

The undisputed political parallels between Krio experience in Sierra Leone, and that of the Saro of both Port Harcourt and Lagos, are much too poignant to be ignored. In all three instances, we are presented with ethnic minority populations with political expectations in inverse proportion to their numbers. There is a tragic sameness about H.C. Bankole-Bright, perhaps the most prominent spokesman for Krio rights in Freetown before independence, Herbert Macaulay, the aforementioned leader of the Nigerian National democratic Party (NNDP), and the Rev. Potts-Johnson.[2] In all three cases, we are confronted with political ambition rooted in expectations of minority preference by the colonial authority, over the claims of much larger indigenous constituencies. Minority claims would be rebuffed in each case. What are some of the lessons to be drawn from the Nigerian parallels?

The Saro experience in Lagos differed from that of Port Harcourt in many crucial areas. Lagos had attracted a far larger group of immigrants, with strong ethnic links in local society. This had greatly facilitated their incorporation, even though local hostility, and resentment of their meddlesomeness and European pretensions were not unknown.[3] Having arrived in Nigeria before the 1890's when a heightened race-consciousness would limit African opportunity in government and related spheres, many had served in prominent capacities in the colonial administration. Lagos Saro proximity to the indigenous population would, of course, also breed resentment in official British circles, as was clearly evident in the celebrated case involving Herbert Macaulay and Eshugbayi Eleko, the Oba of Lagos, in the 1920's and early 1930's.[4] We see at work, in this set of events, the dynamics of cultural immersion open to the Lagos Saro, a facility of social incorporation that was not enjoyed by their more ethnically-alienated counterparts in Port Harcourt. Not only could Herbert Macaulay utilise his detailed knowledge of land matters in Lagos to successfully champion the land claims of the aggrieved Chief Oluwa before the Privy Council, he would also exploit the opportunity of a captive British media to press the demands of the Oba of Lagos for more dignified treatment, and improved remuneration from the British administration.[5] The use by Oluwa, a subordinate chief, and Macaulay, of the Eleko's staff of office (with the Eleko's approval) while in London to enhance the legitimacy of their cause, would generate a major furore in Lagos. The Saro, Macaulay, would be accused of manipulating the House of Dosunmu, of which Eleko was the incumbent. This political crisis would pit indigenous Yoruba against the Saro, but it would also divide the Saro, with Henry Carr, Resident of Lagos and nemesis of Herbert Macaulay, and other educated and influential Saro immigrants, fanning the anti-Eleko embers, and providing scarcely-needed encouragement to a British administration soon to depose the Oba from office.[6]

The Eleko incident is instructive for our purposes on two principal fronts. Firstly, unlike the Port Harcourt situation where Potts-Johnson had few intellectual peers, thus allowing his ideas to go largely unchallenged within the Saro community, Herbert Macaulay was surrounded by an array of Saro luminaries, and he therefore had to make the case for his various positions within as well as outside the Saro group. He could not therefore easily accede to the dominance Potts-Johnson enjoyed in Port Harcourt. Secondly, and perhaps even more significantly, we see in this incident the cultural intimacy that the Lagos situation afforded the Saro, a major element ultimately in their travails, however, as, unlike their Niger Delta counterparts, they could not be seen to be uninvolved in traditional politics. A Niger Delta of a congeries of ethnic communities spared the minority Saro the imperative of cultural attachment to indigenous patrons. A more ethnically homogenous Yorubaland demanded affiliation of the immigrants, thus sharply undermining their autonomy, and limiting their public involvement with Freetown.

In the end, both sets of Saro leaders would find themselves bereft of local political support, for it was the colonial dispensation, not the popular weal, that had fostered their emergence. Herbert Macaulay's quarrel with Chief Oluwa in 1938 marked the beginning of the end for the NNDP. Potts-Johnson's difficulties with the small-scale African traders and their working-class associates in the House Tenants Union, set his fortunes on the slippery slope, even as his allies in the indigenous elite, victims of an underdeveloped class consciousness,[7] reconsidered their involvement with the unpopular immigrants. Both men had been cultural pragmatists, engaged in a dialectical fusion of African and European value. This eclecticism would be woefully inadequate in a nationalist climate that validated only the indigene. In Sierra Leone, Bankole-Bright appears to have suffered from a similar range of contradictions. The image he cut of an Edwardian dandy, his social distance from indigenous society, and his abrasive repudiation of non-Krio claims, ensured for him like rejection when his political fortunes were put to the national test.[8] Political aspirants of minority ethnic communities with ex-slave returnee connections have, generally, had a chequered experience on the African political scene.[9] The life of Potts-Johnson, as with others of his experience, attests ultimately to the enormous difficulties that confronted generations of those once up-rooted from the African continent by slavery. Condemned to a perpetual rootlessness, and for reasons of his own personal contradictions, as well as society's unwillingness to speed his re-incorporation, the returnee could never fully re-enter into his African inheritance.

APPENDIX 1

SIERRA-LEONE UNION, PORT HARCOURT. CONSTITUTION, RULES AND REGULATIONS

1. *Name*:
   The Union shall be called the Sierra-Leone Union, Port Harcourt.
2. *Object*:
   The main object of the Union shall be to seek to unite all Sierra-Leone citizens and descendants resident or domiciled in Port Harcourt with a view to fostering their general welfare, and to serve as a link with the homeland as well.
3. *Membership*:
   (a) Membership shall be open to Sierra-Leonians or their descendants above 18 years of age. New members shall be admitted and registered following the satisfactory completion of the application form of the Union:
   (b) Any eligible person desiring membership shall complete the Union's application form and submit it with the relevant enrollment fee to the Secretary:
   (c) Enrollment fees shall be 50 Kobo flat for both male and female.
4. *General Meetings*:
   General meetings shall be held every second Saturday of each month. Executive meeting shall be held on the Wednesday preceding the general meetings.
5. *Election*:
   Election of officers shall be held annually in the month of March. The Annual Report and the Union Audited Statement of Accounts shall be submitted at the February general meeting.

6. *Officers*:
   The Officers of the Union shall consist of:
   (a) President
   (b) The Vice President
   (c) Secretary
   (d) Assistant Secretary
   (e) Treasurer
   (f) Financial Secretary
   (g) Welfare Officer
   (h) Auditor
   The Officers shall perform all duties normally incidental to their respective offices subject however, to such changes or additions at the direction of the Union.
7. *Resolutions*:
   At every meeting, the decision of the majority shall be final.
8. *Composition of Executive Committee*:
   The Executive shall be composed of all officers and 2 members—one male, one female—to be elected.
9. *Quorum*:
   At the General Meeting, 12 members shall form a quorum.
   (b) At an Executive Meeting 4 members shall form a quorum including the President or the Vice President and the Secretary or the Assistant Secretary.
10. *Monthly Subscriptions*:
    Monthly subscriptions shall be 30 Kobo male and 20 Kobo female.
11. *Distant Members*:
    A distant member who is financial shall enjoy all the privileges of the Union as if he or she was present, but shall not be elected to office.
12. *Forfeiture of Benefits*:
    A member shall forfeit his or her benefits if he or she is in arrears of monthly subscriptions up to three months.
13. *Authorised Officers for Banking of Funds*:
    (a) The signature of the President and Secretary or Treasurer shall be valid on all vouchers and documents of the Union.
    (b) A quarterly Statement of Accounts shall be read to the General Meeting by the Financial Secretary.
    (c) The Treasurer shall be given an Imprest not exceeding N10 to meet expenses in connection with emergencies or urgency cases.
    (d) All monies to be deposited shall be paid into the bank within seven days of the date they are received by the Treasurer.

14. *Discipline*:
   (a) *Lateness*: A fine of 3 Kobo shall be imposed on a late comer to meetings.
   (b) *Absence*: Any member who absents himself or herself from a lawfully convened meeting without previously informing the Secretary of the Union is liable to a fine of 5 Kobo.
   (c) *Misconduct*: Any member proved disturbing or inciting or abetting the disturbance of the proceedings of a meeting or any other functions of the Union shall be deemed guilty of a misconduct and shall be liable to a minimum fine of 10 Kobo or suspension or expulsion or both.
   (d) *Violation*: Any member proved to have deliberately disobeyed any resolutions duly passed by the Union or to have portrayed the Union by word or action, in any way detrimental to the image or good name of the Union outside shall be guilty of violation and shall be suspended or expelled from the Union.

15. *Benefits*:
   (a) Any financial member who observes the funeral obsequies of a deceased husband/wife, child shall be given the sum of N4.20 Kobo (N4.20)
   (b) Cases of members in distress, shall be considered on their merits for purposes of rendering such aid as may be deemed necessary.

16. *Sick Members*:
   Reports shall be made at General Meetings of members who are indisposed so that arrangements may be made to visit them.

17. *Deaths*:
   The death of a member shall be duly reported to the Union immediately it occurs so that arrangements may be made in good time for the funeral ceremony.

18. *Disputes*:
   To maintain cordial relations among members, it shall be the duty of every member to report a dispute known to exist between any two or more members so that arrangements agreeable to the parties in dispute may be amicably effected.

19. *Republic Day*:
   April 19th of every year shall be known as Sierra Leone Republic Day.

20. *Amendments to the Constitution.*
   Any alteration of this constitution shall be made at the general meeting provided that notice of the proposed amendment is circulated to all members of the Union two weeks before the date of the meeting.

Source: SLDUPH

APPENDIX 2

THE DIAMOND CLUB, PORT HARCOURT

Rules and Regulations.

1. Designation.
   (a) The Club shall be called "Diamond Club."
   (b) Motto: "For love, for friendship, and for society."
   (c) Emblem: Crest showing radiance of Diamond.
2. Object.
   The Object of the Club is to promote the Social and intellectual developments and mutual relations among its members.
3. Membership.
   Any African of good repute shall be eligible to become a member of the Club provided he shall upon application through the Secretary accompanied by the entrance fee be proposed and seconded by two members. This rule shall not apply to Honorary members.
4. Candidature.
   The Name of a candidate for admission as an ordinary member with the name of his proposer and seconder shall be circulated seven days before the meeting at which his admission or rejection shall be decided by a vote. The admission of any person as an ordinary member of the Club shall be two thirds or more majority of votes, and should he be rejected his entrance fee shall be returned to him.
5. Classification of Membership.
   Members shall consist of:
   (a) Ordinary members

(b) Temporary members

(c) Honorary members

(d) Distant members

5a. An ordinary member is one who is resident in Port Harcourt and regularly pays monthly subscriptions and other necessary dues for the up keep of the Club. He shall enjoy its rights and privileges.

5b. A Temporary member is one who is not resident in Port Harcourt but comes here for a period of about three months or less. Such a member may upon being duly proposed and seconded be admitted as a Temporary Member of the Club and shall be eligible to the privileges of members except as to voting. Temporary members may not pay entrance fees but will be liable to pay other dues as members. Any gentleman in this category loses his membership immediately he leaves the Township.

5c. A Hon. member is one who is invited by the Club to be a Patron, etc. He is liable neither for entrance fee nor for monthly subscriptions but his donations or services shall be gladly accepted by the Club.

5d. A Distant member is one who leaves the Township for a period of not less than 3 months. Such a member may if he so desires, retain his membership on payment of an annual subscription of 3/-.

6. Entrance Fee.

The Entrance fee for a member shall be 10/-

7. Officers.

The following shall comprise the officers of the Club; President, Vice President, Hon. Secretary, Asst. Secretary, Hon. Treasurer, Hon. Financial Secretary and Auditors.

8 Duties of Officers.

a. It shall be the duty of the President or in his absence the Vice President to order the convening of meetings and to preside at all meetings and to have a casting vote in all matters. He shall sign the minutes of proceedings, and his ruling shall be final on a subject under discussion.

b. The Secretary shall be responsible for the convening of meetings as may be directed by the President. He shall also be responsible for the keeping of the records of the proceedings of all meetings and shall do all Secretarial work appertaining to the Club.

c. The Assistant Secretary shall as far as possible assist the Secretary in the performance of his duties and shall in the latter's absence act for him.

d. The Treasurer shall be responsible for the accurate keeping and accounting of all Club monies, and shall deposit same in the local banking account, and submit a quarterly balance sheet. He shall hold an imprest of not less than 20/-.

e. The Financial Secretary shall collect and receive all fees and hand them to the Treasurer.

f. The Auditors shall audit periodically the books of the Treasurer and shall report to the Club their findings quarterly. All cheques drawn against the Club and all monies expended out of the funds of the Club shall be on the joint signatures of both the Treasurer and the Financial Secretary to be countersigned by the President.

9. Trustees.

The Trustees of the Club shall be the President or the Vice-President, Treasurer and Secretary. All cheques drawn against the Club and all monies expended out of the Club shall be on the joint signatures of the last two officer (sic.) countersigned by the President or Vice-President. They shall operate on the banking account of the Club.

10. Management.

The management of the Club shall be vested in a Committee consisting of the officers of the Club and two un-official members to be appointed at the annual election of officers. The Committee may appoint a Sub-Committee from the members of the Club with such powers and duties as the Committee may determine.

11. Duties of the Committee.

The Committee shall meet at least once a month or as often as occasion arises, to consider the affairs of the Club and shall report to members in the ordinary general meeting, the progress, financial position and general affairs of the Club during the previous month.

a. The Committee may convene Extra-ordinary general meetings of the Club and shall also convene such a meeting upon a written request signed by four or more members who shall specify in the application the purpose for which such a meeting is desired.

b. The Committee shall have power to make supplement to these rules and regulations or frame Bye-Laws for the proper management of the Club. All Bye-Laws shall be binding on the members.

12. Election of Officers.

The Election of officers and Committee members shall take place at the general meeting to be held on the 2nd Thursday in August of every year; this shall be by ballot and the officers and Committee members of the previous year shall be eligible for re-election.

13. Meetings and Quorums.

   a. The ordinary meeting of the Club shall be held on the second thursday of every month, one-fourth of the members including the Secretary or his assistant, shall form a quorum, and all questions shall be decided on a majority of votes.

   b. Emergency or Extra-ordinary meetings may be summoned when necessary; one-fifth of the member (sic.) shall form a quorum; this number shall include the President. No minutes of ordinary meetings shall be read at such a meeting.

   c. Committee Meetings may be summoned when necessary. Half of the members shall form a quorum. This number shall include the President.

   d. There shall be an annual meeting on the second Thursday of August for the election of officers, and to hear the report of the Secretary and the Treasurer.

Every meeting shall be convened by a circular which shall be issued about 4 days before the date of the meeting.

14. Monthly Subscription.

There shall be paid by every member of the Club a monthly subscription of 1/- payable in advance or at most ten days after the end of the month. Distant members pay 3d. per month. Arrears exceeding 3/- render a member liable to suspension.

15. Pledge of submission to the Club.

The Payment of Entrance fee and subscription by an ordinary member and the payment of subscription by a temporary member shall be considered as a declaration of submission to the Rules, Bye-Laws and Regulations of the Club, and the orders of the Committee.

16. Discipline. Penalty for Failure to pay Dues.

Any member who fails to pay his subscription after the prescribed time shall forfeit his rights to enjoying any of the amenities of the Club.

Every Club Member is expected to behave in a most gentlemanly manner at all meetings and functions of the Club.

   a. The use of vernacular or slang is prohibited at all meetings and functions of the Club.

   b. Any member who contravenes any of these rules shall be dealt with by the Committee whose decision shall be final.

   c. All officers are responsible to the Club for the proper and satisfactory performance of their duties. Any neglect of duty on the part of any officer can be reported by any member of the Club through the Secretary to the Committee.

d. The Club may institute legal proceedings against any member or person who fails to discharge his liabilities to the Club. In such proceedings the Secretary or a nominee shall represent the Club.

17. Attendance.

a. Every member shall be expected to attend all the meetings of the Club regularly. Any cause for absence shall be communicated to the Secretary in time to be read at the opening of the meeting from which a member is absent.

b. Every emergent or unforseen cause of absence shall be reported in writing three days at the latest after the meeting from which the member is absent.

c. Every such application shall be considered on its merits.

18. Penalty.

Any member who is absent from a meeting without permission is liable to a fine of 6d. which should be paid within 7 days of its imposition. Any member who deliberately fails or refuses to pay such a fine shall automatically be suspended until payment has been made.

19. Persistent Absence.

Any member who is persistently absent from meetings for a period of three months without permission shall be considered with a view to suspension. No period of suspension shall exceed one month.

20. Late-comers.

Any member who comes in after the reading of the minutes is considered as having been late and shall be liable to a fine of 3d; but every case shall be considered on its merits.

Finance.

21. Control of Expenditure.

Every expenditure of the Club's money shall, in the first instance, be approved in a general meeting or in urgent cases of send off or reception by the Executive Committee.

b. All payment vouchers should be signed by the Secretary and countersigned by the President.

22. Send-off and Reception.

Every send-off or reception shall be arranged by the Committee. Send-off or reception shall be given to members not in arrears, who are not suspended or under any form of punishment whatsoever. Any member proceeding on leave or transfer should notify the Committee through the Secretary at least three days before the actual date of departure.

23. Resignation.

Any member desiring to resign shall submit the resignation in writing through the Secretary for discussion at the general meeting. Any member resigning shall be required to pay all monies he is owing to the Club.

24. Re-admission.

Any member seeking re-admission shall as usual send a written application but may not be required to pay Entrance fee. Arrears of the previous months may be paid.

25. Dismissal.

The Persistent disregard of the rules and regulations of the Club on the part of any member shall render him liable to dismissal. No member shall be dismissed until his case had been discussed at a general meeting or he has had a chance of defending himself at a general meeting.

26. Claims on the Club.

No member who resigns or is dismissed shall have any claim on the Club in respect of subscription or any other payments made.

27. Activities of the Club.

There should be a literary section of the Club which shall involve discussion on subjects such as debates, impromptu speeches, addresses (read or unread) and recitations.

a. The social section shall include concerts, dances, entertainments, in-door games, picnic and athletics.

28. General.

All the employees of the Club are under the direct control of the Secretary who is empowered to inflict punishments on them with the approval of the President. Such punishment must be reported by the Secretary to the general meeting for confirmation or otherwise.

b. Any misconduct on the part of any employee of the Club should be reported by any member to the Secretary who should exercise his discretion and deal with such a report.

29. Amendments.
No addition, alteration, or amendment shall be made to these Rules without a vote of two-thirds of the members present, and no motion to amend shall be acted upon at the same meeting at which it was proposed.
30. Enforcement of Rules.
These rules shall come into force with effect from 1st May 1938 and shall be binding on all the members.
S.E. Orubo, Hon. President
D.E. Iwarimie JaJa, Hon. Secretary

Officers and Members of the Diamond Club

Mr. S.E. Orubo	President
Mr. L. Ade John	Vice President
Mr. D.E. Iwarimie Jaja	Hon. Secretary
Mr. E.G. Pepple	Hon. Treasurer
Mr. A.G.K. Abalo	Fin. Secretary
Mr. J.P. Adeyemi-Cole	Auditor
Mr. B.B.J. Members	Auditor
Mr. R.G. Pepple	Asst. Secretary
Mr. E. Ade-Koku	Asst. Secretary

Distant Members

Mr. J.T. Ogbolu	(Past President)
Mr. I.O. Kuforiji	(Past President)
Mr. Jas. M. Egbuson	(Past Chairman)
Mr. D.C. Osadebay	
Mr. G. Egbuniwe	
Mr. J.T. Awoboh	

Source: SLDUPH

APPENDIX 3

PORT HARCOURT OPTIMISTS RULES AND REGULATIONS

Title

1. PORT HARCOURT OPTIMISTS.

Constitution

2. That this Society shall consist of all Lovers of Music, Male and Female, temporarily or permanently resident in Port Harcourt, in Nigeria, provided they satisfactorily comply with the terms of membership.

Object

3. To promote the Social and intellectual development and mutual relations among its members; and to elevate the technical and general knowledge and proficiency of Musicians therein, and the rendering thereof by means of Services, Lectures, Singing Competitions, Piano Recitals, Dramatical Concerts etc., and generally to watch over and protect the interest of members for the time being of the Society. (sic)

Regular Meeting

4. The Regular Meeting shall be held at the Office of the President on the first Saturday in every month at the hour of 7 o'clock p.m. or any other place and time as the President or his Deputy may determine.

Emergency Meeting

5. Emergency Meeting may at any time be called when necessary on instructions from the President, in his absence, his Deputy.

Officers

6. The officers of the society shall consist of the following: President, Deputy President, Treasurer, Secretary, Financial Secretary, Assistant Secretary, Auditors and a Musical Director.

Duties of Officers

7. The President shall preside and manage the affairs at all meetings of the Society, and in his absence the Deputy President shall communicate with the Secretary for the summoning of Emergent (sic.) Meetings. And on all matters affecting the interest of the society. (sic.) The President shall have a common vote, and a casting vote when necessary.

    (a) The Treasurer shall be responsible to the Society for all monies received by him, from the Secretary and the Financial Secretary, and for a proper account of all authorized disbursement of the same—He shall open a current account with the Bank of British West Africa and shall have as Co-Trustees the President and Secretary. The Treasurer alone shall pay all current and other expenses in connection with the Liabilities of the Society. He shall prepare at the end of every quarter a statement of Accounts to be read at the General Meeting—A pay order Voucher to the Treasurer dully (sic.) signed and approved by the Secretary and President shall support all Payments from the funds of the Society.

All Cheques for withdrawal of monies from the Bank must be counter-signed by the President.

    (b) The Secretary shall be responsible for the convening of all meetings, preparation of all munites, (sic.) the Roll of Membership, General Correspondence of the Society, and the rendering of all half Yearly and Yearly Accounts and Reports i.e. Members on the roll, General changes of members and the financial state of the Society—The Secretary shall pay to the Treasurer all monies collected by him, either at or, out of the meeting, the names of all members in Arrears. (sic.) In the absence of the Secretary, the Assistant Secretary will cover up the duties of the Secretary.

(c) The Auditors shall be appointed annually, at the end of the year, or at any time necessary to Audit all the financial Books of the Society in the hands of the Financial Secretary, the Secretary and the Treasurer, and report their findings to the first regular meeting—There shall be two Auditors.

(d) The Musical Director shall be responsible for conducting, Teaching of Music, Piano Playing, Voice Production, Harmony, Counterpoint, Canon, fugue and the like—He is to submit a monthly report to the General meeting of the conduct and progress of each Artist for the Society's information.

Entrance Fees

8.   The amount payable for entrance fee by each member—Male shall be 5/- (Five Shillings) and Female 2/6 (Two Shillings and six pence).

Monthly Subscription

9.   The amount of monthly subscription payable by each member shall be one shilling (Male) and sixpence (Female) in advance. Any member in arrears for three months, and is not absent from Town, (sic.) nor make any arrangement by which his monthly Fee shall be paid, (sic.) shall automatically cease to be a member and can only be eligible again to become a member by complying with Rule 8.

Application for Membership

10. All applications for membership shall be made in writing through the Secretary. The fee for admission shall be five shillings, if accepted; or returned should the ballot prove unfavourable.

Committee Members

11. The Committee of the Society shall consist of all the Officers and two other members, and shall serve for one Year only. Five shall form a Quorum.

Election of Officers

12. The election of Officers shall be annually at the Regular Meeting by open Vote i.e. on the 1st Saturday in April in each year; but shall be eligible for re-election. (sic.)

Notice of Motion

13. Notice of Motion may be given in writing to the Secretary at least ten days previous to the meeting at which such motion is to be considered and such notice shall be inserted in the Circular Summons.

Resignation of Officers or Members

14. Any member may resign his membership by signing a written notice to that effect to the Secretary or personally signifying at a meeting, his wish to resign, remaining however, responsible for arrears of subscription if any. Such members shall forfeit all claims to every and anything in connection with the Society.

Attendance, etc.

No member shall absent himself or herself from any meeting when duly notified without informing the Secretary of the same, either in writing or otherwise, of his or her inability to attend. Any member absenting himself or herself from two meetings consecutively, without sufficient explanation, shall be liable to a fine of three pence payable forwith or at the next General Meeting. If a member wilfully refuses to pay a fine he or she shall cease to take any active part in the affairs of the Society until the fine shall have been paid. Any member leaving the Town, temporarily or otherwise, shall report the same in writing to the Secretary.

Music and Singing Lessons

16. The Society meets three times a week for the purpose of singing, Piano Playing, Lectures Etc., Members failing to attend these practices will be seriously dealt with by the committee of Management.

Bye Laws

17. No motion for the abrogation or alteration of any of these Bye-Laws or for any addition thereto, shall be considered unless at least one month's previous notice of such motion be given at a regular meeting of the Society, and the notice calling the meeting at which it falls to be considered contain a copy of it. If the proposed alteration be approved by a majority of at least

two-thirds and afterwards be confirmed by the Committee of General Purposes, it shall come into full force and operation.

Adopted and passed at the general meeting held on the 3rd of April, 1939.

O.A. Alakija M.A. B.C.L.
President
Felix Meyer
Deputy President
W. Max. George L.N.C.M. (Lond)
Hon. Secretary and Musical Director

Source: Riv. Prof. 9/1/765, NAE

APPENDIX 4

HOUSE TENANTS UNION PREAMBLE TO THE CONSTITUTION

WHEREAS on Saturday January 6, 1945, a meeting of Tenants was convened by Mr. N.D. Godswille-Hart at the instance of a Co-operative determination between him and two other gentlemen, namely, Messrs. I.W. Osika and B.J. George.

AND whereas the determination culminating on seeking the welfare of House Tenants in Port Harcourt evinced itself by these gentlemen having obtained the use of Enitonna High School room, and having published an announcement in the Eastern Nigeria Guardian resultant in getting together 267 members of the community in the said School room at 5:30 p.m.

AND whereas that particular meeting after having heard the aims and objects of the conveners, and having decided and resolved to get up a constituted body, which should serve to protect the interest of House Tenants in Port Harcourt, resolved that the following be the constitution of the said body. It is, therefore, determined, constituted and declared as follows:

Article 1: Name

1. That the name of this body shall be known and called PORT HARCOURT HOUSE TENANTS UNION.

Article 2: Aims and Objectives

A. It shall be the duty of this union to protect the interest of members who are House Tenants of houses in the Native location exclusive of Government quarters.

B. It shall also be the duty of this union to foster co-operation among all House Tenants who are members of the Union ever always to be ready to contribute legitimate help towards any suffering Tenants in order to restore to him or her the necessary comfort and amenity which he should have from his Landlord and quarters.

C. It shall be the duty of this Union to approach the Government or any other authority of the Government constitutionally, in matters affecting adversely the welfare of Tenants who are members.

D. It shall be the duty of this Union to put up official avenues whereby reasonable information could easily be gathered from reliable sources regarding tenancy in Port Harcourt.

Article 3: Meetings

There shall be known to be functioning the following meetings of the Union:

A. General meeting which shall be held once in the month to be attended by every member.

B. Emergency meeting which shall be held as often as necessary in order to consider matters needing urgent attention.

C. Executive Committee meeting which shall be a meeting of members of the Executive Body who think fit as often as necessary to meet matters of interest in which action should be taken on behalf of the Union as a whole. (sic.) In all meetings a quarter of the number of members shall form a quorum.

Article 4: Membership

A. Any House Tenant may be enrolled as a member of the Union on payment of a registration fee of one shilling as a foundation member, and one shilling and six pence as registration fee for subsequent enrollment of persons who are not foundation members.

B. Any person thus registered shall then become a recognized member of the Union.

C. Every enrolled member shall be issued with a card known as House Tenants Union Membership Identity Card which shall be signed by the President and the Secretary certifying that the particular person whose name is shown on the card is a member of the Union and the cost of the card shall be sixpence.

Article 5: Dues

The following shall be the recognized dues which every member shall pay:

A. *Monthly Subscription:* It shall be the duty of every member to pay into the funds of the Union a monthly due of sixpence.

B. *Emergency Due:* There shall be paid by every member any particular sum of money which is stipulated and made payable for purposes of meeting up an emergent demand such as present funds could not adequately meet up.

C. *Accidental Dues:* Under Bye-Laws any fines which shall be levied on any particular member or members and made payable into the funds shall fall due as accidental dues.

Article 6: Failure to Pay Dues

Any member of this Union who fails to pay any of the dues, as constitutionally approved shall be disconnected forthwith if such member refuses to pay up the said dues after three months.

Article 7: Officers—Election of and Duties

A. The Officers of this Union shall be a president, Vice-president, Secretary, Assistant Secretary, Treasurer, Financial Secretary and 2 Auditors.

B. Election of Officers shall be made from the members of the Union yearly and they shall serve in the capacity for which they are elected. All Officers shall be elected in January for that year and vacancies occurring accidentally in office shall be filled by the Executive Committee for the unexpired term. Election shall be made by ballot or rivavoca (sic.) and in majority of votes shall be required to elect. (sic.).

C. The President shall preside at all meetings of the Union and shall sign all orders and vouchers on the Treasurer duly approved by the Executive Committee, and shall perform all such other duties as pertaining to his office.

D. His Vice-President shall act in the absence of the President and perform such duties as may be assigned to him by the President. In the absence of all the Presidents, one of the members present can be appointed to act instead.

E. The Secretary shall make and keep proper minutes of the proceedings at each meeting of the union and of the Executive Committees, conduct such correspondence as may be directed by the President or his deputy, notify Officers of their appointments, prepare an order of business for each meeting for the use of the President or his deputy, receive list of membership of the Union, give publicity in the Press, of matters to be treated through the Press, and attend to all other matters relating to the Union, such matters as may be referred to him, the Secretary. He shall also be responsible to convene meetings as shall be directed by the President or his deputy and, together with the President or his deputy, and the Financial Secretary, sign all orders and vouchers on the Treasury.

F. The Assistant Secretary shall assist the Secretary by getting to do such duties as shall be assigned to him by the Secretary and shall act in the absence of the Secretary by performing such duties as are already assigned to the Secretary.

G. The Treasurer shall receive and pay into the Bank all monies of the Union, shall keep an accurate account and record of all Receipts and Expenditure, and render a Balance Sheet annually so that the same may be duly audited before the last General meeting of the Union for the year. A copy of the Balance Sheet duly approved by the General Meeting shall be scrutinised by the Executive Committee and passed to be stored in the Archives of the Union.

H. The Financial Secretary shall assist the Treasurer to carry on the secretarial work relating to Finance as may be assigned to him by the Treasurer. It shall also be his duty to receive money of the Union from any legitimate source and pay same into the Treasury through documentary "Hand-over" and to issue Receipts and keep record for all monies received by him.

I. The Auditors shall audit all accounts of the Union quarterly and submit their joint report to the Executive Committee for general meeting.

J. All Officers shall be Ex-officers of both the General Meeting and the Executive Committee.

Article 8: The Executive Committee

This shall be composed of all the Officers and four other elected members of the Union. All acts of the Executive Committee shall be reported at the General Meeting.

Article 9: Funds

The funds of the Union shall be under the custody of the Treasurer together with whom the President or his deputy the Financial Secretary and the Secretary or his Assistant shall sign Vouchers or Orders on the Treasury or the Bank for any withdrawal of any sum of money for business of the union. No sum of money shall be left in the hands of the Treasurer but that all monies except Imprest Cash shall be left in his hands for emergent use of the Union.

B. *Imprest Cash:* A sum of money not more than twenty shillings shall be left with the Treasurer at all times with a view to meeting up emergent needs of the Union. Neither the Treasurer nor the Financial Secretary shall keep with him any sum of money for more than 7 days under his custody so long as such sum of money is unauthorized to be kept by him.

Article 10: Reports

All Officers shall submit brief report of their year's work at the last General Annual Meeting and a copy for each shall be filed by the Secretary.

Article 11: Amendments

The Constitution of this Union may be altered or amended only at a meeting or meetings of the general meeting of the Union. Notice of proposal for any amendment by any member must reach the Secretary not later than 7 days before the general meeting.

Article 12: Patrons, Vice-Patrons & Honorary Members

Persons of respectable or responsible position and others interested in the Housing Problem of Tenants may be invited to become Patrons, Vice-Patrons, or Honorary Members.

B. Upon accepting the invitation they are placed on the same footing as the honorary members except the right to office.

C. A list of the Patrons, Vice Patrons and Honorary Members shall be kept and published by the Secretary of the Union in the local press.

Article 13: Parliamentary Rules

Parliamentary rules shall govern this Union in all cases to which they are applicable and in which they are not inconsistent, more especially during meetings of this Union.

Article 14: Notification by Members for Help

It shall be the duty of any member who is under any adverse circumstance relative to his tenancy or question of building or premises or on rental dues or on a dispute between himself and his House-owner or Care-taker to write immediately or walk up and report the matter in toto to the Secretary, and the President or his deputy stating definitely the fact of the case and the sort of help he needs in order that the Union shall be placed in a position to solve forth-with the difficulty confronting that particular member.

Article 15: Social Obligations by Members

In case of illness or death affecting any member of this Union, it shall be the duty of this Union to give help financial or otherwise such help as shall be decided and approved by the Executive Committee.

B. In any case in which the normal joy of a member is multiplied and if a representative body of the Union is invited, it shall be the duty of the Executive Committee to vote what necessary form of co-operative representation by attendance, donation or otherwise which shall be contributed towards that purpose.

Bye-Laws

Article 1: Late Coming

Any member who at any meeting of the Union who shall come late for fif- teen minutes more than the stipulated time shall pay a fine of one penny. (sic.)

Article 2: Absence at Meetings

Any member who shall absent himself without permission at meeting of the Union shall pay a fine of three pence.

Article 3: Defaulters

Any member who is charged with an offence under the Bye-laws or this Constitution shall be given the chance to explain himself fully before the Executive Committee to show cause why he shall not be punished. If the explanation is accepted by majority of votes of the members present such defaulter shall be left off unpunished.

Article 4: Unbecoming Conduct

Any member who is found to be rude or who exhibits an unbecoming conduct in meetings or in any function of the Union is liable to a fine of one shilling.

Article 5: Official Secrets

Any member who is proved to have divulged an official secret of the Union whereas he knows that such a matter should not be divulged at the Union's expense shall be liable to a fine of two shillings and sixpence.

Read and passed by all members at the General Meeting of the Union held at 150 Victoria Street, Port Harcourt, on the 13th day of February 1945.

President
Secretary

Source: OW5755, Riv. Prof. 9/1/1278, NAE

APPENDIX 5

THE SIERRA LEONE
UNION PORT HARCOURT BRANCH

Secretariat
c/o A.O. Wilson,
No. 8 Bonny Street,
Port Harcourt.

His Excellency,
The High Commissioner for Sierra Leone in Nigeria,
Sierra Leone High Commission,
LAGOS

Your Excellency,

We the undersigned are Sierra Leoneans who are domiciled in what was formerly the Eastern Region of Nigeria in search of our livelihood. Some of us have spent upwards of thirty years in this country and what we say should be taken with the seriousness that it deserves.

First of all we have to say that whatever Mr. Samuel Metzger has stated in Sierra Leone that has made the Prime Minister of Sierra Leone to make the statement attributed to him cannot be regarded as the truth, because nothing which tends to make anyone support the Nigerian rebels cannot be the truth.

Take for instance the question of genocide. No one intends to exterminate the Ibos. Rather, the Ibos in their mad bid for power intended to exterminate any group that opposed them. The coup of January 1966 is a case in point. When in late 1964 and early 1965, they found out that they could not seize power in Nigeria they started planning the Coup. This culminated in the killing of the Sardauna of Sokoto (Sir Ahmadu Bello), the Prime Minister, (Sir Abubakar Tafawa Balewa), Chief Festus Okotie Eboh and Northern and Yoruba high ranking Army personnel. It is significant that no Ibo leader whether military or political was killed.

Major General Aguiyi Ironsi took over the reins of Government and for a time the Ibos were satisfied. Meanwhile in the North, Ibos resident there started to taunt and jeer at the Northerners. You do not know the Iboman as we who lived amongst them do. They can be exasperating. They can goad you into doing something mad.

The Northerners are no angels it is true, but in this case the events of May and September, 1966 were as a result of extreme provocation. You or your leaders killed or cause to be killed my own leaders. Then you now turn round to show me the photograph of one of those killed, especially one whom you know I hold in high esteem, and make such provocative statement as, "Is this not that your God, where is He now"?, and with that you throw the photograph on the ground and stamp upon it. Who will sit by and take such taunts coolly?

By this time Ojukwu had taken over the Governorship of the Eastern Region. We have it in good authority that he was not satisfied with the administration of General Aguiyi Ironsi. He felt the General was too lukewarm in his methods of administration. As a result he was planning a coup that would topple General Ironsi and place himself in the saddle. But the coup of July, 29 that placed Lt. Col. Yakubu Gowon-now Major General-forestalled him. In fact if the hedge that was built around Major General Yakubu Gowon was not such that could be described as impenetrable, we could have been hearing a different story today.

Several attempts were made to get at him, but the soldiers around him were very much alive to their duties.

When Ojukwu discovered that all was lost, at least in so far as his ambition of becoming Lord and master over the Federal Republic had failed, he like Lucifer in Milton's Paradise lost mind (sic) "IT IS BETTER TO RULE THOUGH IN HELL THAN TO SERVE IN HEAVEN". He therefore started making arrangements for his illegal secession. He made his tribesmen believe that they were no longer safe in the Federal Republic of Nigeria. From information received, Ojukwu received a telex message, whilst he was conducting his Consultative Assembly of hand picked people from the former Eastern Region informing him of the Federal Military Government's intentions to create TWELVE STATES in the Federal Republic. A few days afterwards, 27th May, 1967 to be precise, the decree promulgating the creation of TWELVE STATES was made. Three days afterwards the ill-fated Republic of Biafra was declared over the area which had been decreed as the Central Eastern State, Rivers State and South Eastern State.

From that moment onwards the tempo of persecution increased. Anybody who was not of Ibo origin was looked upon as being against the Ibos. We expatriates were treated in the same way as native Nigerians of the South Eastern or Rivers States. One of our members was arrested and thoroughly beaten up by the so called Biafra Militia for no other reason than that he displayed the Sierra Leone Emblem on his door-post.

Another member was detained for hours because he had a misunderstanding with a neighbour of his who was an Iboman. Our houses were searched several times between night fall and sun up.

We do not need to catalogue the indignities which we suffered at the hands of Ibo people. The purpose of this letter as we have said earlier is to remove whatever impressions the mis-statements of Sam Metzger has (sic.) made on the minds of Sierra Leoneans.

We know that Sam Metzger did not on his own accord start peddling unwholesome rumours about the Nigerian Crisis. We know too that he is in the pay or the rebels. We also know that not being physically present at the scene, he received education from the lips of certain misguided Sierra Leoneans who were air-lifted home (Sierra Leone) by the Red Cross at the instance of, we can guess, the rebel High Command.

As we have earlier stated, we wish to impress it on anyone who reads this letter that anything said by a rebel Agent in defence of the rebels should be treated with contempt because anything from that camp is intended to gain the sympathy of the gullible masses of the world.

But as Dr. Azikiwe, a one time rebel envoy from whose eyes the scales have now fallen, has said, "You can fool some of the people some of the time, but you cannot fool all the people all the time".

Before closing this letter we have to express very grave concern at the slight we have so far received at the hands of Your Excellency's Office in Lagos, Nigeria. Sometime ago, the High Commission sent one of its Secretaries to find out whether or not there were Sierra Leoneans in Port Harcourt after the liberation. When he arrived we all rallied round him and made him to understand that indeed and in fact there are still Sierra Leoneans in Port Harcourt. We gave him a list of our names and addresses in the hope that he would keep us informed of day to day activities in our Homeland. He was expected to send us copies of periodicals from Sierra Leone. But up till the present moment nothing has happened.

And again, we were utterly surprised to read from Nigerian Newspapers and the Rivers State Digest Vol. No. 3 that one Mr. Gborie had visited Port Harcourt to see things for himself and report back to the Sierra Leone Parliament. Mr. Gborie did not meet any of us and we are confident that the High Commission in Lagos did not inform him of our presence in Port Harcourt; for if he had been informed, he would have been duty bound to contact us and hear from us a first hand account of the Nigerian Crisis before making his recommendations.

We have now no alternative but to feel that we are a neglected people whose hopes hang in the balance.

It is our earnest desire that our Country should steer clear of the Nigerian Crisis which is purely an internal matter. Let us not break friendship with this great Country that has been in close association with our people since the past decades. We here want to make our stand crystal clear that we are not in support of any vicious moves that may tend to break the unity of this Country.

Long Live One Nigeria
Long Live Sierra Leone—Nigeria Friendship
for: SIERRA LEONE COMMUNITY IN PORT HARCOURT

1. (A. Ola Wilson)
2. (T. Jos. Wilson)
3. (P.O'Dwyer Macaulay)
4. (W.S. Byron)
5. (B.R. Browne)
6. (Joe Barnes)
7. (J.T. Akibo Betts)

cc: His Excellency,
Military Governor of Rivers State.
Mr. H.O. Gborie, Secretary-General APC/DPC (sic.)
Sierra Leone.

NOTES

Notes to Introduction

1. Robert W. July, "Nineteenth-Century Negritude: Edward W. Blyden", in *Journal of African History*, V, 1, 1964, pp. 80-81; E.A. Ayandele, "James Africanus Beale Horton, 1835-1883: Prophet of Modernization in West Africa", *African Historical Studies*, IV, 3, 1971, and *The Educated Elite in the Nigerian Society* (Ibadan, 1974); and Leo Spitzer, *The Creoles of Sierra Leone: Responses to Colonialism, 1870-1945*, (Madison, Wisconsin, 1974) p. 113.

2. C. Magbaily Fyle and Isabella Heroe, "Krio Traditional Belief", *Africana Research Bulletin*, vii, 3, June, 1977.

3. S.J.S. Cookey, "West African Immigrants in the Congo, 1885-1896", *Journal of the Historical Society of Nigeria*, 3, 2, Dec. 1965; and Akintola J.G. Wyse, "The Place of Sierra Leone in African Diaspora Studies" in J.F. Ade Ajayi and J.D.Y. Peel (eds.) *African History: Essays in memory of Michael Crowder* (London, 1992), p. 108. See also Kenneth Little, "The Significance of West African Creole for Africanist and Afro-American Studies", *African Affairs*, 49, 1950, pp. 308-19; K.A.B. Jones-Quartey, "Sierra Leone's role in the development of Ghana, 1820-1930", *Sierra Leone Studies*, (new series), 10, June 1958, pp. 73-83; and J.D. Hargreaves, "Senegal: Another Creole Frontier, 1889", *Journal of the Historical Society of Sierra Leone*, 1, 2, July 1977.

4. Akintola J.G. Wyse, "The Sierra Leone Krios: A Reappraisal from the Perspective of the African Diaspora", in Joseph E. Harris (ed.) *Global Dimensions of the African Diaspora*, (Washington, D.C., 1982) p. 313.

5. P. Amaury Talbot, *The Peoples of Southern Nigeria* (Oxford, 1926); R. R. Kuczynski, *Demographic Survey of the British Colonial Empire*, vol. 1, (Oxford, 1948).

6. Kuczynski, *op. cit.* pp. 552, 556, 583, 610, 612 and 616.

7. In all, the author located only three non-Krio Saro families in Port Harcourt in the period up to independence from British rule.

8. For a discussion of the female hearth-hold sphere as distinct from the male-ruled household, see Felicia Ekejiuba, "Contemporary Households and Major Socio-Economic Transitions in Eastern Nigeria: Towards a Reconceptualization of the Household", in *Conceptualizing the Household: Issues of Theory, Method, and Application*, workshop organised at Harvard University, Nov. 1984, and coordinated by Jane I. Guyer and Pauline E. Peters.

9. For some of the possibilities in this process, see Justin Willis, *Mombasa, the Swahili and the Making of the Mijikenda* (Oxford, 1993).

10. See, for instance, M. Herskovits, *The Myth of the Negro Past* (New York, 1941); George Padmore, *Pan-Africanism or Communism* (London, 1956); Howard Brotz, *The Black Jews of Harlem* (New York, 1964); Hollis Lynch, *Edward Wilmot Blyden: Pan Negro Patriot* (London, 1967), Winthrop Jordan, *White Over Black: American Attitudes Toward the Negro*, 1550-1812 (Baltimore, 1968); Okon E. Uya, *Black Brotherhood* (Lexington, Mass. 1971); John W. Blassingame, *The Slave Community: Plantation Life in the Antebellum South* (New York, 1972), and Nathan Huggins, *Black Odyssey: The Afro-American Ordeal in Slavery* (New York, 1977).

Notes to Chapter 1

1. C. Fyfe, *History of Sierra Leone* (London, 1962); and *Sierra Leone Inheritance* (London, 1964); J. Hargreaves, *A Life of Sir Samuel Lewis* (London, 1958); Paul Hair, "Africanism": The Freetown Contribution", *The Journal of Modern African Studies*, v. 1967, pp. 521-39; Arthur Porter, *Creoledom* (London, 1963); J.E. Peterson, *Province of Freedom: A History of Sierra Leone*, 1787-1870 (Evanston, Ill., 1969); L. Spitzer, *The Creoles of Sierra Leone: Responses to Colonialism* 1870-1945 (Wisconsin, 1974); A.P. Kup, *Sierra Leone: A Concise History* (London, 1975); C. Magbaily Fyle, *The History of Sierra Leone* (London, 1981); and J.A.D. Allie, *A New History of Sierra Leone* (London, 1990); Various other notable contributions have been made by Robert Clarke, A.B.C. Sibthorpe, J.U.J. Asiegbu, and other scholars.

2. Wyse, *The Krio*, p. 65-66.

3. *Ibid*, p. 67.

4. R. Olaniyan, (ed.), *Nigerian History and Culture* (Ibadan, 1985), pp. 138-61.

5. J.F.A. Ajayi, *Christian Missions in Nigeria, 1841-1891: The Making of a New Elite* (Evanston, Il., 1965); E.A. Ayandele, *The Missionary Impact on Modern Nigeria*, 1842-1914 (London, 1966), *Holy Johnson: Pioneer of African Nationalism*, 1836-1917 (New York, 1970), and *The Educated Elite in the Nigerian Society* (Ibadan, 1974); J.H. Kopytoff, *A Preface to Modern Nigeria* (Wisconsin, 1965); Pauline Baker, *Urbanization and Political change: The Politics of Lagos*, 1947-67 (Berkeley, 1974); and O.U. Kalu (ed.) *The History of Christianity in West Africa* (London, 1980).

6. Akintola Wyse, *op cit.*, p. 20.

7. *Ibid.* p. 21.

8. There was much resentment of the Saro among the indigenes of Yorubaland over the influence the immigrants came to have in the traditional ruling houses. See Patrick Cole, *Modern and Traditional Elites in the Politics of Lagos* (Cambridge, 1975), pp. 127-28.

9. Cole, *Modern and Traditional Elites*, p.95.

10. Kalu Ezera, *Constitutional Developments in Nigeria* (Cambridge, 1960), p. 22-23.

11. James C. Coleman, *Nigeria: Background to Nationalism*, (Berkeley, 1960), pp. 191-2; Ezera, *Constitutional Developments*, pp. 23-24.

12. J. Ayodele Langley, *Pan Africanism and Nationalism in West Africa*, 1900-1945 (Oxford, 1973), p. 256.

13. Cole, *Modern and Traditional Elites*, p. 124.

14. Ezera, *Constitutional Developments*, p. 26.

15. Coleman, *Nigeria*, p. 196; and Ezera, *Constitutional Developments*, p. 27.

16. Akintola J.G. Wyse, "The Place of Sierra Leone in African Diaspora Studies", in J.F. Ade Ajayi and J.D.Y. Peel (eds.) *Peoples and Empires in African History: Essays in Memory of Michael Crowder*, (London, 1992), pp. 111-112.

17. E.M.T. Epelle, *The Church in the Niger Delta* (Port Harcourt, 1955).

18. E.A. Ayandele, *Holy Johnson: Pioneer of African Nationalism*, 1836-1917 (New York, 1970).

19. *Ibid.* p. 235.

20. *Ibid.* pp. 237-243.

21. *Ibid.* p. 264.

22. *Ibid.* p. 253.

23. *Ibid.* pp. 357-362.

24. C.N. Anyanwu, "The Growth of Port Harcourt, 1912-1960", in W. Ogionwo (ed.), *The City of Port Harcourt*, (Ibadan, 1979), pp. 15-19.

25. R.F. Burton, *Wanderings in West Africa from Liverpool to Fernando Po* (London, 1863).

26. Wyse, *The Krio*, p. 46.

27. *Ibid.* pp. 34-35.

28. Ayandele, *Holy Johnson*, and M.K. Akpan, "The Return to Africa-Sierra Leone and Liberia", *Tarikh*, 20, V, (4), 1981.

29. Cole, *Modern and Traditional Elites*, p. 72, and Kopytoff, *Preface*, pp. 208-14.

30. Cole, *Modern and Traditional Elites*, p. 75.

31. Wyse, *The Krio*, p. 46.

32. *Ibid.* p. 63.

33. Anyanwu, "Port Harcourt, 1912-1960", pp. 19-20.

34. *Ibid.* pp. 24-25.

35. Interviews with Mrs. Clementina Manly-Rollings.

36. Olaniyan, *Nigerian History*, p. 141.

37. Interviews with Mrs. Clementina Manly-Rollings; see also Anyanwu "Port Harcourt, 1912-1960", p. 22.

38. Pauline H. Baker, *Urbanization and Political Change* (Berkeley, 1974). See also Akin L. Mabogunje, *Urbanization in Nigeria* (London, 1968).

39. Kenneth Little, *West African Urbanization* (Cambridge, 1965), pp. 27-102; see also Coleman, *Nigeria*, pp. 72-73.

40. See Nancy J. Hafkin and Edna G. Bay, *Women in Africa* (Stanford, 1976), pp. 4-9, and 14; also Kenneth Little, *African Women in Towns* (Cambridge, 1973) and Sharon Stichter and Jane Parpart (eds.) *Patriarchy and Class* (Boulder, Colorado, 1988).

41. Little, *African Women*, pp. 76-101; also Claire Robertson, "Women in the Urban Economy", in Margaret Jean Hay and Sharon Stichter, (eds.), *African Women South of the Sahara* (New York, 1995), p. 55.

42. Little, *African Women*, p. 33.

43. Otonti Nduka, "Educational Development in Port Harcourt: Retrospect and Prospects", in W. Ogionwo, (ed.), *The City of Port Harcourt* (Ibadan, 1979), p. 37.

44. *Ibid.* pp. 36-38.

45. P. Amaury Talbot, *The Peoples of Southern Nigeria*, (London, 1926), pp. 10 and 131.

46. Interviews with Mrs. Clementina Manly-Rollings.

47. Bade Onimode, *Imperialism and Underdevelopment in Nigeria* (London, 1983), p. 45.

48. *Ibid.*

49. A.G. Hopkins, *An Economic History of West Africa* (New York, 1973), pp. 133-34.

50. OW 236/16 Ref. H. Riv. Prof. 8/4/18[B], Quarterly Report on Port Harcourt, March, 1916, National Archives, Enugu, (hereafter NAE).

51. CO 583/37, Lugard to Bonar Law, Secretary of State for the Colonies, 6 Oct. 1915, Public Records Office, Kew Gardens, London (hereafter, PRO).

52. *Ibid.*

53. Co 583/75, Petition addressed to Secretary of State, through the Acting Governor of Nigeria, 7 April, 1919, PRO.

54. *Ibid.* A.G. Boyle to Viscount Milner, 7 May, 1919.

55. OW 449/19, Riv. Prof. 8/7/126, Station Magistrate, Port Harcourt to Commissioner of Police, 13 Nov. 1919, NAE.

56. *Ibid.* J.M. Metzger to Sir Hugh Clifford, 22 Oct, 1919.

57. Riv. Prof 8/10/493, Station Magistrate, Port Harcourt to Resident, Owerri Province, 11 July, 1922, N.A.E. Macauley's mother was subsequently located, and his personal effects, in four boxes, were handed over to another Saro, a customs clerk called Walker, for onward transmission to the bereaved mother.

58. OW 583/16. Riv. Prof. 8/4/550, Quarterly Report on Port Harcourt, July-September, 1916, NAE.

59. CO 583/78, Visit of Governor and Lady Hugh Clifford to Port Harcourt, 16 October 1919, P.R.O.

60. *Ibid.*

61. OW449/19. Riv. Prof. 8/7/126, Petition of I.R. Benjamin to Governor Clifford, 16 October, 1919, N.A.E.

62. OW 583/16.H Riv. Prof. 8/4/550, Quarterly Report on Port Harcourt, July-September, 1916, NAE.

63. O. Nduka, "Educational Development in Port Harcourt: Retrospect and Prospects", in W. Ogionwo (ed.) *The City of Port Harcourt* (Ibadan, 1979), pp. 35-51.

64. Annual Report of the Wesleyan Methodist Missionary Society (WMMS), 1943. See also Synod Minutes of the Wesleyan Methodist Missionary Society, Eastern Nigeria, 1933. Microfiche Box 14, Library of the London School of Oriental and African Studies (hereafter, SOAS).

65. The work of the Saro, Rev. L.R. Potts-Johnson, will soon be reviewed. In September 1932, a uniting conference brought the Primitive Methodists and Wesleyans into the same congregation in Eastern Nigeria. See Wesleyan Methodist Missionary Archives, Correspondence, Eastern Nigeria, 1932-38, Microfiche Box 23, SOAS.

66. OW 242/16 Riv. Prof. 8/4/194, B.P. Langley, Church Secretary to District Officer, 17 April 1916.

67. The Nigerian Observer, 11 Jan. 1930.

68. The Nigerian Observer, 6 May, 1933.

69. The Nigerian Observer, 21 May, 1932.

70. Riv. Prof 8/14/117, Minutes of the Township Advisory Board (hereafter, TAB), 19 Feb. 1926.

71. CO 583/15, Lugard to Secretary of State, 19 June, 1914, PRO.

72. CO 583/45, Lugard to Bonar Law, 6 Apr. 1916, PRO.

73. T.S. Gale, "The Disbarment of African Medical Officers by the West African Medical Staff: A Study of Prejudice", *Journal of the Historical Society of Sierra Leone*, 4, 1 and 2, Dec. 1980, pp 33-44.

74. CO 583/66, Confidential Report for 1917 on I.G. Cummings, by A. Clough, Acting Principal Medical Officer, PRO.

75. Riv. Prof. 8/14/117, Minutes of the meeting of the TAB, 19 Feb. 1926.

76. Riv. Prof. 8/13/189, Handing over notes, Station Magistracy, D.O'Conner to J.M. Pollen, 18 June, 1925, NAE.

77. Riv. Prof. 8/18/40, Vincent to Station Magistrate, 13th Feb. 1930; Commissioner of Police, Port Harcourt to Resident, Owerri Province, 11 March, 1930; District Officer, Degema to Resident, Owerri Province, 18 July, 1930; Resident, Owerri Province to Secretary, Southern Provinces, Enugu, 16 Sept. 1930, NAE.

78. *Ibid.* Alicia Williams to Resident Owerri Province, through Station Magistrate, Port Harcourt, 2 Oct. 1930.

79. David Meredith, "Government and the Decline of the Nigerian oil-palm export industry, 1919-1939", *Journal of African History*, 25, 1984, p. 318.

80. *Ibid.* p. 323.

81. F.K. Ekechi, "Aspects of palm oil trade at Oguta (Eastern Nigeria), 1900-1950", *African Economic History*, no. 10, 1981, p. 57.

82. David Meredith, *op cit.*, pp. 325-326.

83. There is urgent need for a full-length biography of Potts-Johnson, and it is hoped that this study will help to channel some research efforts into that endeavor. While in Port Harcourt, the author heard rumours of the existence of Potts-Johnson's private papers, which are to be released, enigmatically, at "the appropriate time" by the family. He got no confirmation of this from family members.

84. Enquiries into Potts-Johnson's parentage yielded no useful results. We know nothing of substance about his parents. His mother died in Conakry, Guinea, on 8 April, 1905. He had a brother, Ernest, of whom, again, little is known. See the Nigerian Observer, 9 Apr. 1932. There was also a sister, Caroline Mary Johnson, who turned up in Port Harcourt shortly after Potts-Johnson's death.

85. This was gleaned from obituary notices published in Nigerian newspapers in 1949 when Potts-Johnson died, to which more ample references will be made later. It also comes from interviews in Port Harcourt with W. Byron (10 Feb. 1985), and Mr. and Mrs. T. Jos. Wilson (17 Feb. 1985), who knew Potts-Johnson well. The author failed to locate any personal papers of Potts-Johnson during his six-year sojourn at the University of Port Harcourt during which most of the fieldwork on this project was done.

86. See *Alphabetical Arrangement of Wesleyan Methodist Ministers*, 1912, p. 30. SOAS.

87. District Synod meeting, Lagos, 9-20 Feb, 1914. See Wesleyan Methodist Missionary Society, Synod Minutes, 1912-37, Microfiche Box 13, SOAS.

88. *Ibid.*

89. Annual Report of the Wesleyan Methodist Missionary Society (hereafter, WMMS), 1913-14, p. 169. SOAS.

90. *Ibid.*, p. 172.

91. Annual Report of WMMS, 1915, p. 171.

92. *Ibid.*

93. Oliver Griffin to Hartley, 20 Mar. 1915. WMMS, Synod Minutes, 1912-37, microfiche, Box 13, SOAS.

94. WMMS Synod Minutes, 1912-37, microfiche Box 13, SOAS.

95. *Ibid.*

96. WMMS Annual Report, 1920, pp. 81-82.

97. *Ibid.*

98. WMMS, Synod Minutes, Lagos District, March, 1920, microfiche Box 13, SOAS.

99. *Ibid.*

100. *Ibid.*

101. *Ibid.*

102. *Ibid.* London Missionary Committee to Lagos District Synod, 10 Jan. 1922.

103. *Ibid.*

104. *Ibid.* Synod Minutes, Lagos District, 16 Feb.–6 March, 1922.

105. *Ibid.*

106. *Ibid.* Minutes of meeting of Local Committee, 15 March, 1922.

107. *Ibid.* Report of E.K. Ajai Ajabe on a visit to Opobo, 6 Dec.–24 Jan., 1922.

108. *Ibid.*

109. *Ibid.*

110. *Ibid.* Missionary Committee to Lagos Synod, Dec. 1922.

111. *Ibid.*

112. *Ibid.*

113. *Ibid.* Minutes of Lagos Synod meeting, 25 Jan.–9 Feb. 1923.

114. *Ibid.* Missionary Committee to Lagos Synod, 19 Dec. 1923.

115. *Ibid.*

116. *Ibid.* London Missionary Committee to Lagos Synod, 10 Dec. 1924.

117. *Ibid.*

118. *Ibid*

119. *Ibid.* Minutes of meeting of Lagos Synod, 29 Jan.–14 Feb. 1925.

120. *Ibid.* London Missionary Committee to Lagos Synod, 7 Feb. 1927.

121. *Ibid.* Minutes of Lagos Synod meeting, 2-22 March, 1927.

122. *Ibid.* Minutes of Lagos Synod meeting, 19 Jan.–6 Feb. 1928.

123. *Ibid.* Missionary Committee, London, to Nigerian Synod, through Rev. John Stewart, 1 Dec. 1928.

124. *Ibid.*

125. *Ibid.*

126. *Ibid.* Annual letter of the Nigerian District Synod to the Missionary Committee, London, 2 Feb, 1929.

127. *Ibid.* Potts-Johnson left the church at the same time as one D.A. Tekoe. See Missionary Committee, London, to Nigerian Synod, 16 Dec. 1929.

128. Paul Hair has expressed much surprise at the Methodist church's unusual tolerance of Potts-Johnson's conduct. Personal communication with Paul Hair, November, 1996.

129. E.A. Ayandele, *Holy Johnson*, pp. 286-87; Edward W. Blyden, *Christianity, Islam, and the Negro Race*, second edition, (London, 1888), and *African Life and Customs* (London, 1908).

130. Wyse, *The Krio*, p. 52.

131. At Uzuakoli, in January, 1938, he was listed as an African member of the Synod in charge of the Education Committee. In 1940, his wife, Nancy Eniton, was at Synod as lay African member. In 1941, Potts-Johnson's term on the Synod education committee ended, and his official involvement with Synod ceased. See Methodist Missions, Eastern Nigeria, Minutes of Synod, 1938, held at Uzuakoli; Minutes of Synod 1940 and 1941. Microfiche Box 15, SOAS.

132. See Akintola Wyse, *The Krio*. p. 43.

133. Over the years, Potts-Johnson would pass on some editorial responsibility to two other Saro: Kelfallah Sankoh (1932-38), and Egerton Shyngle (1939). Informants pointed out, however, that it was widely known that he personally wrote most editorials, especially those of a political nature for which the editor could be liable.

134. The Nigerian Observer, 4 Jan. 1930.

135. *Ibid.*

136. C. Magbaily Fyle and I. Heroe, "Krio Traditional Beliefs", *Africana Research Bulletin*, 7,3, June, 1977; see also Wyse, *The Krio*, p. 11, and A. T. Porter, *Creoledom* (London, 1963).

137. See Wyse, "The Place", p. 112.

138. Coleman, *Nigeria*, p. 213.

139. Fyfe, *History*, p. 292.

140. Kopytoff, *Preface*, pp. 97 and 115.

141. *Ibid*, p. 130. See also Cole, *Modern and Traditional Elites*, p. 48.

142. The Nigerian Observer, 15 March, 1930.

143. The Nigerian Observer, 22 March and 12 April, 1930.

144. For a detailed review of the life of Dandeson Coates Crowther, see E.M.T. Epelle, *The Church in the Niger Delta* (Port Harcourt, 1955) pp. 119-128.

145. The Nigerian Observer, 3 May, 24 May, and 4 Oct. 1930.

146. The Nigerian Observer, 14 Feb. 1931. Crowther addressed another February gathering on the subject "Reminiscences on the Delta"—see the Nigerian Observer, 7 Feb. 1931.

147. The Nigerian Observer, 21 Feb. 1931.

148. The Nigerian Observer, 4 April and 9 May, 1931.

149. The Nigerian Observer, 1 Nov. 1930.

150. The Nigerian Observer, 12 Sep. 1931. For a discussion of the Eleko affair which caused some British officials great embarrassment, see Patrick Cole, *Modern and Traditional Elites*. pp. 122-131. The Sierra Leone Union of Port Harcourt lost the bulk of its minutes and records of other activities during the Nigerian civil war of the late 1960's.

151. The Nigerian Observer, 9 Aug. 1930; 21 and 28 May, 1932.

152. See above, n.2.

153. Riv. Prof. 8/9/365. Township Report for 1 Jan-31 March 1921.

154. OW 236/16 Ref. H. Riv. Prof. 8/4/18^B, Quarterly Report, Port Harcourt, March 1916, NAE.

155. Riv. Prof. 8/5/227. OW 212/17. Handing-over notes. Burrough to Macgregor, 26 Apr. 1917, NAE.

156. Howard Wolpe, *Urban Politics in Nigeria: A Study of Port Harcourt* (Los Angeles, 1974), p. 95.

157. O. Adewoye,, "Sierra Leonean Immigrants in the Field of Law in Southern Nigeria, 1856-1934", *Sierra Leone Studies*, 26, Jan, 1970 p. 26.

158. Riv. Prof. 8/13/189, Handing over notes, Station Magistracy, Port Harcourt. D. O'Conner to J.M. Pollen, 18 June, 1925, NAE.

159. Not to be confused with S.T. Ikiroma-Owiye, Owner of Reasonable Stores, P.O. Box 95, Port Harcourt.

160. Riv. Prof. 8/12/53, Handing over notes, A.L. Weir to J.M. Pollen, 6 Jan. 1923, NAE.

161. Riv. Prof. 8/13/43, Resident, Owerri Province to Secretary, Southern Province, Lagos, 29th June, 1925, NAE; see also the Eastern Nigerian Guardian, 12th Nov. 1951, and the Nigerian Observer, 16 Nov. 1951, NAE.

162. Cole, *Modern and Traditional Elites*, p. 46.

163. Riv. Prof. 8/15/69, TAB minutes for meeting of 7 March, 1927, in Resident, Owerri to Secretary, Lagos, March 1927; NAE.

164. *Ibid.*

165. *Ibid.*

166. Riv. Prof. 8/14/49, Town Planning sub-committee meeting, 2 July 1926, NAE.

167. Riv. Prof. 8/16/17, Minutes of TAB meeting of 12 Jan. 1928, NAE.

168. *Ibid.*

169. Riv. Prof. 8/17/11, Minutes of TAB meeting, 10 Jan. 1929, NAE.

170. *Ibid.*

171. Coleman, *Nigeria*, pp. 178-82.

172. *Ibid.* pp. 180-82.

173. *Ibid.* p. 197

174. See L. Spitzer and La Ray Denzer, "I.T.A. Wallace-Johnson and the West African Youth League", *International Journal of African Historical Studies*, 6, Nos. 3 & 4, 1973; also Akintola J.G. Wyse, *H.C. Bankole-Bright and Politics in Colonial Sierra Leone*, 1919-1958 (Cambridge, 1990).

175. Riv. Prof. 8/13/189, Handing over notes, D. O'Conner to J. Pollen, 18 June, 1925, NAE.

176. *Ibid.*

177. *Ibid.*

178. *Ibid.*

179. Riv. Prof. 8/13/137, APU to Governor, 9 March, 1925, NAE.

180. *Ibid.*

181. *Ibid.*

182. *Ibid.*

183. *Ibid.*

184. *Ibid.* The signatories were Alhaji I.B. Davies (President), from Lagos; William E. Bailey (Vice President) from Sierra Leone; K.A. Lanipekun (Secretary), from Sierra Leone; Lawan Balogun (Treasurer), from Lagos; A.D. Grant (Financial Secretary) from Sierra Leone; B.N. Tom West, from New Calabar; Okoro Ocher, an Igbo; Ikunadu Okon, an Igbo; Malam Belarabi, a Hausa; and George Meffle, from the Gold Coast.

185. *Ibid.* Station Magistrate to Resident, Owerri Province, 19 March, 1925.

186. *Ibid.*

187. *Ibid.* APU to Governor, 23 May, 1925. The APU was apparently referring here to the case of the German trader, W. Kunze, who had enjoyed official protection in setting up his business, and was "said to have ousted the other firms completely in the hardware trade which is quite considerable". Monopoly control by Kunze meant, of course, higher prices for African residents. Thus the concern. See Riv. Prof. 8/13/310, Owerri Province Annual Report, Jan to Dec. 1925, NAE.

188. Riv. Prof. 8/13/137, APU to Governor, 23 May, 1925, NAE.

189. *Ibid.* Resident Owerri to Secretary, Southern Provinces, Lagos, 11 Apr. 1926.

190. *Ibid.* For APU respresentations on trading sites and forestry fees, see Riv. Prof. 8/15/69, minutes of TAB meeting of 18 Feb. 1927.

191. Riv. Prof. 8/15/69. Minutes of the TAB meeting of 6 Oct. 1927, NAE.

192. Cole, *Modern and Traditional Elites*, p. 141.

193. Riv. Prof. 8/13/137, APU to Governor, 28 Apr. 1928, NAE.

194. The first set of homes were established on 50 x 100 and 30 x 60 plots, with occupation licenses of £1 and 10s respectively. *Ibid.* APU to Lieutenant Governor, 24 Sept. 1928. . . .

195. *Ibid.*

196. *Ibid.*

197. *Ibid.* This petition was signed by the following members of the "Lagos Section" who gave their occupations as "trader": Alhaji I.B. Davies, Gbadamosi Ope, K.O. Adeogun, Yisa Agbasi, Amusa Ajasa, Alufa Brima, Osini Sumonu Falahun, S. Fella, Siberu Ajiboka, Sanusi Dabri, Sefa Kadini, Aseni Ajoke, Seibu, Kosumu Akonbi, Belo Maja, Salami Bale, and Abu Bakare. The only non-trader to sign the petition was the Saro contractor, E. Odu Thomas. A "Delta Coast town Residential Union", an Efik Section, an Igbo section (among Igbo members were Moses Obi, S.O. Njemanze, and S.O. Akuna) also supported the petition.

198. *Ibid.* Minutes of the meeting between the APU and Lieutenant Governor, 25 Sept. 1928.

199. *Ibid.*

200. *Ibid.*

201. *Ibid.*

202. Riv. Prof. 8/16/17, Minutes of the TAB meeting of 8 March 1928, NAE.

203. *Ibid.* Minutes of the TAB meeting of 15 Nov. 1928.

204. *Ibid.*

205. Small-scale traders supported the APU which offered them a voice against the more capitalised African entrepreneurs such as I.B. Johnson and Ikiroma-Owiye, who enjoyed most bank credit.

206. J.B. Webster, "African Political Activity in British West Africa, 1900-1940", in J.F.A. Ajayi and Michael Crowder (eds.)., *History of West Africa* vol. II

(Longman, Essex, 1987), pp. 642-651; also D.C. Dorward, "British West Africa and Liberia" in A.D. Roberts (ed.,) *The Cambridge History of Africa*, vol. 7, (Cambridge, 1986), p. 432.

207. Interviews with Mrs. Clementina Manly-Rollings.

208. Dorward, "British West Africa", p. 447; also Cheryl Johnson, "Class and Gender: A Consideration of Yoruba Women during the Colonial Period", in Claire Robertson and Iris Berger (eds.) *Women and Class in Africa* (New York, 1986) pp. 242-243.

Notes to Chapter 2

1. Riv. Prof. 8/13/137, APU to the Governor, 12 March 1929.

2. The Nigerian Observer, 25 Jan, 1930. In its issue of 4 Jan., 1930, the paper had asked why the water supply of the town was so inadequate, and why so many stand-pipes were kept "permanently closed".

3. The Nigerian Observer, 22 Feb. and 26 July, 1930. Potts-Johnson's use of "masses" here is instructive, and an index of his political orientation. See the Nigerian Observer, 30 Aug. 1930.

4. Riv. Prof. 8/13/137, extract from the Nigerian Observer of 1 Feb. 1930, NAE.

5. *Ibid.* APU to the Resident, 28 July, 1930.

6. *Ibid.*

7. *Ibid.*

8. See chapter 1, note 61.

9. See chapter 1, note 181.

10. The Nigerian Observer, 8 Feb. 1930.

11. Riv. Prof. 8/13/137, R.S. Ajagbe, Secretary, APU to Resident, Port Harcourt, 1 Aug. 1930.

12. Wesleyan Methodist Missionary Society, (WMMS), Synod Minutes, Feb. 28-7 March, 1933, Microfiche box 14, SOAS.

13. *Ibid.* Annual letter from the Eastern District Synod to the Methodist Missionary Committee, London, 22 Jan. 1935. These measures were adopted after funding from the London headquarters was cut by 10% starting 1936.

14. Informants in Port Harcourt repeatedly commented to the author of Johnson's lack of warmth and passion. He came through as a rather shy and distant character, who was almost self-effacing socially. Some interpreted this as a ploy to ward off the many requests for material help that came his way. A number though vouched for his generosity, and support of beggars and the disabled.

15. Riv. Prof. 8/17/11, TAB minutes for meeting of 23 Apr. 1936, NAE.

16. *Ibid.* TAB minutes for meeting of 17 Sept. 1936.

17. *Ibid.* TAB minutes for meeting of 17 Nov. 1936.

18. The Nigerian Observer, 30 May and 18 July, 1931.

19. The Nigerian Observer, 19 Sept. 1931.

20. The Nigerian Observer, 7 May, 1932.

21. Robert W. July, "Nineteenth-Century Negritude: Edward W. Blyden", *Journal of African History*, V, 1, 1964, p. 85

22. The Nigerian Observer, 26 Nov. 1932.

23. See J.F.A. Ajayi and M. Crowder, (eds.), *A History of West Africa*, vol. II. (London, 1985)

24. J.B. Webster, "African Political Activity in British West Africa, 1900-1940", in J.F. Ade Ajayi and Michael Crowder (eds). *History of West Africa* (Essex, 1987) pp. 648-51.

25. Webster, "African Political Activity", p. 649; also Akintola J.G. Wyse, *H.C. Bankole-Bright and Politics in colonial Sierra Leone*, 1919-1958 (Cambridge, 1990) p. 84.

26. The Nigerian Observer 14 Jan, 1933.

27. The Nigerian Observer, 21 and 28 Oct. 1933. Potts-Johnson's political gradualism, and the political elitism common to his class in the West Africa of this period, are fully apparent in these observations. See A. Ajayi and M. Crowder (eds.) *A History of West Africa*, vol. II. (London, 1985)

28. See the Nigerian Observer of 11 Feb. 1933 (on the need for more water stand pipes); 8 Sept. 1934 (on overcrowded rented accomodation where "men are housed liked cattle in a pen"); and 12 Jan. 1935 (on hospital facilities).

29. Akintola Wyse, *The Krio of Sierra Leone* (London, 1989), pp. 85-7.

30. James S. Coleman, *Nigeria: Background to Nationalism* (Berkeley, 1960), p. 157.

31. Missionary Committee, London, to Eastern Nigeria District Synod, Dec. 1933. WMMS Synod, microfiche box 14, SOAS.

32. Minutes of the Synod of 1938, WMMS, microfiche box 15, SOAS.

33. Riv. Prof. 9/1/578, Annual Report of the Education Department, 1937, NAE.

34. The Eastern Nigerian Guardian, 8 Jan. 1949.

35. *Ibid.*

36. Riv. Prof. 13/1/3[D]. ACL to the Lieutenant-Governor, 21 Oct. 1935, NAE.

37. *Ibid.* E.K. Williams (for ACL) to Resident, Owerri Province, 10 Feb. 1936.

38. Lower rents at the Palladium would mean cheaper tickets for its African patrons.

39. Riv. Prof. 13/1/3[D], E.K. Williams (for ACL) to Resident, Owerri Province, 10 Feb. 1936, NAE.

40. *Ibid.*

41. *Ibid.* Memorandum of the Resident, Owerri Province, 24 Sept. 1936.

42. *Ibid.* E.K. Williams to Resident, 26 Sept. 1936.

43. *Ibid.*

44. *Ibid.*

45. *Ibid.* E.K. Williams to Resident, 28 Oct. 1936.

46. *Ibid.*

47. *Ibid.* Local Authority to Resident, Owerri province, 2 Dec. 1936. Local resentment of the Igbo was a matter of long-standing record in official memory.

48. *Ibid.* E.K. Williams to Resident, Owerri Province, 28 Oct. 1936. The ACL wanted six of its members to sit on the TAB.

49. The TAB had obviously reconsidered its earlier aversion to African lawyers. See chapter 1, note 109.

50. Riv. Prof. 8/18/16, TAB minutes for meeting of 18 Feb. 1937, NAE.

51. The Nigerian Observer, 6 March, 1937.

52. Riv. Prof. 8/18/16, Minutes of the TAB meeting of 27 May, 1937, NAE.

53. *Ibid.* Expenditure on the bus shelter was later judged to be prohibitive, and the idea was dropped. See TAB minutes of the meeting of 24 June, 1937.

54. Riv. Prof. 13/1/3^D, E.K. Williams to Resident, Owerri, 25 Feb. 1937, NAE

55. *Ibid.* The Resident wrote: ". . . regret to hear of the sudden death of the Rev. E.K. Williams. I wish to express my sympathy to all members of the Port Harcourt Community League". See Resident to S.O. Ogundipe, ACL's secretary, 3 Aug. 1937.

56. The Nigerian Observer, 7 Aug. 1937.

57. F.W. Dodds to Ayre, 3rd Aug. 1937, WMMS, Correspondence from Eastern Nigeria, 1932-38, microfiche box 23, SOAS.

58. The Nigerian Observer, 14 Aug. 1937. Although there were many Saro at the funeral, there is no reference in the reports to the official group involvement of the Sierra Leone Union in the funeral activities. The Union may well have been going through one of its moribund phases at this time.

59. Commander Causer proposed, and Dr. Clark seconded the following resolution: "That it is the unanimous desire of this board to convey to the relatives in Freetown of the late Rev. E.K. Williams, an expression of their deep sympathy . . . on the occasion of his death and to express their regret at the loss of a member of the Board who always took a great interest in the public welfare of Port Harcourt". See Riv. Prof 8/18/16, TAB minutes of meeting of 27 Aug 1937, NAE.

60. *Ibid.* Minutes of the TAB meeting of 27 Aug. 1937.

61. *Ibid.*

62. Riv. Prof. 9/1/66. Handing-over notes, D.E.R. M. Lambert, Local Authority to C.T. Ennals, 6 Nov., 1937, NAE.

63. The Nigerian Observer, 9 April 1943.

64. Riv. Prof. 8/18/16, Minutes of the TAB meeting of 27 Jan. 1938, NAE.

65. *Ibid.* Minutes of the TAB meeting of 24 Feb. 1938. See above, note 47.

66. *Ibid.*

67. The Nigerian Observer, 23 Apr. 1938.

68. See the Nigerian Observer, 2 April, 1938.

69. Riv. Prof. 13/1/3[D], L. Nicholls, Senior Assistant Conservator of Forests to Local Authority, Port Harcourt, 6 Apr. 1938; NAE.

70. The Nigerian Observer, 14 May, 1938.

71. Akintola Wyse, *The Krio of Sierra Leone* (London, 1989), pp. 76-7; also "The 1919 Strike and Anti-Syrian Riots: A Krio Plot?" *Journal of the Historical Society of Sierra Leone*, III, 1 and 2, Dec. 1979, pp. 1-14.

72. The Nigerian Observer, 18 June, 1938.

73. J.D.Y. Peel, *Ijeshas and Nigerians* (Cambridge, 1983), p. 184.

74. See above, discussion of the APU.

75. Kalu Ezera, *Constitutional Developments in Nigeria* (Cambridge, 1966), p. 55

76. See chapter 1; Azikiwe was born in Zungeru, Northern Nigeria, in 1904, attended schools in Lagos, and left for studies in the United States in 1925. After his education at Lincoln University, Howard, and at Columbia, he failed to get a job as tutor at King's College, Lagos. He subsequently took to journalism. See Ezera, *Constitutional Developments*, p. 53.

77. Ezera, *Constitutional Developments*, pp. 55; see also Coleman, *Nigeria*, pp. 224-5; and J. Ayodele Langley, *Pan-Africanism and Nationalism in West Africa* (Oxford, 1973), p. 238.

78. Leo Spitzer and La Ray Denzer, "I.T.A. Wallace-Johnson and the West African Youth League", *International Journal of African Historical Studies*, VII, 3, 1973; Leo Spitzer, *The Creole of Sierra Leone* (Madison, 1974) Ch. 6; S.K.B. Asante, *Pan-African Protest: West Africa and the Italo-Ethiopian Crisis*, 1934-1941; and M.H.Y. Kaniki, "Politics and Protest in colonial West Africa: The Sierra Leone Experience", *The African Review*, IV, 3, 1974, pp. 423-58.

79. Wyse, *The Krio*, pp. 94-5.

80. Atanda Pratt, a dispenser, and L.A. John, Cashier of Barclays Bank, were executive members. See Riv. Prof. 2/1/48, copy of a report of Inspector A.C. Willoughby on a meeting at Port Harcourt, held on 17 Nov. 1938.

81. The Nigerian Observer,9 and 16 July, 1938.

82. Riv. Prof. 8/18/16, see minutes of TAB meeting of 8 Sept. 1938.

83. *Ibid.* Minutes of the TAB meeting of Oct.1938.

84. The Nigerian Observer, 5 Nov. 1938.

85. Riv. Prof. 2/1/48, copy of a report by Inspector A.C. Willoughby of a meeting at Port Harcourt, 17 Nov. 1938, NAE.

86. *Ibid.* On the platform with Potts-Johnson at this meeting were the following: A.O. Alakija; Alihu Madaiki (Hausa Chief); Yisa Agbansi (Yoruba chief); Suberu Ajibola (Yoruba Headmen); Nkonsong (representing the Efik); Aduba, a nurse (representing Igbo); Trezise, Vice-Chairman, Youth Movement; A. Pratt, Secretary; Y. Mov. A. Agbor, (representing Gold Coasters); A. Willoughby, Inspector of Police, who was said to be "rigidly invited" (sic.)

87. *Ibid.* Resident, Port Harcourt to Secretary, Southern Province, Enugu, 18 Nov. 1938.

88. Spitzer, *The Creole*, p. 185.

89. The Nigerian Observer, 17 Dec. 1938.

90. Riv. Prof. 9/1/680, Annual Report, Port Harcourt, 1938, NAE.

91. Potts-Johnson had expressed disquiet over Germany's withdrawal from the League of Nations over disagreements on re-armament. He had cautioned. "We have been basking in an atmosphere of comparative peace during the last fourteen years, and it is the duty of the world's statesmen to be alive to their responsibilities and to calculate before hand the results of any steps they may take. Any false steps . . . will lead not only themselves, but millions of weak, helpless, innocent and defenseless people who took no part in their mad competition for armaments, to incalculable sufferings and calamities". See the Nigerian Observer, 18 Nov. 1933.

92. The Nigerian Observer, 10 and 31 Dec. 1938.

93. Webster, "African Political Activity", pp. 651-55.

94. *Ibid.*

95. The Nigerian Observer, 25 Jan. 1930.

96. Akintola Wyse, *The Krio of Sierra Leone*, pp. 36-7.

97. See Nnamdi Azikiwe, *Zik: A Selection from the speeches of Nnamdi Azikiwe* (Cambridge, 1961).

98. The Nigerian Observer, 25 Jan. 1930.

99. The Nigerian Observer, 26 Apr. and 23 Aug. 1930. Potts-Johnson had long made a connection between race and African socio-economic deprivation.

100. The Nigerian Observer, 3 Oct. 1931.

101. The Nigerian Observer, 10 Oct. and 14 Nov. 1931. Elaborate social expenditure was a highly sensitive area for the immigrant commentator, and Potts-Johnson's ability to articulate a position reflects both his social immersion, and his acceptance in the local community, as well as his penchant for controversy. Incidentally, observers may find these remarks of some contemporary relevance.

102. The Nigerian Observer, 19 Dec. 1931.

103. The Nigerian Observer, 19 March, 1932.

104. The Nigerian Observer, 16 and 23 Apr. 1932.

105. The Nigerian Observer, 23 Apr. 1932.

106. The Nigerian Observer, 29 Apr. and 27 May, 1933.

107. The Nigerian Observer, 14 Apr. 1933.

108. David Meredith, "Government and the decline of the Nigerian oil-palm export industry, 1919-1939", *Journal of African History*, 25,1984, p. 326.

109. The Nigerian Observer, 19 May and 16 June, 1934.

110. David Meredith, "Government and decline of the Nigerian oil-palm export industry" etc., p. 326.

111. The Nigerian Observer, 16 June, 1934.

112. R.J. Southall, "Farmers, Traders and Brokers in the Gold Coast Economy", *Canadian Journal of African Studies*, 12, 1978; also J. Miles, "Rural

Protest in the Gold Coast: Cocoa Hold-ups of 1908-38", in C. Dewey and A.G. Hopkins (eds.), *The Imperial Impact* (London, 1978).

113. The Nigerian Observer, 23 June and 13 Oct. 1934; also 9 Feb. 1935.

114. The Nigerian Observer, 1 June, 1935. Potts-Johnson wanted more Africans as Senior Officers in the WAFF.

115. The Nigerian Observer, 27 July, 1935.

116. The Nigerian Observer, 28 Sept. 1935 and 21 March 1936. For a discussion of an earlier phase of this problem, see J.F. Ade Ajayi,"The Development of Secondary Grammar School Education in Nigeria", *Journal of the Historical Society of Nigeria*, II, 4, Dec. 1963, pp. 524-529.

117. The Nigerian Observer, 22 Aug. and 12 Sept. 1936; also 3 Sept. 1938.

118. The Nigerian Observer, 17 Sept. and 22 Oct. 1938; also 29 July 1939.

119. The Nigerian Observer, 21 Jan. 1939.

120. Riv. Prov. 8/18/16, see minutes of TAB meeting of 2 March, 1939. European members of the Board seemed opposed to any further relief.

121. The Nigerian Observer, 29 April and 1 July, 1939.

122. Riv. Prof. 8/18/16, Minutes of the TAB meeting of the 7 Sept. 1939.

123. *Ibid*.

124. The Nigerian Observer, 9 Sept. and 11 Nov., 1939.

125. Riv. Prof. 9/1/817, Annual Report, Port Harcourt, 1939, NAE.

Notes to Chapter 3

1. See chapter 1, n. 136.

2. Interviews with Mrs. Clementina Manly-Rollings.

3. Otonti Nduka, "Educational development in Port Harcourt: Retrospect and prospects" in W. Ogionwo (ed.) *The City of Port Harcourt* (Ibadan, 1979), pp. 36-38.

4. The Nigerian Observer, 8 March, 1930.

5. The Nigerian Observer, 12 April 1930.

6. See Nancy J. Hafkin and Edna G. Bay (eds.) *Women in Africa* (Stanford, 1976), p. 4.

7. The Nigerian Observer, 11 Oct. 1930 and 7 Feb. 1931.

8. The Nigerian Observer, 28 Feb. 1931.

9. The Nigerian Observer, 16 Dec. 1933. See Nancy Eniton's memorial to her late father.

10. The Nigerian Observer, 5 Dec. 1931.

11. E.A. Ayandele, "James Africanus Beale Horton, 1835-1883: Prophet of Modernization in West Africa", *African Historical Studies*, IV, 3, 1971, p. 697; Robert July, "Africanus Horton and the Idea of Independence in West Africa", *Sierra Leone Studies*, 18, Jan. 1966, p. 10; also J. Ayodele Langley, "The Gambia

Section of the National Congress of British West Africa", *Africa*,XXXIX, 4,Oct. 1969, p. 391.

12. J.F.A. Ajayi, "The Development of Secondary Grammar School Education in Nigeria", *Journal of the Historical Society of Nigeria*, II, 4, Dec. 1963, p. 525.

13. *Ibid.* p. 526; also J.S. Coleman, *Background to Nationalism* (Berkeley, 1960), p. 118.

14. R.W. July, "Nineteenth Century Negritude: Edward W. Blyden", *Journal of African History*, V, 1, 1964, p. 78.

15. The Nigerian Observer, 23 Jan 1932; Aggrey was born in the Gold Coast, and would obtain several degrees in the United States, emerging as a leading pan-Africanist with passionate views on African pride and identity. See P.O. Esedebe, *Pan-Africanism*, (Washington, D.C. 1982) pp. 99-100.

16. The Nigerian Observer, 19 and 24, Mar. and 9 Apr. 1932.

17. The Nigerian Observer, 16 Apr. 1932.

18. The Nigerian Observer, 7 May 1932. Among the guests were Mrs. Potts-Johnson, Messrs. G.F. Spiff, T.E. Spiff, I.B. Johnson, Dr. De Marra, Mr. Williams, the druggist, Messrs. A.W. Porter, Fred O. Jack, Dandeson Green, I.T. Ikiroma-Owiye, and Osika.

19. The Nigerian Observer, 27 Aug. and 12 Nov. 1932.

20. The Nigerian Observer, 6 and 13 May, 1933.

21. The Nigerian Observer, 22 Apr. 1933.

22. The Nigerian Observer, 9 Sept. 1933; also 5th May and 15 Dec. 1934.

23. The Nigerian Observer, 9 March, 1935.

24. The Nigerian Observer, 20 Apr. 1935. Sankoh, as already indicated, was once on the editorial Board of the Nigerian Observer. The Saro and others called him "Professor". A Freemason and ex-pastor, Sankoh's life deserves review in a biographical study. He died in Port Harcourt on November 14, 1940.

25. Akintola Wyse, *The Krio of Sierra Leone* (London, 1989), p. 52.

26. The Nigerian Observer, 20 Apr. 1935.

27. The Nigerian Observer 3 Aug 1935, 25 Apr. 1936, and 17 Jul. 1937.

28. The Nigerian Observer, 1 Jan. 1938.

29. The Nigerian Observer, 12 Nov. 1938.

30. The Nigerian Observer, 5 Aug. 1939.

31. His involvement in plans for a Girls School to be built in memory of the Ven. Arch. D.C. Crowther would ultimately result in the Arch. Crowther Memorial Girls School, Elelenwa, just outside Port Harcourt. (See the Nigerian Observer, 14 May 1938). When plans were made for a muslim school in Port Harcourt, Potts-Johnson commended the idea. He wrote: "As subjects of a United empire, the time has come when all religious bias should be set aside and all, irrespective of denomination, creed or religion, should pull together to draw the race nearer to the goal we all aim at". (See Nigerian Observer, 15 Aug. 1936).

32. The Nigerian Observer, 24 Apr. 1942.

33. The Nigerian Observer, 4 May, 1945.

34. Filomina Chioma Steady, "Protestant Women's Associations in Freetown, Sierra Leone", in Hafkin and Bay, *Women in Africa*, pp. 213-237.

35. Kenneth Little, *African Women in Towns* (Cambridge, 1973), p. 61.

36. The Nigerian Observer, 14 Mar. 1931.

37. The Nigerian Observer, 30 Jan. 1932 and 21 May 1933.

38. The Nigerian Observer, 6 May, 1 July, and 12 Aug. 1933. In 1933, the Methodist Synod reported the commencement of work on Banham Memorial Church, and a much smaller Wesley Church. The new Banham building was unveiled late in 1933 to a congregation of 1,474. In February 1934, the Wesley facility was dedicated, with plans for a larger building later. See WMMS Synod minutes, March 1933, and Annual Report of the Port Harcourt Circuit, 1933, in microfiche box 14, SOAS.

39. The Nigerian Observer, 23 June and 21 July 1934; also WMMS, Annual Report to Synod on Port Harcourt, 1936, microfiche box 14, SOAS.

40. The Methodism of the Nigerian Observer's proprietor might partly explain this.

41. The Nigerian Observer, 4 Jan 1930 and 17 and 24 March, 1934.

42. The Nigerian Observer, 5 Apr., 3 May, and 27 Sept. 1933; also 2 Dec 1933 and 17 Mar. 1934.

43. The Nigerian Observer, 7 Apr. and 21 July 1934; also 6 July and 7 Sept. 1935; and 17 Apr. 1937.

44. Interviews with Mrs. Clementina Manly-Rollings and other members of the Sierra Leone Descendants Union.

45. The Nigerian Observer, 8 June 1940.

46. The Nigerian Observer, 2 Oct. and 27 Nov. 1942; also 10 Sept. 1943.

47. The Nigerian Observer, 4 Jan. 1930.

48. *Ibid.*

49. The Nigerian Observer, 24 May 1930. Potts-Johnson would identify the Ven. Arch. D.C. Crowther as one of the culprits. See the Nigerian Observer, 27 Jan. 1934.

50. The Nigerian Observer, 14 Feb. 1931. Rising juvenile delinquency was criticised repeatedly. See the Nigerian Observer, 2 Feb. 1945, which discussed a TAB meeting at which the subject was addressed.

51. The Nigerian Observer, 25 July 1931.

52. The Nigerian Observer, 26 Dec. 1931. The Observer once offered tips to drunks on methods to recover their sobriety (see the paper for 21 March 1936). It also welcomed the idea of introducing temperance societies to Port Harcourt, and condemned the over-use of alcohol by the youth: "Young men and even women indulge in alcoholic drinks and . . . get entirely out of control. . . . Free use is made of filthy language, blows are sometimes exchanged, and what follows can be better imagined than described". See the Nigerian Observer, 31 Oct. 1936.

53. This came through unsolicited in most interviews. Potts-Johnson fathered children out of wedlock. The author met two of them while in Port Harcourt,

and Olu Potts-Johnson, a son, has always been very active in the affairs of the Sierra Leone (Descendants) Union.

54. This position might well explain some of his earlier problems with the authorities of his church (see chapter 1); also the Nigerian Observer, 13 Feb. 1932).

55. Interviews with members of the Sierra Leone Descendants Union.

56. The Nigerian Observer, 7 May 1932.

57. The Nigerian Observer, 16 July 1932.

58. In 1934, Potts-Johnson had referred to Blyden's ideas on race consciousness, and in October 1935, during the unveiling at the EHS of a portrait of Aggrey, he had devoted an editorial to that Pan-Africanist. See the Nigerian Observer, 20 Oct 1934, and 12 Oct. 1935.

59. The Nigerian Observer, 6 Aug. 1932.

60. The Nigerian Observer, 25 Feb. 1933.

61. The Nigerian Observer, 25 Feb. 1933. "Show boby" is "expose part of a breast", in titillating style, in Krio. By 1935, the Saro, Mrs. Hamilton Leigh was the most sought after seamstress in town. For a review of her range of fashions, see her advert in the Nigerian Observer, 7 Dec. 1935.

62. The Nigerian Observer, 8 Apr. 1933.

63. The Nigerian Observer, 12 Aug. 1933; also Felix K. Ekechi, *Tradition and Transformation in Eastern Nigeria* (London, 1989), pp. 189-90. The Osu system was formally abolished, in 1956, by the Eastern Regional government of Nigeria. This did not, however, end belief in the practice.

64. The Nigerian Observer,17 March 1934.

65. Governors Clifford and Graeme Thompson came in for much criticism. See the Nigerian Observer, 31 March, 1934.

66. The Eastern Nigerian Guardian, 19 May, 1944.

67. The Nigerian Observer, 12 Jan. 1945.

68. See Niara Sudarkasa, "From Stranger to Alien: The Socio-political history of the Nigerian Yoruba in Ghana, 1900-1970", in William Shack and E.P. Skinner (eds.) *Strangers in African Societies* (Berkeley, 1979) pp. 152-158.

69. The offertory at the divine service went to the St. Cyprian's building fund. See the Nigerian Observer, 15 Apr. 1933.

70. The Nigerian Observer, 7 July 1934.

71. The Nigerian Observer, 17 Aug. 1940.

72. The Nigerian Observer, 25 June, 1943.

73. The Nigerian Observer, 28 Jan. 1944.

74. The Nigerian Observer, 5 Jan. and 8 June, 1945.

75. The Nigerian Observer, 21 Sept. 1945.

76. Traditional foods of *Akara, Olele, Agidi, Furrah, pap,* jollof rice, rice bread, and ginger beer, featured prominently in these affairs. In 1934, the Nigerian Observer, in a piece reminiscent of Freetown Krio experience, discussed the habitual thieving activity that invariably accompanied these communal cooking festivities. See the Paper for 21 July 1934.

77. Sule Mansaray and his family arrived in the early 1970's. There are several references to their involvement in Sierra Leone (Descendants) Union (SLDU) activity in the 1970's and 1980's. See minutes of the Union's Executive and General meetings, 14 August 1971, 14 April, 1973, 6 August, 1975, and 8 August 1981. These papers are housed in the Secretariat of the SLDU in Port Harcourt (hereafter referred to as SLDUPH). Unfortunately, the author only learned of the Kallays after leaving Port Harcourt.

78. They operated in a situation of binary ethnicity.

79. See, for instance, Barbara E. Harrell-Bond, Allen M. Howard and David E. Skinner, *Community Leadership and the Transformation of Freetown, 1801-1976* (The Hague, 1978), p. 192.

80. E. Frances White, "Women, Work and Ethnicity: The Sierra Leone Case", in Edna G. Bay (ed.) *Women and Work in Africa* (Boulder, 1982), p. 28.

81. In its edition of 27 Feb. 1932, the Nigerian Observer warned of the evils of gossip (in Krio, *Kongosa*). It called gossip "the breaker of societies, of friendship and good feeling". Gossip, it claimed had "smashed many peaceful homes", and "put pastor and flock at variance". To further interest in Krio culture, Potts-Johnson periodically published aphorisms in Krio in the paper's more expansive anecdotal moments. See "One thing and another"—Nigerian Observer, 21 July 1934.

82. The Nigerian Observer, 15 Jan. 1938.

83. Interview with T. Jos. Wilson, 17 Feb. 1985.

84. Claire Robertson and Iris Berger (eds.) *Women and Class in Africa*, (New York, 1986), pp. 14-15.

85. Bay, *Women and Work*, p. 2.

86. Sharon B. Stichter and Jane L. Parpart (eds.) *Patriarchy and Class*, (Boulder, 1988), pp. 14-17.

87. For some discussion of the methods employed by women to overcome their exploitation, see Janet M. Bujra, "Urging Women to Redouble their Efforts: Class, gender and capitalist transformation in Africa", and Jane L. Parpart, "Class and Gender on the Copperbelt", in Robertson and Berger, *Women and Class*.

88. Interviews with Mrs. T. Jos Wilson, 17 Feb. 1985.

89. *Ibid.* Potts-Johnson's name always featured in these conversations.

90. See the Nigerian Observer, 9 March 1945.

91. The Nigerian Observer, 18 Sept. 1937 and 20 Oct. 1939.

92. The Nigerian Observer, 30 March 1940. Roger Williams (26 years of age) was jailed for 3 years in the mid-1920's. See the petition for his release from his brother, Allen, in Riv. Prof. 8/14/18, Allen Williams to Sir Graeme Thompson, Governor, 27 Apr. 1926, NAE.

93. The Nigerian Observer, 18 Feb. 1944. Browne's murderer was sentenced to death. See the Nigerian Observer, 7 Apr. 1944.

94. The Nigerian Observer, 21 Aug. 1942.

95. The Nigerian Observer, 3 Dec. 1948.

96. The Nigerian Observer, 1 April 1949.

97. Dublin Green who would serve on the Township Advisory Board in the late 1940's, retired as a government hospital dispenser, and later became a private druggist.

98. The Nigerian Observer, 16 Aug. 1930.

99. See the Nigerian Observer, 5 Dec. 1947.

100. The Nigerian Observer, 13 Dec. 1930.

101. The Nigerian Observer, 28 Feb. 1931.

102. The Nigerian Observer, 20 Aug. 1932.

103. The Nigerian Observer, 20 May 1932.

104. The cast was predominantly Saro. See the Nigerian Observer, 23 Sept. and 9 Dec. 1933.

105. The Nigerian Observer, 18 Aug and 22 Dec. 1934.

106. The Nigerian Observer, 28 Sept. 1935.

107. The Nigerian Observer, 13 March and 4 Sept. 1938; see also Riv. Prof. 9/1/765, the Optimists to the Resident, Owerri Province, *undated*; and Riv. Prof. 9/1/765, Resident to Max George, 9 Oct. 1939, NAE. Port Harcourt also had a Sierra Leone Benevolent Society. See the Nigerian Observer, 29 July and 19 Aug. 1939.

108. The Nigerian Observer, 4 Feb. 1944.

109. The Nigerian Observer, 1 Apr. 1933.

110. The Nigerian Observer, 17 Nov. 1934.

111. The Nigerian Observer, 17 April, 1937

112. The Nigerian Observer, 20 Apr. 1940.

113. The Nigerian Observer, 9 April, 1943.

114. At this time, alumni of the Sierra Leone Grammar School (SLGS) were being invited to contribute "statement of facts", anecdotes, photographs, and other material toward "A History of the SLGS". Alumni in Port Harcourt were requested to send their contributions to T.C. Luke in Freetown. See the Nigerian Observer, 5 May 1944 and 9 March 1945.

115. Akintola Wyse, *The Krio*, p. 37. see also K.A.B. Jones-Quartey, "Sierra Leone's role in the development of Ghana, 1820-1930", *Sierra Leone Studies* (New series), 10, June 1958, p. 79.

116. The Nigerian Observer, 17 Apr. 1937, refers to Potts-Johnson as "the Postal Agent".

117. The Nigerian Observer, 20 May and 10 June, 1933; also 14 July 1934; see also obituary to Potts-Johnson, Eastern Nigerian Guardian, 20 June, 1949.

118. Potts-Johnson had a birthday celebration in February 1931, and a similar low-key affair marked Eniton's birthday in September 1931. See the Nigerian Observer, 7 Feb. and 19 Sept. 1931.

119. The Nigerian Observer, 20 Feb. 1937.

120. This came through repeatedly in interviews with W.S. Byron (10 Feb. 1985), and T. Jos. Wilson (17 Feb. 1985).

121. The Nigerian Observer, 1 Oct. 1932 and 7 Jan. 1933; see also WMMS.Synod minutes, 1938, microfiche box 15, SOAS.

122. The Nigerian Observer, 15 Aug. and 5 Sept. 1941.

123. The Nigerian Observer, 9 July, 1943.

124. The Nigerian Observer, 22 Feb. 1941 and 14 Apr. 1944.

125. The Nigerian Observer, 8 Feb. 1930.

126. Riv. Prof. 9/1/65. Handing-over notes, H.M.S. Brown to J. Cook, 11 May 1932, NAE; see also the Nigerian Observer, 1 March 1930; also 27 Feb. and 7 May 1932.

127. The Nigerian Observer, 7 Jun. 1930.

128. See the Nigerian Observer, 2 Jan and 2 Apr. 1932; also 15 Sept. 1934.

129. Mrs. Taylor visited twice, in 1933, and again in 1937. See the Nigerian Observer, 13 May and 2 Sept. 1933; also 12 June 1937 and 30 Apr. 1938.

130. The Nigerian Observer, 20 Oct. 1934.

131. The Nigerian Observer, 10 July 1937 and 11 Feb. 1939.

132. The Nigerian Observer. 13 Apr. 1940.

133. The Nigerian Observer, 29 Jan. 1943.

134. The Nigerian Observer, 4 June 1948. Dr. Johnson would later marry the local lawyer and indigene, A.C. Nwapa, a decision that did not meet with her parent's approval, according to informants.

135. C. Fyfe, *A History of Sierra Leone*, (London, 1962), pp. 472, 602, and 617-18.

136. The Nigerian Observer, 24 Mar. 1944.

137. See chapter 2; also the Nigerian Observer, 24 March 1944 and 2 Feb. 1945.

138. The Nigerian Observer, 3 Oct. and 5 Dec. 1947.

139. The Nigerian Observer, 16 and 23 July 1948; also 6 Aug. 1948.

Notes to Chapter 4

1. See Olajide Aluko, "Politics of decolonisation in British West Africa, 1945-1960", in J.F. Ade Ajayi and Michael Crowder, (eds.) *History of West Africa* (Essex, 1987), pp. 693-735.

2. James S. Coleman, *Nigeria: Background to Nationalism* (Berkeley, 1960), p. 227; also Kalu Ezera, *Constitutional Developments in Nigeria* (Cambridge, 1960), p. 56.

3. Ezera, *Constitutional Developments*, pp. 57-78.

4. *Ibid.* pp. 78-9.

5. *Ibid.* pp. 79-81.

6. Riv. Prof. 1/9/4, Secret circular from the Secretary, Southern Provinces, 1 March, 1926, NAE.

7. This was an area of some local experience. In 1931, Bowari Brown, the local correspondent of the Daily Times, had attracted much attention. The District officer had minuted of him: "[he has] permitted his journalistic zeal to outstrip his discretion. This has resulted in the publication of garbled and exaggerated accounts of local incidents . . . [he] loudly and frequently voices his loyalty to government, and his desire to assist the administration . . . it is hoped that his exuberance may in the future be kept within reasonable bounds". *Ibid.* District Officer, Aba Division to Senior Resident, 28 Feb. 1931.

8. Riv. Prof. 13/1/58, Act. Resident Mylius to Potts-Johnson, 6 Sept. 1939, NAE.

9. *Ibid.*

10. Riv. Prof. 2/1/44, Secret Intelligence report for period 22 Sept. -7 Oct. 1939, NAE.

11. Interviews with W. Byron (10 Feb. 1985), and T. Jos. Wilson (17 Feb. 1985).

12. The Nigerian Observer, 15 June 1940.

13. We have already reviewed Krio/Saro resentment of the Levantines. See chapter 2, n. 71; also Riv. Prof. 20/1/6, meeting of the Win-the-War fund committee (hereafter WTWF), 22 July 1940.

14. *Ibid.* WTWF Committee meetings of 29 July and 15 Aug. 1940.

15. The Nigerian Observer, 31 Aug. 1940.

16. The Nigerian Observer, 7 Sept. 1940.

17. Riv. Prof. 20/1/6, meeting of the WTWF, 19 Dec. 1940, NAE; also the Nigerian Observer, 7 Dec. 1940, and 3 and 17 May, 1941.

18. *Ibid.* Igbo traders had organised a show at the Rex Hall, and the proceeds had not been donated.

19. *Ibid.* Meeting of the WTWF Committee, 9 March, 1942.

20. The Nigerian Observer, 16 Oct. 1942.

21. The Nigerian Observer, 17 Nov. 1944.

22. Riv. Prof. 9/1/984, Annual Report, Port Harcourt, 1940, NAE.

23. Riv. Prof. 9/1/1301, Annual Report, Port Harcourt, 1945, NAE.

24. Interviews with members of the Sierra Leone Descendants Union.

25. Riv. Prof. 9/1/984, Annual Report, Port Harcourt, 1940, NAE.

26. Riv. Prof. 8/18/16, Minutes of the meeting of the TAB, 10 Jan. 1940, NAE. The out-spoken indigene, Z.C. Obi, joined the TAB in August, 1940. *Ibid.* Minutes of TAB meeting, 8 Aug. 1940; see also the Nigerian Observer, 6 April, 1940.

27. In 1940, the total tax return was assessed at £1815.19s, and £1418.13s. was realised after collection. See Riv. Prof. 9/1/984, Annual Report, Port Harcourt, 1940, NAE.

28. The Nigerian Observer, 5 Oct. 1940.

29. The Nigerian Observer, 29 March, 1941.

30. Akintola Wyse, *The Krio of Sierra Leone* (London, 1989), pp. 76-7.

31. Riv. Prof. 9/1/883, Extract from the Daily Service of 11 Aug. 1941, NAE. Those were prophetic observations in the light of the economic indigenisation measures Nigeria would adopt after independence in 1960. See also H.L. Van Der Laan, *The Lebanese of Sierra Leone* (The Hague, Mouton, 1975).

32. Interviews in 1985 with W. Byron, T. Jos. Wilson, and other members of the Sierra Leone Descendants Union. Saro relations with the Syrians were rather ambivalent. I.B. Johnson and other members of the Saro elite had close associates among the Syrians and Lebanese. Even the poorer Saro looked kindly on Levantine traders who allowed them credit facilities. When the popular Syrian trader, George Breedy, died in 1940, many of the Saro leaders turned out for the funeral. See the Nigerian Observer, 17 Feb. 1940.

33. The Nigerian Observer, 21 Aug. 1942.

34. The Nigerian Observer, 23 Oct. 1942.

35. See Chapter 1, notes 179, 180 and 181.

36. The Nigerian Observer, 4 Nov. 1942.

37. *Ibid.*;also the Nigerian Observer, 11 Dec. 1942.

38. The Nigerian Observer, 13 Nov. 1942.

39. With Potts-Johnson and Dr. Ajibade on the ACL delegation were Z.C. Obi, I.B. Johnson, C. Egerton Shyngle, and Chief Taiwo. See the Nigerian Observer, 20 Nov. 1942.

40. The Nigerian Observer, 27 Nov. 1942.

41. The Nigerian Observer, 11 Dec. 1942.

42. The Nigerian Observer, 1 Oct. 1943.

43. See the paper's editorial of 15 Oct. 1943.

44. Carried in the Nigerian Observer, 22 Oct. 1943.

45. *Ibid.*

46. The Nigerian Observer, 29 Oct. 1943.

47. The Eastern Nigerian Guardian, 26 May, 1944.

48. The Eastern Nigerian Guardian, 27 May, 1944.

49. The Eastern Nigerian Guardian, 16 Nov. 1944.

50. Riv. Prof. 9/1/1145, undated memorandum of the post-war municipal development sub-Committee, NAE.

51. For the vote of confidence, see above, no. 46; for details of the meeting, see the Nigerian Observer, 5 Nov. 1943.

52. The Nigerian Observer, 5 Nov. 1943.

53. The Nigerian Observer, 26 May 1944 and 19 Jan. 1945.

54. See the Union's constitution in the appendices.

55. The Eastern Nigerian Guardian, 11 Nov. 1946.

56. See chapter 3, n. 108.

57. Riv. Prof. 9/1/1323, annual Report, Port Harcourt, 1946, NAE.

58. *Ibid*; also Riv. Prof. 12/8/3, Minutes of the TAB meeting, 19 Dec. 1946, NAE.

59. Riv. Prof. 9/1/1278, Memorandum to the government from the House Tenants Union, Nov. 1947, signed by Union President, A. Dabulo, and others, NAE.

60. *Ibid.*

61. Riv. Prof. 13/1/200, Annual Report, Port Harcourt, 1947, NAE.

62. *Ibid.*

63. *Ibid.*

64. *Ibid.*

65. In May 1943, Potts-Johnson wrote: "Empty vaseline bottles are filled with burnt palm oil,and sold as vaseline. Pomades are treated in the same way. . . . Tins of Cuticura powder . . . are emptied half-way and then adulterated with powdered chalk." See the Nigerian Observer, 7 May, 1943.

66. See the Nigerian Observer, 5 Dec. 1941 and 14 Aug. 1942.

67. The Nigerian Observer, 25 Dec. 1942.

68. The Nigerian Observer, 13 Nov. 1942. Potts-Johnson also called for a Rate Payer's Association of all who paid over £12 annually. *Ibid.*

69. See the representations of Potts-Johnson, O. Ajibade, and Z.C. Obi to the Governor in November 1942. The Nigerian Observer, 27 Nov. 1942 and 18 June, 1943.

70. The Nigerian Observer, 11 June, 1943.

71. The Nigerian Observer, 12 Nov. 1943.

72. Riv. Prof. 9/1/1212, Annual Report, Port Harcourt, 1943, NAE.

73. The Nigerian Observer, 26 Nov. and 10 Dec. 1943. Relations were not helped by allegations at this time that the Senior Resident had referred to the ACL as an organisation ridden with bribery. See Riv. Prof. 13/1/3^D, Dr. O. Ajibade to the Senior Resident, 1 Dec. 1943, NAE.

74. The Nigerian Observer, 10, Dec. 1943.

75. The Nigerian Observer, 26 Feb. 1943.

76. The Nigerian Eastern Mail, 15 Jan. 1943- extract in Riv. Prof. 13/1/3^D, Mylius to Secretary, Eastern Provinces, 31 Dec. 1943, NAE.

77. Riv. Prof. 3/1/107, S.D. Akanibo, Secretary, Rivers Division People's League, to the Resident, 7 Jan. 1944, NAE.

78. Among the people present were the following: R.T.E. Wilcox, Arch. E.T. Dimieari, J.B. Ketebu, Chief Bowari Brown, S.D. Akanibo, Chief G.D. Fiberesima, D.E. Iwarime-Jaja, E.M.T. Epelle, N. Ikuru, and Chief N.G. Yellowe. Other officials of the League were M.A. Abasa, D.K. Achebbe, C.K.D. Abangesi, M.D. Selema, H.N. Alagoa, and E.D. Brown. *Ibid.* An indigene-based Women's Political Action Committee, led by Mrs. M.F. Ene, was formed in December, 1948. See Riv. Prof. 13/1/276, Resident, Rivers Province, to Mrs. M.F. Ene, Dec. 1948. NAE.

79. The Nigerian Observer, 28 Jan. 1944.

80. The Nigerian Observer, 4 Feb. 1944. The Saro, S.B. Rhodes, was not to be replaced by another Saro, Potts-Johnson.

81. The Nigerian Observer, 10 March, 1944.

82. CO583/268/30453/1, ACL to Secretary of State, 5 Apr. 1945, PRO.

83. See the Nigerian Observer's report (1 Dec. 1934) when the Igbo Union welcomed Azikiwe to Port Harcourt.

84. The Eastern Nigerian Guardian, 1 July, 1946.

85. The Nigerian Observer, 20 Sept. 1946.

86. *Ibid.*

87. See Howard Wolpe, *Urban Politics in Nigeria: A Study of Port Harcourt* (Los Angeles, 1974), pp. 120 and 124. The term "Zikist" was coined from "Azikiwe", the name of the NCNC leader. See also Ehiedu Iweriebor, *Radical Politics in Nigeria, 1945–1950: The Significance of the Zikist Movement* (Zaria, 1996).

88. See details of one such rally in the Nigerian Observer, 23 Jan. 1948.

89. The Nigerian Observer, 6 Dec. 1946.

90. The Eastern Nigerian Guardian, 7 Dec. 1946.

91. *Ibid.*

92. Proceedings of the Eastern House of Assembly (hereafter PEHA), 10 Jan. 1947, p. 37, NAE.

93. The Nigerian Observer, 5 Sept. 1947.

94. *Ibid.* This observation would later bring Potts-Johnson into conflict with local ex-servicemen.

95. PEHA, 19 Dec. 1947, NAE.

96. *Ibid.*

97. See chapter 2, n. 27.

98. A rather trusting, loyal, and conservative Potts-Johnson had warned. "Gandhi with his calibre and world-wide fame has a somewhat precious life and he should be the last man to pursue his political activities in such a way as would leave no other course open to the authorities save that of incarcerating him. He may become an idol and even a martyr . . . but all right thinking people may begin to doubt his ability as a real political leader . . . the lesson we in British West Africa are to learn from Indian affairs therefore is one of *Festina Lente*. . . . we should go slowly and step by step. Fortunately our lot is cast with sympathetic people, who as soon as they realise that we are in a position to manage our own affairs will pack up bag and baggage. Our destiny is in our own hands, and we will only have ourselves to blame if we fail to profit by recent events in India". See the Nigerian Observer's editorial of 16th Jan. 1932.

99. The Eastern Nigerian Guardian, 23 Dec. 1948.

100. *Ibid.*

101. See his application for plot 174f. for the construction of staff quarters to the value of £1000; Riv. Prof. 12/8/3, TAB meeting, 14 Feb. 1947, NAE.

102. The Eastern Nigerian Guardian, 19 Feb. 1947.

103. Riv. Prof. 12/8/3/, TAB meeting, 17 Apr. 1947, NAE; also the Eastern Nigerian Guardian, 24 May, 1947. He would similarly dispel rumour in November 1948 that 1,100 British settlers were about to take up permanent residence in Nigeria. This rumour which stemmed from the Clay report on an Oil Seeds Com-

mission, came out of speculations over the governments's plans for small-scale agriculture in the Kontagora region. See the Eastern Nigerian Guardian, 13 Nov. 1948.

104. The Eastern Nigerian Guardian, 19 March, 1947. Potts-Johnson was no stranger to the problems of those who dealt in fish. He had led a protest of female fish traders to see the Local Authority, in March 1942, when the women faced unfair male competition. See the Nigerian Observer, 27 March, 1942.

105. Riv. Prof. 12/8/3, TAB meeting, 18 Sept. 1947, NAE; see also the Nigerian Observer, 5 Sept. 1947, which carried Potts-Johnson's speech before the Eastern House on the subject in August 1947. Potts-Johnson considered it "petty and autocratic" for the Methodist Council to oppose sunday viewing in Port Harcourt.

106. The Eastern Nigerian Guardian, 4 Jan. 1949.

107. The Nigerian Observer, 7 Jan. 1949.

108. The Eastern Nigerian Guardian, 26 Feb. and 3 March, 1949.

109. The Nigerian Observer, 11 Feb. 1949.

110. Interviews with W. Byron, T. Jos. Wilson, and other members of the Sierra Leone Descendants Union.

111. See the Nigerian Observer, 24 March, 19 and 26 May, 1944.

112. Riv. Prof. 2/1/81, Resident to Secretary, 8 Aug. 1946.

113. Local Streets were renamed, in August, 1942, for such heroes as "Asinobi", "Yoko", "Ugoji", "Alozie", "Akwiwu", and others, but the administration could not overlook "Potts-Johnson", and "I.B. Johnson". The Saro got honored as well. See the Nigerian Observer, 21 Aug. 1942.

114. See above, n. 94.

115. The signatories of the veterans petition were R.J.O. Chukayere, B.A., P.K. Okarafor, L.D. Chukuezi, and F.D. Wambu. See the Nigerian Eastern Mail, 17 Feb. and 13 March, 1948; also the Nigerian Observer, 23 April 1948.

116. See Aluko, "Politics of Decolonisation", pp. 693-735.

117. So the author gathered from interviews with the members of the Sierra Leone Descendants Union.

118. The Eastern Nigerian Guardian, 25 June, 1948.

119. The Nigerian Observer, 17 Sept. 1948.

120. The Eastern Nigerian Guardian, 17 Jan. 1949.

121. *Ibid.*

122. This came through in all interviews with the older SLDU members.

123. The Eastern Nigerian Guardian, 5 March, 1949.

124. The Nigerian Observer, 11 May, 1945.

125. The Nigerian Observer, 5 Oct. 1945.

126. Riv. Prof. 9/1/1301, Annual Report, Port Harcourt, 1945, NAE.

127. Riv. Prof. 2/1/81, Resident to Secretary, Enugu, 8 Aug. 1946.

128. Riv. Prof. 12/8/3, TAB meeting, 23 Sept. 1947, NAE.

129. *Ibid.* TAB meeting, 2 Oct. 1947.

130. The Government's proposal of a 9ᵈ increase in the tax rate for 1948 caused much consternation. Potts-Johnson again appealed for a spirit of sacrifice while conceding that the increase was untimely, coming as it did on the eve of elevation to municipal status. See the Nigerian Observer, 5 Dec. 1947.

131. The Nigerian Observer, 28 Jan. 1949.

132. Riv. Prof. 13/1/200, TAB meeting, 24 Feb. 1949, NAE. The author could not establish whether Potts-Johnson's design was ultimately adopted.

133. See the Eastern Nigerian Guardian, 14 and 16 May, 1949.

134. The Eastern Nigerian Guardian, 11 June, 1949.

135. The Eastern Nigerian Guardian, 20 June, 1949. Many attributed Potts-Johnson's sudden death to the exhaustion that came from the tour, on local government matters, that he had embarked upon on his return from Sierra Leone. See the Nigerian Observer, 24 June, 1949.

136. See the editorial of the Eastern Nigerian Guardian of 20 June, 1949.

137. The Eastern Nigerian Guardian, 23 June, 1949.

138. See excerpts from Ndaguba's tribute in the Eastern Nigerian Guardian of 25 June, 1949.

139. The Nigerian Observer, 24 June, 1949.

140. *Ibid.*

141. *Ibid.* For details of the wake-keeping ceremony preceding the funeral, which was a mix of "native dancers", hymns, and chants, befitting Potts-Johnson's cultural eclecticism, see the Nigerian Observer, 8 July, 1949.

142. The Nigerian Observer, 24 June 1949. The following provided wreaths for the graveside: the government of the Eastern Province, the Sierra Leone Union, Mrs. N.E. Potts-Johnson, the staff of the Nigerian Observer, the Calabar Improvement League, the Okrika Masonic Lodge, Mrs. Esther Adesigbin, "Mrs. Pratt's class", Mrs. A. O. Egonu, Mrs. Phyllis Macaulay, Gauge O'Dwyer, the Ira Brights, the Port Harcourt Women's Political Action Committee, M.N. Itigwe Akobundu, Mrs. Prince, Mrs. E.D. Spiff and children, the Enitonna Ex-students Association, Ohe and Aina Johnson, the technical staff of the Nigerian Observer, Mrs. Garrick, the Kallays, the Manly-Rollings family, the Yoruba section of Wesley church, the A.S. Williams', N.J.C. Cline and family, the Ijaw Union, the Port Harcourt Community League, the staff and students of the EHS, Mrs. Reffell and family, the Methodist Boys High School, Freetown, and Dr. Abayomi Cole's family, also of Freetown. *Ibid.*

143. *Ibid.* Another of Potts-Johnson's students, Okechuku Okoro, called on Mrs. Potts-Johnson to keep the EHS as a memorial to her husband's efforts on behalf of "[the] Ibo as a tribe, and Nigeria as a country." See the Nigerian Observer, 1 July, 1949.

144. So boasted the paper's masthead.

145. See the paper's editorial for 24 June, 1949. The paper would cease publication in 1953.

146. The Nigerian Observer, 8 July, 1949.

147. The Nigerian Observer, 15 July 1949. We know nothing about Potts-Johnson's sister, Caroline. In October 1949, another memorial service was held at the Tinubu Methodist church, Lagos, in Potts-Johnson's memory. The service was arranged by EHS alumni resident in Lagos. The Chief Secretary, H.M. Foot, attended the service, and paid glowing tribute to Potts-Johnson's life and work. See the Nigerian Observer, 21 Oct. 1949.

Notes to Chapter 5

1. For some discussion of the immigrant experience of these groups, see the following: H.L. Van Der Laan, *The Lebanese Traders in Sierra Leone*. (Mouton, Hague, 1975); Michael Twaddle, (ed.) *Expulsion of a Minority: Essays on Ugandan Asians* (London, 1975); Mahmood Mamdani, *From Citizen to Refugee* (London, 1972); and C.P. Fitzgerald, *The Third China: The Chinese Communities in South-East Asia* (London, 1965).

2. Mamdani, *Citizen to Refugee*; and Margaret Peil, "Host Reactions: Aliens in Ghana", in William A. Shack and Elliott P. Skinner (eds.), *Strangers in African Societies* (Berkeley, 1979), pp. 123-140.

3. E.P. Skinner, "Strangers in West African Societies", *Africa*, vol. 33, no. 4, 1963, pp. 307-320.

4. Shack and Skinner, *Strangers*, p. 1; see also Donald Levin, *Georg Simmel: On Individuality and Social Forms* (Chicago, 1971).

5. E.P. Skinner, "Theoretical Perspectives on the Stranger", paper presented at the conference on Strangers in Africa, October, 1974, Smithsonian Conference Center, Belmont, Maryland, pp. 8-9.

6. For some review of the deprived indigenes' animus toward the stranger, see William A. Shack, "Open Systems and Closed Boundaries: The Ritual Process of Stranger Relations in New African States", in Shack and Skinner, *Strangers*, pp. 45-46.

7. Proceedings of the Eastern House of Assembly (PEHA), December, 1949; also H. Wolpe, "Port Harcourt: Ibo Politics in Microcosm", *Journal of Modern African Studies*, 7, 3, 1969.

8. CO 583/311/9, Report on the working of Port Harcourt Town Council, July 1949-June 1950, PRO.

9. *Ibid*.

10. *Ibid*.

11. Riv. Prof. 13/1/3^D, Secretary, ACL, to the Resident, Rivers Province, 5 Aug. 1950, NAE.

12. *Ibid*. Secretary, ACL, to Resident, 25 Aug. 1950

13. This was not unlike the views indigenous Ivorians held of Dahomeyan immigrants in their midst in the colonial period. See Herschelle Sullivan Challenor,

"Strangers as Colonial Intermediaries: The Dahomeyans in Francophone Africa", in Shack and Skinner, *Strangers*, pp. 78 and 80.

14. See K.O. Dike, *Trade and Politics in the Niger Delta, 1830-1885* (Oxford, 1956); T.M. Tamuno and E.J. Alagoa (eds.) *Eminent Nigerians of the Rivers State* (Ibadan, 1980); E.J. Alagoa, "Long-distance trade and States in the Niger Delta", in the *Journal of African History*, XI, 3, 1970, and "The Development of Institutions in the States of the Eastern Niger Delta", *Journal of African History*, XII, 2, 1971; Also Howard Wolpe, "Port Harcourt: Ibo Politics in Microcosm", *The Journal of Modern African Studies*, 7, 3, 1969, p. 488.

15. R. First, *The Barrel of the Gun: Political Power in Africa and the Coup d'Etat* (Harmondsworth, 1970); J. de. St. Jorre, *The Nigerian Civil War* (London, 1972); B.G. Dudley, *Instability and Political Order: Politics and Crisis in Nigeria* (Ibadan, 1973); B. Gbulie, *Nigeria's Five Majors: Coup d'Etat of 15th January 1966: First Inside Account* (Onitsha, 1981); and T. Falola and J. Ihonvbere, *The Rise and Fall of Nigeria's Second Republic, 1979-84* (London, 1985).

16. See S.M. Nyovele, (for Secretary to the Military Government) to W. Byron, Secretary, SLU, 13 June, 1969, Papers of the Sierra Leone Descendants Union of Port Harcourt (hereafter, SLDUPH).

17. Interview with T. Jos. Wilson (17 Feb. 1985). Mrs. Wilson was the former Mrs. C.E. Garrick. When, in April 1970, Archbishop M.N.C.O. Scott of Sierra Leone visited the Saro, the war experience was widely narrated and reviewed. See welcome address to Arch. Scott, 17 April, 1970, SLDUPH.

18. Interview with T. Jos Wilson, 17 Feb., 1985. The author called at the Wilson home regularly during his stay in Port Harcourt, and got to know the couple very well.

19. Interview with W. Byron, 10 Feb. 1985.

20. Sam Metzger was a prominent journalist and political commentator in Freetown after independence in 1961.

21. A.O. Wilson to High Commissioner of Sierra Leone, Lagos (Undated), SLDUPH. See full text in the appendices.

22. *Ibid.*

23. *Ibid.*

24. Victoria Pratt to J.O. Barnes, Ag. Secretary, SLU, 17 Nov. 1969, SLDUPH.

25. J.O.Barnes to Mrs. V. Pratt, (undated), SLDUPH.

26. See, for instance, the custody controversy over the home of Mrs. Annet Williams which would lead to accusations of financial impropriety against W. Byron, SLU secretary and care-taker of the property. The subsequent rift with Byron would keep him away from the SLU for several years. See J.E. Davies to Byron, 12 May 1972; also minutes of SLU general meetings, 13 May, 8 July, 12 Aug. and 14 Oct., 1972, and 15 June and 14 Sept. 1974, SLDUPH.

27. General meeting of the SLU, 14 Nov. 1970; also Byron to Attorney-General, Rivers State, 28 Nov. 1970, SLDUPH.

28. See copy of the Gazette in SLDUPH papers. It would appear from this release that indigenous women married to Saro males were being regarded as Sierra Leoneans, and thus subject to the same treatment.

29. Emergency meeting of the Executive of the SLU, 28 July, 1973, SLDUPH.

30. W.H. Fitzjohn to Secretary, SLU, 12 Oct. 1973, SLDUPH.

31. E. Johnson to the Governor, Rivers State, 11 March, 1974, SLDUPH.

32. General meeting of the SLU, 12 April, 1974; meeting of the SLU Executive, 11 June, 1975, SLDUPH; also interview with W. Byron, 10 Feb. 1985.

33. General meeting of the SLU, 10 Oct. 1970, SLDUPH.

34. Sis. P.M. Udeogu to secretary, SLU, 4 Nov. 1970, SLDUPH.

35. Byron to the High Commissioner of Sierra Leone, 28 June, 1971, SLDUPH.

36. Christine L.A. Harding to Fitzjohn, Lagos, 28 July 1972; also R.A. Wokoma to SLU, 3 Oct. 1972, SLDUPH.

37. See above n. 26.

38. The Nigerian Observer, 13 Jan. 1950.

39. See chapter 1, n. 55.

40. Interviews with the T. Jos Wilsons.

41. These apprehensions, common in the 1960's and 1970's, were communicated with much gravity in interviews with the older Saro such as Byron and the Wilsons.

42. General meeting of the SLU, 14 March, 1970, SLDUPH.

43. See, for instance, SLU involvement in the marital problems of the Akibo-Betts'. See letter from Bro. O.I. Akibo-Betts to the president, SLU, 10 Oct. 1970. Also Byron to Akibo-Betts, 26 Nov. 1970, SLDUPH.

44. See the constitution of the SLU in the appendices.

45. General meeting of the SLU, 13 June, 1970; Executive meeting of the SLU, 5 July, 1972, SLDUPH. On average, only twenty of the Union's sixty registered members attended meetings regularly in the early 1970's.

46. General meeting of the SLU, 13 Jan. 1973, SLDUPH.

47. Interviews with T. Jos. Wilson.

48. SLU members were divided into four groups with rotational responsibility to entertain the membership at monthly general meetings. The following groups were formed: Group I: Sis. T. Wyse, G.H.S. Bucknor, Sis. C. Rollings, S.F. Cole, Sis. P.O. Macaulay, Sis. S.A. Bright, Ben Williams, Sis. P. Udeogu, and D. Battey. Group II: Sis. S.I. Boyle, T.J. Wilson, G. Ulzen, Sis. T. Davies, Sis. J.A. Bull, C. Williams, R. Williams, A.L.O. Thompson, Sis. E.E. Alagoa, and G.O. Garrick. Group III: Sis W.R. Cline, C. Hazeley, E.V. Meheux, J.N. Coker,Sis. E. Wyse, J.A. Bull, J.E. Davies, Sis. M.T. Marshall, Sis. E. Green, E.O. Williams, and G.B.A. Hamilton. Group IV: S.O. Johnson, Sis. G.E. Betts, A.A. Williams, Sis. V.E. Ogan, Sis. J.L. Jibunoh, Banke Johnson, C.J. Marshall, Sis. Domo-Spiff, Thomas Benjamin,and Sis. Sarian Barnes. See J.E. Davies to Group Leaders (undated), SLDUPH.

49. *Ibid.* A probationary period prior to full membership for new applicants had been adopted in December 1970 on Wilson's insistence, but this had clearly proved inadequate. See minutes of SLU general meeting, 12 Dec. 1970.

50. See SLU executive meetings 11 June and 9 July, 1975; also SLU general meeting, 11 Sept. 1974, SLDUPH.

51. Interviews with T. Jos. Wilson.

52. General meeting of the SLU, 13 Feb. 1971, SLDUPH.

53. J.E. Davies, Secretary, SLU to Fitzjohn (undated); A. Renner Thomas, Head of Chancery to J.E. Davies, 17 Oct. 1972; and Executive meeting, SLU, 8 Aug, 1973, SLDUPH.

54. Bishop Y. Fubara to A. Renner Thomas, 17 Sept. 1973, SLDUPH.

55. Fitzjohn to SLU, 12 Oct. 1973, SLDUPH.

56. When subsequently Daniel Williams, brother of the late Ben Williams, offered part reimbursement of the funerary expenses, it was accepted very reluctantly by the SLU membership which saw its support of the Williams' as compatriotic duty. See General meeting of the SLU, 8 May 1976; SLU, Calabar, to SLU, Port Harcourt, 4 June, 1976; also, general meeting of the SLU, 14 Aug. 1976.

57. See, for instance, the application for Sierra Leone citizenship by Augustine Battey, a Cameroonian spouse of a Saro. A.E. Battey to Executive of the SLU, 7 May 1971; also Battey to SLU, 21 July, 1971, SLDUPH.

58. Interviews with T. Jos. Wilson. The Saro, G.H.S. Bucknor, with a mother from Andoni, was similarly valued.

59. Exccutive meetings of the SLU, 7 Feb. and 7 March, 1973, SLDUPH.

60. Edward Davies, Secretary, SLU, to Olu Potts-Johnson, 16 April 1973, SLDUPH.

61. Executive meeting of the SLU, 24 April, 1971, SLDUPH.

62. The SLU enlisted the help of the Saro Union, Lagos, in re-drafting the constitution. See J.E. Davies to Secretary, Saro Union, Lagos (N.T. Deen, 20 Layeni Street, Lagos), 21 Oct. 1972; also Deen to SLU, 21 Nov. 1972, SLDUPH.

63. General meeting of the SLU, 13 Dec. 1975, SLDUPH. That this matter generated a "heated debate", and had to be deferred indicates, perhaps, the plurality of views even on cultural matters in an increasingly differentiated Saro community.

64. Executive meeting of the SLU, 11 June, 1975, SLDUPH.

65. General meeting of the SLU, 8 July, 1972, SLDUPH.

66. Interviews with W.S. Byron, (10 Feb. 1985), and Mrs. T. Jos. Wilson (17 Feb. 1985).

67. J.O. Barnes to A.B. Mansaray, 5 Nov. 1969, SLDUPH.

68. Executive meeting of the SLU, 23 Sept. 1970, SLDUPH.

69. See despatch to the SLU from the High Commission regarding Prime Minister Stevens' broadcast in Freetown of 23 Oct. 1970; also Byron to High Commissioner, 29 Sept. 1970, SLDUPH; and interviews with members of the SLDU.

70. G.E. Taylor to SLU, 16 April 1971; also Executive meeting of the SLU, 24 April 1971, SLDUPH.

71. Emergency general meeting of the SLU, 17 April 1971; also Executive meeting of the SLU, 24 April 1971, SLDUPH.

72. Byron to High Commissioner, 5 Aug. 1971, SLDUPH.

73. Byron acknowledged receipt of the travel papers. The SLU president also contacted the High Commission to determine whether "he could sponsor and sign on behalf of any member wishing to obtain a passport". See general meeting of the SLU, 11 Sept. 1971; also Byron to High Commissioner, 14 Oct. 1971, SLDUPH.

74. Releases from the Sierra Leone High Commission, 9 Nov. 1971 and 23 March 1972, SLDUPH.

75. Emergency general meeting of the SLU, 15 April 1972, SLDUPH. The Nigerian government had no public reaction to this development.

76. W.O. Ochi, Secretary, Military Government, to B.R. Browne, 27 July, 1973, SLDUPH. Interviews with T. Jos. Wilson.

77. General meeting of the SLU, 10 Aug. 1974, SLDUPH.

78. Press release of radio broadcast by President Stevens, 1 July, 1975, SLDUPH; Interviews with W. Byron and T. Jos. Wilson.

79. General meeting of the SLU, 15 Nov. 1975, SLDUPH.

80. Executive meeting of the SLU, 7 March, 1973, SLDUPH.

81. *Ibid.*

82. The returns were as follows:

B.R. Browne	President
Sis. Allagoa	Vice-President
Ebun Johnson	Secretary
Noble Johnson	Chief Welfare Officer
G.H.S. Bucknor	Deputy Welfare Officer
Sis. Boyle and Udeogu	Welfare Officers
Sis. V. Ogan	Treasurer
E. Davies	Financial Secretary
T. Jos. Wilson	Auditor
Sis. M.C. Wilson	Ex-offcio member
G.B.A. Hamilton	Ex-officio member

See general meeting of the SLU, 10 June 1973, SLDUPH.

83. See discussion of a letter to the late Sis. Macaulay's survivors (Justice and Mrs. Johnson of Ibadan, and Mrs. G. Douglas) regarding purchase of "No. 35" Executive meeting of the SLU, 8 Aug. 1973, SLDUPH.

84. Executive meetings of the SLU, 22 Nov, 1973 and June 1974; also general meeting of the SLU, 10 Nov. 1973, SLDUPH. Modupe Davies, a Union member, later installed fans at the premises.

85. General meeting of the SLU, 14 June, 1975, SLDUPH.

86. Executive meeting of the SLU, 6 Aug. 1975, SLDUPH.

87. Challenor, "Strangers as Colonial Intermediaries", pp. 74-82.

88. Van Der Laan, *The Lebanese Traders*, pp. 253-260.

89. Peil, "Host Reactions", p. 134.

90. Jessica Kuper, "Goan" and "Asian" in Uganda: An Analysis of Racial Identity and cultural Categories", in Shack and Skinner, *Strangers*, p. 256.

91. Niara Sudarkasa, "From Stranger to Alien: The Socio-Political History of the Nigerian Yoruba in Ghana, 1900-1970", in Shack and Skinner, *Strangers*, p. 163.

92. See Table 5-1.

Notes to Chapter 6

1. For reports on Saro weddings, christenings, memorial services, naming ceremonies, funerary observances, and such activities of these years, see general meetings of the SLU/SLDU, 10 April 1976, and 12 Sept. 1981; also Executive meeting of the SLU, 7 July, 1976, SLDUPH.

2. A.L.O. Thompson to High Commissioner, Lagos, 2 June 1977, SLDUPH.

3. The Sierra Leone Elements, c/o The Sierra Leone Union, to Chairman, Abandoned Property Implementation Panel, 7 June, 1977, SLDUPH.

4. *Ibid.*

5. Most governments in West Africa were at this time out to rid their nations of illegal residents. An Economic Community of West African States (ECOWAS) had been established in 1975, and efforts were being made to sanitise the populations of participating members as new protocols were implemented. See A.B. Akinyemi, S.B. Falegan, and I.A. Aluko, (eds.) *Readings and Documents on ECOWAS* (Ibadan, 1984).

6. A.R. Wurie to A.L.O. Thompson, 11 May 1978, SLDUPH.

7. F.G.T. Cole to Browne, 6 Nov. 1979, SLDUPH.

8. Letter from 1 Cole Street, Onitsha, to SLU, SLDUPH (undated, no name).

9. Most informants were reluctant to discuss the final terms of their settlement and the agonising complications of their experience.

10. Executive meeting of the SLU, 7 July, 1976, SLDUPH.

11. A leaking roof and repairs to the pantry at "No. 35", in October 1976, cost the Union 150 naira. See Executive meeting of the SLU, 6 Oct. 1976, SLDUPH.

12. Executive meeting of the SLDU, 6 Dec. 1979, SLDUPH.

13. Olu Potts-Johnson to Head of Chancery, Lagos, 11 Dec. 1979, SLDUPH. The government of Sierra Leone did not oblige.

14. General meeting of the SLDU, 12 Sept. 1981, SLDUPH.

15. *Ibid.*

16. *Ibid.*

17. The committee was made up of G.H.S. Buckner, W.S. Byron, and Batubo Johnson. See general meeting of the SLDU, 11 Sept. 1982, SLDUPH.

18. General meeting of the SLDU, 9 Oct. 1982, SLDUPH.

19. See programme of activities for April 1983 celebrations, SLDUPH.

20. SLDU to Deputy Governor, 22 April, 1983, SLDUPH.

21. *Ibid.*

22. Bucknor appears to have been the first Saro to obtain a chieftaincy title.

23. SLDU Trustees to Chief M. Okilo, Governor, Rivers State, 5 Nov. 1983; also, general meeting of the SLDU, 12 Nov. 1983, SLDUPH.

24. General meeting of the SLDU, 31 March, 1984, SLDUPH.

25. General meeting of the SLDU, 12 May, 1984, SLDUPH.

26. R.E. Mondeh to A.L.O. Thompson, 30 March, 1977, SLDUPH.

27. General meeting of the SLU, 9 April, 1977.

28. Annual Anniversary report, 1977; also, Executive meeting of the SLU, 11 May, 1977, SLDUPH.

29. General meeting of the SLU, 11 June, 1977, SLDUPH; the Saro reached out to other Sierra Leonean descendants, and resident Sierra Leoneans, as it worked on its programme of celebrations for 1978. Among the guests invited were the following: Hon. Justice and Mrs. Okoro-Idogu, Mr. and Mrs. S. Matturi, Mrs. E. Diete-Spiff, Mr. and Mrs. Albert Norman, Dr. and Mrs. S.B.S. Afiesimama, Mr. and Mrs. T.C. Manly-Rollings, Dr. and Mrs. C. Wari-Toby, Mr. and Mrs. R. Ogali, Mrs. K. Wakama, Mr. and Mrs. George Samuels, Mr. and Mrs. Hector Omealey, and Mr. and Mrs. S. B. Wellington. See Invitation to Sierra Leone Descendants, 19 April, 1978, SLDUPH.

30. General meeting of the SLU, 10 June, 1978, SLDUPH. Interview with the T. Jos. Wilsons, 17 Feb. 1985.

31. Letter to delinquent members, 13 June, 1979, SLDUPH.

32. General meeting of the SLDU, 9 June, 1979, SLDUPH.

33. The Bonny Ibiminaunyo Ereogbu to the SLDU, Dec. 1979; General meeting of the SLDU, 9 Feb. 1989, SLDUPH; also interviews with Union members.

34. J. Coker to SLDU, 29 Oct. 1980, SLDUPH.

35. The Secretary, SLDU, to N. Coker, 55 Bende Street (undated); also, general meeting of the SLDU, 10 March, 1984, SLDUPH.

36. The results were as follows:

B.R. Browne	President
Sis. G.C. Douglas	Vice-President
Olu Potts-Johnson	Secretary
Sis. S.C. Udom-Imeh	Assistant Secretary
Sis. V. Sonny Joe	Financial Secretary
Sis. W.R. Cline	Treasurer
A.L.O. Thompson	Chief Welfare Officer
Sisters C. Ulzen, S. Barnes, T. Davies, and M. Udeogu	Welfare Officers

W.S. Byron and
Sis. S. Wilson.   Ex-officio members

T. Jos. Wilson was also listed among the Ex-officio members although he was in Freetown at the time.

37. Sisters V. Ogan, H. Domo-Spiff, G.C. Douglas, and M.C. Wilson, appear to have been the more outspoken female members who held their own in debates with the men. Their education and/or relative affluence were the key to their prominence.

38. General meetings of the SLDU, 12 Dec. 1981 and 12 March, 1983, SLDUPH.

39. General meeting of the SLDU, 9 April, 1983, SLDUPH.

40. Interviews with female members of the SLDU.

41. Interviews with T. Jos Wilson, 18th Feb. 1985. The author was a regular visitor to the Wilson household.

42. See chapter 5, n. 17.

43. T. Jos. Wilson to SLDU, 11 April 1979, SLDUPH; also, interviews with Mrs. M.C. Wilson, who stayed back in Port Harcourt when her husband returned to Freetown (17 Feb. 1985), and W.S. Byron (10 Feb. 1985).

44. General meeting of the SLDU, 10 April 1982, SLDUPH.

45. Wilson also experienced problems with his passport. See general meeting of the SLDU, 10 July, 1982, SLDUPH.

46. General meeting of the SLDU, 11 Sept. 1982; Interview with T. Jos. Wilson and W. Byron, 17 Feb. 1985.

47. General meeting of the SLDU, 14 April, 1984, SLDUPH.

48. General meeting of the SLDU, 12 June, 1982, SLDUPH.

49. Interviews with T. Jos Wilson and W. Byron, 17 Feb. 1985.

50. Bucknor was president of the SLDU throughout the author's stay in Port Harcourt in the 1980's. See general meeting of the SLDU, 11 Dec. 1982, SLDUPH.

51. Interviews with T. Jos. Wilson; also general meeting of the SLDU, 12 Feb. 1983, SLDUPH.

52. General meeting of the SLDU, 12 March, 1983, SLDUPH.

53. Programme of Activities, Republican Anniversary/Union's golden Jubilee, April 1983, SLDUPH.

54. For details, see Toyin Falola and Julius Ihonvbere, *The Rise and Fall of Nigeria's Second Republic, 1979-84* (London, 1985).

55. General meetings of the SLDU 10 and 31 March, 1984, SLDUPH.

56. A.L.O. Thompson to the family of the late Sis. C. Williams, 14 July, 1984, SLDUPH. The author did not establish how this impasse was resolved.

57. A.L.O. Thompson to all members of the SLDU, 6 Oct. 1984, SLDUPH.

58. A.L.O. Thompson to Chief Information Officer, Rivers State, 13 Oct. 1984, SLDUPH.

59. General meeting of the SLDU, 9 Feb. 1985, SLDUPH.

Notes to Conclusion

1. Interviews with W. Byron and T. Jos. Wilson, February, 1985.

2. See Akintola J.G. Wyse, *H.C. Bankole-Bright and Politics in Colonial Sierra Leone, 1919-1958* (Cambridge, 1990).

3. E.A. Ayandele, *The Educated Elite in the Nigerian Society* (Ibadan, 1974), pp. 27, 29-31, 34-37. Also, Patrick Cole, *Modern and Traditional Elites in the Politics of Lagos* (Cambridge, 1975), p. 49.

4. Patrick Cole, *Op cit.*, pp. 122-151.

5. *Ibid.*

6. *Ibid.* See also chapter 1, note 150. Carr's partiality to European forms and observances poignantly foreshadows the later preferences of Port Harcourt's aloof patrician, I.B. Johnson. Although he was himself very critical of Herbert Macaulay's pursuit of culthood in Lagos, Potts-Johnson also bears much resemblance to that Lagos politician of the Saro.

7. On the dangers of intra-class rivalries in such amorphous situations, see Ali Mazrui, "Casualties of an Underdeveloped Class Structure: The Expulsion of Luo Workers and Asian Bourgeoisie from Uganda", in William Shack and Elliott P. Skinner (eds.) *Strangers in African Societies*, (Berkeley, 1979), p. 277.

8. Akintola Wyse, *H.C. Bankole-Bright*, pp. 176-178.

9. The experience of the Americo-Liberian rulers of Liberia who, from 1847-1980, had a long and controversial period of rule in that territory, also comes to mind. Here, the returnee grossly violated the public trust by a reckless mis-use of power, thus further compounding his "illegitimacy" in the estimation of the indigenous population. See G. Kieh, "Causes of Liberia's Coup", *TransAfrica Forum*, 1989, pp. 37-47.

SELECT BIBLIOGRAPHY

Books and Articles

Books

Ajayi, J.F.A., *Christian Missions in Nigeria, 1841-1891: The Making of a New Elite* (Evanston, Illinois, 1965).

——, and M. Crowder, eds., *A History of West Africa*, vol II (London, 1985).

Akinyemi, A.B., S.B. Falegan, and I.A. Aluko, eds., *Readings and Documents on ECOWAS* (Ibadan, 1984).

Alie, J.A.D., *A New History of Sierra Leone* (New York, 1990).

Ayandele, E.A., *The Educated Elite in the Nigerian Society* (Ibadan, 1974).

——, *Holy Johnson: Pioneer of African Nationalism, 1836-1917* (New York, 1970).

——, *The Missionary Impact on Modern Nigeria, 1842-1914* (London, 1966).

Azikiwe, Nnamdi, *Zik: A Selection from the Speeches of Nnamdi Azikiwe* (Cambridge, 1961).

Baker, Pauline, *Urbanization and Political Change: The Politics of Lagos, 1947-67* (Berkeley, 1974).

Blassingame, John W., *The Slave Community: Plantation Life in the Antebellum South* (New York, 1972).

Brotz, Howard, *The Black Jews of Harlem* (New York, 1964).

Cole, Patrick, *Modern and Traditional Elites in the Politics of Lagos* (Cambridge, 1975).

Coleman, James C., *Nigeria: Background to Nationalism* (Berkeley, 1960).

Dike, K.O., *Trade and Politics in the Niger Delta, 1830-1885* (Oxford, 1956).

Dudley, B.G., *Instability and Political Order: Politics and Crisis in Nigeria* (Ibadan, 1973).

Ekechi, Felix K., *Tradition and Transformation in Eastern Nigeria* (London, 1989).

Epelle, E.M.T., *The Church in the Niger Delta* (Port Harcourt, 1955).

Esedebe, P.O., *Pan-Africanism* (Washington, D.C., 1982).

Ezera, Kalu., *Constitutional Developments in Nigeria* (Cambridge, 1960).

Falola, Toyin, and J. Ihonvbere, *The Rise and Fall of Nigeria's Second Republic, 1979-84* (London, 1985).

First, Ruth, *The Barrel of the Gun: Political Power in Africa and the Coup d'Etat* (Harmondsworth, 1970).

Fitzgerald, C.P., *The Third China: The Chinese Communities in South-East Asia* (London, 1965).

Fyfe, Christopher, *A History of Sierra Leone* (London, 1962).

————, *Sierra Leone Inheritance* (London, 1964).

Fyle, Magbaily C., *The History of Sierra Leone* (London, 1981).

Gbulie, B., *Nigeria's Five Majors: Coup d'Etat of 15th January, 1966: First Inside Account* (Onitsha, 1981).

Hafkin, Nancy J., and Edna G. Bay, eds., *Women in Africa* (Stanford, 1976).

Hargreaves, J., *A Life of Sir Samuel Lewis* (London, 1958).

Harrell-Bond, Barbara E., Allen M. Howard, and David E. Skinner., *Community Leadership and the Transformation of Freetown, 1801-1976* (The Hague, 1978).

Herskovits, M., *The Myth of the Negro Past* (New York, 1941).

Hopkins, A.G., *An Economic History of West Africa* (New York, 1973).

Huggins, Nathan, *Black Odyssey: The Afro-American Ordeal in Slavery* (New York, 1977).

Iweriebor, Ehiedu, *Radical Politics in Nigeria, 1945–1950: The Significance of the Zikist Movement* (Zaria, 1996).

Jordan, Winthrop, *White over Black: American Attitudes toward the Negro, 1550-1812* (Baltimore, 1968).

Jorre, J. de St., *The Nigerian Civil War* (London, 1972).

Kalu, O.U., ed., *The History of Christianity in West Africa* (London, 1980).

Kopytoff, J.H., *A Preface to Modern Nigeria* (Wisconsin, 1965).

Kuczynski, R.R., *Demographic Survey of the British Colonial Empire*, vol.1. (Oxford, 1948).

Kup, A.P., *Sierra Leone: A Concise History* (London,1975).

Langley, J. Ayodele, *Pan-Africanism and Nationalism in West Africa, 1900-1945* (Oxford, 1973).

Levin, Donald, *Goerg Simmel: On Individuality and Social Forms* (Chicago, 1971).

Little, Kenneth, *African Women in Towns* (Cambridge, 1973).

————, *West African Urbanization* (Cambridge, 1965).

Lynch, Hollis, *Edward Wilmot Blyden: Pan-Negro Patriot* (London, 1967).

Mamdani, Mahmood, *From Citizen to Refugee* (London, 1972).

Olaniyan, R., ed., *Nigerian History and Culture* (Ibadan, 1985).

Onimode, Bade, *Imperialism and Underdevelopment in Nigeria* (London, 1983).

Padmore, George, *Pan-Africanism or Communism* (London, 1956).

Peel, J.D.Y., *Ijeshas and Nigerians* (Cambridge, 1983).

Peterson, J.E., *Province of Freedom: A History of Sierra Leone, 1787-1945* (Evanston, Illinois, 1969).

Porter, Arthur, *Creoledom* (London, 1963).

Robertson, Claire, and Iris Berger, eds., *Women and Class in Africa* (New York, 1986).

Shack, William, and Elliott P. Skinner, eds., *Strangers in African Societies* (Berkeley, 1979).

Spitzer, L., *The Creoles of Sierra Leone: Responses to Colonialism, 1870-1945* (Wisconsin, 1974).

Stichter, Sharon, and Jane Parpart, eds., *Patriarchy and Class* (Boulder, 1988).

Talbot, P. Amaury, *The Peoples of Southern Nigeria* (Oxford, 1926).

Tamuno, T.O., and E.J. Alagoa, eds., *Eminent Nigerians of the Rivers State* (Ibadan, 1980).

Twaddle, Michael, ed., *Expulsion of a Minority: Essays on Ugandan Asians* (London, 1975).

Uya, Okon E., *Black Brotherhood* (Lexington, Mass., 1971).

Vail, L., ed., *The Creation of Tribalism in Southern Africa* (Berkeley, 1989).

Van Der Laan, H.L., *The Lebanese of Sierra Leone* (The Hague, Mouton, 1975).

Willis, Justin, *Mombasa, the Swahili and the Making of the Mijikenda* (Oxford, 1993).

Wolpe, Howard, *Urban Politics in Nigeria: A Study of Port Harcourt* (Los Angeles, 1974).

Wyse, Akintola J.G., *H.C. Bankole-Bright and Politics in Colonial Sierra Leone, 1919-1958* (Cambridge, 1990).

————, *The Krio of Sierra Leone* (London, 1989).

Articles

Adewoye, O., "Sierra Leonean Immigrants in the Field of Law in Southern Nigeria, 1856-1934", *Sierra Leone Studies*, 26, Jan., 1970, pp. 11-26.

Ajayi, J.F.A., "The Development of Secondary Grammar School Education in Nigeria", *Journal of the Historical Society of Nigeria*, 2, 4, Dec. 1963, pp. 517-535.

Akpan, M.K., "The Return to Africa: Sierra Leone and Liberia", *Tarikh*, 20, v, 4, 1981, pp. 92-116.

Alagoa, E.J., "The Development of Institutions in the States of the Eastern Niger Delta", *The Journal of African History*, 12, 2, 1971, pp. 269-278.

————, "Long-Distance Trade and States in the Niger Delta", *The Journal of African History*, 11, 3, 1970, pp. 319-329.

Aluko, Olajide, "Politics of Decolonisation in British West Africa, 1945-1960", in J.F. Ade Ajayi and Michael Crowder, eds., *History of West Africa*, vol ii, (Essex, 1987), pp. 693-735.

Anyanwu, C.N., "The Growth of Port Harcourt, 1912-1960", in W. Ogionwo, ed., *The City of Port Harcourt* (Ibadan, 1979), pp. 15-34.

Ayandele, E.A., "James Africanus Beale Horton, 1835-1883: Prophet of Modernization in West Africa", *African Historical Studies*, iv, 3, 1971, pp.691-707.

Bujra, Janet M., "Urging Women to Redouble their Efforts: Class, Gender and Capitalist Transformation in Africa", in Claire Robertson and Iris Berger, eds., *Women and Class in Africa* (New York, 1986), pp.117-140.

Campbell, Carl, "John Mohammed Bath and the Free Mandingos in Trinidad: The Question of their Repatriation to Africa, 1831-1838", *Journal of African Studies*, 4, Winter, 1975/76, pp. 467-95.

Challenor, Herschelle Sullivan, "Strangers as Colonial Intermediaries: The Dahomeyans in Francophone Africa", in William Shack and Elliott P. Skinner, eds., *Strangers in African Societies* (Berkeley, 1979), pp. 67-84.

Cookey, S.J.S., "West African Immigrants in the Congo, 1885-1896", *Journal of the Historical Society of Nigeria*, 3, 2, Dec. 1965, pp. 261-70.

Dixon-Fyle, M. "The Saro in the political life of early Port Harcourt, 1913-49", *The Journal of African History*, 30, 1, 1989, pp. 125-38.

———, "The Sierra Leone (Descendants) Union of Port Harcourt, 1933-86", *Africana Research Bulletin*, XIV, 3, 1985, pp. 76-82.

Dorward, D.C., "British West Africa and Liberia", in A.D. Roberts, ed., *The Cambridge History of Africa*, vol.7 (Cambridge, 1986), pp. 399-459.

Ekechi, F.K., "Aspects of Palm Oil Trade at Oguta (Eastern Nigeria), 1900-1950", *African Economic History*, 10, 1981, pp.35-65.

Ekejiuba, Felicia, "Contemporary Households and Major Socio-Economic Transitions in Eastern Nigeria: Towards a Reconceptualization of the Household", in Conceptualizing the Household: Issues of Theory, Method, and Application, workshop organised at Harvard University, November, 1984, and co-ordinated by Jane I. Guyer and Pauline E. Peters.

Fyle, Magbaily C., and I. Heroe, "Krio Traditional Beliefs", *Africana Research Bulletin*, 7, 3, June, 1977, pp. 3-26.

Gale, T.S., "The Disbarment of African Medical Officers by the West African Medical Staff: A Study of Prejudice", *Journal of the Historical Society of Sierra Leone*, 4, 1 and 2, Dec. 1980, pp. 33-44.

Hargreaves, J.D., "Senegal: Another Creole Frontier, 1889", *Journal of the Historical Society of Sierra Leone*, 1, 2, July, 1977, p. 65.

Hair, Paul, "Africanism: The Freetown Contribution", *The Journal of Modern African Studies*, v, 1967, pp. 521-39.

Johnson, Cheryl, "Class and Gender: A Consideration of Yoruba Women during the Colonial Period", in Claire Robertson and Iris Berger, eds., *Women and Class in Africa* (New York, 1986), pp. 237-54.

Jones-Quartey, K.A.B., "Sierra Leone's Role in the Development of Ghana, 1820-1930", *Sierra Leone Studies* (new series), 10, June 1959, pp. 73-83.

July, Robert W., "Africanus Horton and the Idea of Independence in West Africa", *Sierra Leone Studies*, 18, Jan., 1966, pp.2-17.

———, "Nineteenth-Century Negritude: Edward W. Blyden", *Journal of African History*, v, 1, 1964, pp. 73-86.

Kaniki, M.H.Y., "Politics and Protest in Colonial West Africa: The Sierra Leone Experience", *The African Review*, iv, 3, 1974, pp. 423-58.

Kieh, G., "Causes of Liberia's Coup", *TransAfrica Forum*, 1989.

Kuper, Jessica, "'Goan' and 'Asian'" in Uganda: An Analysis of Racial Identity and Cultural Categories", in William Shack and E.P. Skinner, eds., *Strangers in African Societies* (Berkeley, 1979), pp.234-59.

Langley, J. Ayodele, "The Gambia Section of the National Congress of British West Africa", *Africa*, xxxix, 4, Oct., 1969, pp. 382-95.

Lonsdale, J.M., "Some Origins of Nationalism in East Africa", *The Journal of African History*, ix, 1, 1968, pp.119-146.

Mazrui, Ali A., "Casualties of an Underdeveloped Class Structure: The Expulsion of Luo Workers and Asian Bourgeoisie from Uganda", in William Shack and Elliott P. Skinner, eds., *Strangers in African Societies* (Berkeley, 1979), pp. 261-78.

Meredith, David, "Government and the Decline of the Nigerian Oil-Palm Export Industry, 1919-1939", *The Journal of African History*, 25, 1984, pp. 311-29.

Miles, J., "Rural Protest in the Gold Coast: Cocoa Hold-ups of 1908-38", in C. Dewey and A.G. Hopkins, eds., *The Imperial Impact* (London, 1978).

Nduka, O., "Educational Development in Port Harcourt: Retrospect and Prospects", in W. Ogionwo, ed., *The City of Port Harcourt* (Ibadan, 1979), pp. 35-51.

Parpart, Jane, L., "Class and Gender on the Copperbelt", in Claire Robertson and Iris Berger, eds., *Women and Class in Africa* (New York, 1986), pp. 141-160.

Peil, Margaret, "Host Reactions: Aliens in Ghana", in William Shack and Elliott P. Skinner, eds., *Strangers in African Societies* (Berkeley, 1979), pp. 123-140.

Robertson, Claire, "Women in the Urban Economy", in Margaret Jean Hay and Sharon Stichter, eds., *African Women South of the Sahara* (New York, 1995), pp. 44-65.

Shack, William, "Open Systems and Closed Boundaries: The Ritual Process of Stranger Relations in New African States", in William Shack and Elliott P. Skinner eds., *Strangers in African Societies* (Berkeley, 1979), pp. 37-47.

Southall, R.J., "Farmers, Traders and Brokers in the Gold Coast Economy", *The Canadian Journal of African Studies*, 12, 2, 1978, pp. 185-211.

Spitzer, L., and La Ray Denzer, "I.T.A. Wallace-Johnson and the West African Youth League", *International Journal of African Historical Studies*, 6, nos. 3 and 4, 1973, pp. 413-52.

Steady, Filomena Chioma, "Protestant Women's Associations in Freetown, Sierra Leone", in Nancy J. Hafkin and Edna G. Bay, eds., *Women in Africa* (Stanford, 1976), pp.213-37.

Sudarkasa, Niara, "From Stranger to Alien: The Socio-Political History of the Nigerian Yoruba in Ghana, 1900-1970", in William Shack and Elliott P. Skinner, eds., *Strangers in African Societies* (Berkeley, 1979), 141-167.

Webster, J.B., "African Political Activity in British West Africa, 1900-1940", in J.F.A. Ajayi and Michael Crowder, eds., *History of West Africa*, vol. II (Longman, Essex), pp. 635-64.

White, E. Frances, "Women, Work, and Ethnicity: The Sierra Leone Case", in Edna G. Bay, ed., *Women and Work in Africa* (Boulder, 1982), pp.19-33.

Wolpe, Howard, "Port Harcourt: Ibo politics in Microcosm", *The Journal of Modern African Studies*, 7, 3, 1969, pp. 469-93.

Wyse, Akintola J.G., "The Place of Sierra Leone in African Diaspora Studies", in J.F. Ade Ajayi and J.D.Y. Peel, eds., *Peoples and Empires in African History: Essays in Memory of Michael Crowder* (London, 1992), pp. 107-120.

————, "The Sierra Leone Krio: A Reappraisal from the Perspective of the African Diaspora", in Joseph E. Harris, ed., *Global Dimensions of the African Diaspora* (Washington, D.C., 1982), pp. 309-337.

Unpublished Documents

Official

National Archives of Nigeria, Enugu (NAE).

This proved to be a rich collection of official reports, and minutes of Board meetings. The most useful series was the "Riv-Prof" files, a collection of predominantly official quarterly and annual reports, handing-over notes, petitions, and Township Advisory Board minutes, 1916-1949. See Riv-Prof 1/9, 2/1, 8/4, 8/5, 8/7, 8/10, 8/12, 8/13, 8/14, 8/15, 8/16, 8/17, 8/18, 9/1, 12/8, 13/1, and 20/1.

Public Records Office, London (PRO).

The CO 583 series: Governors and other official reports, correspondence with the Secretary of State, and confidential reports on officials, 1915-1950. See documents in the following series: CO 583/15, 583/16, 583/37, 583/45, 583/66, 583/75, 583/78, 583/268, and 583/311.

Unofficial

The Collection of the Methodist Church, located at the School of Oriental and African Studies, London University, (SOAS).

1.   Annual reports of the Wesleyan Methodist Missionary Society (WMMS), 1912-1950.

2.   On microfiche, WMMS Synod minutes, London Missionary Committee reports, and Lagos Synod reports, 1912-1950. See boxes 13, 14, 15, and 23.

Papers of the Sierra Leone Descendants Union of Port Harcourt (SLDUPH), 1969-85, in the custody of the Union's secretariat, Victoria Street, Port Harcourt.

1.   Minutes of Executive and General meetings.

2.   Correspondence with Nigerian Federal and State government officials.

3.   Correspondence with the Sierra Leone High Commission, Lagos.

Newspapers: National Archives of Nigeria, Ibadan.
1.　The *Nigerian Observer*, 1930-1953.
2.　The *Eastern Nigerian Guardian*, 1944-1951.

Oral Informants.

I held formal interviews with my principal informants (listed below), but also derived a wealth of detail from informal conversations with the members of the Sierra Leone Descendants Union. I attended several Union meetings between 1985 and 1988, paid a number of home visits, and continued these conversations at "socials", weddings, funerals, and at the annual Union and Sierra Leone republican anniversary celebrations. Key interviews were taped, and notes were taken at others.

Principal Informants.

1.　Mrs. Mercy Alagoa: Interviewed on several informal occasions between 1985 and 1988.
2.　Mr. W. Byron: Taped interview on 10 Feb. 1985; frequent discussions during a series of home visits between 1984 and 1988.
3.　Mr. Cecil Manly-Rollings: Interviewed on regular home visits, 1983-88.
4.　Mrs. Clementina Manly-Rollings: Interviewed informally on several occasions between 1983 and August 1988.
5.　Mrs. Margaret Constance Garrick-Wilson (wife of T. Jos Wilson): Taped interview on 17 Feb. 1985; many conversations during home visits between Jan. 1984 and her death in Port Harcourt on 4 Jan 1986.
6.　Mr. T. Jos. Wilson: Taped interview on 17 Feb. 1985; several informal interviews at his residence between Jan. 1984 and October 1985, when he passed away.
7.　Various informal conversations with the officers and members of the Sierra Leone Descendants Union of Port Harcourt.

INDEX

A Saro Community in the Niger Delta, 1912–1984: The Potts-Johnsons of Port Harcourt and Their Heirs reviews the history of Sierra Leoneans in the Niger Delta from the time of their migration there in the early twentieth century. The Saro, a Nigerian term for immigrants from Sierra Leone, settled in the newly established British-administered city of Port Harcourt, bringing with them their western education and enjoying undisguised British support. They easily dominated the indigenous population in several socio-economic fields: education, civil service, and trade. The Saro celebrated their cultural exclusivity and revelled in their civic and professional prominence, albeit in alliance with a small indigenous elite. As might be expected, Saro dominance engendered much resentment, though tensions were largely defused before World War II. After the war, immigrant dominance came increasingly under local challenge as Nigeria approached independence.

By focusing on the Reverend L. R. Potts-Johnson, the unofficial leader of the Saro community, the work provides an inside view of the trends, thus enhancing the treatment of many important issues to be considered when researching African history, among them intra-African migration, status of and dominance by elites (both indigenous and immigrant), women's roles in social relationships, and preservation of family and cultural values under extreme socio-economic stress.

Advance praise:

A Saro Community in the Niger Delta, 1912–1984 shows in detail how the settler community introduced their own distinctive form of Christian, anglicized culture, and how they interacted with the indigenous communities, the British colonial administration, and the Nigerian administration. The narrative centers around the unofficial leader of the community, the Reverend L. R. Potts-Johnson; since few biographies of Africans of this period have appeared, this study of a remarkable African is particularly welcome.

—Christopher Fyfe, Author of *A History of Sierra Leone*

A Saro Community in the Niger Delta, 1912–1984 is a very important and valuable study. It provides a clear illustration of the African initiative (a popular theme in African historiography), and it increases our knowledge and understanding of the Saro experience in particular and comparative immigration history in general. The book will appeal to Africanist historians, scholars, and students interested in ethnic or migration studies, to sociologists, and to those interested in women's studies.

—Felix K. Ekechi, Professor of History, Kent State University

MAC DIXON-FYLE received his Ph.D. from the School of Oriental and African Studies at London University. His work on the colonial political-economy and nationalist politics of the Plateau Tonga of Northern Rhodesia/Zambia led to his dissertation and several articles in *The Journal of African History, The International Journal of African Historical Studies*, and other journals. He is co-author of *Sierra Leone at the End of the Twentieth Century: History, Politics, and Society*, due to be published later this year. He has taught at the University of Sierra Leone and the University of Port Harcourt, and is currently Professor of History at DePauw University.